Political Liberalism and Plurinational Democracies

The current context of developed societies is characterised by a number of phenomena, the most significant of which are processes of economic globalisation, information technologies, increasing multiculturalism and the emergence of cases of national pluralism which require full political accommodation both within democracies and in the international sphere.

The book examines the current state of affairs concerning the political recognition and constitutional accommodation of national pluralism in liberal democracies in the global era of the twenty-first century. The aim of this volume is to reveal the normative, analytical and institutional shortcomings of liberal democracies in multinational contexts and to offer alternatives that theoretically refine and practically improve the recognition and political accommodation of national pluralism within the democratic polity. Through a series of analyses linked to the development of political liberalism in contemporary states the contributors analyse the direct impact on the way that democracies have treated, and continue to treat, national pluralism in modern-day societies.

Bringing together leading scholars in the field to explore the different debates and approaches to this important issue, this volume will interest researchers and students of nationalism, federalism and multiculturalism, as well as political actors and policy makers with a particular interest in the management of diversity in present-day liberal democracies.

Ferran Requejo is Professor of Political Science at Universitat Pompeu Fabra, Barcelona. **Miquel Caminal** is Professor of Political Science at Universitat de Barcelona.

Nationalism and ethnicity/Routledge studies in nationalism and ethnicity

Formerly known as Cass series: nationalism and ethnicity, ISSN 1462–9755

Series Editor: William Safran
University of Colorado at Boulder

This new series draws attention to some of the most exciting issues in current world political debate: nation-building, autonomy and self-determination; ethnic identity, conflict and accommodation; pluralism, multiculturalism and the politics of language; ethnonationalism, irredentism and separatism; and immigration, naturalisation and citizenship. The series will include monographs as well as edited volumes, and through the use of case studies and comparative analyses will bring together some of the best work to be found in the field.

Nationalism and ethnicity

Ethnicity and Citizenship
The Canadian case
Edited by Jean Laponce and William Safran

Nationalism and Ethnoregional Identities in China
Edited by William Safran

Identity and Territorial Autonomy in Plural Societies
Edited by William Safran and Ramón Maíz

Ideology, Legitimacy and the New State
Yugoslavia, Serbia and Croatia
Siniša Malešević

Diasporas and Ethnic Migrants
Germany, Israel and Russia in comparative perspective
Rainer Munz and Rainer Ohliger

Ethnic Groups in Motion
Economic competition and migration in multiethnic states
Milica Z. Bookman

Post-Cold War Identity Politics
Northern and Baltic experiences
Edited by Marko Lehti and David J. Smith

Welfare, Ethnicity and Altruism
New findings and evolutionary theory
Edited by Frank Salter

Routledge studies in nationalism and ethnicity

Ethnic Violence and the Societal Security Dilemma
Paul Roe

Nationalism in a Global Era
The persistence of nations
Edited by Mitchell Young, Eric Zuelow and Andreas Sturm

Religious Nationalism in Modern Europe
If God be for us
Philip W. Barker

Nationalism and Democracy
Dichotomies, complementarities, oppositions
Edited by André Lecours and Luis Moreno

Pathways from Ethnic Conflict
Institutional redesign in divided societies
Edited by John Coakley

Political Liberalism and Plurinational Democracies
Edited by Ferran Requejo and Miquel Caminal

Political Liberalism and Plurinational Democracies

Edited by Ferran Requejo and
Miquel Caminal

LONDON AND NEW YORK

First published 2011
by Routledge
2 Park Square, Milton Park, Abingdon, Oxon OX14 4RN

Simultaneously published in the USA and Canada
by Routledge
270 Madison Avenue, New York, NY 10016

Routledge is an imprint of the Taylor & Francis Group, an informa business

© 2011 Institut d'Estudis Autonòmics (IEA); individual contributors
Stephen Tierney and José Woehrling, their contributions.

Typeset in Times by Wearset Ltd, Boldon, Tyne and Wear
Printed and bound in Great Britain by TJI Digital, Padstow, Cornwall

British Library Cataloguing in Publication Data
A catalogue record for this book is available from the British Library

Library of Congress Cataloging in Publication Data
Political liberalism and plurinational democracies/edited by Ferran
Requejo and Miquel Caminal.
p. cm. – (Nationalism and ethnicity/Routledge studies in nationalism and
ethnicity)
Includes bibliographical references and index.

1. Democracy. 2. Federal government. 3. Cultural pluralism. 4.
Nationalism. 5. Minorities–Civil rights. 6. Minorities–Political activity. I.
Requejo Coll, Ferran. II. Caminal i Badia, Miquel.
JC423.P5645 2010
321.8–dc22   2010013783

ISBN: 978-0-415-56450-2 (hbk)
ISBN: 978-0-203-84183-9 (ebk)

Contents

Contributors

Miquel Caminal is Professor of Political Science at Universitat de Barcelona.

Montserrat Guibernau is Professor of Politics, Queen Mary College, University of London.

Will Kymlicka is currently the Canada Research Chair in Political Philosophy at Queen's University in Kingston, Canada.

John Loughlin is currently Professor of Politics at Cardiff University.

Ramón Máiz is Professor of Political Science at the University of Santiago de Compostela, Spain.

Wayne Norman is the Mike and Ruth Mackowski Professor of Ethics in the Kenan Institute for Ethics and the Department of Philosophy at Duke University, North Carolina.

Bhikhu Parekh was until recently Centennial Professor at the London School of Economics and is currently Professor of Political Philosophy at the University of Westminster.

Ferran Requejo is Professor of Political Science at the Universitat Pompeu Fabra, Barcelona.

Michel Seymour is Professor of Philosophy at the Université de Montréal, Canada.

Stephen Tierney is Professor of Constitutional Theory, School of Law, University of Edinburgh and Director of the Edinburgh Centre for Constitutional Law.

José Woehrling is Professor of Canadian and Comparative Constitutional Law at the Université de Montréal, Canada.

Series editor's foreword

This volume deals with an important topic: democracy and nationalism in ethnically mixed countries of Europe and North America. It contains the thinking of a group of internationally prominent social scientists who explore the relationships among democracy, liberalism, nationalism, and cultural pluralism. Using theoretical, historical, institutional, and case-study approaches, and focusing primarily on member states of the European Union, the contributors provide a richly documented comparative perspective by contrasting unitary with federal polities and the monocultural polity of Jacobin France with multicultural ones such as Spain; and they assess the role of language, religion, and ideology in the development of nationalism and nationhood. They discuss the often controversial juxtapositions between national unity and subnational particularisms, between majority rule and minority claims, and between individual and group rights. Particular attention is paid to the rights of ethnic minorities and immigrants, including the right to be represented and to vote. The authors provide multiple analyses of the processes of democratic nation-building, paying careful attention to varying historical situations and contexts. All the contributors, each in their own way, analyze theories of the interplay between democracy and nationalism, and they unravel a number of concepts in the light of modern developments, such as globalization, immigration, and multiculturalism, and the challenge these pose to the individualistic bias of traditional liberal democracy and to long-held notions of the state and of collective identity. They provide a reexamination of normative theories of classic and modern thinkers about sovereignty, majority rule, and minority representation in the light of contemporary realities. They assess the claims of ethnic minorities for justice and fairness, including the right to secession, and the role played by institutional arrangements, economic policy, and territorial constraints in dealing with them. One chapter – on France – compares liberal and authoritarian concepts of nationhood and traces their respective roots; another compares constitutional patriotism with traditional national patriotism; and still another shows that there is no absolute distinction between civic and ascriptively based nationalism. The book is a major contribution to the study of democracy.

William Safran
University of Colorado at Boulder

1 Liberal democracies, national pluralism and federalism

Ferran Requejo and Miquel Caminal

1 Democracy and national pluralism

In recent decades it has become increasingly clear that nowadays *liberal democracies* have no rivals when they are compared with other political systems. However, these types of democracy are political entities whose construction has been based on states that developed over the preceding centuries. Therefore, *theories of democracy* have traditionally been theories of the democratic state. This is not a neutral issue in theoretical terms, above all when societies have become much more complex and plural than those that existed when the earliest versions of the main contemporary political theories were formulated.

The current context of developed societies is characterised by a number of phenomena, the most significant of which are processes of economic globalisation, information technologies, increasing multiculturality and the emergence of cases of national pluralism which require full political accommodation both within democracies and in the international sphere. Nowadays, some of the traditional political and constitutional regulations, as well as some of the basic features of traditional theories of the state, are no longer adequate. It is to be expected that democratic institutions and the principal contemporary political ideologies – mainly liberal, social democratic, conservative, Christian Democrat and nationalist – encounter difficulties when they attempt to understand what is happening and attempt to formulate normative and political proposals in order to "improve" democratic systems and the international sphere.

The construction of political systems that are increasingly refined in national and cultural terms constitutes one of the most prominent challenges of the normative and institutional revision of modern democracies. New issues are appearing on the agenda: how can the spheres of institutions, symbology or self-government regulate plurinational states in constitutional terms? How should such classic concepts as representation, participation, or popular sovereignty be approached and defined in plurinational and multicultural contexts? How should the rights of immigrant peoples be regulated within the linguistic and educational policies of the host states?

One way of describing the history of democratic liberalism is to interpret it as the history of the progressive recognition of different social and cultural sectors.

We know that the abstract and universalist language that underlies the liberal values of liberty, equality and pluralism has contrasted, in practical terms, with the exclusion of a number of *voices* with regard to the regulation of specific liberties, equalities and pluralisms of contemporary societies. Historically, this was the case of those who did not own property, women, indigenous people, as well as ethnic, linguistic and national minorities, etc. In fact, most of the first liberals – until the end of the nineteenth century – opposed the recognition of democratic rights such as universal suffrage or freedom of association. These rights, which today seem to be almost "obvious", had to be wrested from liberal constitutionalism from the second half of the nineteenth century onwards following decades of confrontations by, above all, the political and trade union organisations of the working classes. This would later be followed by the generalisation of rights of a social nature which form the foundations of the welfare states that were created after the Second World War.

In recent years, new political *voices* have emerged that have pointed out their lack of recognition and accommodation in terms of equality and liberty in democracies. Among these, it is necessary to highlight the cases of minorities or minority national and cultural groups; that is, those national and cultural identities that do not coincide with the identities of majority and hegemonic groups within democracies.

This has meant that liberal democracies must now deal with the accommodation of their own internal national and cultural pluralism in the institutional and collective decision-making spheres, despite the fact that these issues have been largely ignored by traditional democratic liberalism and other political ideologies, such as the different variants of classic socialism, republicanism and conservatism. The most significant cases are those relating to immigrant peoples, minority nations (or stateless nations), and indigenous groups. Each of these movements gives rise to specific questions regarding the *recognition* and *political accommodation* (group rights, self-government, defence of particular cultural values, presence in the international arena, etc.) faced with which classic political ideologies often reveal themselves to be resistant, puzzled or disoriented.

In general terms, it can be said that national and cultural pluralism has introduced a "new agenda" of issues into the democratic debate which can no longer be dealt with by the main concepts and legitimising discourse that these ideologies use. These issues include individual rights, the principle of non-discrimination before the law, popular sovereignty, the *public virtues* of the republican tradition, the emancipation of productive relations, etc. With regard to specific questions of a cultural nature, what seems increasingly untenable is not what traditional democratic liberalism and other classic ideologies say, but what they do not say because they take it for granted: a series of theoretical assumptions and common practices of a "stateist" nature that characterise the nation-building processes that impregnate the symbols, language, institutions, collective decision-making processes, the territorial distribution of powers, etc., in addition to the practical concretion of the values of liberty, equality and pluralism of liberal democracies. In fact, all states have been and continue to be nationalist and nationalising agencies.

Unfortunately, too often the official responses have treated national and cultural differences within democracies as "particularist deviations". But in clear contrast to the versions that defend a supposed laissez-faire attitude to cultural matters, or an equally questionable superiority or modernity of the values of the majority, experience indicates that the state has never been, nor is, nor can ever be neutral regarding cultural matters. Too often the practical development of the majority of liberal democracies has been to promote the cultural assimilation of minorities in the name of their political integration. In other words, the practical consequence has been the undermining and marginalisation of state national and cultural minorities in favour of "universalist" versions of "equality of citizenship", "popular sovereignty" or "non-discrimination". These versions have acted in a highly unequal, discriminating and partial way by favouring the *particular* characteristics of the culturally hegemonic or majority groups of the state (which do not always coincide with the hegemonic groups or sectors in the socio-economic sphere).

Today we can say that we are faced with a new national and cultural element of the political equity that *theories of justice* talk about. This is an aspect that is essential when one attempts to move towards democracies with a greater degree of ethical quality. Or, in other words, the idea is currently gaining ground that uniformity is the enemy of equality, and that cosmopolitanism means establishing an explicit and wide-ranging recognition and accommodation of the national and cultural pluralism of democracies (of both majorities and minorities).

Among the elements that characterise the weaknesses and national and cultural biases of the liberal-democratic tradition (and of other political ideologies which we do not deal with here) and condition both the concretion of the values and organising principles of democracies and their institutional regulations, we will highlight the following:

- The absence of a theory of the *demos* in the theories of democracy of these traditional ideologies (whether they be of a more liberal or a more republican nature). Neither have these theories developed any conceptions regarding legitimate demarcations (borders).
- An almost exclusive approach to "justice" from the theoretical perspective of the *paradigm of equality* in socio-economic terms, without taking into account the *paradigm of difference* in national and cultural terms. The inclusion of the latter is necessary for the democratic regulation of culturally plural societies. This is the contrast between what is sometimes called the *paradigm of redistribution* and the *paradigm of recognition and difference* (a contrast which, within theories of democracy, is manifested in the approaches called Liberalism 1 and Liberalism 2).
- The assignment of cultural pluralism to the private sphere. The public sphere does not participate in this kind of pluralism: "political" marginalisation of minority cultures. Differences in the evolution of liberal attitudes

focused on cultural *assimilation*, on political *integration* and, more recently, the political *accommodation* of the internal cultural diversity of democracies.

- The processes of state nation-building established in all democracies. A universalist language is often applied to a particular state group which is presented internally as a homogeneous national reality. The consequence is the presence of a uniformising state nationalism in cultural terms that often constitutes the "hidden" element of traditional democratic liberalism in the regulation of the rights and duties of "citizenship", of "popular sovereignty" and of the territorial division of power (also in the majority of federations).
- The limitations of the language and the interpretation of the values and democratic institutions by the more complex liberal-democratic theories (Rawls, Habermas) when confronted with demands for recognition and normative and institutional accommodation from national and cultural pluralism movements of a territorial nature (minority nations, indigenous peoples).

In order to solve a problem, the first thing one needs to do is define it well. And defining a problem requires at least three things: first of all, knowing what the basic, the decisive, question is. Obviously, in addition to this question there are likely to be a whole host of other aspects which are closely related to the first question: economic development, inequalities in income, supranational integration processes (such as the European Union), the multicultural character of the society, etc. But it is not advisable to mix all these issues together from the outset. Second, defining a problem also involves knowing how to describe it as precisely as possible. This involves both an accurate treatment of a conceptual and historical nature and of the most important empirical data. And, third, defining a problem is also knowing where to go to find possible solutions, both in the theoretical and in the comparative political spheres. Isaiah Berlin said that the questions we ask ourselves in the fields of philosophy, history or the social sciences in general are only intelligible if we know where we have to go to find the answers. In other words, when we have a question and we do not know where to go to find the answers, this normally means that we are on the wrong track from an epistemological point of view.

2 National pluralism and federalism

In our case, the basic political question to be addressed is how a liberal democracy can be turned into a plurinational reality. We understand this type of reality to be one in which a group of citizens recognise themselves as belonging to a nation that does not coincide with the nation constructed by the state. The "classical" answers to this question can be summarised by the following three responses:

1   federalism (in a broad sense, including federations, associated states, federacies, confederations and even regional states).

2   institutions and processes of a "consociational" nature (based on consensus between the majorities and the minorities). (Examples of these can be found in the systems of Switzerland and Belgium, in these cases in conjunction with federal solutions.)
3   secession.

Identifying the most suitable solution will depend on the context of each specific case (history, international situation, type of actors and political culture, etc.). However, if one does not wish (or at least not at first) to embark on the radical solution of secession, the key question for a plurinational liberal democracy is to establish, not how the *demos* can become the *cratos* – that would be the traditional view of democracy – but how the different *demoi* (majorities and minorities) that co-exist within the same democracy can be politically and constitutionally recognised and accommodated on equal terms. In other words, how the different *demoi* interrelate with the different *cratos* and, at the same time, how both the two interrelate among themselves. This involves aspects of both a "democratic" (participation of majorities and minorities in the "shared governments of the democracy") and, above all, "liberal" nature (protection and development of minorities in the national and international spheres, in contrast to the "tyranny of the majority").[1] On the other hand, in plurinational realities there will always be elements of a nationally competitive legitimising nature. It is counterproductive, as well as useless, to attempt to redirect this question by means of notions such as "post-nationalism" or other similar concepts which attempt to ignore it or to "overcome" it. These are poorly equipped attempts, empirically speaking, and in practice end up legitimising the status quo.

Modern-day societies have become too complex to be described using political conceptions that were designed for a much lower level of social, national and cultural diversity than that which currently exists. Nowadays it is necessary to establish a much more refined interpretation of the most basic values of the liberal and democratic tradition (liberty, equality, pluralism, and justice) than that offered by traditional constitutionalism. This complexity demands theories that are more sensitive to variations in empirical reality when one wishes to concretise its basic legitimising values. And, above all, it demands practical, institutional and procedural solutions which are far more suitable for the pluralism of modern-day societies. Political theory and comparative politics are fields that need to be interrelated in order to conduct better theory and better comparative politics. At the beginning of the twenty-first century, the recognition and political accommodation of plurinational democracies continue to be unresolved issues on the agenda of the liberal democracies.

In general terms, one fact relating to comparative politics in the 1990s shows that conflicts of a territorial nature constitute the largest group of armed conflicts that have occurred in the world. Furthermore, the emergence of a large number of new states in Europe was brought about following the collapse of two empires: the Austrian Empire, after the First World War, and the USSR, during the last decade of the twentieth century. In contrast, few states belonging to the group of western European democracies have achieved independence during the twentieth century – Norway (1904), Ireland (1921) and a few islands (Cyprus, Malta, etc.).

Empirical studies on democracies show, moreover, the importance of the interaction of constitutional solutions with a whole series of factors of an economic, social, historical, institutional nature and political culture for democratic success and stability. Thus, for example, it is clear that given certain levels of development – calculated to be around $8,800 per capita income in purchasing power of the year 2000 – those states that have implemented democratic systems do not regress towards autocratic systems.[2] Moreover, studies of federal systems carried out independently of those mentioned above have revealed similar features: above a similar income level federations display low indices of violence in territorial conflicts (with some exceptions), whereas below an income level of around $3,000 federalism does not achieve a better accommodation of territorial disputes than unitary states.[3]

In western democracies, the armed conflicts in the Basque Country and Northern Ireland are the exception: the majority of territorial disputes in favour of higher levels of self-government by national minorities are peaceful in nature. This is the case, for example, of Scotland, Quebec, Catalonia and Flanders. In all these territories there are those who are in favour of achieving independence by democratic means, despite the small number of states that have achieved this over the last 100 years and the role in favour of maintaining the status quo played by transnational organisations such as the European Union. In conceptual terms, there is nothing that prevents the subject of where borders should be drawn from forming part of the democratic debate. But empirically speaking it is clear that liberal-democratic states are highly possessive of their territories, an issue on which they behave more like states than like liberal democracies.

Some of the conclusions of these comparative political studies are more or less obvious, but others, however, are more subtle. On the one hand, it has been shown that the degree of socio-economic development is not a necessary condition for access to democracy. In fact, in recent years new democracies (or semi-democracies) have emerged in countries with low levels of development. On the other hand, empirical studies demonstrate that in the sphere of democratic states territorial disputes show no tendency to disappear – in contrast to what some theories of modernisation with liberal or Marxist roots had predicted – and that quite the opposite tends to occur. Moreover, above a certain level the degree of development of a plurinational democracy is not a useful factor for predicting a greater or lesser degree of success in the political accommodation of its internal national minorities. Other factors are more decisive for making this prediction: among the factors that affect the accommodation of federal democracies the following are particularly important:

- the specific history of the interaction between the affected groups;
- the presence or absence of specific institutions, such as federalism and the existence of "consociational" clauses (institutions shared by the different territorial groups in the composition of governments, courts, etc., propor-

tional electoral systems, rights of veto and procedural "alarm bells" (examples can be found in the current constitutional regulations of Switzerland and Belgium);

- the degree of consensus or coercion of the federations;
- the establishment or not of a broad and protected sphere of self-government by the minorities;
- the possibility or not of establishing institutions that coordinate the policies and strategies of the federated units in relation to the central power (an example – December 2003 – is the Canadian Council of the Federation);
- the existence or not of a "federal culture" in the interactions between the main political actors;
- the heterogeneity or not of the party systems of the federated units and the federation;
- the congruence or lack thereof between the executives of the two levels of government;
- in parliamentary systems, the difficulty or not to attain absolute majorities in the composition of the central parliament;
- the degree of political independence of the supreme or constitutional courts;
- the existence or not of an effective system of fiscal federalism.

From the perspective of political theory, it is important to point out two components of the current debate which also affect the better or worse political accommodation of the national pluralism of a democracy. The first involves the two intellectual traditions from which federalism has traditionally been approached; the second is related to the interpretation of the basic values of liberal democracies in contexts of national and cultural pluralism. These two components are very closely linked.

In very general terms, it is possible to establish the existence of two different approaches to federalism, which we will associate, on the one hand, with the school of thought represented by Althusius and Montesquieu and, on the other hand, with the American authors of the *Federalist Papers* (Madison, Hamilton and Jay). The former are more linked with what we might call the spirit of confederations and consociational federalism. The classical notion of sovereignty is understood here in terms of negotiation and is of a shared nature. One of the aims of the "federal pact" will be the preservation of the plurality of the particular identities of the subjects of the pact. This establishes an ascending order in the structuring of powers that at one extreme involves a consecutive process of federalisation (Althusius, *Politica Methodice Digesta* (1614), VIII). In line with the classical juridical formula of Roman law known as the "quod omnes tangit" formula, which establishes that that which affects everyone must be agreed by everyone, it translates in federal terms into the introduction of the right of veto by the federated collectivities.[4] Here, the polity is associated with a commitment of a consensual nature which is permanently negotiated.

On other hand, the American federalist tradition associated with the creation of the first federal state of the contemporary era based its approach to federalism on much more federal than confederal foundations. Here the centre of gravity is located in the governance of a modern nation-state and the subsequent supremacy of the central power over the federated powers. One of the explicit objectives is to avoid the instability that confederations have repeatedly displayed at an empirical level. In contrast with the school of thought represented by Althusius and Montesquieu, the establishment of the federation should not involve existing social and territorial divisions but should attempt to construct a new polity that subsumes the old divisions by establishing new processes of state-building and nation-building. The union is more important than the units.[5] This tradition that has been reinforced by the later actions of the Supreme Court, although in the last decade some of the rulings of this court indicate a "friend-lier" attitude towards the states which does not involve constitutional changes.

Depending on the federal conception we locate ourselves within, we will obtain different conclusions in all the spheres of territorial accommodation. This question has also been highlighted in the debate regarding (federal or non-federal) democracies in contexts of cultural pluralism. Thus, the interpretation of the values of liberty, equality and pluralism will be different depending on whether one is dealing with uninational or plurinational liberal democracies, above all with regard to collective or group liberties and rights, the subjects of equality or the type of pluralism which is to be protected or guaranteed. Let us look at the present, for example. The classical questions "equality, of what?" or "who are the equals?" will receive different "federal" responses depending on where we situate ourselves in the Althusian or Madisonian tradition of federalism, and depending on where we situate ourselves in a conception that is linked to Liberalism 1 or Liberalism 2 of the analytical and normative debate on liberal democracies.

This volume

The chapters of this book develop these issues. The contributions of Ferran Requejo and Bhikhu Parekh focus on the approaches adopted by the traditional theories of political liberalism, democracy and federalism. They highlight some of the main weaknesses of these theories when they are faced with plurinational realities, realities which were not originally part of their theoretical backgrounds when these theories were established and developed. The two authors emphasise new concepts and values with a view to refining both analytical and normative aspects of liberal-democratic theories in order to achieve fairer and more plausible collectivities in plurinational contexts.

John Loughlin conducts an analysis of the evolution of democratic states in western Europe and points out those transformations that affect the relationship between democracy and national pluralism. Will Kymlicka contrasts the concepts of justice and security in conceptions of the accommodation of minority nations and national minorities in western and eastern Europe, indicating shortcomings in legitimisation in the discourses of different state entities and international organisations when they attempt to deal with national pluralism. Michel

Seymour focuses his analysis on the concepts of post-nationality and constitutional patriotism (which is also analysed in the last section of the chapter by Ferran Requejo) showing the moral and analytical inadequacies of the two concepts from a liberal-democratic perspective in nationally diverse states.

Stephen Tierney analyses the classical concept of sovereignty in plurinational and increasingly globalised democratic contexts. His approach proposes a "reframing" of this concept in the field of constitutional arrangements, as well as a revision of legitimising constitutional language in plurinational democracies which has implications both *within* and *beyond* the state. In his chapter, José Woehrling discusses whether the protection of rights and freedoms is compatible with federalism. He believes that this is the case when rights are seen as resulting from a process in which interests are balanced and opposing claims adjusted in a democratic manner. However, when rights are seen as resulting from a restriction of the democratic process, federalism has a more conflicting logic in relation to majority mechanisms, while when rights are seen as pre-political it will be very difficult for them to vary from one jurisdiction to another due to their universal scope.

Ramón Máiz's chapter deals with civic patriotism and focuses on the case of French state nationalism over recent decades. Finally, Wayne Norman analyses theories of secession in plurinational contexts, arguing in favour of the federal regulation of the right of secession as a legitimate and useful way to prevent secessionist processes in liberal democracies, while Montserrat Guibernau shows the relationships between nationalism and cosmopolitanism and Miquel Caminal highlights the overlaps between nationalism and federalism.

The classic question "What is Enlightenment?" today demands more plural responses than those offered by the classic political theories. As a whole, the aim of this volume is to reveal the analytical, normative and institutional shortcomings of liberal democracies in plurinational contexts and to offer alternatives that theoretically refine and practically improve the recognition and political accommodation of national pluralism within the democratic polity. It is a series of analyses linked to the development of political liberalism in contemporary states that has a direct impact on the way that democracies have treated, and continue to treat, national pluralism in modern-day societies.

Notes

1 See Requejo (2005, 2001); Caminal (2002). In this volume, we prefer to use the term "plurinational" instead of using the most common "multinational". The reason is two fold. First, "plurinational" refers both to the descriptive side of the concept (the fact that some democracies include different national societies within them) and to the prescriptive side of the concept (the claim for recognition and protection of plurination in liberal democracies – national pluralism, in this case). In contrast, the term "multinational" only covers the descriptive side of the concept.
2 See Diamond (1999); Przeworski *et al.* (2000).
3 See Karmis and Norman (2005); Amoretti and Bermeo (2004); Gagnon and Tully (2001).
4 This conception has points in common with the recent "republican" theory of collective

negative liberty, known as the "neo-Roman" conception following the work of Q. Skinner.
5 See, for example, *Federalist Papers*, 10, 37, 51 (Madison), and 9, 35 (Hamilton).

References

Amoretti, U. and Bermeo, N. (eds) (2004) *Federalism and Territorial Cleavages*, Baltimore, MD: Johns Hopkins University Press.

Caminal, M. (2002) *El Federalismo Pluralista*, Barcelona: Paidós.

Diamond, L. (1999) *Developing Democracy: Toward Consolidation*, Baltimore, MD: Johns Hopkins University Press.

Gagnon, A. and Tully, J. (eds) (2001) *Multinational Democracies*, Cambridge: Cambridge University Press.

Karmis, D. and Norman, W. (eds) (2005) *Theories of Federalism. A Reader*, New York: Palgrave Macmillan, Houndsmills.

Przeworski, A., Alvarez, M., Cheibub, J.A. and Limongi, F. (2000) *Democracy and Development: Political Institutions and Well Being in the World, 1950–1990*, Cambridge, New York: Cambridge University Press.

Requejo, F. (ed.) (2001) *Democracy and National Pluralism*, London, New York: Routledge.

Requejo, F. (2005) *Multinational Federalism and Value Pluralism*, London, New York: Routledge.

2 Shadows of the Enlightenment

Refining pluralism in liberal democracies

Ferran Requejo

The irruption of recent phenomena such as economic and technological globalization and cultural pluralism movements means that the classic question "What is Enlightenment?" demands far more plural responses than those provided by traditional forms of political liberalism, democracy, federalism and constitutionalism. This is not the first time that the "shadows" associated with these responses have been pointed out. For instance, in the interwar years of the twentieth century, the Frankfurt school highlighted important shortcomings in the social sciences and classical philosophy when they spoke of "progress" or "emancipation". Their target was the way that the "enlightened" tradition (including Marxism) had developed up until that time. In Hegelian terms and taking a pessimistic view of modern societies – although they distanced themselves from a conception of history seen as a "rational" process and Hegel's philosophy of identity – authors like Adorno, Horkheimer and Marcuse criticized the positivist suppositions associated with a clear separation between science and ideology and the philosophies that established unquestionable normative principles.

In opposition to the different versions of orthodox Marxism, political economy could no longer be considered *the* science of human emancipation. Instead of being the solution, Marx was part of the problem. The way forward was to be found in interdisciplinary work which was far more aware of its own limitations and analytical complexities. In fact, according to the Frankfurt school, the Enlightenment itself, which wished to demythologize the world, has in turn become a myth. Confidence in the advent of an era of reason and enlightenment in contrast to suffering, ignorance and injustice is more an expression of faith than a reasonable perspective. The means that were proposed, domination of nature, have become the ends. The domination of capitalism and socialism over nature result in uncivilized forms of behaviour in the name of reason – exploitation, new kinds of dependence, ecological crises, etc. Enlightened reason leads to irrationality. The essence of historical rationality can only be negative or, in other words, "critical". In order to conduct good theory one must pay attention to contexts, which are always particular, and these require interdisciplinarity, the use of induction, and more modest epistemological pretensions than the suppositions of abstract theories of enlightened origin. It is necessary, say those of the Frankfurt school, to recover the sceptical element in Hegelian thought, that which shows the biased nature of any scientific or political "representation". The universal can only be examined at the particular level, not "above" or "beyond" it. Validity is always limited and inconclusive, etc.

This criticism of the "shadows" of the Enlightenment referred to questions of a "socio-economic" nature. But together with their tendency to break away from and encourage political emancipation from the *Ancien Régime*, the "enlightened" declarations and political ideas associated with the French Revolution also spoke of a "nation of citizens", understood in culturally homogeneous terms. This is something that the empirical evidence of liberal democracies constantly denies in many cases. Since the last decade of the twentieth century there has been a normative revision of the legitimising bases of these democracies, a revision which is associated with the re-emergence of a set of practical phenomena that broaden the "socio-economic criticism" of the "enlightened shadows" mentioned above towards a "national and cultural" dimension. Phenomena such as the treatment that liberal democracies dispense to indigenous peoples, minority nations (Quebec, Scotland, Flanders, Catalonia, etc.), transnational immigrant peoples, etc. reveal normative and practical deficiencies – of both an instrumental and procedural nature – in the "enlightened" suppositions of traditional democratic liberalism and practical constitutionalism.

This is a revision and a series of phenomena that have established a "new agenda" of issues – issues which have been barely or badly addressed (or not addressed at all) by classic theories of democracy and by theories of justice and federalism (the rights, recognition and accommodation of permanent national and cultural minorities). These theories are cloaked in new "shadows" in terms of their interpretation and concretion of values such as individual dignity, liberty, equality or pluralism. It is clear that these theories lack sufficiently conceptual, analytical and normative resources to offer responses that may be considered to be both just and workable when faced with the challenges posed by this new agenda of issues, an agenda which takes political issues into dimensions that until recently were largely neglected. One of these "shadows" refers to the interrelationship between *monism* and *stateism* which runs through traditional forms of democratic liberalism and constitutionalism. Monism, says Berlin, is at the root of all extremism – extremism, we might add, that may also be established in democratic terms.

What follows is a synthesis of a brief set of analytical elements of the theory of democracy which identify a number of "shadows" or flaws that exist in the normative and institutional bases of plurinational liberal democracies, as well as a number of elements related with the revision of these bases in order to carry out a *political and constitutional recognition* and *accommodation* of the national pluralism of this kind of democracy. This is an attempt to focus attention on some of the aspects that have been addressed by the traditional theories of liberal democracy with regard to national pluralism and which it is important to take into account when embarking upon a revision of federalism in plurinational contexts (section 1). Second, we will focus on the idea of moral cosmopolitanism and national minority rights taking into account the Kantian philosophical perspective that is usually present in traditional liberal approaches. Kantian concepts of cosmopolitism, nationalism and patriotism will be here the main points of reference. Although Kant's philosophy contains some elements, such as the *unsocial sociability* of humans beings and the *Ideas of Reason*, to overcome the failures of Kantism regarding cosmopolitism and national minority rights, I will point out the need for a more Hegelian perspective in the normative and institutional analysis of plurinational democracies (section 2).

1 Liberal democracies in plurinational societies: 20 shadows of the Enlightenment

1   Currently, no political theory of democracy, justice, etc. has the capacity to synthesize the normative complexity involved in the legitimacy of liberal democracies and even less so if institutional and procedural issues such as federalism are added to the equation. We have rather partial theories for particular issues. Traditional liberal-democratic theories and theories of federalism are usually analytically and normatively flawed when they attempt to deal with plurinational and multicultural issues.[1]

2   In order to obtain more refined and realistic results, it would be better to combine the theoretical analyses with those of an empirical nature (comparative analyses or case studies). Empirical information usually includes elements that are important from a normative perspective in specific contexts that abstract analyses usually fail to take into account. It would also be advisable to take a fresh look at and pluralize the *ethical* dimension of practical rationality, which links up with values and practices in specific contexts that are always particular (*Sittlichkeit*, in classic Hegelian terms), together with the more common *pragmatic* (instrumental) and *moral* (*Moralität*) dimensions of this rationality, which are based more on criteria that are independent of the context. This *ethical* dimension has usually been neglected by traditional theories of political liberalism (from Locke to Rawls), which have tended to uncritically accept a "state communitarian" perspective.

3   In general terms, both the recent debate regarding the relations between liberal democracies and national pluralism and empirical analyses have revealed the obsolescence of approaching the normative and institutional discussion in terms of a contrast between "democratic liberalism" on the one hand and "nationalism" on the other. At the normative level, discussion about national pluralism in democracies is currently located between two conceptions of democratic liberalism, known as Liberalism 1 and Liberalism 2. The latter is more sensitive to the demands for the recognition and accommodation of national and cultural minorities.[2] At an empirical level, it is clear that the citizens of most minority nations in plurinational democracies usually defend values and conceptions which are as liberal (or as illiberal) as the citizens of majority nations. Currently, the notion that

minority nationalisms promote policies which are contrary to liberal-democratic values is inappropriate (in fact it is really the Jacobinism implemented by the majority of specific democracies which emits non-liberal signals with regard to the way they treat minorities).[3]

4   Plurinational democracies are political collectivities containing two or more nations that aspire to be recognized and accommodated politically as such within political and constitutional rules.[4] They, therefore, are not uninational realities with "regional" subunits that belong to a single national *demos*. They are "different societies" (in the sense that they display distinctive features and express a desire to be distinguished from other societies). It is more correct here to speak of a plurality of *demoi* than of a single *demos* (although the latter may describe itself internally as "plural"). The general challenge of plurinational democracies is *one polity, several demoi*. However, while theories of democracy have usually failed to address or respond to the question of who should constitute the *demos* of a democracy, theories of justice do not usually address or respond regarding to which collectivity "basic justice" should apply. In both cases, the two concepts are usually uncritically defined in advance in relation to the state (regardless, moreover, of the historical process through which this has been formed). In the majority of theories of liberal justice (Rawls) it is understood that the citizens are united through a common acceptance of a series of "principles of justice", and not through issues of national, cultural or historical identity. This is somewhat naïve in the theoretical sphere of democracies and biased in their practical sphere.

5   Majority and minority national realities are both internally plural. Empirical citizens, moreover, sometimes hold several national identities. This conveniently avoids the need to address, analytically and normatively, the contraposition between the national collectivities of plurinational democracies in terms of a contrast between internally homogeneous blocks. Individual and collective "identities", furthermore, do not constitute a fixed reality either. They construct themselves and change over time.

6   All liberal democracies have carried out and continue to be involved in processes of state nation-building (specific collective values, institutions, decision-making processes, specific policies). Some of the nation-building processes used by democracies in the past are unacceptable nowadays in normative terms (assimilation, deportation, repression, stigmatization of minorities, etc.). Traditional democratic liberalism and constitutionalism have failed to develop the question of the regulation of *permanent* national minorities in democracies with regard to their recognition and political accommodation.[5]

7   Those democracies which display internal national pluralism usually display distinct simultaneous processes of nation-building. These processes will, at least partly, be of an agonistic nature. This does not appear to be surmountable by referring to a form of political liberalism based on the "aggregation of interests" or on attempted processes of "rational consensus". Moreover,

the fact that two societies share the same values is not particularly informative regarding their willingness to live together (examples: the secessions of Norway and Sweden at the beginning of the twentieth century, and Slovakia and the Czech Republic in the 1990s).

8 Two general objectives to be achieved with regard to a "just and workable" regulation of national pluralism in plurinational democracies are the explicit constitutional *recognition* of that pluralism and an *equitable political accommodation* of the majority and of national minorities in relation to the rights, institutions and decision-making processes of these democracies (a fair accommodation of the different processes of nation-building of the majority and of the minorities). The distinction between "civic" and "ethnic" nationalisms is not very fruitful from a conceptual or empirical standpoint in the case of liberal-democratic nationalisms. All liberal-democratic majority and minority nationalisms introduce cultural factors into public life (symbols, languages, historical references, etc.).

9 In the analysis of legitimacy in plurinational contexts, there is a juxtaposition of perspectives between the so-called *paradigm of equality* (equality vs. inequality) and the *paradigm of difference* (equality vs. difference). The main legitimizing liberal-democratic values (dignity, liberty, equality, pluralism): (i) are internally complex (e.g. negative and positive liberties; equality, of what? between whom?; pluralism, of what?; etc.); and (ii) cover both individual and collective dimensions. The politics of recognition of different national and cultural differences is part of the struggle for human dignity (*Human Development Report*, United Nations 2004).[6]

10 Nowadays it also seems to be generally accepted that the sphere of "national and cultural" justice is different from the sphere of "social justice". The concepts, questions and values of "social justice" do not coincide with those of "national and cultural justice" (redistribution vs. recognition). Some institutions and policies are able to improve the former, but have hardly any effect on the latter and vice versa. Occasionally there are interrelations between these two spheres of justice, but the phenomena associated with each are different. These two spheres refer to distinct values, objectives, actors, institutions, practices and policies. There have been historical experiences in which groups that are socio-economically dominant in a territory can at the same time be dominated themselves in the cultural and linguistic sphere of the state. Political cleavages that are present in empirical cases may reinforce or diminish national tensions.[7]

11 Traditional theories of democracy display a *stateist* bias, which is favourable to majorities, in relation to: (i) the conceptions of the kinds of individualism, pluralism and universalism that they defend; and (ii) the use of legitimizing notions usually of a monist (not pluralist) nature, such as "equality of citizenship", "national sovereignty" or "popular sovereignty". The advisability of considering *national pluralism* not only as a political fact which has to be managed, but as a specific type of normative pluralism that democratic systems must recognize, protect and facilitate.

12   The different kinds of legitimising *values, identities* and *interests* present in plurinational democracies are also difficult to synthesize. The classic debate on the "incommensurability of values" is joined by the achievable compatibility (only partial and pragmatic?) between different national identities; the importance of reaching *modus vivendi* agreements (practical agreements which seek to achieve peaceful coexistence) which depend on historical and specific political conditions.

13   The criticism of individualistic "atomism" and the "subject who chooses" of traditional political liberalism underlines the often flawed approach of traditional liberal-democratic theories to issues of a national and cultural nature.[8] The idea that human beings are autonomous individuals that choose their (national, ethnic, linguistic, religious, etc.) identities is to a large extent a myth of traditional liberalism. In other words, they are usually not chosen. In reality, they are the foundations on which one's choices are based. They are the political, social and cultural contexts in which individuals socialize, and are usually the result of processes that include historical events of both a peaceful and violent nature (wars of annexation, territorial conquests, etc.). These processes are often at the root of present-day struggles for the recognition and accommodation of minority nations.

14   The issue of borders has rarely been considered by theories of democracy and federalism. The establishment of constitutional rules in liberal democracies is preceded by a self-awarded collective right: the right to self-determination for the state collective (regardless, once again, of the (sometimes coercive) historical process which has created the state itself). This is a right that democracies usually deny internal national collectives of the state polity.[9] A number of minorities currently question the legitimacy of the state's monopoly of the right to collective self-determination and defend their own "right to decide".

15   The idea that the democratic state is a culturally "neutral" entity is another liberal myth that is no longer defended by the majority of authors who espouse traditional liberalism. It is an idea that cannot be approached in terms of a form of separation like that which (theoretically) governs the relations between the state and the different religions in the majority of liberal democracies. All states impose particular national, linguistic and cultural features on their citizens. Minority nations also do this when they have their own institutions of self-government.

16   Cultural and national liberties, which include both individual and collective dimensions, are an essential value of the *democratic quality* of a society and people's individual development and self-esteem. These liberties are not protected by the mere application of civil, participatory and social rights which are usually included in the liberal-democratic constitutions of the twentieth century.

17   The classic liberal-democratic institutional "solutions" to achieve recognition and political accommodation in nationally diverse democracies are federalism, consociationalism and secession. Questions regarding institutional

issues in plurinational contexts appear to require solutions that are "open" to evolution over time. There is a little practical and normative plausibility to want to "close" territorial issues in plurinational federations.[10]

18 It is important to establish the motives and objectives on which a federalization process is based. These motives and objectives are unlikely to coincide in the case of uninational and plurinational polities. Federated units of a national nature often coexist in a plurinational federation with others of a regional (of the majority nation) nature. In theories of federalism, moreover, there is a clear contrast between those that situate the normative centre of gravity in the "union" that emerges from the federal agreement, and those that situate it with the parties that obtain the agreement. Broadly speaking, this is the contrast between the approaches of J. Madison and J. Althusius, respectively) which are more closely linked with what we might call the spirit of confederations and consociational federalism.[11] One of the aims of the "federal agreement" would, in this case, be the preservation of the identities of the subjects of the agreement.[12] On the other hand, American federalist tradition associated with the creation of the first contemporary federal state, has interpreted the agreement from a much more unitary–federal than confederal perspective. The centre of gravity is located in the governance of a "nation-state" (new processes of state-building and nation-building), and in the subsequent supremacy of the central power over the federated units. Here, the Union is more important than the units.[13] It is obvious that different normative and institutional conclusions will be obtained depending on which of these two traditions of federalism is adopted (questions about liberty: individual and collective, positive and negative; about equality: the equality of national entities? the equality of federated units?, etc., and how these responses interrelate).

19 The political accommodation of minority nations through rules and federal procedures will, in general terms, require both the institutional concretion of the *self-government* of these minorities and a kind of specific protection and participation in the *shared government* of the federation. The legitimation of federal institutions and processes in plurinational federations (national pluralism, recognition, accommodation, etc.) differs from and widens the usual legitimation of constitutionalism in uninational federations. When there is a clear de facto asymmetry in the national pluralism of the state and/or when the number of federated entities is high constitutional asymmetric solutions or practices of *opting in* and *opting out* may offer a suitable framework for the political accommodation of this form of pluralism.

20 Federalism is directly affected by supra-state processes of political and economic integration (e.g. the European Union). The dissolution of the state monopoly on the principle of territoriality and the exclusive dualism between state and non-state processes of nation-building are two elements that have an influence on the institutional accommodation of national pluralism in a globalized political, economic and technological context.

The creation of liberal democracies that are increasingly refined from a moral and institutional point of view in terms of their *national* and *cultural pluralism* is one of the challenges of present-day democratic and federal systems. This requires a more in-depth review of the theoretical revision and practical reformulations carried out over recent years in some plurinational democracies (Belgium, Canada, Spain, the United Kingdom, etc.). This would tackle questions such as: what implications does the regulation of national pluralism have for the symbolic, institutional and self-government spheres?[14] What does accepting plurinationality in an international society mean? I will focus on this latter question in the next section following the path of *cosmopolitism* and its relation with national minorities. Kant's philosophy is here an obvious point of reference.

2   Moral cosmopolitanism and national minority rights

Global Justice has usually been understood to mean institutional and social justice (political and redistributive issues on a global scale). In contrast, issues involving different national and cultural identities are usually marginal in reflections on global justice. This occurs despite the fact that charters of human rights include political, social *and* cultural rights. This section links a conception of global justice, *moral cosmopolitanism*, with plurinational democracies. It is possible that conclusions reached regarding political, social and national/cultural issues in relation to global justice will not be identical, as there are clear differences between: (1) the values and the kind of pluralism involved, (2) the actors and empirical cases involved, and (3) the variable degree of difficulty in achieving normative and institutional consensus for these issues. The shadows of the Enlightenment show here an international face.

2.1 Moral cosmopolitanism

Broadly speaking, cosmopolitanism is the idea that all human beings belong to the same moral collectivity. This is primarily a normative conception that creates obligations towards the other members of that collectivity, regardless of specific characteristics such as nationality, language, religion, etc., that individuals may possess (moral cosmopolitanism). Second, cosmopolitanism also refers to a more political idea, one that advocates the creation of links between human collectives through a "league or federation of states" and an "international system of justice" (political and institutional cosmopolitanism). It is well known that these general ideas on moral, political and institutional cosmopolitanism usually are linked to Kant's work.

More recently, T. Pogge has offered a specific version of moral cosmopolitanism, linking it with three basic elements: (a) *individualism* (the fundamental moral reference are persons, not groups, families, tribes, etc.); (b) *universality* (morality concerns all human beings in equal measure, not only those of a specific ethnic group, nation, religion, etc.); and (c) *generality* (the moral implication is understood to concern all individuals, not only compatriots, members of the same religion, etc.).[15]

Criticisms of the positions of cosmopolitanism can be broken down into criticisms of each one of these components.[16] One of the most established criticisms of moral cosmopolitanism is that which questions its implicit anthropological roots. Behind the most common versions of moral cosmopolitanism one usually finds preconceived ideas about human nature and a certain intellectual tendency to approach moral questions more in *monist* than in *pluralist* terms.[17] So, cosmopolitanism would be flawed in at least two ways: on the one hand, because it does not match the empirical motivations of moral behaviour: it would be a "moralist" position based on a flawed conception of human beings; and on the other hand, because of its excessively abstract, and therefore empirically impoverished, position. It would fail to satisfactorily include the specific contextual elements with which human individuals and groups make "rational and reasonable" decisions according to their specific *values*, *identities* and *interests*. The defence of human dignity and political liberty, for example, probably does not have the same consequences in different contexts (e.g. in uninational societies, like Germany or Portugal, or in plurinational societies, like Belgium, Spain or Canada). I think that the solution, however, is not to reject moral cosmopolitanism, but to refine and adjust it according to the contexts of its application. Our main theoretical point of reference is here Kant's work.

2.2 Cosmopolitanism, patriotism and nationalism. A revision of Kant

Kant's work is commonly used as a reference point in theoretical discussions on cosmopolitanism, patriotism and nationalism. However, I am not sure that these constant references to Kant's work are always accompanied by an acceptable degree of analytical precision. On the one hand, many authors who claim to be cosmopolitan defend a version of "civic patriotism", although often without justifying the compatibility between these two positions. On the other hand, it is worth mentioning the general defence that cosmopolitan authors make of liberal "national patriotism" (at times juxtaposed with and not very well distinguished conceptually from civic patriotism), especially when some aspect of their "national identity" is threatened.

Generally speaking, it is possible to say that in relation to cosmopolitanism and patriotism, Kant's work postulates:

- a kind of moral cosmopolitanism (in the terms previously mentioned).
- a moderate type of political cosmopolitanism, linked to the "league of nations", constitutional law and "hospitality" between nations and with respect to "foreigners". As is well known, it is a form of cosmopolitanism which does not include a coercive power (whether it be executive, legislative or judicial), but simply the voluntary adoption of supra-state organizations and their rules.

- an explicit line of reasoning on the compatibility between moral cosmopolitanism and republican-style *civic patriotism*. Both positions generate different duties, but they are two normative ensembles that are harmonious or compatible.
- a line of reasoning in favour of a form of *national patriotism* based on belonging to a specific national group founded on a common ancestry, one's own customs, etc., and on a set of specific collective values.

The last two aspects mentioned point out the discussion about moral cosmopolitanism and its compatibility with two basic types of patriotism – civic and national – in plurinational contexts.

2.2.1 Civic patriotism

Kant's *civic patriotism* is related to the *state patriotism* and the *citizen's patriotism* of the republican tradition. The basic values here are liberty, equality, *res publica* and self-government – echoes of classical thought. This is a form of patriotism that generates duties that would like to believe they are compatible with the duties associated with moral cosmopolitanism. Here Kant must confront a serious difficulty. Kant appears to believe he has overcome the possible incompatibility between duties, mainly by pointing out that both kinds of duties in fact lead us towards the same cosmopolitan objective: to get ever closer to "perpetual peace".[18] However, Kant's approach raises a number of questions about whether this compatibility is as harmonious as Kant would wish it to be (not to mention that Kant thinks in an institutional *liberal* republic). The following are a number of critical questions on this issue: which of the two duties is more important when, in practice, resources are scarce?; why should the state, the republican "polity", be considered unquestioningly as a collectivity characterized by solidarity and, moreover, one that takes precedence over all the other collectivities?; are their, more consensual or more coercive, historical formation processes morally relevant for the legitimacy of states?; does this alleged civic patriotism – today we would say this "constitutional patriotism" – which ignores linguistic, cultural, historical, etc. characteristics, which are present in all states, really exist?[19] It would seem that attempting to base the solidarity of a polity on the "interaction" that exists between its citizens is difficult to defend in moral terms, as this interaction may itself be based on previous coercion practised on particular collectives (wars of annexation, mass deportations, exterminations of specific peoples, etc.). In other words, coercion may have preceded interaction (European history is full of examples of this kind).

2.2.2 National patriotism

Basically, Kant observes the psychological difficulty of attempting to be linked only to cosmopolitan duties and postulates a rejection of this position. Using a line of reasoning reminiscent of Hume, Kant posits the need to exercise the duties based on some empirical focus which supposes an emotive implication in our moral actions. The lack of emotive implications in this nucleus would be an obstacle for moral action. From here on, Kant simply identifies the group of co-nationals as this empirical focus, which also generates duties compatible with those linked to moral cosmopolitanism. But, as Kleingeld points out, neither the assimilation of co-nationals as members of the polity, nor the identification between the reference empirical focus and the national collectivity seem justified here. Other alternative empirical foci can be used.[20] Here, Kant's argument fails to meet his usual own high analytical standards. Nevertheless, it points towards a proven fact: concretion and emotivity are common ingredients of moral motivation.

In the case of plurinational societies, we always find several at least partially competitive, nation-building processes. This is reflected in the different political positions that emerge when one attempts to establish the constitutional recognition of plurinationality itself, the level of the self-governments, how to regulate the use of political symbols, how the international relations of the state and minority nations should be regulated, which historical reconstruction most faithfully reflects past reality in school curricula, etc. I believe that any "monist" moral conception is bound to fail here – as is any pluralist conception which attempts to establish a complete arrangement for values and for *all* practical cases. In fact, values related to empirical processes of nation-building are agonistic – they compete with each other – making it impossible to establish "rational" hierarchies of a *generic* nature among them.

The conclusion is that, despite the fact that with the "civic" version of patriotism Kant finds it easier to argue in favour of the compatibility between this version and moral cosmopolitanism, this line of reasoning is not without its difficulties. It creates conceptual, empirical and institutional difficulties. Civic patriotism does not appear to pass the test of institutional practice (like the majority of "republican" notions when there are different boundaries for the republic and for the nations). Moreover, it is a concept that grants hegemony to national majorities in detriment to minorities, and which therefore acts as a legitimizing tool for the status quo of states, wherever the boundaries between them may be. However, Kant's work makes it possible to incorporate and enrich moral cosmopolitanism from foundations that are more "agonistic" and better adapted to the *empirical* world (and more sensitive to the rights of minority nations than the usual versions of moral cosmopolitanism). We are entering a theoretical context in which it is advisable to introduce the perspective of Berlin's *value pluralism* and Taylor's *politics of recognition* into the rules of cosmopolitism.[21] Both reflect the "deep diversity" of national pluralism. In order to do so, it is useful to introduce into the discussion: (1) an analytical perspective associated with the Kantian concept of *"unsocial sociability"* of human beings, put forward in *Idea for a Universal History from a Cosmopolitan Point of View* (1784); and (2) an analytical approach of the *Ideas of Pure Reason*, developed in the *Transcendental Dialectics* of the first *Critique*, especially when this use is related to the form of cosmopolitanism postulated in Kant's "historical writings". The section that follows discusses these two Kantian approaches from the perspective of national minority rights.

2.3 The concept of "unsocial sociability" and the Ideas of Pure Reason *as elements of the moral and institutional refinement of cosmopolitanism in plurinational democracies*

2.3.1 The "unsocial sociability" of mankind

One of the main attractions of Kant for current political theory – especially for theories of justice and theories of democracy in a globalized world – is that he is an author who is by no means lacking in realism. We are not faced with a "moralist" work in the utopian sense, one that is disconnected from reality. Neither are we in the presence of someone who shrinks from dealing radically with the components of the behaviour of individuals and human collectives. The world is characterized by conflict and evolution in a non-linear fashion. Kant would not have been surprised by Darwin's theory of evolution. I believe that, at times, some of Kant's devotees do not fully appreciate this theoretical approach from an author they venerate. Fortunately, with Kant we are a long way from any "angelic" conception of mankind and societies. Kant's cosmopolitanism has less in common with Rousseau than with the tragic authors (from Aeschylus to Shakespeare). In other words, we are a long way from an ingenuous kind of rationalism and moralism.

This is reflected in the title of the small paper *Idea for a Universal History from a Cosmopolitan Point of View* and in its very first phrase: "Whatever concept we may have, on a metaphysical plane, of free will, its phenomenal manifestations, human actions, are determined, like other natural phenomena, by the general laws of Nature". History is neither linear nor moves towards a pre-established objective. No harmonious society is waiting for us in the future. This is not the horizon of the "cosmopolitan society" that Kant postulates.

One of the key concepts established in *Idea for…* is the notion of "unsocial sociability" which characterizes mankind. Today we would say that the genetic "hardware" with which we are born is characterized by an internal antagonism in our "natural dispositions" to be in society, put another way, to be in *any society* that transmits a set of specific cultural "software" to us. Conflict, rivalry, competition for resources and for power are ingredients of social relations. And it is all beyond our will. At times, human beings desire harmony, but our nature desires something else. And in this dual human condition of "supportive egoists" are the roots of progress. But they are tragic roots.

Without action there is no tragedy, Aristotle said. It is like the board on which the game of our political and moral decisions is played. And the human condition is contradictory, among other reasons because the values with which we attempt to order the world morally are often irreconcilable. Love, justice, liberty, duty or friendship are desirable values, but they cannot be synthesized in a harmonious way. Viewed in isolation they lead to dogmatism.

In this way, the tragedies show what moral and political theories usually keep quiet about: our instrumental reason is strong, our morality fragile. Practical actions are never decided in a totally rational way. But Creon, Antigone, Orestes,

Brutus, Henry IV or King Lear cannot but act, despite the fact that their questions have a number of possible rational and moral responses. The "agonistic" nature of morality and politics becomes "tragic" not only because any action that we embark upon involves some kind of loss, but also because we will not be able to avoid the fact that any action we take will have negative effects, whatever it is that we decide to do. Human morality reflects an insurmountable pluralism of values,[22] linked to our *unsocial sociability.* This is one of Kant's most penetrating and fruitful concepts for the political sphere which allows us to better define cosmopolitan society. Progress towards a *cosmopolitan society,* towards a society that "applies law universally", is slow and plagued by setbacks. In fact, this progress may be seen as: (1) progress towards a form of political liberalism in the international sphere (international rule of law), and (2) progress towards liberal democracies which are more refined morally and institutionally. Both aspects require one to understand: (a) that *value pluralism* constitutes an insurmountable framework when partially agonistic values and identities which should find their own accommodation among themselves come into conflict; and (b) that it is morally desirable to go deeper into a *politics of recognition* of deep diversities (among them those that reflect the national pluralism in some polities) as an ingredient of the moral and institutional refinement of liberal democracies at the beginning of the twenty-first century.[23]

2.3.2 The "Ideas of Reason" and cosmopolitanism

Another aspect of Kant's work that has received very little attention is that relating to the potential of the first *Critique* for political theory, and, more specifically, that which is linked with the role of the Ideas of Pure Reason developed in the "Transcendental Dialectics". As is well known, unlike the "Transcendental Analytics", where scientific knowledge based on the conjunction between theoretical categories and empirical information predominates, the Reason of the "Transcendental Dialectics" offers us Ideas. We can define these Ideas, although we are unable to obtain "knowledge" from them because there is a lack of empirical experience at this epistemological level.[24] The Ideas function as a framework for ordering our experience and activity because they give us a global vision of the world. In this way, we humans know a lot less than we think. The problems posed by Kant's Reason cannot be resolved unequivocally, nor rejected.[25] Thus, "metaphysics" is here understood as a disposition.[26] Ideas provides points of reference for our experience. They are not arbitrary inventions, but constructions based on the same nature as human reason.[27] Among these Ideas are those of a *cosmopolitan society* and *perpetual peace.*

Today we know that language and thought is what most distinguishes us as a species, but is probably not what most defines us as individuals. It is a characteristic of this strange primate, the product of evolution, who calls himself *sapiens* but whom it continues to be relatively easy to deceive and who is adept at deceiving himself.[28] How? For example, when the use of the Ideas goes beyond its functions – something that can happen quite easily. For Kant, humans make correct and incorrect use of the Ideas of Reason. The correct uses are those which limit the function of the Ideas to a *regulative* use, while incorrect uses establish a *constitutive* use of them; in other words, a use which attempts to obtain a "knowledge" from them which they are epistemologically forbidden to provide. This incorrect use has disastrous consequences in the practical sphere (moral and political).[29] In this sense, *cosmopolitan society* is a *regulative* Idea which protects against *constitutive* uses of Reason that result in the desire to attain an absolute order.

One of Kant's most decisive contributions is to have seen that the *constitutive* use of the Ideas – those which attempt to take human reason beyond its limits – cannot be eradicated. This is a "metaphysical impulse" of human reason related with its agonistic underpinnings. One must accept the inevitable existence of this impulse and endeavour to combat its excesses, the tendency to overstep rational limits[30] both in theory – for which it is necessary to have freedom of criticism and enlightened education – and in practice – for which one needs rights and *liberal* institutions (not "republican").

Kant's Ideas of Reason are not invented problems[31]; "imagined communities" are not "invented" communities. Kant puts forward a complex philosophical version, expressed in modern language, of the aim to protect against the two main practical dangers detected in classical Greece: anarchy and tyranny. For Kant, the theoretical correlate of anarchy is scepticism and the correlate of tyranny (or despotism) is dogmatism. Cosmopolitanism represents an achievement for the human race, in other words, an objective for mankind (*First Critique*) which encourages the species' progress towards *perpetual peace* in the empirical world (*Historical Writings*). In this way, cosmopolitanism (and civic patriotism) would act, for example, as a restriction on the fanaticism (Schwärmerei) and obsession (Wahn) of national patriotism (whether this is exercised by the majority or by a minority). However, it will be better to defend moral cosmopolitanism, as Kant perceives it, while at the same time accepting the radical pluralism of a set of national (not civic) and, predictably to some extent, competitive patriotisms, which are searching for mutual accommodation both in the sphere of democracies and internationally.

2.4 Moral cosmopolitanism and minority rights in plurinational democracies. Refining justice and institutions on a global and domestic scale

It is obvious that both state and non-state "nationalisms" have provoked practices that fail to respect the propositions of moral cosmopolitanism. One only needs to take a look at the history of the twentieth century to find examples where nationalist positions have been used to justify totalitarian practices and the extermination of peoples, such as Nazism, Stalinism, Maoism, the events that occurred in the former Yugoslavia, etc. However, nationalism is not intrinsically alien to cosmopolitan tenets. In fact, the concepts of "nation" and "citizen" originate from the same historical experiences in the American and French revolutions of the eighteenth century. Both concepts were and continue to be linked to a large extent to states (to existing states, to demands for the creation of new states and to reform existing ones).

Moral cosmopolitanism has its own roots deep in this modern and enlightened tradition, but we know that "progress" has also its darker side. This darker side sometimes reveals itself because the gap which always exists between what the theories say and what empirical institutions do (the liberal language of the "free and equal men" has contrasted with exclusions based on gender, class, religion, ethnicity, etc., of empirical societies which called themselves liberal). It is as much of a mistake to believe that liberalism and cosmopolitanism are all sweetness and "light", as it is to believe that moral "principles" should be insensitive to context. In fact, today we know that despite the fact that a plurinational liberal democracy may respect the civil, political and social rights of its citizens, the latter are not usually treated equitably in national and cultural terms.

In this context, moral cosmopolitanism has sometimes functioned as a "conservative" philosophy, that is to say, as a way of legitimizing the status quo of the national and cultural characteristics dominant in contemporary societies. This happens when cosmopolitanism turns a blind eye to, or, in other words, when it fails to question or challenge examples of domination exercised by human groups over others regarding national and cultural issues. This situation means that cosmopolitanism is sometimes associated in practice with a lack of respect for *individual dignity* and a deficient treatment of the kinds of *universal equality* and *generality* that supporters of moral cosmopolitanism defend.

Therefore, the three elements of moral cosmopolitanism mentioned above – individualism, universal equality and generality – demand special attention when *national pluralism* is introduced into the "fact of pluralism" of some contemporary societies:

1   *Individualism.* National pluralism introduces an anthropological normative dimension which affects people because, precisely, they are "the ultimate units of concern ... rather than, say, family, tribes, ethnic, cultural or religious communities, nations or states" (Pogge). This means recognizing people as moral subjects, without ignoring them or deciding their characteristics for them.

2   *Universal equality.* This second element indicates that the individualism mentioned above refers "to every living being equally – not merely to some sub-set, such as men, aristocrats, Aryans, whites...". In our case, this would mean enlarging the list of "men, aristocrats..." to include persons with a "hegemonic national identity in their own state". This is precisely the dimension of political liberty which is marginalized or ignored in the traditional theories of political liberalism and cosmopolitanism.

3   *Generality of application.* This condition would require the inclusion of minority national identities in the cosmopolitan rules of juridical recognition and guarantee. All national minorities – and not only the largest ones in a state – should be the object of normative and institutional protection on a global scale.

Political power has often become despotic due to the same tendency of human reason to "go beyond its limits". Political liberalism successfully carried out the task of regulating a series of rights and putting limits on the exercise of political power. Thus, it is not a question of establishing a relativist or "multicultural" alternative to liberally based moral cosmopolitanism, but to refine it intellectually and morally so that its characteristics of individualism, universal equality and generality can find better practical expression in nationally diverse societies (in the intellectual and moral sense of the term "better"). My proposal for the case of plurinational societies is a form of cosmopolitanism that:

1   at the *analytical* and *normative* level, is a kind of cosmopolitanism that is much more sensitive, both in its *concepts* and in the interpretation of its *values*, to empirical information that has crucial moral and political relevance for individuals who are part of minorities; a kind of cosmopolitanism that displays the will to "optimize" national diversity morally and politically (without uncritically sanctioning the simple reality of existing states in the international sphere). Both conditions would encourage greater respect for the individual *dignity* of individuals themselves, and development of the individual and collective dimensions which are usually excluded from the values of *liberty*, *equality* and *pluralism* established in the political and constitutional practices of present-day democracies

2   at the *institutional* level, is a kind of cosmopolitanism that recognizes and guarantees the "pluralism of values and identities" of these societies as well as establishing recognition, juridical guarantees and wide-ranging self-government for national minorities in its constitutional rules (recognition of the plurality of *demoi* existing in the polity; collective rights and liberties, a division of powers through consociational and/or federal rules establishing constitutional asymmetries when demographic, historical or cultural conditions require it, or even with clear rules for secession).

There is no guarantee, as Kant knew, that "mankind will progress constantly towards a better future". Conflicts are inherent to human collectivities. The important thing is to have institutions capable of settling conflicts between legitimate values, interests and identities. In this field, we humans have invented nothing better than the charters of rights and institutional practices that have their origins in the political liberalism of modern times. Although this is not the subject of this chapter, I am personally sceptical, for both theoretical and practical reasons, about the advisability of establishing institutions of "global democracy". Having said that, I believe that moral and political "progress" for the twenty-first century should consist in setting up institutions of "political liberalism", in other words, institutions to guarantee rights and the rule of law on a global justice scale. These global rights and rules should take into account the national and cultural rights of national minorities (charters of rights which include the option to appeal to international courts, which would have the capacity to impose sanctions on offenders). This is a indispensable requirement to ensure that we progress towards the kind of democracies and international relations that are more in tune with the cosmopolitan ideal.[32]

In short, I advocate the establishment of a kind of moral cosmopolitanism which is more attentive to the *normative* and *empirical* pluralism of contemporary societies in a world in which globalization is transforming economic, political and cultural relations. It is a question, in theoretical terms, of putting, so to speak, Berlin and Taylor inside Kant; and, in practical terms, of establishing: (1) constitutions based on respect for national minorities and which put them on an equal footing with the majorities, and (2) international institutions based on a global rule of law (charters of rights, courts, etc.) to which the citizens of minority groups can have recourse when they believe that their rights have been violated. This should be a kind of cosmopolitanism that is firmly rooted in the *unsocial sociability* of mankind, in what moves people to act in empirical contexts (values, but also bonds and identities), and understood, not as a "utopian ideal", but as a regulative function of one of the Ideas of Kantian Reason. In this way, a global cosmopolitanism that includes the moral and institutional perspective of plurinational societies will gradually enlarge the themes and the scope of this "society which applies the rule of law universally" of which Kant was speaking over two centuries ago. However, I think that a "Hegelian turn" (recognition, ethicity and moral collectivism) needs to be introduced to this approach in order to overcome the conceptual and ontological "shadows" linked to the individualist and "universalist" perspective present in most Kantian approaches.[33]

Notes

1 Berlin's criticisms of the theoretical and moral prejudices of Western philosophy can be summarized in his well-known statement that from the time of Classical Greece and Christianity until the rationalism of the Enlightenment, this tradition takes the following three assertions for granted: (1) that there is a unique rational response to all true questions; (2) that there is a way to discover these truths; and (3) that all these true responses are compatible among them. Each one of these assertions is questionable (see Berlin 1998). For a previous approach to the liberal-democratic shortcomings related to plurinational polities, see Requejo (2010d).

2 Normative complexity entails both a "pluralism of values" and a "plurality of perspectives" (Hobbesian, liberal, democratic, social, multicultural, national, federal, post-materialist, etc.). For an approach to normative pluralism in liberal democracies through "nine normative poles", see Requejo (2005, chap. 1).

3 See Taylor (1992). Moments of contrast between theories related to "justice" and "truth" (Plato, Kant, Rawls) and reactive theories associated with "virtue" and the "community" (Aristotle, Hegel, Taylor) are common in the history of political thought.

4 The so-called Liberalism 2 criticizes the notions of individualism, universalism, citizenship or nationalism associated with traditional political liberalism for being normatively biased in favour of majority national groups. Traditional political liberalism displays a "stateist" bias. For arguments of a normative nature, see Norman (2006); Máiz and Requejo (2005); Parekh (2000); Taylor (1992); and for arguments of an empirical nature, see McGarry (2002); Nagel (2004).

5 For a description of minority nations from a normative and empirical perspective, see Requejo (2010a).

6 See Tierney (2004); Gagnon and Tully (2001); Requejo (2010a, 2010b); Tully (1994).
7 See Berlin (1998, 1976); Taylor (2001).
8 See Guibernau and Hutchinson (2001).
9 M. Walzer identifies three "exaggerations" associated with political liberalism: the subject who chooses, confidence in deliberation, and the use of reason in politics. See Walzer (1999).
10 The federations of Ethiopia, St Kitts & Nevis and the federation of Serbia and Montenegro (defunct since the referendum in Montenegro in 2006) are exceptions to this rule. Canada occupies an intermediate position due to the *Opinion* issued by the Supreme Court in the *Secession Reference* (1998).
11 See Gagnon and Iacovino (2007); Burgess (2006).
12 See Hueglin (2003). A third type of federal theory is rooted in Kant. Probably, the "Transcendental Dialectics" of the first *Critique* – which prefigures the theorems of the limitations of contemporary logic (Tarski, Gödel, etc.) – and Kant's "Historical Writings" – which prefigure the ambivalences of human sociability – provide a more suitable theoretical framework for a moral refinement of liberal democracies than that of their "aggregative" or "consensual–deliberative" approaches. This framework is better at incorporating the double normative dimension of equal *respect* and equal *recognition* in the practical political expressions of human dignity.
13 The classic juridical formula of Roman law known as "*quod omnes tangit*" (that which affects everyone should be decided by everyone) establishes, in federal terms, the introduction of a right of veto by the federated collectivities. See Althusius, *Politica Methodice Digesta* (1614), VIII. This is a conception which presents a similar approach to the recently revalued republican theory of collective negative liberty, which Q. Skinner refers to as a "neo-Roman" conception. See Skinner (1998).
14 See *Federalist Papers*, 10, 37, 51 (Madison); 9, 35 (Hamilton). See also the "Introduction" in Karmis and Norman (2005).
15 Pogge (1994: 90).
16 I do not develop this point here. See Caney (2005, chaps 3–5).
17 See J. Tully (1994); Taylor (1992); Parekh (2000, chap. 1); Requejo (2005a, chap 1).
18 P. Kleingeld posits a third type of patriotism in Kant's work, "trait-based patriotism" (Kleingeld 2003: 305). Despite the analytical plausibility of her arguments, I believe that the main types of patriotism in Kant are the other two (civic and national). The third type is linked to the second and can be subsumed within it. I will omit here this third type of patriotism.
19 For a criticism of the *Esperanto-concept* of "constitutional patriotism", see Requejo (2005b: 97–100).
20 On this point, I concur with P. Kleingeld's analysis (2003: 311–314).
21 Berlin (1998); Taylor (1992).
22 The performance of tragedies, as Aristotle saw, is always accompanied by understanding the characters and by the fear that the action arouses in the audience. Shakespeare situated this plurality of motives within his characters. We are morally trapped inside ourselves, and outside, there is nothing else.
23 I think that Kantian cosmopolitism is more fruitful than remaining in the Rousseauian perspective of "constitutional patriotisms", "communities of dialogue" or the renewed faith in "deliberative politics". In this sense, I believe that Kant's work is more politically fruitful if it is understood as a key point within the Montaigne–Shakespeare–Hobbes–Hume–Berlin–Taylor line of reasoning than in that of Rousseau– Kant–Marx–Habermas.
24 *Critique of Pure Reason (CPR)*, B 395, Kant's note; Reason orders (B 671), regulates (B 672) and plans (B 814, B 730). It does not work only "at dusk", after knowledge, but precedes it, regulates it and directs it (B 708). The philosopher is the legislator of Reason, not its creator" (B 867). Here there is a kind of "Kantian revenge": Kant

could say to Hegel and Marx that "precisely because you show 'reason' when you criticise me, you have to return to me".

25 *CPR*, A VII. In *Idea for*. Kant clearly states: "men do not move, like animals, by pure instinct, nor, like rational citizens of the world, according to a pre-arranged plan. It does not seem to be possible to construct a history of mankind according to a plan" (2nd paragraph).

26 *CPR*, A XI. See also B 295.

27 *CPR*, A669; B697.

28 Requejo (2005a, final remark).

29 The Spanish painter Francisco de Goya (1746–1828), a contemporary of Kant, expressed the same idea in the painting *The Dreams of Reason Engender Monsters*.

30 *CPR*, B 421.

31 *CPR*, B 386.

32 In recent years I have defended the possibilities of federal models to achieve this objective. Not all these models are equally effective. Normally, minority nations will not be politically accommodated unless they have at their disposal specific constitutional recognition and a singular position through techniques of asymmetric federalism. See Requejo (2005a, chaps 3 and 4).

33 I have developed this "Hegelian turn" as a philosophical framework for establishing a better political recognition and constitutional accommodation of national pluralism in liberal democracies, in Requejo (2010c).

References

Berlin, I. (1976) *Vico and Herder: Two Studies in the History of Ideas*, London: Hogarth Press.

Berlin, I. (1998) "My Intellectual Path", *New York Review of Books*, 14 May.

Burgess, M. (2006) *Comparative Federalism. Theory and Practice*, London: Routledge.

Caney, S. (2005) *Justice Beyond Borders*, Oxford: Oxford University Press.

Gagnon, A. and Iacovino, R. (2007) *Federalism, Citizenship and Quebec*, Toronto and London: University of Toronto Press, Buffalo.

Gagnon, A. and Tully, J. (eds) (2001) *Multinational Democracies*, Cambridge: Cambridge University Press.

Guibernau, M. and Hutchinson, J. (2001) *Understanding Nationalism*, Cambridge: Polity.

Hueglin, T. (2003) "Federalism at the Crossroads: Old Meanings, New Significance", *Canadian Journal of Political Science* 36(2).

Karmis, D. and Norman, W. (eds) (2005) *Theories of Federalism. A Reader*, New York: Palgrave Macmillan, Houndsmills.

Kleingeld, P. (2003) "Kant's Cosmopolitan Patriotism", *Kant-Studien* 94: 299–316.

McGarry, J. (2002) "Federal Political Systems and the Accommodation of National Minorities", in Neremberg and Griffiths, *Handbook of Federal Countries*, Montreal: McGill, Queens University Press, pp. 416–447.

Máiz, R. and Requejo, F. (eds) (2005) *Democracy, Nationalism and Multiculturalism*, London and New York: Routledge.

Nagel, K.J. (2004) "Transcending the National/Asserting the National: How Stateless Nations like Scotland, Wales and Catalonia React to European Integration", *Australian Journal of Politics and History* 50(1): 58–75.

Norman, W. (2006) *Negotiating Nationalism*, Oxford: Oxford University Press.

Parekh, B. (2000) *Rethinking Multiculturalism. Cultural Diversity and Political Theory*, London: Macmillan.

Pogge, T. (1994) "Cosmopolitanism and Sovereignty in Brown", *Political Restructuring in Europe: Ethical Perspectives*, London: Routledge.

Requejo, F. (2005a) *Multinational Federalism and Value Pluralism*, London and New York: Routledge.

Requejo, F. (2005b) "Multinational not 'postnational' federalism", in R. Máiz and F. Requejo (eds) *Democracy, Nationalism and Multiculturalism*, London and New York: Routledge.

Requejo, F. (2010a) "Federalism and Democracy. The Case of Minority Nations: A Federalist Deficit", in M. Burgess and A. Gagnon (eds) *Federal Democracies*, London: Routledge.

Requejo, F. (2010b) "The Crooked Timber of Liberal Democracies is still too Straight", in N. Walker, B. Shaw and S. Tierney (eds) *Europe's Constitutional Mosaic*, Oxford: Hart Publishing.

Requejo, F. (2010c) "Three Theories of Liberalism for Three Theories of Federalism. A Hegelian Turn", in M. Seymour (ed.) *Democracy, Liberalism and Federalism* (provisional title), CREQC, Montréal (forthcoming).

Requejo, F. (2010d) "Revealing the Dark Side of Traditional Democracies in Plurinational Societies: The Case of Catalonia and the Spanish 'Estado de las Autonomías' ", *Nations and Nationalism* 16(1): 148–168.

Skinner, Q. (1998) *Liberty before Liberalism*, Cambridge: Cambridge University Press.

Taylor, Ch. (1992) "The Politics of Recognition", *Multiculturalism and the "Politics of Recognition"*, Princeton, NJ: Princeton University Press.

Taylor, Ch. (2001) "Plurality of Goods", in R. Working, M. Lilla and R. Silvers, *The Legacy of Isaiah Berlin*, New York: New York Review Books.

Tierney, S. (2004) *Constitutional Law and National Pluralism*, Oxford: Oxford University Press.

Tully, J. (1994) *Strange Multiplicity. Constitutionalism in an Age of Diversity*, Cambridge, Cambridge University Press.

Walzer, M. (1999) *Vernunft, Politik und Leidenschaft* (Reason, Politics and Passion), Frankfurt am Main: Fischer Taschenbuch Verlag.

3 Liberal democracy and national minorities

Bhikhu Parekh

As the past and present experiences show, liberal democracies find it difficult to cope with the demands of territorially concentrated national minorities and often provoke resistance and instability. In this chapter I explore why this is so and how liberal democracy needs to be reconceptualised and reconstituted if it is to come to terms with them.

By a national minority I mean a community that has a strong historically based sense of collective identity and forms part of a larger political unit. It is a *national* community because it has a more or less distinct way of life, institutions, traditions, history, etc. And it is a *minority* because its membership is numerically smaller than that of the rest of the country. A national minority might be territorially concentrated or dispersed. In the former case, it takes the form of a minority nation, and raises problems not shared by dispersed national minorities. Since these problems are more intractable and sources of much instability, I shall concentrate on them.

1 Liberal democracy

Liberalism and democracy can be combined in two different ways, giving rise to two different kinds of political system. One might privilege democracy, give it a conceptual and moral priority, and allow it to set the limits of liberalism. This is democratic liberalism. Or one might do the opposite, and allow liberalism to set the limits of democracy. This is liberal democracy, that is democracy defined and structured within the framework of liberalism.[1] In this chapter I am concerned with the latter, the most common form of combining liberalism and democracy. Although liberal democracy takes different forms in different societies depending on their history, traditions and social structure, several basic features are common to them all and define their conception of the good society. I shall briefly highlight three of these that are relevant to our discussion.

First, unlike the Athenian and almost all other pre-modern societies which took the community as their starting point, defined the individual in terms of it, and had a communitarian orientation, liberal democracy takes the individual as the ultimate and irreducible unit of society and defines the latter in terms of it. For it the individual is conceptually and ontologically prior to society, transcends or is capable of transcending it in varying degrees, and his or her interests are the *ultima ratio* of society. Society 'consists' or is 'made up' of individuals, and refers to the totality of them and their relationships. Individuals are the sole sources of moral claims, and social and political institutions are judged in terms of these.

Second, in the liberal democratic view human beings share a common nature, and hence certain common fundamental interests. These interests are the basis of their claims to corresponding rights, which it is the job of the state to establish and safeguard. Since the interests and rights are derived from and represent the necessary demands of human nature, they are assumed to be universal in their validity. The liberal democratic state is believed to represent the realm of rationality in two important and related senses. The rights and interests it protects are not parochial or local and culturally contingent but arrived at by rational reflection on human nature. The state, furthermore, is a deliberative organisation based on discussion and debate and guided by public reason. As an institution embodying reason in its guiding principles and mode of operation, liberal democracy is believed to represent a higher level of collective existence than the tribal, traditional and other pre-modern societies in which traditions, customs, etc. are thought to hold sway.

Third, the liberal democratic state represents a homogeneous legal space within which its citizens move freely and enjoy identical basic rights irrespective of where they are settled. The same laws apply throughout the state and all citizens are equally subject to them. Citizens might belong to different ethnic, religious, linguistic and other communities, but the state takes no official cognizance of them and grants them no official status. These communities, largely seen as voluntary associations belonging to the civil society, are entirely their private business and do not affect their status and rights as citizens. The state transcends them, represents an independent realm of its own, and its members are expected to rise above their other affiliations when conducting themselves as citizens. While the liberal democratic state allows, even cherishes, the ethnic, religious, the regional, cultural and other identities, it privileges political identity or the identity of the citizen, and subordinates other identities to it. The unity of the state is taken to require that all its citizens should identify with it and share a singular, unitary and undivided political identity. The political identity is articulated in terms of shared institutions and values. All citizens are expected to subscribe to these, and in so doing constitute a single *demos* or people. The people collectively wield and exercise the sovereignty that is inherent in the state. Since unanimity is often impossible, the majority of them are authorised to speak and decide in their name.

These three features play a crucial part in defining the guiding ideals of liberal democracy. Every liberal democracy seeks to realise them, judges itself in terms of them, and feels disturbed when for some reason it falls short of them. Since this is not easy in societies divided along religious, cultural, national and other lines, every liberal democracy had to find ways of dealing with them. As for religious differences, Western liberal democracies privatised them and expected the state to be secular or at least religiously neutral, an arrangement that has worked well but now faces serious difficulties in the face of the increasingly assertive Christianity and the arrival of Islam. Cultural differences cannot be privatised, and the state made culturally neutral. The liberal democratic state therefore has gone about creating and consolidating a common national culture by embodying it in its legal, political, educational and other institutions; an arrangement that has worked well but is coming under strain because of the increasing cultural diversity brought about by individualism, globalisation and immigration. An even more acute challenge is posed by territorially concentrated national minorities,[2] and in the rest of the chapter I shall concentrate on them.

2 National minority

There are scores of examples of territorially concentrated national minorities. They include the Walloons in Belgium, Quebec and the original nations in Canada, Catalonia, the Basque country and Galicia in Spain, the Tamils in Sri Lanka, Tibet in China, the Baluchis in Pakistan and Afghanistan, the Kurds in Turkey, Kashmir and the North Eastern tribal states in India, the Moros in the Philippines, the Bougainvilleans in Papua and New Guinea, the Karens and Shans in Burma, and many such groups in parts of Eastern Europe, Africa, Russia, Latin America and Central Asia. These communities aspire to express, maintain and transmit their way of life and seek an appropriate restructuring of the wider political community.

They demand different degrees of autonomy and want their identity to be suitably reflected in the country's self-understanding and symbols. They seek adequate representation in the central institutions of the state, and the right of veto over measures affecting their vital cultural and other interests. Many of them also seek the right to control immigration not only from abroad and but also from other regions of the country to avoid being outnumbered or marginalised. They want to restrict the linguistic and other choices of immigrant children lest these should over time undermine their way of life. Some of these minorities also want to ban outsiders from buying land in their territory to avoid being taken over by them or losing control over their affairs. My concern in this chapter is not to discuss these and other rights and powers, some of which are suspect, but rather to explore whether the general demand for autonomy from which they derive their legitimacy is justified and, if so, why it is often resisted in a liberal democracy.

There are several good reasons to meet this demand. First, in some cases there is a historical obligation to do so. The national minorities joined the state on the explicit or implicit understanding that their identity would be respected and accommodated, as, for example, in the cases of Quebec and Kashmir. In some other cases they were conquered, colonised, annexed or subjected to forcible occupation, and seek to redress past injustices.

Second, meeting the minority's demand for autonomy facilitates its integration. People are unlikely to see a state as theirs if it humiliates them, mocks their legitimate aspirations, and consigns them to a shadowy existence. By contrast they are more likely to want to become part of it if it respects their identity, values their differences, and gives them a secure space for self-expression. Historically speaking few national minorities have been successfully suppressed for long, even in such highly repressive societies as Stalin's Soviet Union and Franco's Spain. Violence or forcible assimilation heightens the minority's sense of identity, leaves a legacy of hatred, and encourages secession, precisely what one wishes to avoid. Croatia denied autonomy to the Serbian-populated Krajina. When the latter took up arms, Croatia relented after considerable bloodshed, but by then the Serbs had come to feel that the 'concessions' were too little and too late. By contrast Ukraine bargained with its Russian population in Crimea, resisted the pressure to resort to military and police action, and gave the peninsula the status of an autonomous republic, which was readily accepted.

Third, the national minority's demand for autonomy has much to commend it on moral and political grounds. It aims to create a form of government with which its members can identify and whose institutions, language of public discourse and political culture reflect their ways of thought. This increases their commitment to it, promotes political participation, and deepens democracy. It also fosters their individual and collective self-respect, and helps them feel at ease with themselves. Feeling secure about their way of life, they acquire the confidence to take a critical view of it, challenge and change its ugly practices, and open up spaces for dissent. It is a common experience that when a minority feels besieged or is subjected to assimilationist pressure, it closes ranks, becomes intolerant, and demands total conformity lest its disagreements should be used by outsiders to undermine it. Furthermore when a minority is no longer obsessed with its cultural survival, its members are able to concentrate on other issues. Institutions of civil society tend to flourish, the literary, cultural, and other areas of life release new creative energies, political and other differences are freely aired, and the normal processes of social life resume their rhythm. A vibrant and self-confident national minority also adds to the richness of the collective life, and checks the process of excessive centralisation to which homogeneous societies are generally prone.

The minority demand is also justified on grounds of justice.[3] Justice is concerned with the distribution of rights and opportunities not only between individuals but also between groups, which is why we talk of justice between states and nations. Contrary to the conventional liberal democratic argument, the minority community does not usually face a neutral and rational state made up of de-ethnicised individuals. Rather it faces a majority nation or a national majority, another community like it with its distinct history, language, values and identity and whose national particularity is presented in the idiom of universality and neutrality. Quebec does not confront Canada but the Anglophones whose historical experiences, understanding of what Canada is about, values, etc. have shaped and are reflected in the country's dominant institutions. The Catalonians do not face Spain but the Castilians who have put their stamp on Spanish life and defined it in a certain way. Since the dominant group enjoys the right of self-expression and shapes the state in its image, justice between communities requires that the national minority too should enjoy that right. Although one is in a majority and the other in a minority, and that makes some difference to their claims, both alike are national communities and, qua communities enjoy a basic equality.

3 Reason for resistance

Prima facie there is thus a good case for accommodating the national minority's demands for self-government and special status within the larger political framework, and for the resulting asymmetrical federation. This raises the question why that demand is either rejected outright or met with the greatest reluctance and after much delay and bloodshed. Reasons for resistance are both prudential and moral.

First, it is argued that autonomy is the thin end of the wedge and leads to eventual secession. Once a community gets used to the power and trappings of autonomy, it is tempted to ask for more. It also acquires the confidence that it can exist and even flourish on its own, and sees no reason why it should continue to live in the shadow of another. Its leaders develop new ambitions, and build up vested interests that can only be satisfied by an independent state. This is particularly the case with those unable to make much headway through the normal political processes. Large and even small grievances are made the basis of mass mobilisation around the cause of independence, widely presented as an answer to all the community's problems. What is more, once a state concedes a minority's demand for autonomy and allows its unity to be challenged, it encourages all kinds of expectations and has no moral and political defence left against secession by the community concerned and even perhaps by others.

Although this argument is not without its merit, it is flawed.[4] The fact that autonomy might one day lead to secession is not a conclusive argument against it unless we assume that the unity of the state is the only or even the highest value. It is in fact one value among others, and it is a value because and insofar as it promotes human well-being. If it involves repression or egregious violence against a national minority, as it is bound to do if the latter remains deeply discontented, the unity of the state is hardly worth its cost and is in any case unlikely to last long. Furthermore, meeting a national minority's demand for autonomy is often the best way to secure its loyalty, and is a step towards political integration rather than disintegration. The minority gets what it wants and enjoys the additional economic, political, diplomatic, military and other advantages of belonging to a larger unit. Autonomy tends to lead to secession when it is long denied and granted after considerable bloodshed. The minority's struggles and sacrifices intensify its sense of identity, unite its otherwise divided members, release powerful passions, leave a lasting legacy of hatred, and create a situation in which its members have no desire to remain within the state concerned.

The danger of secession cannot of course be ruled out altogether. Unlike the traditional nation state which is built on the presumption of 'continuing in perpetuity' as John Rawls put it, a plurinational state lives in the shadow of secession. The way to deal with it is not to be obsessed by it and allow it to shape all one's policies but rather to build countervailing forces. These include interregional cooperation, greater economic investment and subsidies to the minority region, drawing its elite into the mainstream, giving it generous representation in the federal institutions, and offering incentives that would be withdrawn in the event of secession. When members of a national minority are settled in other parts of the country and are well treated, they too act as a powerful force against secession. The Sikhs in the rest of India had a dampening influence on their co-religionist's struggle for an independent Sikh state. The French-speaking minority outside Quebec was and is a significant moderating factor on the Quebecois separatists. The Luo in Kenya are concentrated in the western part of the country and resent the Kikuyu domination. However they have never contemplated a Biafra-type secession because many of their tribesmen hold influential positions in other parts of the country, especially Nairobi and Mombasa, and have not been made to feel insecure or unwanted.

The second reason for resistance to the minority demand for autonomy has to do with the difficulties involved in running an asymmetrical federation.[5] The latter sometimes leads to such a complex division of powers and functions that citizens often do not know who is responsible for what. There is also a constant tension between the federal government and the minority region over their respective powers and jurisdictions, especially when they are run by different political parties. The state risks becoming so loose that it lacks a clear sense of purpose and is unable to pursue long-term goals and mediate interregional conflicts. There is also the much-debated question of what issues the minority representatives at the federal level are entitled to speak and vote on. Should the Quebec members of federal Parliament, for example, be allowed to vote on measures that do not apply to their province, such as the immigration policy? Should the Scottish members of Parliament vote on matters that pertain to England alone? The question becomes particularly important when the minority vote on an issue is decisive and tilts the balance. If minority representatives are not allowed to vote on certain matters, they feel marginalised and do not see themselves as part of the country. However if they are allowed to vote, they appear to exercise an unacceptably disproportionate influence, and might even legitimise the wider society's similar interventions in their own affairs.

Although some of these difficulties are acute and sometimes make a federation, especially an asymmetrical one, an administrative nightmare, they are not insoluble. All federations have to deal with divisions of powers and jurisdictions, and we have a considerable historical experience of what systems work. The asymmetrical federation complicates the situation, but does not represent a wholly novel entity. The powers of the minority region can be specified reasonably clearly as, for example, they are in the case of Quebec in Canada, Kashmir and the North Eastern states in India, and Catalonia, the Basque country and Galicia in Spain. If a national minority region includes smaller minorities, they might be given autonomy in important areas, as the multi-level Indian federation has done in recent years. When a national minority enjoys considerable autonomy and is exempted from federal jurisdiction in significant areas, its say in federal matters could be reduced. Puerto Rico, which enjoys greater autonomy than the states do in the US, is not considered a state like the others, is not allowed to vote in Presidential elections, and has only one representative in the Congress in the form of a Commissioner who has a right to speak but not to vote except in committees. Several such arrangements in other countries work reasonably well.

Although federal representatives of the national minority might rightly be asked not to speak and vote in certain areas, it is important not to be too rigid in these matters, and to rely on conventions and good sense rather than detailed constitutional provisions. The important thing is to create a climate of trust, and that requires generosity on the part of the wider society and the spirit of accommodation on that of the minority. As the national minority feels reassured and sees itself as part of the wider political community, petty differences and squabbles over powers and jurisdictions tend to diminish. In the ultimate analysis national minorities confront us with a difficult but inescapable choice. We either learn to cope with the messy and sometimes contentious politics of compromise and accommodation, or live with constant instability and violence. There is little to be said for the latter.

Third, it is argued that the national minority seeks group or collective rights, and privileges them over individual rights, both of which subvert the basic principles of liberal democracy. The argument is mistaken on both counts. Group rights are an integral part of every state including liberal democracy.[6] A state's right to independence is a collective right in the sense that it does not belong to its members individually but collectively, as a community. They do not as individuals have the right to independence which they can be said to transfer to the state. Rather they enjoy it only insofar as they form part of the community, and exercise it collectively. This is also the case with the state's rights to maintain its way of life, control immigration, and to fight for its survival in external and civil wars. The collective right demanded by a national minority is no different.

It is true that some national minorities might deny or severely restrict basic individual rights. However this is not true of all of them, and is not inherent in their right to autonomy. In any case they could be granted autonomy on condition that they respect basic individual rights, as well as the rights of such minorities as they include. Furthermore, rights vary greatly in their importance. To lump them all together and call all of them basic, human or fundamental is to lack a sense of proportion. Some rights are central to human dignity and wellbeing and may never be restricted or only under rare circumstances: for example, the rights to life, equality of treatment, and to freedom of expression and association. Others, such as the choice of the medium of instruction and the freedoms to buy and sell property or settle in any part of the country are not of this kind and may be subjected to greater restrictions. The fact that the distinction is not always easy to draw does not deny either its validity or its importance. Rights also come into conflict, and there is no universal and 'truly rational' way of resolving it. A national minority cherishes and seeks to maintain its way of life. While it may not violate basic individual rights, it may prioritise other rights differently and place greater restrictions on some of them. The way of life of indigenous peoples, for example, is integrally bound up with land. If outsiders were free to buy its land, they might with their greater resources end up buying all or a substantial part of it, and undermine the indigenous way of life. If immigrants to Quebec were to have an unrestricted right to demand education for their children in English, French would over time become a minority language and Quebec's identity would be subverted. If we value a community's right to its identity, we cannot consistently deny it the right to impose such restrictions, provided, of course, that they are proportionate and necessary to maintain its identity.

In a liberal democracy individual rights are highly prized, and there is a general tendency to subsume the demands of a national minority under their rubric. It is assumed that once individual rights of the national minority members are assured, they neither need nor are entitled to the right to autonomy. This argument is only partially valid. It dissolves the minority community into a collection of individuals and fails to appreciate its collective nature and identity. The national minority is a historic community with its distinct culture, language, etc., in terms of which its members are bonded and define their shared identity. They constitute it even as it constitutes them. While they are self-determining individuals and need individual rights, they are also part of the community and need the right to continue as one if they so wish. It is a mistake to stress either alone, as the liberals and communitarians do from their opposite perspectives. We need both individual and minority rights, and any well-considered statement of human rights should include both.

The fourth liberal objection to the national minority's demand for autonomy has to do with the liberal theory of rationality and progress. For many liberals, national minorities are backward groups, tribal, closed, custom-bound, anti-modern, driven by ethnic nationalism, and an obstacle to progress. Since they are supposed to be doomed to extinction under the impact of modernisation, their desire to maintain their identity, although understandable, deserves no sympathy. They should rather be assimilated into the liberal democratic state, and made fit for a life of rationality and universality. This widely held view underpinned the European 'civilising mission', underlies the current distinction between civic and ethnic nationalism, and at least partly explains the widespread liberal hostility to minority autonomy. J.S. Mill put it with characteristic simplicity and eloquence:[7]

> Nobody can suppose that it is not more beneficial to a Breton, or a Basque of French Navarre, to be bought into the current of ideas and feelings of a highly civilised and cultivated people – to be a member of French nationality, admitted on equal terms to all the privileges of French citizenship, sharing the advantages of French protection, and the dignity and prestige of French power – than to sulk on his own rocks, the half-savage relic of past

times, revolving in his own little mental orbit, without participation or interest in the general movement of the world. The same remark applies to Welshman or the Scottish Highlander as members of the British nation.

The contrast between the reactionary nature of national minority and the rational character of liberal democracy is overdrawn and ultimately untenable. Grading ways of life is a notoriously difficult exercise, and there is no noncircular way of showing that liberal democracy represents the most rational form of life. Furthermore, not all national minorities are tribal and hidebound and it is wrong to homogenise them and dismiss their claims indiscriminately. Some of them cherish important liberal and democratic values, but differ in the way they reconcile them with certain collective goals. Some others are not as liberal as liberals wish, or aim at different forms of liberalism, or prefer democratic liberalism over liberal democracy, but that does not make them irrational or even illiberal. As for liberal democracy itself, it neither consists of constantly self-examining individuals of the Millian imagination nor represents rationality in its pristine form. It often has an ethnic basis in the shape of a particular people with whose history, values, language, culture, etc. it is bound up and whose traditional culture shapes its institutions, practices, and view of rationality. This is why different liberal democracies have different institutional structures and views of the world, differently define and prioritise their shared values, and differently structure their political and moral discourses.

Fifth, liberals argue that accommodating the claims of the national minority within an asymmetrical federation violates the principle of equal citizenship. Since the minority region offers a different set of rights or imposes greater restrictions on some of them, citizens in different parts of the country do not enjoy equal rights. This argument misunderstands the nature and implications of equal citizenship. Equal treatment does not entail identical treatment, and the same general right may entail different second order rights, if the needs and circumstances of those involved are dissimilar. Giving special status to a national minority is intended to show it the same respect and concern as the national majority. However since its needs and circumstances are different, its equal right to self-expression entails different powers.

In every state equal citizenship is rightly qualified in several ways. Gay teachers or militant atheists may not be employed by orthodox religious schools, and Sikhs may carry their traditional dagger which non-Sikhs may not. The case of national minority is not very different, except that the difference here is territorially articulated. This is a common phenomenon in a federal state. Subject to the constraints of the principles and rights enshrined in the constitution, its constituent units are free to organise areas falling within their jurisdiction as they consider proper, and may and do enact different laws. In the US, for example, one can buy and sell pornographic material in some states but not in others, and enjoy more welfare benefits in some than in others. A federation would have no point if such differences were disallowed. An asymmetrical federation introduces greater diversity but it is qualitatively no different.

Those liberals who are sympathetic to the minority demand for autonomy but remain committed to the principle of equal citizenship argue that rather than give a special status to the national minority, we should give all other federal units the same powers as are demanded by it. This view, dubbed *café para todos* (coffee for all) by some Catalonian writers, is open to two objections.[8] It misses the point of the national minority's demand, which is not only about powers but also about the recognition of its identity and all that it entails. Acknowledgement of its special status has a great symbolic significance, and ensures that the majority's understanding of the national minority is in broad harmony with the latter's own. Symbols are never purely formal and devoid of substantive content because they confer public legitimacy on minority aspirations and can be used to justify other demands.[9]

Giving other units the same power as the minority region is at one level an empty and at another a mischievous measure. In the absence of a separate language, culture or way of life to protect, they are unlikely to use these powers, and the national minority, which will want to use them, would be seen as odd, illiberal and put under pressure not to do so. More importantly, if other units decide in future to surrender these powers to the federal government, the principle of equality would require that the national minority should do so as well, and that would negate the very purpose of equalising its powers. This is not at all an uncommon experience in federal states. The US began as a highly decentralised federation, but over time it became one of the most centralised, with the federal government acquiring powers wittingly or unwittingly ceded to it by the constituent states. In Canada there was a similar trend for decades, but it was thwarted by Quebec's insistence on its distinct identity. In the Russian federation, its fifty-six regional units have limited interest in their autonomy, and not only do not see centralisation as a threat but even welcome it. By contrast Tartarstan, North Ossetie and other national minority regions are highly jealous of their powers and fear the creeping centralisation. In Spain the Autonomous Communities of Catalonia, the Basque country and Galicia fear and resist centralisation whereas most of the other fourteen Autonomous Communities generally do not mind transferring their powers to the federal government. In short, unless the national minority enjoys a special status, which the liberal democratic version of equal or rather uniform citizenship disallows, it has no protection against the centralising and assimilationist pressures of the rest of the country.

Sixth and finally, liberals sometimes argue that in a democracy the will of the majority is sovereign and should prevail. Since the special status demanded by the national minority exempts it from the majority will in certain important areas, it is considered undemocratic. Their argument is doubly flawed. First, the majority is not free to do what it likes in a democracy, especially a liberal one, and is expected to respect constitutionally enshrined rights. The prior question therefore is to decide what is included in these rights. If we agree that they should include a national minority's right to autonomy, then clearly the majority will is limited by it in a democracy.

More importantly, liberal democracy takes a homogeneous view of people. It assumes a single and indivisible people, which it equates with the totality of citizens. In a plurinational state peoplehood is articulated at two levels, that is, there is more than one *demos*.[10] At one level all citizens constitute a single people, and are governed by the majority principle. At another level, the national minority constitutes and sees itself as a distinct people, whose members share a common history, institutions, culture, language, etc. and identify with each other. Peoplehood is not a closed and exclusive category, and there is no reason why one cannot belong to more than one people. Since there are at least two peoples in a plurinational state, the majority principle is articulated at two levels, within the country as a whole and within the national minority, and the former does not hold an unqualified sway. The majority of the wider society is decisive in areas where the whole society constitutes a single people, and that of the national minority in those where it constitutes a people. The task of the Constitution is to demarcate the two areas and define the jurisdictions of the two majorities.

Since a plurinational state has at least two peoples, members of the national minority have two political identities. They are Scots as well as British, Catalonians and Spaniards, Kashmiris and Indians, Walloons and Belgians. Since liberal democracy allows only one political identity, it feels deeply uncomfortable with such a dual identity and resorts to familiar devices. Sometimes it seeks to suppress the narrower identity; sometimes it recognises it provided that it is ethnicised and not given political salience; on other occasions it allows its political articulation only if it is subordinated to the wider identity. Members of a national minority are often asked if they feel 'more' British or Scottish, more Spanish or Catalonian, and so on. Such discomfort with a dual political identity springs from the mistaken belief that unless the political identity is singular, the unity of the state remains insecure. The belief owes its origin to the ideology of the nation state which informs liberal democracy. In a plurinational state, a dual political identity is not only a common occurrence but lies at its basis.[11]

Since members of a national minority have two political identities, whereas the rest of their fellow citizens might have only one, their relation to the country is asymmetrical. When the English ask the Scots why they cannot all be 'just British', their apparently egalitarian demand often conceals an inequality. Britishness as it is conventionally defined is generalised Englishness in the sense that its content is English in nature. While it involves no loss on the part of the English, it denies the Scots a deeply valued political identity. A plurinational state is most stable when it values both identities and finds ways of harmonising them.[12] As the two identities interact, they do not remain mutually indifferent. Each shapes and is shaped by the other. One is a Scot or a Catalonian but within a British or Spanish context. Conversely one is British or Spanish but in a Scottish or Catalonian way. As the two identities dovetail and become inseparable, members of the national minority come to define themselves in terms of both and feel part of two overlapping peoples.

In plurinational states members of a national minority stand in a complex relationship with the rest of the country. Barring the separatists, most of them see themselves as part of the country, but they also wish to retain a measure of distance from it. They are not foreigners, but nor are they as assimilated and indistinguishable as the rest. Thanks to the hold of the ideology of the nation state, they are sometimes accused of being anti-national or taking an instrumental view of the country, and viewed with suspicion and subjected to discrimination. Such treatment generates a sense of marginality, weakens their attachment to the country, and paves the way for secession, which neither they nor the rest of the country want. In a plurinational state we need to appreciate that some groups of citizens will define their place in and relate to the country differently from the rest, and that this is the only moral and political basis on which its unity can be constructed.[13]

For centuries European states insisted that their members should share a common religion, and doubted the loyalty of those who did not. Over time and after much bloodshed, they realised that this was unfair and counterproductive, and that the best way to win over their citizens' loyalty was to respect their religious differences within a suitably broadened conception of citizenship. A similar lesson needs to be learnt in relation to the ethnic and especially national differences. It is harder to learn because, unlike religious groups, territorially concentrated national minorities compete with the state on their own terrain and demand an effective share in the exercise of its sovereignty. Unless we find ways of accommodating their demand by redefining the traditional theory of sovereignty and the unitary view of the state, we run the risk of provoking a cycle of secessionist violence and undermining the very unity and stability in whose name the demand is resisted.

4 Conclusion

In the light of our discussion, we need to reconsider some of the basic principles of liberal democracy, particularly the three listed at the beginning of this chapter, if it is to be stable, do justice to its national minority (or minorities), and benefit from its (or their) cultural diversity and decentralising influence. It might be argued that it would not then be a liberal democracy but something wholly different. This is so only if liberal democracy is defined in narrowly individualist terms and tied to the ideology of the unitary and politically and culturally homogeneous nation state. Such a view equates liberal democracy with one particular tradition of it, and renders it irrelevant to much of the contemporary world. Liberal democracy has rich conceptual and institutional resources. Not to explore and exploit them out of blind loyalty to a particular historical version of it is to fall prey to the very vice of dogmatism it takes pride in condemning, and from which it claims to be free.

Notes

1 Sometimes the conflict between the state and its national minority is about these two versions of liberal democracy. In Canada, for example, Anglophones insist on liberal democracy, whereas Quebec is keen on democratic liberalism. This resembles but is not quite the same as Charles Taylor's well-known distinction between two forms of

liberalism in his 'The Politics of Recognition' in A. Gutmann (ed.) *Multiculturalism*, 1994 (Princeton: Princeton University Press).

2 Keating, Michael, *Nations Against the State: The New Politics of Nationalism in Quebec, Catalonia and Scotland*, second edition, 2001 (Basingstoke: Palgrave) pp. 17ff.

3 Kymlicka, Will, *Politics in the Vernacular*, 2001 (Oxford: Oxford University Press) Ch. 4.

4 Kymlicka, Will, 'Federation and Secession: East and West,' in Ramón Máiz and Ferran Requejo (eds) *Democracy, Nationalism and Multiculturalism*, 2005 (London: Frank Cass).

5 Kymlicka, Will, *Politics in the Vernacular*, op. cit.

6 Parekh, Bhikhu, *Rethinking Multiculturalism*, second edition, 2006 (Basingstoke: Palgrave Macmillan) pp. 213ff.

7 Mill, J.S., *Utilitarianism, Liberty, and Representative Government*, 1964 (London: Everyman's Library) p. 363.

8 Guibernau, Montserrat, *The Identity of Nations*, 2007 (Cambridge: Polity Press) p. 46.

9 Symbols are never merely symbolic. George Santayana rightly spoke of their 'deadly significance'; cited in Donald Harowitz, *Ethnic Groups in Conflict*, 1985 (Berkeley, CA: University of California Press) p. 210.

10 Requejo, Ferran, 'Political Liberalism in Multinational States: The Legitimacy of Plural and Asymmetrical Federalism', in Alain-G. Gagnon and James Tully (eds) *Multinational Democracies*, 2001 (Cambridge, UK: Cambridge University Press).

11 Ibid.

12 For a fuller discussion, see my 'Being British', *Government and Opposition* Vol. 37, number 3, Summer 2002.

13 Resnick, Philip, 'Accommodating National Differences within Multinational States', in Ramón Máiz and Ferran Requejo, op. cit. See also Karmis, Dimitrios and Gagnon, Alain-G., 'Federalism, Federation and Collective Identities in Canada and Belgium: Different Routes, Similar Fragmentation', in Gagnon and Tully, op. cit.

4 The transformation of the democratic state in Western Europe[1]

John Loughlin

1 The concept of democracy and its institutional expression in Europe

1.1 Our common European heritage

'Democracy' is a European invention with its roots in the political systems of the ancient Greek city-states. It has several meanings, the most important of which for modern states are representative, direct and participatory democracy[2] (Pateman 1970; Gaudin 2007) and representative or liberal democracy (Held 1987). In its modern expression it owes much to the philosophies of the Enlightenment with their exalted role of the individual (Mendras 1997), but also to Montesquieu's doctrine of the separation of powers. This latter doctrine found its fullest institutional expression in the new USA and formed the basis of the 1787 American Constitution, which separated the different arms of representative and executive government and the judiciary. Rousseau[3] was also important for the development of the modern concept of democracy in his championing of the individual against absolute power and his concept of the *general will*, although his relationship with the Enlightenment is ambiguous (Garrard 2003). Nevertheless, the ideas of both the Enlightenment and of Rousseau were taken over and transformed into the doctrine of the Rights of Man and the Citizen at the French Revolution that forms the basis of modern liberal democracy (Boudon 2006). A key development during the Revolution was the invention of the concept of the 'nation-state' which became the dominant form of political organization in the modern world and with which liberal representative democracy has been closely associated (see below).

This is not to suggest that the concepts of the nation-state and liberal democracy are ones on which a consensus has always existed. On the contrary, the very diverse philosophical heritage underlying democracy and its association with the nation-state have led to a number of ambiguities and it has been a much contested concept. It has been opposed by those groups, such as the hierarchy of the Catholic Church and the European aristocracies, who rejected the modern nation-state, especially in its republican form, as well as democracy.[4] Associated with these forces were other political movements and ideologies such as regionalism and, towards the end of the nineteenth century, federalist movements seeking to reunify Europe (Gras and Livet 1977; Brugmans 1965).

The Catholic Church began to accept the modern nation-state with Pope Leo XIII's encyclical *Rerum Novarum* (1891). This allowed Catholics to accept modern liberal democracy after having fought it throughout the nineteenth century. It then led to the foundation of Catholic trade unions and groups such as *Ordre Nouveau* which brought together Catholic (and some Protestant intellectuals) in the inter-war period.[5] *Ordre Nouveau* played an important role in laying the foundations for one strand of European federalism during and after the Second World War, but it retained a suspicion of liberal democracy and the nation-state. This type of European federalism, which later became known as *le fédéralisme intégral*, wished to see the nation-state, which it held responsible for three European wars (the Franco-Prussian war in 1870–71; and the First and Second World Wars), replaced by a European federation of smaller entities such as regions. The original idea of a 'Europe of the Regions' was formulated by Denis de Rougement (1968) and a similar idea of a 'Europe des Ethnies' by Guy Héraud (1993). The philosophical tradition underlying this strand of European federalism was known as 'personalism',[6] which was meant to be a mid-way position between liberal individualism and the collectivist ideologies of Marxism, Fascism and Nazism. The integral federalists did have a concept of democracy but it took the form of corporatism. Indeed, some of the members of this movement had sympathies with the corporatist ideas of Italian fascism but, despite the movement's name, *Ordre Nouveau*, it was not on the extreme right and a majority of its members joined the resistance against Nazism.

More serious rejections of democracy (because attempts were made to put them into practice) are political ideologies and movements such as Marxism, Fascism and Nazism. They opposed democracy in principle and, once in power, dismantled the institutions of the liberal democratic state. Soviet socialism, despite the appellation of 'peoples' democracies', opposed any kind of democracy in practice, preferring one party rule behind a façade of 'democratic' constitutions and constitutional guarantees of civil liberties. The collapse of the Soviet system in the late 1980s revealed their hollowness and their own peoples' alienation.

But even in established liberal democracies there remain ambiguities with different understanding of the meaning of the term democracy. There is a tension between individualist and communitarian conceptions, that is, whether it is the free expression of the rights of individuals, or whether it is an expression of the existence of 'communities', defined in different ways, of which the individual is part and which may, in certain respects, supersede his or her individual interests. Another way of phrasing this is to ask whether in democratic practice emphasis should be given to 'individual' autonomy or to 'communitarian' autonomy (Lapidoth 1997). An early version of the communitarian approach may be found in the personalist movement mentioned above. A contemporary expression is the communitarian movement founded in the United States by Amitai Etzioni (1993). The thought of the Catholic philosopher Charles Taylor (1989, 1991) has some affinities with communitarianism, although he denies being part of the movement. This tension is at the heart of the epistemological, methodological and normative debates[7] within the contemporary social sciences (Frazer 1996; MacIntyre 1984) and underlies the difficulties of finding the appropriate institutional expression of democracy in practice.

1.2 The link between liberal democracy and the nation-state

There is a close link between liberal democracy and the nation-state, which emerged as the dominant form of political organization in the nineteenth and twentieth centuries (Alter 1994). It is true that there have also been nation-states that were not democratic as in the cases of Fascist Italy and Nazi Germany and, indeed, of communist states such as Albania and Romania (Bogdani and Loughlin 2007). Democracy could also develop in societies that were not nation-states in the classical sense of the word as, for example, in the United Kingdom (see below for a discussion of the problems of defining the UK as a nation-state). Nevertheless, there seems to be a close correspondence between it and liberal democracy. Although the nation-state is pre-eminently a way of organizing the political system (the state) and of relating this to society (nation), it also suited the nature of capitalist economic production as it developed during the Industrial Revolution, which necessitated the creation of wider markets and the harmonization of factors such as weights, measures and time zones – what Karl Polanyi has termed 'The Great Transformation' from pre-market forms of economic organization to the market system (Polanyi 1944). The Industrial Revolution was driven by the industrial bourgeoisie, many of whom espoused the political ideology of liberal nationalism. The liberal democratic nation-state, one among several forms of political organization (Spruyt 1994), became dominant probably because it best served the needs of these new elites who were replacing the aristocracy and the Church as the leaders of European society. What is certain is that almost all our modern political institutions – executives accountable to representative assemblies; political parties elected to these assemblies in free elections; Weberian-type public administration systems[8]; and the various 'freedoms' – of speech, of assembly, of the press, of movement and so on – emanate from the nation-state.

If the nation-state was contested as it established itself, it continues to be so today. Its imminent disappearance is predicted by various commentators (Ohmae 1995; Guéhenno 1995). It is claimed that the forces of globalization and Europeanization from above and the new regionalism and the new localism from below are squeezing it out of existence. It is, however, too soon to write its obituary. It is still alive and kicking but it is being transformed as a result of wider transformations: in public administration and public policy (New Public Management), in the economy (neo-liberalism and globalization) and in society (increasing societal fragmentation and individualism) (Loughlin 2004). Indeed, the fate of the nation-state – its continuing existence or its transformation – is the main question facing the social sciences today (Le Galès 1999).

If we accept the link between the modern nation-state and liberal democracy and if the former is, indeed, being significantly transformed, then this has profound consequences for liberal democracy. Some authors have argued that one response to the challenges from 'above' – globalization and Europeanization – is to develop a 'cosmopolitan' democracy (Held 1993; Cerny 1999; Beck 2000; Habermas 2003). There has been less reflection on the question of subnational democracy and how these challenges might affect it (Loughlin *et al.*, 2001). The purpose of this chapter is to offer some reflections on the issues involved. It will first confront the question: is subnational democracy even possible within a political system dominated by the nation-state?

1.3 Is subnational democracy possible?

Liberal democracy has been so closely associated with the nation-state, that it might be defined as *national* democracy. In other words, democratic legitimacy might be regarded as deriving from the existence of a *national* polity with its particular state organs of representation and administration. This raises the question of whether it is possible for liberal democracy to be present when these conditions are not met – for example, in regions or localities which are not national such as the north-east of England or Rhônes-Alpes, or in nations without states such as Catalonia, Scotland or Wales. Does the legitimacy of subnational democratic government derive from the national government of the state in which it is situated, or from the national, regional or local community in which it is expressed?

Different countries will give different answers to this question. In the case of France, the answer is clear: the French allow no deviation from the principle that all democratic legitimacy derives only from the nation-state and this is true even of those societies, such as Corsica, which have a distinctive character (Loughlin 2007). Most Corsicans would define themselves as a 'people', and some would say they are a 'nation' and that this is the basis of the democratic legitimacy of a Corsican Assembly.[9] The French Constitutional Court rejected this interpretation and argued that it infringed the French Constitution which only recognizes one 'people' in France – '*le peuple français*'. But other cases are less clear-cut. Historically, nation-states developed mainly at the expense of the autonomy of other forms of territorial organization – towns, cities, communes, provinces, regions, etc. – which had existed for much longer periods of time than nation-states. A striking example is Scotland which was an independent national monarchy before being joined to England in the union of the crowns in 1603 and of the parliaments in 1707. This raises the question as to the basis of democratic legitimacy of today's restored Scottish Parliament. Does this derive from the referendum of the Scottish people in 1997, which approved the principle of restoring the Scottish Parliament, or the Scotland Act in 1998 of the Westminster Parliament by which the Parliament was established? Scottish nationalists hold the first position, unionists the second. In Spain, many Basques, Catalans and some Galicians question the legitimacy of the Spanish Constitution which defines

Spain as a 'one and indivisible nation' and which adds 'regions and nationalities', normally taken to refer to the Basque Country, Galicia and Catalonia. At least the Basques and Catalans (the Galicians are less forthright) reject the description of themselves as 'nationalities' and claim full 'nationhood'. Negotiations in 2007 between Prime Minister Zapatero's government and the centre-left government of Catalonia led to a formula which recognized the 'national character' of Catalonia but without defining it fully as a 'nation'. The Basques also wish to reform their relationship with the Spanish state. The radical nationalists of Herri Batasuna/ETA seek to set up an independent Basque nation-state through armed struggle. The more moderate Partido Nacionalista Vasco (PNV) seek to reconfigure the relationship through peaceful means: first by a relationship inspired by the 1998 Good Friday Agreement in Northern Ireland then; and when this failed, through a system of sovereignty-association, similar to what Quebec nationalists had attempted in Canada (Letamendia and Loughlin 2006). At root, the problem lies in conflicting interpretations of democratic legitimacy and nationhood. For Spanish nationalists, whether of the left or the right, this is derived from the Spanish nation. For Catalan and Basque nationalists, it derives from their own nations.

There has been little systematic theoretical work on the question of regional and local democracy in European states.[10] Most theoretical work on local democracy, or urban politics, seems to have originated in the United States, migrated to the United Kingdom, to be applied in a piece-meal fashion to other European countries. This is, however, highly problematic and unsatisfactory as the political histories, institutions and conditions of European states are quite different from those of North America.[11] At root the problem here is one of a lack of awareness of the importance of state traditions and, in particular, of the differences that exist between the Anglo-American state tradition and the state traditions of continental Europe (Kickert and Stillman 1999). The Anglo-American approach has provided a number of important concepts such as policy networks, new public management and the idea of 'governance' as something wider than 'government'. Undoubtedly, these concepts and the research which they underpin have produced significant results in empirical analysis as they have permitted scholarship to go beyond a merely constitutional–legal understanding of political institutions and to look behind these at the deeper issues of power relationships and actual practice.[12]

But this needs to be supplemented by an analytical approach that recognizes the existence of the state and of different state traditions (Dyson 1980; Loughlin and Peters 1997; see below for further details). These lead to different configurations of central–local relations (Page and Goldsmith 1987) but also influence both the meaning and practice of democracy.

1.4 Different concepts of nationhood

In the French case, it was thought that the state also existed to create the nation (Hayward 1983). But citizenship is also based on the voluntary decision to accept to be part of the nation. This has sometimes been called the voluntaristic concept (one chooses one's nationality) or nation as *demos*. It was graphically expressed by Renan who said, in his *Qu'est-ce une Nation?*, that the French nation is 'a daily plebiscite' of the French people.

The 'Germanic' concept of 'nation' was rather different and was based on Herder's notion of sharing a common linguistic culture (even if this was divided into many mutually incomprehensible dialects) – the *Kulturnation*, or nation as *ethnos*. At the time of the Revolution, France already had a fairly high degree of political centralization (albeit with a great deal of administrative diversity) because of the centralizing activities of the French monarchs. On the other hand, it was culturally and linguistically quite diverse.[13] The case of 'Germany' was quite different. Here, there was to some extent a common linguistic culture, but politically a great variety of territorial arrangements (from large and powerful empires such as Austria–Hungary and kingdoms such as Prussia and Bavaria to city-states such as Bremen or Hamburg). Nationalism in Germany and, later in Italy, which was quite similar in this respect, meant the attempt to build a unified political state on the basis of this alleged common culture.

The two notions of nation as *demos* and nation as *ethnos* in practice tend to shade into one another – in France, membership of the French nation eventually came to mean that an individual was expected to assimilate the French culture and language. In Germany, cultural nationhood, finally found expression during the Weimar Republic, in a democratic system, or nation as *demos* – which can be said to have consolidated only in the second half of the twentieth century.

The United Kingdom differed from both the French and German experiences in that it retained the pre-modern arrangement of a plurinational state albeit with a modernizing system of public administration. Rokkan and Urwin have called this a 'union' state, differing from either federal states such as the United States or Switzerland, and unitary states such as France, as it was formed through a series of Acts of Union (Rokkan and Urwin 1982). But this has meant a great deal of ambiguity over the concepts of 'nation' and 'state'. It is a kingdom with three nations (England, Scotland and Wales) and part of a nation (Northern Ireland is part of the Irish nation), but is there a *British* 'nation'? It is here that the confusion arises as research on national identities, known as the 'Moreno question', has shown (Moreno 2006). Most English people define themselves first as British and second as English, while most Scots and Welsh define themselves as first Scottish and Welsh and second as British. The majority of Scots who see themselves as Scottish first is a higher percentage than the majority of Welsh who see themselves as first Welsh. In Northern Ireland, the majority of Protestants define themselves as first British and second as Northern Irish, 'Ulster' or Irish; most Catholics see themselves as Irish and not at all British.

1.5 State traditions and territorial governance

There is not an infinite variety of forms of territorial governance in European states. Page and Goldsmith (1987) distinguish between northern and southern

European states in their study of central–local relations and between 'political localism' characteristics of southern European countries and 'legal localism' found in northern European countries. In a system characterized by legal localism, there is a high degree of administrative regulation from above, while where there is political localism, informal relationships between such as clientelism or more formal settings such as the French *cumul des mandats* become important. A different typology, closer to those of Dyson and Loughlin/Peters, was developed by Hesse and Sharpe (1991) who distinguished between three types of state: an Anglo group (UK, Ireland, North America); a Franco group (France, Italy, Spain, Belgium, Portugal and, to some extent, Greece); and a northern and middle European group (Scandinavian countries, NL, and Germany).

The Page/Goldsmith typology, while useful in drawing attention to the different legal or political bases of local government in Europe, is somewhat 'broad brush'. The Hesse/Sharpe analysis refines the analysis with a three-fold typology. Dyson (1980), like Hesse and Sharpe, distinguishes three 'state traditions' in Europe, the Anglo-Saxon, the Germanic, and the Napoleonic. Loughlin and Peters (1997) follow Dyson's lead, but add a fourth tradition, the Scandinavian. Dyson's approach was basically an exploration of the philosophical traditions underlying different state forms while Loughlin and Peters attempt to give this a more focused empirical application and to situate different aspects of state and political features within these underlying traditions and cultures.

Each of these state traditions, grouping a number of 'families' of states, gives rise to a particular type of territorial organization – unitary, federal and 'union'. It must, however, be remembered that, within each of these 'families', there exist distinct *national* traditions as well. In southern Europe, there is a common heritage deriving from the Napoleonic state but also important differences among the different countries in their historical development, their political and administrative cultures, and their understanding of democracy itself. There are thus key differences in both the *understanding* and *practice* of democracy within each state tradition. We have already noted the differences between French, German and British understandings of nation and state. To a large extent, the understanding of citizenship and democracy will be influenced by these traditions. In France, and those countries influenced by the French tradition, the citizen is seen as an individual who chooses his or her adherence to the French nation and does not possess any other defining features such as language, religion, ethnicity and even gender. The French also reject any representation through intermediary bodies such as trade unions or churches. The German approach, on the other hand, is characterized by corporatism – the citizen is indeed an individual but may also be a member of a corporate body and these bodies are closely intertwined with the state. The British tradition, like the French, also emphasizes the individual but places society or, rather, commerce and the market, above government and so has a weakly developed state. If we wished to assign philosophers who provided the ideas underlying these three main traditions, we might choose Rousseau, Hegel and Locke respectively, although each tradition is in fact a complex interplay of historical evolution, political circumstances and a variety of intellec-

Table 4.1 State traditions

Feature	Tradition			
	Anglo-Saxon	Germanic	French	Scandinavian
Is there a legal basis for the state?	no	yes	yes	yes
State–society relations	pluralistic	organicist	antagonistic	organicist
Form of political organization	union state/limited federalist	integral/organic federalist	Jacobin, 'one and indivisible'	decentralized unitary
Basis of policy style	incrementalist, 'muddling through'	legal corporatist	legal technocratic	consensual
Form of decentralization	'state power' (USA), devolution/local government (UK)	cooperative federalism	regionalized unitary state	strong local autonomy
Dominant approach to discipline of public administration	political science/sociology	public law	public law	public law (Sweden), organization theory (Norway)
Countries	UK, USA, Canada (not Quebec), Ireland	Germany, Austria, Netherlands, Spain (post-1978), Belgium (post-1988)	France, Italy, Spain (pre-1978), Portugal, Quebec, Greece, Belgium (pre-1988)	Sweden, Norway, Denmark, Finland

Source: Loughlin and Peters (1997).

Table 4.2 Central–local relations in EU member states

Type of state	State	Political region[a]	Administrative/ planning regions[b]	Right of regions to participate in national policy-making	Right of regions to conclude foreign treaties[c]	Political/legislative control over subregional authorities
Federal	Austria	Länder (10)		yes	yes (but limited)	yes (not absolute)
	Belgium	Communities[d] (3)		yes	yes (but limited)	no
		Regions (3)		yes	yes (but limited)	yes (not absolute)
	Germany	Länder (16)			yes (but limited)	yes (not absolute)
Regionalized unitary	Italy[e]	Regioni[g] (20)		consultative	no	yes
	France	Régions[h] (21)		consultative	no	no
	Spain	Comunidades autonomas (17)		no	no	yes
	United Kingdom[f]	Scottish Parliament Welsh National Assembly Northern Ireland Assembly	English standard regions	no with regard to English regions still unclear with regard to Scotland, Wales, and NI	no at present, but may evolve	yes in Scotland and NI no in Wales (so far)
Decentralized unitary	Denmark	Faroe Islands	Groups of Amter	no	no	no
	Finland	Aaland Islands	Counties have a regional planning function	no	no (but has a seat in the Nordic Council)	yes
	Netherlands	Rijnmond region[i]	Landsdelen	consultative	no	no
	Sweden		Regional administrative bodies	no	no	no
Centralized unitary	Greece	Island regions[j]	Development regions (13)	no	no	no
	Ireland		Regional authorities (8)	no	no	no
	Luxembourg		Potential planning regios	no	no	no
	Portugal					

Notes

a This refers to regions and nations (as in Scotland, Wales, Catalonia, the Basque Country, and Galicia) with a directly elected assembly to which a regional executive is accountable.

b This refers to regions without a directly elected assembly, which exist primarily for administrative/planning purposes.

c There is a sharp distinction between the federal and non-federal states in this regard; however, the majority of non-federal states may engage in international activities with the approval of, and under the control of, the national governments.

d The Flemish linguistic community and the Flanders economic region have decided to form one body; the French-speaking community and the Walloon region remain separate.

e Italy is currently undergoing a process of political reform that involves the transformation of the old state into a new kind of state with some federal features. However, although the position of the regions will be strengthened, this will not be a federal state such as Germany or Belgium.

f The United Kingdom was, until the referendums in Scotland and Wales in September 1997, a highly centralized 'union' state. However, the positive outcome of the referendums means that there will be a Scottish Parliament and a Welsh National Assembly by 1999. A referendum in 1998 on a Greater London Authority with an elected mayor was also successful, and this is seen as a precursor to possible regional assemblies in England. The successful outcome of the Northern Ireland peace process means there will be a Northern Ireland Assembly as well as other new institutions linking together the different nations and peoples of the islands.

g In Italy there are 17 'ordinary' regions and five regions with a special statute because of their linguistic or geographical peculiarities: Sicily, Sardinia, Trentino-Alto Adige (South Tyrol, large German-speaking population), Val d'Aosta, and Friuli-Venezia Giulia.

h There are 21 regions on mainland France. However, to this one must add Corsica and the overseas departments and territories (the DOM and TOM). Since 1991 Corsica has a special statute and is officially a *Collectivité territoriale* rather than a region. The TOM too have special statutes, and one of them, New Caledonia, has recently (May 1998) been permitted to accede to independence within a period of 20 years.

i In 1991 it was decided to set up a new metropolitan region with an elected government in the Rotterdam area to replace the *Gemeente* of Rotterdam and the Province of South Holland. However, this was rejected by a referendum held in Rotterdam.

j Portugal, while making provision in its Constitution for regionalization, has so far only granted autonomy to the island groups of the Azores and Madeira. The mainland remains highly centralized.

tual influences. The Scandinavian tradition is a mixture of Germanic corporatism and Anglo-Saxon individualism. The place of subnational government also varies considerably across the different traditions as well as in other ways. Different state traditions express subnational political systems in different ways. The two extremes are the Napoleonic tradition, expressed most fully in France, which allows little variation across its national territory and the Anglo-Saxon tradition which tolerates wide variations, as in the United Kingdom.

1.6 Variations in federal and unitary states

There is a classical distinction between federal and unitary states. However, these two basic forms of state need to be further differentiated. There exist different types of federation, such as 'dual federalism', where the different levels of the federation operate independently of each other, as in Belgium or the United States, and 'cooperative federalism', where the levels operate in close conjunction with each other, as in Germany (Burgess 2006; Hueglin and Fenna 2006). Elazar (1987) and Watts (1999) have explored the different forms that federalism, and a range of intermediate federal-type arrangements which they label 'federacies', have taken (Loughlin 2008). Requejo (2005) has developed the concept of 'multinational federalism' with particular reference to Spain but the concept could also be applied to Canada.

'Unitary' states also need to be differentiated. First, the United Kingdom, as we saw above, has been described as a 'union' rather than a unitary state. Among the rest, there is a variety of central–local relationships giving rise to distinct models of unitary state: centralized unitary, decentralized unitary, regionalized unitary (Bullmann 1996; Loughlin 1996b, 1998). There thus emerges a complex picture of the variety of expressions of democracy at the national and subnational levels within the member states of the European Union. All of these state forms, operating within state traditions, would claim to be 'nation-states' but, clearly, this general concept has been interpreted in a variety of ways.

The importance of state traditions for the understanding and expression of democracy lies in the ways in which the institutions of liberal democracy and the practices of policy-making have developed. Thus, although it is outside the scope of this chapter to do so, we also need to revisit in this light the various typologies of electoral and party systems that have been developed in past decades such as Lijphart's distinction between majoritarian and consociational forms of democracy (Hendriks 2006).

2 The concrete expression of subnational democracy

The great variety of institutional and political traditions has given rise to different concrete expressions of democratic practice. There are several different ways of electing political parties, and the role and functions of parties in political systems display a great variety, but also a capacity for evolution and change (Broughton and Donovan 1999). There is a variety of methods used for electing political leaders, from presidents and prime ministers to the mayors of communes.

In some cases, the regional and local political systems replicate the national, in others it is different. In the United Kingdom, for example, there are, as a result of the devolution reforms, different electoral systems in operation – the 'first-past-the-post' or plurality system at the national level and in most local government, the single transferable vote (STV) system of proportional representation in Northern Ireland and in Scottish local elections, and in the Scottish Parliament and the Welsh National Assembly there is a mixed 'additional-member' system alongside the 'first-past-the-post' system. In federal and regionalized states, such as Germany, Belgium, Italy and Spain, there may be different party systems at the subnational level with the existence of regionally based parties, such as the Bavarian *Christlich Sozial Union* (CSU, Christian Social Union), the Catalan *Convergencia i Unio* (CiU, Convergence and Union), and the Basque *Partido Nacionalista Vasco* (PNV, Basque Nationalist Party).[14] Such regionally based parties may also play a role at the national level as in Spain when the Catalan and Basque representatives in the Cortes have enjoyed some leverage in hung parliaments of both the left and the right and have used this to wring concessions (increased autonomy) from the national government. In the United Kingdom, there has always been a different party system in Northern Ireland, where, until recently, the British parties did not organize (in recent years, the Conservative Party has permitted a Northern Irish branch). With devolution, the tendency to develop regionalized political cultures and party systems in Scotland and Wales has intensified as the dividing cleavages vary from nation to nation or region to region. In Scotland, for example, the 'national question' is generally regarded as 'settled' in the sense that most of those living within Scotland regard their society as constituting a 'nation' distinct from the other nations and regions of the UK. The political cleavage of the future is likely to concern the political expression and relationship of the Scottish nation to the rest of the UK: the current status quo, independence within Europe, or a federal United Kingdom. In Wales there is no sense of 'settled nationhood' and the primary cleavage (among others) was much more between those who supported devolution and those who opposed it, although this is now changing as the majority of Welsh people now seem to have accepted, albeit not very enthusiastically, the existence of the National Assembly for Wales. In Northern Ireland, the cleavage is different again: even if the Good Friday Agreement seems to have ended the overt conflict for the time being, there is still a fundamental difference between the longer-term political aspirations of unionists and nationalists.

Similar regionalization and differentiation of political systems is taking place across Europe: Catalan and Basque politics are as different from each other as they both differ from Madrid; Bretons and Corsicans are as different from each other as are Bretons and Parisians, and so on. This is reinforced by the development of regional or subnational branches of national parties that take on different characteristics from the party at the national level as, for example, with the Catalan section of the Spanish Socialist Party differing from the national party, or the Scottish and Welsh Conservatives being now more in favour of devolution than their English counterparts. There are of course wide variations in this regard. In some cases, such as those just mentioned, the regional system may develop in an autonomous manner. In others, the regional and local systems are completely dominated by the national parties who control local politics from the centre. This is largely the case in Ireland and France and, even in the decentralized United Kingdom, the central organs of the Labour Party have difficulty in letting go of control over the parties in the periphery. In France, there is a weak local party system and, in some respects, through the *cumul des mandats* system of multiple office-holding and the role of the Senate, the local may, in some respects, dominate the national (Loughlin 2007).

A final point to be made with regard to changing local patterns of governance is that there is in western and central Europe a tradition of local self-government and autonomy that predates the emergence of the nation-state (Le Galès 2002). One thinks, for example, of the cities of the Hanseatic League or the Italian city-states such as Florence and Venice. Although these communes were not democratic in the modern sense, as they were often ruled by local oligarchies, nevertheless the tradition of communalism may be regarded as a forerunner of local democracy. Without accepting the thesis of a neo-mediaevalism (because of the very 'modern' or 'post-modern' nature of these developments) it is clear that one of the consequences of the changing nature of the nation-state and the loosening of central–local bonds is that this tradition is reasserting itself today.

2.1 The implications of membership of the European Union for democratic practice

A further complication has entered the equation with the creation and development of the European Union. The background to this was the devastation of the Second World War, but also the experience of the collapse of democracy in Germany and Italy and the threat to liberal democracy from the Soviet Union. One of the primary reasons for the setting up of the Community, therefore, was to protect democracy in the states where it had existed and to strengthen it in those countries that had experienced dictatorship. Indeed, one of the conditions of entry into the Union today is that candidate states should possess the characteristics of liberal democracy outlined above. Most commentators agree that the Union has been successful in achieving most of these aims. All of its member states are successful functioning democracies, even if they all contain imperfections of various kinds.

It is ironic that, despite these successes, the Union has itself failed to develop into a fully democratic system. One of the major criticisms levelled against it is its serious 'democratic deficit'. Despite efforts to fill this deficit, such as strengthening the role of the European Parliament and the creation of the Committee of the Regions, the European system still lacks the democratic legitimacy characteristic of the nation-states which comprise its members. One of the reasons for this deficit is that liberal democracy, as has been pointed out above, has grown up along with the nation-state form of political organization, whether this is federal or one of the kinds of unitary state. However, it is unlikely that the EU will develop into such a nation-state or even into a federation such as Germany or Austria. One of the problems with filling the EU's democratic deficit is that this is measured against the democratic system of nation-states, that is, liberal representative democracy. But if the EU is not, and has little chance of becoming, a nation-state, then such a comparison is inappropriate. Rather, new mechanisms of democratic accountability need to be found that are appropriate to the kind of decision-making system into which the Union has evolved. The challenge is, therefore, both to strengthen the democratic institutions that do exist within the member states and to create new mechanisms whereby democratic control might be strengthened at the European level.

It is true that the European Parliament, as a directly elected body, has been able to fill the democratic deficit to some extent and, through the co-decision procedure, does participate in the decision-making processes of the Council of Ministers. Nevertheless, it still lacks the legislative powers of control and accountability characteristic of national parliaments.[15] Furthermore, it is unable to table initiatives or drafts for legislation such as directives. It can only ask the Commission to present such proposals. The creation of the Committee of the Regions in 1994 also goes some way toward filling the democratic deficit by allowing, for the first time, the representation of regional and local authorities at the European level of decision making (Loughlin 1996a). However, while this is an important breakthrough, and the Committee of the Regions has managed to establish a niche for itself in the decision-making architecture of Europe and this has been gradually strengthened, it still has no more than consultative powers and its Opinions *may* be ignored.[16]

Despite these cautionary comments, two points should be made. First, the democratic gains of the European Union outweigh any democratic losses given the general success of the democratic systems of the member states. Furthermore, the EU has been an important factor in bringing about social and economic development, the *sine qua non* of democratic practice, in many European countries and regions, including the older core states.[17] The second point is that, especially since the 1980s, the European Union has developed into a policy-making system in its own right and that the decisions made by the EU institutions have an important and direct impact on the member states (Cram 1997). One of these institutions is the Committee of the Regions which brings together regional and local politicians from all of the member states. Undoubtedly, this is a forum of intense learning and exchange and is the means by which different democratic experiences and examples of best practice can be shared across Europe. Nevertheless, these developments have still not solved the problem of democratic practice at the European level and more thought should be given to this problem in terms of institutional design.

2.2 The role of the Council of Europe and the European Charters of Local and Regional Self-government

The EU is not the only body which has encouraged the development of democracy in Europe. In fact, we can see that its contribution in this regard is rather ambiguous and, in some ways, it might even be an obstacle to subnational democracy.[18] The same could not be said of the other main European organization, the Council of Europe, founded in 1949 with the aims of promoting democracy and human rights. Originally with a membership of just ten states[19] it now has 47 member states, including almost all the states of the former Soviet bloc (the exceptions are Belarus and Kazakhstan). The Council of Europe has developed the notion of *local* democracy through its European Charter of Local Self-government, a short document of 18 articles which define the conditions of effective autonomy for local authorities. The Charter was first promulgated in 1985 and first signed by member states in 1988. Today, almost all the member states have signed and ratified the Charter and this means that it may be used as a benchmark by which to assess the state of play of local democracy in a particular state. A committee of independent experts attached to the Council's Congress of Local and Regional Authorities of Europe has the task of monitoring the application of the Charter in all of the member states. A similar Charter of Regional Self-government is still in draft form and has run into strong opposition from a number of member states, although the Congress has passed a number of resolutions supporting regional autonomy.

An attempt was made by the UN-Habitat organization in the 1990s to draw up a World Charter of Local Self-government based on the European Charter. This, however, did not succeed because of opposition from a number of states, albeit the reasons for opposition differed in each case: the United States and the UK, China, the Arab and Muslim states. In 2003, a new committee of experts was formed[20] to attempt to advance this idea. The result was, not a binding Charter like that of the Council of Europe, but a set of 'Guidelines on Effective Decentralization' which was approved by the Governing Council of UN-Habitat at its meeting in Nairobi in 2007. This illustrates that decentralization and local democracy are now seen as essential elements of 'good democratic governance'.

2.3 The role of citizens: representative vs. participatory democracy

It is citizens who 'practise' democracy through electing leaders but also seek to influence decision making and the running the affairs of their communities or localities in a variety of other ways. Although theorists such as Schumpeter looked askance at *participatory* democracy, in the contemporary period (at least since the 1960s), the practice of democracy has been closely related to the existence of an *informed* and *involved* citizenry[21] (Pateman 1970), and, therefore, the attitude of ordinary citizens toward their subnational levels of government is extremely important. To what extent do citizens get involved in subnational government? This may express itself in a number of ways: electoral turnout, standing for election, contacting the council, maintaining an awareness of council decisions and activities. In some countries, voting is compulsory and, therefore, not a true indicator of commitment to democratic practice at this level.

Democracy is rarely practised in a manner that is completely faithful to the liberal democratic schema outlined above, whereby elected representatives legislate and their decisions are translated into policies and executed by local administrators. Some authors, in the American pluralistic tradition of social science, have gone as far as to speak of 'post-parliamentary democracy' arguing that democracy might occur through the competition of elites or of policy networks (Jordan and Richardson 1985). The neo-corporatist literature of the 1980s also pointed to a shift away from formal parliamentary decision making to a system involving concertation between governments, employers' associations and trade unions (Lehmbruch and Schmitter 1982). Here the American and British debate between elitists and pluralists is useful to some extent in pointing to the dimension of power relations in political systems: is power widely diffused as pluralists would argue or is it concentrated in the hands of a few as elitists maintain? With regard to the subnational level, the neo-corporatist analysts claimed to find a tendency towards 'meso-corporatism' (Cawson 1985). Although these debates occurred in the context of the period of the welfare state, either in expansion (pluralists vs. elitists) or in decline (neo-corporatists), and this kind of state has significantly changed under the pressure of neo-liberalism, nevertheless they are useful in pointing to the more hidden mechanisms of the distribution and exercise of power and decision making and in relativizing the role of elected assemblies.

The distinction currently found in the literature between 'government' and 'governance' may be useful here as it points to these wider dimensions of the way in which power is exercised (Kohler-Koch 1996; Rhodes 1997; Le Galès 1999). 'Governance' refers to the phenomenon that decisions are often taken within policy networks and communities, including non-elected participants, who constitute a 'system' that is wider than the institutional structures of 'government'. Outside of these policy networks and communities, pressure groups of various kinds often attempt to have an influence on these decisions. Whether this is 'post-parliamentary democracy' or 'non-democracy' (a new form of elitism) is what the current debate needs to clarify but certainly this form of decision making radically affects the nature of democratic practice. It may also help to clarify the nature of the EU as a system of governance and how this affects subnational democracy. The EU is clearly not a 'government' but, equally clearly, it is a system of decision making and governing, that is, a system of 'governance' with distinct patterns of institutions, actors and processes. What has emerged, therefore, in recent years, is a complex set of overlapping and nested systems of governance involving European, national, regional and local actors, groups and networks. This has been described as 'multilevel governance' (Hooghe and Marks 2001).

These developments have profound implications for the practice of liberal representative democracy and government. It is methodologically difficult to identify the existence and ascertain the effects of such policy networks and pressure groups on democratic practice and it is important not to set up 'government' against 'governance' as if the latter was somehow displacing the former. On the contrary, one of the features of contemporary government is that it co-exists with governance. This presents a challenge to the traditional concepts of liberal democracy: representation, legitimacy and effectiveness. The question thus becomes how a wider system of governance will affect the democratic features of traditional government. It could be argued, for example, that the influence of these more or less hidden networks and pressure groups undermines representation, legitimacy and effectiveness and should be reduced. On the other hand, it could be argued that it is impossible to avoid this type of decision-making system and it is more necessary to democratize it. A third approach might be to try to combine both traditional liberal democratic approaches with forms of representation and involvement that recognize more explicitly the role of groups and give them a clearer institutional form. Whatever the response, it is not always easy even to recognize the existence and influence of these more or less hidden groups and it is even more difficult to design institutional systems that might reconcile to two aspects of governing in ways that are compatible with democracy.

3   Challenges and opportunities to regional and local democracy

So far we have outlined the more static aspects of democratic government: the historical traditions and institutional settings that provide the context within which change occurs. It is essential, however, to recognize that these systems are under continual pressure and change continuously. Change may be the result of a gradual and incremental adjustment to various stimuli from within and without states. Or it may be the result of explicit and deliberate reform programmes such as French decentralization in the 1980s, British neo-liberal reforms by Margaret Thatcher the 1980s and 1990s or the recent devolution reforms of the Blair period. Whatever the case, our governmental systems never simply stand still.

Our argument here is that national, regional and local democratic systems have, in recent years, faced a number of challenges. Some of these challenges are common to all states while others are specific to particular states. Sometimes a general challenge may take a particular configuration in an individual state. Among the most important of the challenges common to all states are the following.

3.1   Globalization/regionalism

This rather nebulous and contested term has been the subject of a vigorous debate among social scientists. Basically, there are those, mainly on the left but also some traditional nationalists, who argue that the concept 'globalization' refers to nothing that is new but is used as a way of disciplining, demoralizing and undermining political and social movements that might in some way threaten capitalist development (Hirst 1997; Hirst and Thompson 2002). This is because these movements grew up in the context of the nation-state and attempted to influence decision making at that (key) level. If globalization undermines the nation-state, then the activities of these groups are also reduced to insignificance. According to this approach, 'globalization' refers to little more than global trade flows and has existed at least since the end of the nineteenth century. Furthermore, they argue, national governments still retain a great deal of control over decision making in many areas. They point out too that most multinational corporations – the alleged purveyors of globalization – are, in fact, nationally based companies who happen to have a global outreach and national governments can influence and affect their activities if they so choose. The counter-argument to this, probably accepted by most social scientists, is that globalization refers today to a specifically new set of developments that have changed the nature of our societies, political systems and international relations (for a good summary of the arguments see Beck 2000). We may like or dislike the phenomenon from both right and left points of view but it is here to stay. This is the position taken in this chapter. On the other hand, it seems equally clear that globalization does not simply mean the creation of a single world market but is rather a world dominated by three large economic 'blocs': the USA, Japan and Western Europe. Nevertheless, in practical terms, for the majority of the world's nations, the hegemony of these three blocs and their increasing interdependence and the power of international financial markets mean that there is a de facto world economic system. This discussion is extremely relevant to the question of democratic government and practice as it raises the question as to the fate of the nation-state faced with globalization, and the fate of the nation-state is central to the fate of democracy. It is essential therefore to clarify what is going on at this level.

Part of the confusion surrounding the debate is that globalization refers to several different kinds of phenomena: economic, financial, cultural, political, and social processes. The relationships among these are not always very clear. It is also true that some aspects of globalization have indeed been around for a very long time – in some cases we might even refer to the Renaissance as the starting point, in others to early financial capitalism, to the spread of industrial capitalism in the nineteenth century, and so on. What seems to be new today is their combination into a powerful set of forces that have become increasingly mutually reinforcing and dominant over other forms and processes of political, economic and social organization. Underlying them all has been the successful transformation of capitalism itself following the crisis in the 1970s of the Keynesian welfare state model of economic management and the subsequent development of neo-liberal models of free trade, the end of protectionism and the rapid spread of new technologies, communications and productive systems around the world. All of these developments have radically changed the context within which national governments operate. In all cases, the latter are now constrained by new factors that did not exist before. However, this does not necessarily mean they are weaker – simply that national governing elites must now develop new political strategies often in partnership with their counterparts in other states and sometimes with subnational elites as even large or medium-sized states, such as Germany and the UK, have proved incapable of responding effectively by themselves to these processes.

Globalization also affects subnational levels of government and administration. Some authors give a positive spin to this and link globalization to the emergence of a new model of economic development that stresses the importance of the regional and the local and the return of 'territory' as an important variable (a good summary of this work is found in Le Galès 1999). This linking of the global and the regional/local is sometimes referred to as 'glocalization', in which the key *loci* of economic development are specific regions or localities such as Silicon Valley in the USA or the Dutch Randstadt. 'Regions' here do not necessarily, and usually do not, correspond to political or administrative regions. On the other hand, globalization has led to greater competition among regions and cities even within the same state, while many national governments, influenced by neo-liberal approaches to public policy, have cut down or abolished regional aid programmes that might have helped subnational levels of government cope with the changes. What seems to have happened is that the stronger regions, such as the south-east of England or the Dutch Randstad, have become even stronger while weaker regions, such as those in southern Italy and Spain or in Greece or in the northern parts of Great Britain, have become weaker. On the other hand, some previously peripheral regions and countries such as Ireland and Portugal and parts of Spain have managed to use the new developments to achieve economic performances that are quite spectacular.[22] What is clear is that the old conceptualization of centres and peripheries, dear to authors such Rokkan and Urwin, no longer holds and that the very concepts of space and territory need to be radically reformulated.

These developments are central to the attempt to grasp the challenges facing regions and localities as they respond to globalization. First, globalization seems to have encouraged approaches to public action that are more sympathetic to competition and markets than to solidarity and equalization among territories. Second, regional development is sometimes viewed in purely economic or financial terms rather than in a wider sense as social, political and cultural development. This has favoured the influence of economic or business elites rather than other sections of the community (this is really what is meant by 'governance'). Third, the concepts of 'citizenship' and 'democracy' have become defined in different ways emphasizing the elements of public choice and consumerism. Fourth, as economic processes seem to dominate over political and as economic regions and localities no longer correspond to political and administrative structures, the latter have greater difficulty in providing democratic control over the former. Finally, globalization has exacerbated tendencies toward societal fragmentation and social exclusion. This both harms the communitarian basis of democratic politics and creates extra burdens on subnational authorities who have to deal with the consequences. The ineffectiveness of regional and local governments, and the withdrawal of citizens from active involvement in politics, are both harmful to the democratic legitimacy of subnational governance.

3.2 Europeanization and the 'new' regionalism

The relaunch of Europe in the 1980s, with the 1992 Single European Market project, is often interpreted as a response by national governments and business elites to the perceived threat of a global economy dominated by the United States and Japan. However, it was also the result of intense lobbying by governmental actors and other elites who wished to see the strengthening of the federal elements of an integrated Europe (Pinder 1995; Loughlin 1996b). Concurrent with these processes of integration and federalization was the re-emergence of the notion of a 'Europe of the Regions' in the 1990s. What is important here is not the rather sterile debate as to whether there is a 'Europe of the Regions' or not, but the fact that the intensifying of European integration through the 1987 Single European Act and the revisions of the EC treaties at Maastricht, Amsterdam and Nice, and now (2009) the ratification of the Lisbon Treaty, have created a new administrative and legal environment for local and regional authorities, to which they have been obliged to adapt. This new environment is neither the arrival of a European-wide nation-state nor a European federation but what might be described as a European system of governance that has both state-like and federal-type characteristics. This creates both challenges but also new opportunities for regional and local authorities.

In this new context, regionalism has found a second wind and some authors have spoken of a 'new' regionalism (Keating and Loughlin 1997; Keating 1998). There is, of course, an 'old' regionalism, which was both a political idea or ideology and a set of political movements the origins of which are to be found in the nineteenth century. Many of the early regionalists were opposed to the modern nation-state and even to the forms of liberal democracy with what they regarded as its levelling tendencies and breaking up of natural communities. In recent years and certainly since the 1960s, there developed another more 'progressive' form of regionalism, which may be conceived as a 'modernizing' project (Keating 1998). This kind of 'new' regionalism has received a stimulus from the increased level of integration of the European Union and the challenges and opportunities opened up by the Single European Market and Economic and Monetary Union. These have been in part responsible for the strengthening of regional and structural action policy and the reinforcement of the principles of subsidiarity and partnership.

It would be going too far, nevertheless, to say that we are witnessing the emergence of a 'Europe of the Regions'. There are great difficulties with the notion of a Europe of the Regions. First, there are many ways of defining what a region is (Loughlin 1996a) and, consequently, of the problem of: a Europe of *which* regions? Second, national governments show no signs of disappearing but are, on the contrary, still the most powerful actors in the new system of European governance. Third, their representation at the European level,

through the Committee of the Regions or via DG Regio of the European Commission or the European Parliament, still remains quite weak and marginal.
Nevertheless, despite these limitations, regions and other local authorities have
found a new place in the new Europe: we can speak of a 'Europe *with* the
Regions', in the sense that subnational authorities have today a greater salience
in policy-making terms and a new-found freedom to operate on a broader
European scale than was hitherto the case (Hooghe and Marks 1996). This is
quite different from the previous situation when most subnational authorities
were more or less completely restrained by their national governments as to
the kinds of activities they might engage in and which were firmly limited to
within the boundaries of the nation-state. Now, subnational authorities in most
countries have discovered a new freedom to develop links both with the EU
institutions themselves and also with their counterparts in the rest of Europe
and beyond, through associations such as the Assembly of European Regions,
the Conference of Peripheral Maritime Regions, and many others. This new
situation of regions and local authorities in Europe was formally recognized by
the Treaty on European Union (Maastricht), which set up the Committee of the
Regions in 1994 (Loughlin 1996a; Loughlin and Seiler 1999). The Committee
of the Regions also plays a role in strengthening democracy in the EU, as it
has the potential to bring the processes of European decision making closer to
the ordinary citizens.

3.2.1 Governance in flux

The consequences of these developments are that the role, nature, and functions
of different levels of government – supranational, national, regional, and local –
are in a state of flux. Some already strong nations and regions are likely to
become even stronger, while the weaker may suffer further deprivation. Nevertheless, the new situation may also be an opportunity for regions and local
authorities to formulate new models of regional and local development based
more on a judicious use of resources that are both endogenous – including
regional and local cultures and lifestyles – and exogenous – for example, European structural funds (Cooke and Morgan 1998).

3.3 Societal changes

Western societies are undergoing continual and rapid change with a radical
upheaval in terms of attitudes, values, and lifestyles (Mendras 1997; Loughlin
1998). There has been a decline in traditional forms of association, particularly
those based on social class such as trade unions and political parties and a
growth of individualism. This is an ambiguous phenomenon. On the one hand, it
might mean a decline in willingness to participate in traditional forms of collective action such as political parties, churches and trades unions. However, it
might also mean a search to find new forms of participation and a desire to
replace some of the more traditional institutions. The development of car owner-

ship and cheaper foreign travel has led to much greater levels of mobility and new residential patterns in cities and the countryside. New forms of entertainment, through television, video and the internet, are also centred on the possibility of individual choice and have encouraged people to stay at home. It has been claimed that there has been a decline in the sense of, and commitment to, community in many Western societies although, of course, it is notoriously difficult to operationalize the concept of 'community' in this context since forms might be evolving. Related to this is the problematic concept of 'social capital', developed by Robert Putnam originally in his analysis of Italian regions (Putnam *et al*. 1993) but subsequently applied to the United States. These societal changes, especially the trend toward individualism, have had important consequences for democratic practice and may to some extent explain the apathy and withdrawal from politics that has been evident in recent years. They also represent a challenge to traditional politics, which developed in a much more stable and communitarian society. Some authors, however, (for example, Frazer 1996) are uneasy and believe that the emphasis on local 'community' might in fact be retrogressive in terms of civil liberties as these communities might be morally and politically conservative and, therefore, might be unwilling to tolerate what they would regard as the gains of the new individualism, for example in the area of sexual behaviour or orientation.[23]

However, 'individualism' may also be an opportunity as the masses of the population (at least in most of Europe and other parts of the developed world) are today better educated and healthier than was the case in previous generations. They are also much better informed than were their forebears – news is now available almost instantaneously from every part of the world. The challenge for policy makers and citizens is to translate these positive features into new forms of commitment and institutional design. Many regional and local authorities are experimenting with different methods of bringing citizens more into the political system at this level (Loughlin *et al*. 2001).

3.4 Technological developments

The period since the Second World War has seen enormous technological changes in telecommunications, transport, and forms of economic production. This process of change seems to accelerate exponentially as new developments feed into each other at an extraordinary rate. The societal changes noted in the previous paragraph are to some extent the result of these changes, which seem to have removed many of the limitations of space and time in human existence as well as enhancing the capacity of choice of the individual. It is also true that governments at all levels – European, national, regional, and local – have great difficulty in controlling and mastering these changes and seem to be continually trying to catch up with them. In other words, the locus of power in important areas has shifted from the political domain to the manufacturers of new technologies and new lifestyles (one can think of the 'manufacture' of lifestyles by advertisers, TV and film producers, popular magazines, etc.).

3.5 Meeting the challenges; the principle of subsidiarity

The question is, of course, whether governments *ought* to try to control or at least influence these processes of change in the name of the (or *a*) common good as some of the changes might be considered harmful. If the answer is yes, then greater thought needs to be given to the level at which control can take place. The principle of subsidiarity may be useful as a guide to which level of government (or governance) is appropriate to which kind of activity and decision making. The regional and local are the appropriate levels for dealing with specific kinds of problem while the national and supranational are appropriate for other kinds. The problem is to apply effectively the principle and to draw up criteria which help us to decide which level is appropriate or not. At least one element in these criteria is the democratic involvement of those who live in a region or locality. This is particularly the case with regard to problems such as the environment, urban policy, spatial planning, or tourism. The answer to this problem may lie in devising new forms of institutional design more appropriate to a system of governance than a system of government. It may be that the latter, based on hierarchy, routine and slow responses, needs to be complemented by a system that is more flexible, horizontal and open and that can respond to the ever increasing challenges of a turbulent environment.

Besides these general challenges faced by all regional and local authorities (and indeed by national governments and Europe as well), there exist a certain number of challenges that are particular to each member state. In some cases, this may be conflictual central–local relations that have hampered the development of regional and local democracy. In others, there has been the problem of a low level of institutional capacity at the regional or local level. This is caused either by the existence of too many small councils that lack the resources and expertise to respond to the problems of modern government or by a general lack of institutional capacity in the public-administration tradition of that state in general. For example, in some states not all local authorities have been able to manage and use the quite considerable funds that have arrived from the European Union for purposes of regional and local development. These have lain unused and development has not occurred.

4 Conclusions

A number of conclusions may be drawn from this chapter. First, the concept of democracy itself has several different meanings. The primary meaning, associated with the arrival of the nation-state as the dominant form of political organization, is liberal representative democracy expressed primarily at the national level. There are, however, other types of democracy such as direct and participatory democracy. Second, the variety of national and state traditions has led to a variety of understandings of democracy. These are not infinite in number but may be grouped in a small number of clusters with distinctive features: French, German, Anglo, and Scandinavian. Although states within these clusters share a number of features, there also exist important differences within them. These national and state traditions and the variations within them give rise to different types of territorial organization and define the position of subnational authorities within the states. This, too, will affect the expression of subnational democracy in any particular state. Third, despite these complex variations, there are also a number of general phenomena which affect all states and influence how they give expression to both national and subnational democracy. The most important of these general trends are: globalization and, in Europe, Europeanization; societal and economic changes; and technological changes. These forces have considerably modified the traditional central position of national governments and, while they pose a serious challenge to subnational authorities as well, also open up possibilities for the latter to enter into new types of activity and new relationships with actors both inside and outside their own nation-states.

Notes

1 This chapter is a completely revised and updated version of 'Introduction: The Transformation of the Democratic State in Western Europe', in J. Loughlin *et al.* (2001).
2 Almost sometimes treated as synonyms these two forms of democracy are not identical. Or rather, participatory democracy is always direct, while direct democracy, such as referendums, may not be participatory.
3 The influence of Rousseau is ambiguous and his ideas may be used to justify participatory democracy when applied to small-scale societies such as his native Geneva but become problematic when applied to large countries such as France. This did not stop the French Jacobins from using his thought in their formulation of the 'one and indivisible Republic'.
4 The Catholic Church and the aristocracy were not homogeneous bodies in the eighteenth and nineteenth centuries and some members of both supported the Revolution as well as the nation-state and democracy. But it is probably the case that the majority opposed them and liberalism in general. Pope Pius IX was sympathetic to liberalism when he was elected Pope in 1846, but changed his mind when he witnessed the Revolutions two years later and the threats to the Papal States from the Italian Risorgimento. His infamous *Syllabus of Errors*, condemning almost every aspect of modern liberalism, was promulgated in 1864 when the Papacy was besieged by the Italian nationalists.
5 Associated with this movement were theologians such as the Jesuit Henri de Lubac, the Dominican Yves Congar, the philosophers Jacques Maritain and Etienne Gilson, political theorists such as Raymond Dandieu and Robert Aron. The Swiss Protestant Denis de Rougement was also associated with it as was the European federalist Alexandre Marc, a Jewish convert to Catholicism. Among the young members was Emmanuel Mounier (Loughlin 1988).
6 The term is sometimes confused by speakers of Romance languages such as Italian with 'clientelism'. It means, in fact, a certain understanding of the nature of the human person, as the individual *rooted* in a particular society – the family, the commune, the region, a religion – but opening out to other persons in society. This double movement – returning to roots but then transcending them – was called by these philosophers the 'federalist dialectic'.
7 Epistemologically, the debate concerns the manner in which our minds grasp reality, either analytically or synthetically, or at least which of these two aspects is dominant. Methodologically, the debate is between 'methodological individualism', which usually takes the form of rational choice approaches, and approaches that are

more structuralist, culturalist or institutionalist (whatever the differences among the latter group). Normatively, in terms of public policy, the question is whether democratic practice can be based on the notion that the individual citizen is a member of a collectivity or whether he should be seen as a consumerist, rational individual making choices with regard to the use of public services. If the latter model is adopted, 'public' services are increasingly redefined in a more 'privatized' fashion.

8 Of course, Weberian-type administrations may exist in non-democratic states, such as nineteenth-century Prussia. However, the 'rational' basis of this kind of public administration was admirably demonstrated as the underpinning of the executive branch of liberal democratic government.

9 The issue in Corsica came to a head with the 1982 decentralization reforms under which Corsica was granted a special statute (Statut Particulier) which established a Regional Assembly. Before this, François Mitterrand, who had been presidential candidate, referred to the Corsican 'people' while, later, in an attempted reform of the Corsican Statut Particulier in 1991 by then Minister of the Interior Pierre Joxe in which Corsica was described as a 'peuple' this was deemed unconstitutional by the Constitutional Court (see Hintjens et al. 1995).

10 The first general survey seems to have been the report for the Committee of the Regions drawn up by this author with Eliseo Aja, Udo Bullmann, Frank Hendriks, Anders Lidstrom and Daniel-L Seiler and published in 1999 (Committee of the Regions 1999). This was subsequently revised and published as Loughlin et al. (2001).

11 This statement might be qualified in two ways. First, the United Kingdom and Ireland do share a number of features of a general 'Anglo-Saxon' state tradition as argued in this chapter. Second, Canada, despite its proximity to the United States, which remains a strong influence on it, has many features more similar to European traditions, for example, its stronger, albeit declining, welfare state tradition. Within the Canadian federation, Quebec is even more strikingly similar to European countries especially France.

12 A good example of this is the study of American federalism known as 'Intergovernmental Relations' (IGR) pioneered by Deil S. Wright (1988).

13 It has been estimated that, at the Revolution, the majority of people living in France spoke a language other than French, a situation which lasted until the end of the nineteenth century.

14 For the Spanish case, see Hanley and Loughlin's Spanish Political Parties (2006) which is mostly about the political parties in the Autonomous Communities.

15 This is true even if there has been a significant decline in the powers of national parliaments such as the French Assemblée Nationale, which remains extremely weak under the Constitution of the Fifth Republic, or even the Westminster Parliament, allegedly the exemplar of parliamentary democracy, which has increasingly become dominated by the Cabinet and executive thanks to the two-party majoritarian system. The European Parliament compares rather poorly with these. But it may be that one should not be comparing it with national parliaments since it is the parliament, not of a nation-state but of a quite different kind of political system.

16 In practice, there seems to be a close working relationship between the Committee of the Regions and DG XVI (now renamed as DG Regio); the latter is responsible for Regional Policy and ensures that most of the Committee of the Region's Opinions are taken into account. The Committee of the Regions has also developed a positive relationship with the European Parliament.

17 It is also true that European regions are still divided into 'leaders' and 'laggards' and that, in the latter, EU Regional Funds have not brought about the transformation that was hoped for.

18 For example, because it deals mainly with national governments, it may disempower subnational government in important policy areas.

19 Belgium, Denmark, France, Ireland, Italy, Luxembourg, the Netherlands, Norway, Sweden and the United Kingdom.
20 The author chaired this committee.
21 In the Schumpetarian model, the role of 'citizens' was to elect their political leaders and decision makers and, in the event of the latter failing to live up to their expectations, 'to cast the rascals out' (Held 1987). 'Participation' interfered with the good running of government.
22 Ireland is the most spectacular of all and is sometimes referred to as the 'Celtic Tiger' by analogy with the Asian tigers – see the chapter on Ireland in this book.
23 A striking example of this kind of ideological and moral conflict occurred recently in Scotland when the Scottish Labour Government, supported by the British Labour Government at Westminster, proposed removing Clause 28 of the 1988 Education Act which forbids 'homosexual propaganda' in schools. Civil liberties and homosexual rights groups had been bitterly opposed to this clause on the grounds that it discriminated against homosexuals. The problem was that a large majority of the Scottish population, according to opinion polls, were strongly opposed to dropping the clause even though a majority of parliamentarians in the Scottish Parliament were in favour of dropping it. Given the 'traditional' position of most Scots on this issue, which course would have been more 'democratic'?

Bibliography

Alter, P. (1994) *Nationalism*, 2nd edn, London: Edward Arnold.

Beck, U. (2000) *What is Globalization?*, Cambridge: Polity Press.

Bogdani, M. and Loughlin, J. (2007) *Albania and the European Union: The Tumultuous Journey to Integration and Accession*, London: I.B. Tauris.

Boudon, J. (2006) *Les Jacobins: Une Traduction des Principes de Jean-Jacques Rousseau*, Paris: Librairie Générale de Droit et de Jurisprudence (LGDJ).

Broughton, D. and Donovan, M. (eds) (1999) *Changing Party Systems in Western Europe*, London: Pinter.

Brugmans, H. (1965) *L'Idée Européenne, 1918–1965*, Bruges: De Tempel.

Bullmann, U. (1996) 'The Politics of the Third Level', *Regional and Federal Studies* 6(2): 3–19.

Burgess, M. (2006) *Comparative Federalism: Theory and Practice*, London: Routledge.

Cawson, A. (ed.) (1985) *Organized Interests and the State: Studies in Meso-corporatism*, London: Sage.

Cerny, P. (1999) 'Globalization and the Erosion of Democracy', *European Journal of Political Research* 36(1): 1–26.

Committee of the Regions (1999) *Regional and Local* Democracy *in the European Union*, Luxembourg: Official Publications Office of the EU [J. Loughlin with the collaboration of Eliseo Aja, Udo Bullmann, Frank Hendriks, Anders Lidstrom and Daniel-L Seiler].

Cooke, P. and Morgan, K. (1998) *The Associational Economy: Firms, Regions and Innovation*, Oxford: Oxford University Press.

Cram, L. (1997) *Policy-Making in the European Union: Conceptual Lenses and the Integration Process*, London: Routledge.

Dyson, K. (1980) *The State Tradition in Western Europe: a Study of an Idea and Institution*, Oxford: Martin Robertson.

Elazar, D. (1987) *Exploring Federalism*, Tuscaloosa, AL: University of Alabama Press.

Etzioni, A. (1993) *The Spirit of Community: Rights, Responsibilities and the Communitarian Agenda*, New York: Crown Publishers.

Frazer, E. (1996) 'The Value of Locality', in D.S. King and G. Stoker (eds) *Rethinking Local Democracy*, London: Macmillan, pp. 89–110.

Garrard, G. (2003) *Rousseau's Counter-Enlightenment: a Republican Critique of the Philosophes*, Albany, NY: State University of New York Press.

Gaudin, J.-P. (2007) *La Démocratie Participative*, Paris: Armand Colin.

Gras, C. and Livet, G. (eds) (1977) *Régions et Régionalisme en France: du XVIIe Siècle à nos Jours*, Paris: Presses Universitaires de France.

Guéhenno, J.-M. (1995) *The End of the Nation-State*, London: University of Minnesota Press.

Habermas, J. (2003) Toward a Cosmopolitan Europe, *Journal of Democracy* 14(4): 86–100.

Hanley, D. and Loughlin, J. (eds) (2006) *Spanish Political Parties*, Cardiff: Wales University Press.

Hayward, J.E.S. (1983) *Governing France: The One and Indivisible Republic*, 2nd edn, London: Weidenfeld & Nicolson.

Held, D. (1987) *Models of Democracy*, Cambridge: Polity Press.

Held, D. (1993) 'Democracy: From City-states to a Cosmopolitan Order', in D. Held (ed.) *Prospects for Democracy*, Cambridge: Polity Press.

Hendriks, F. (2006) *Vitale Democratie: Theorie van Democratie in Actie [Living Democracy: a Theory of Democracy in Action]*, Amsterdam: Amsterdam University Press.

Héraud, G. (1993) *L'Europe des Ethnies*, 3rd edn, Bruxelles: Bruylant; Paris: LGDJ.

Hesse, J.J. and Sharpe, L.J. (1991) 'Local Government in International Perspective: Some Comparative Observations', in J.J. Hesse (ed.) *Local Government and Urban Affairs in International Perspective*, Baden-Baden: Nomos Verlagsgesellschaft, pp. 603–621.

Hintjens, H., Loughlin, J. and Olivesi, C. (1995) 'The Status of Maritime and Insular France: the DOM-TOM and Corsica', in J. Loughlin and S. Mazey (eds) *The End of the French Unitary State: Ten Years of Regionalization in France*, London: Frank Cass, pp.110–131.

Hirst, P. (1997) *From Statism to Pluralism: Democracy, Civil Society and Global Politics*, London: UCL Press.

Hirst, P. and Thompson, G. (2002) 'The Future of Globalization', *Cooperation and Conflict* 37(3): 247–265.

Hobsbawm, E. (1992) *Nations and Nationalism since 1780: Programme, Myth, Reality*, 2nd edn, Cambridge: Cambridge University Press.

Hooghe, L. and Marks, G. (1996) '"Europe *with* the Regions". Channels of Interest Representation in the European Union', *Publius* 26(1): 73–91.

Hooghe, L. and Marks, G. (2001) *Multi-level Governance and European Integration*, Lanham, MD; Oxford: Rowman & Littlefield.

Hueglin, T. and Fenna, A. (2006) *Comparative Federalism: A Systematic Inquiry*, Peterborough, Ontario: Broadview Press.

Jordan, G. and Richardson, J. (1985) *Governing under Pressure: The Policy Process in a Post-parliamentary Democracy*, Oxford: Blackwell.

Keating, M. (1998) *The New Regionalism in Western Europe: Territorial Restructuring and Political Change*, Cheltenham: Edward Elgar.

Keating, M. and Loughlin, J. (eds) (1997) *The Political Economy of Regionalism*, London: Frank Cass.

Kickert, W. and Stillman, R.J. (eds) (1999) *The Modern State and Its Study: New Administrative Sciences in a Changing Europe and United States*, Cheltenham: Edward Elgar.

Kohler-Koch, B. (1996) 'The Strength of Weakness: The Transformation of Governance in the EU', in S. Gustavsson and L. Lewin (eds) *The Future of the Nation-state: Essays in Cultural Pluralism and Political Integration*, London: Routledge.

Lapidoth, R. (1997) *Autonomy; Flexible Solutions to Ethnic Conflicts*, Washington, DC: University of Washington Press.

Le Galès, P. (1999) 'Crise de Gouvernance et Globalisation', *Revue Internationale de Politique Comparée* 4.

Le Galès, P. (2002) *European Cities: Social Conflicts and Governance*, Oxford: Oxford University Press.

Lehmbruch, G. and Schmitter, P. (eds) (1982) *Patterns of Corporatist Policy-making*, London: Sage.

Letamendia, F. and Loughlin, J. (2006) 'Lessons for Northern Ireland: The Peace Processes in the Basque Country and Corsica', in M. Cox and A. Guelke (eds) *A Farewell to Arms? From War to Peace in Northern Ireland*, Manchester: Manchester University Press.

Loughlin, J. (1988) 'Personalism and Federalism in Inter-war France', in P. Stirk (ed.) *The Context of European Unity: the Inter-war Period*, London: Francis Pinter, pp.188–200.

Loughlin, J. (ed.) (1994) *Southern Europe Studies Guide*, London: Bowker-Saur.

Loughlin, J. (1996a) 'Representing Regions in Europe: The Committee of the Regions', *Regional and Federal Studies* 6(2): 147–165.

Loughlin, J. (1996b) 'Europe of the Regions and the Federalization of Europe', *Publius* 26(4): 141–162.

Loughlin, J. (1998) 'Autonomy is Strength', in R. Wilson (ed.) *Hard Choices: Policy Autonomy and Priority Setting in Public Expenditure*, Belfast: Democratic Dialogue/ Eastern Health & Social Services Board/Northern Ireland Economic Council.

Loughlin, J. (2004) 'The "Transformation" of Governance: New Directions in Policy and Politics', *Australian Journal of Politics and History* 50(1): 8–22.

Loughlin, J. (2007) *Subnational Government: The French Experience*, Basingstoke: Palgrave Macmillan.

Loughlin, J. (2008) 'Unitary, Federal, and Local Government Institutions', in D. Caramani (ed.) *Comparative Politics*, Oxford: Oxford University Press.

Loughlin, J. and Peters, B.G. (1997) 'State Traditions, Administrative Reform and Regionalization', in M. Keating and J. Loughlin (eds) *The Political Economy of Regionalism*, London: Frank Cass.

Loughlin, J. and Seiler, D. (1999) 'Le Comité des Régions et la Supranationalité en Europe', *Etudes Internationales*, décembre.

Loughlin, J. [with the collaboration of Eliseo Aja, Udo Bullmann, Frank Hendriks, Anders Lidstrom and Daniel-L Seiler] (2001) *Subnational Democracy in the European Union: Challenges and Opportunities*, Oxford: Oxford University Press.

MacIntyre, A. (1984) *After Virtue; A Study in Moral Theory*, 2nd edn, Indiana: University of Notre Dame.

Mendras, H. (1997) *L'Europe des Européens*, Paris: Gallimard.

Moreno, L. (2006) 'Scotland, Catalonia, Europeanization and the "Moreno Question" ', *Scottish Affairs* 54(Winter).

Ohmae, K. (1995) *The End of the Nation State: The Rise of Regional Economies*, London: HarperCollins.

Page, E. and Goldsmith, M. (eds) (1987) *Central and Local Government Relations*, London: Sage Publications.

Pateman, C. (1970) *Participation and Democratic Theory*, Cambridge: Cambridge University Press.

Pinder, J. (1995) *European Community: The Building of a Union*, 2nd edn, Oxford: Oxford University Press.

Polanyi, K. (1944) *The Great Transformation*, Boston: Beacon Press.

Putnam, R.R. Leonardi and Nanetti, R. (1993) *Making Democracy Work: Civic Traditions in Modern Italy*, Princeton, NJ: Princeton University Press.

Requejo, F. (2005) *Multinational Federalism and Value Pluralism: The Spanish Case*, London: Routledge.

Rhodes, R.A.W. (1997) *Understanding Governance: Policy Networks, Governance, Reflexivity and Accountability*, Buckingham: Open University Press.

Rokkan, S. and Urwin, D. (eds) (1982) 'Introduction: Centres and Peripheries in Western Europe', *The Politics of Territorial Identity: Studies in European Regionalism*, London: Sage, pp. 1–17.

de Rougement, D. (1968) 'Vers une Fédération des Regions', *L'Europe en Formation* July: 210–223.

Spruyt, H. (1994) *The Sovereign State and its Competitors: An Analysis of Systems Change*, Princeton, NJ: Princeton University Press.

Taylor, C. (1989) *Sources of the Self: The Making of the Modern Identity*, Cambridge, MA: Harvard University Press.

Taylor, C. (1991) *The Ethics of Authenticity*, Cambridge, MA: Harvard University Press.

Watts, R. (1999) *Comparing Federal Systems*, Montreal: Ithaca. Published for the School of Policy Studies, Queen's University by McGill-Queen's University Press.

Wright, D. (1988) *Understanding Intergovernmental Relations: Public Policy and Participants' Perspectives in Local, State, and National Governments*, 3rd rev. edn, Pacific-Grove, CA: Brooks-Cole.

5 Liberal multiculturalism and human rights

Will Kymlicka

The past 40 years have witnessed dramatic changes around the world in the status and treatment of ethnocultural minorities. Older models of assimilationist and homogenizing nation-states have been increasingly challenged, and often displaced, with newer "multicultural" models of the state. This is reflected in the spread of a wide range of minority rights, such as land claims and self-government rights for indigenous peoples, language rights and regional autonomy for national minorities, and accommodation rights for immigrant groups. It is also reflected in the emergence of minority rights norms at the international level, including Declarations and Conventions on minority and indigenous rights at the United Nations, the Council of Europe, and the Organization of American States.[1]

These changes have been controversial, and remain vulnerable to backlash and retreat. A number of objections have been raised to multiculturalism and minority rights, but in this chapter I want to focus on one issue in particular – namely, the relationship between minority rights and human rights. Many critics worry that minority rights conflict with human rights, and that the spread of multiculturalism is threatening to erode the hard-fought successes of the human rights movement. According to Alain Finkielkraut, for example, the UN's embrace of multiculturalism has involved abandoning Enlightenment universalism for cultural relativism:

> The United Nations, founded to propagate the universalist ideals of Enlightened Europe, now speaks on behalf of every ethnic prejudice, believing that peoples, nations and cultures have rights which outweigh the rights of man. The "multicultural" lobby dismisses the liberal values of Europe as "racist", while championing the narrow chauvinism of every minority culture.[2]

Similarly, Pascal Bruckner has recently stated that

> In multiculturalism, every human group has a singularity and legitimacy that form the basis of its right to exist, conditioning its interaction with others. The criteria of just and unjust, criminal and barbarian, disappear before the absolute criterion of respect for difference.[3]

On this view, the moral logic of multiculturalism fundamentally contradicts that of universal human rights. The former grants each group an unconditional right to maintain its cultural traditions, even at the expense of individual human rights; the latter insists that cultural difference is only legitimate if it respects the inherent moral worth of individuals, as embodied in norms of universal human rights. Multiculturalism, in short, is the enemy of human rights.

Defenders of multiculturalism, however, often argue the opposite position – namely, that multiculturalism emerged out of, and is an extension of, the broader human rights revolution. To be sure, there are many examples around the world in which the language of multiculturalism and minority rights is used by local elites to perpetuate gender and caste inequalities, or to legitimize unjust cultural practices and traditions. However, this is said to be an abuse of the original meaning and goal of multiculturalism. On this view, multiculturalism properly understood is a natural and logical evolution of the norms of universal human rights, and operates within the constraints of those norms. As Tariq Modood puts it, "Multiculturalism is a child of liberal egalitarianism", and is therefore both guided and constrained by a foundational commitment to principles of individual freedom and equality.[4] Some unscrupulous leaders or thinkers may attempt to distort multiculturalism for their own illiberal purposes, but the sorts of minority rights that have actually been adopted within the Western democracies, and that are now increasingly enshrined in international norms, are rooted in the ethos of human rights and liberal-democratic values.

So we have two quite different accounts of the relationship between multiculturalism and human rights: some see the rise of multiculturalism as an abandonment of the principle of universal human rights, others see it as inspired by that principle. Much of the literature on multiculturalism for the past 15 years has centred on the clash between these two interpretations.

Which is the correct account? In this chapter, I will defend the second account, by tracing some of the most important connections between multiculturalism and human rights. Some of these connections are quite clear and explicit. This is particularly true at the level of international law. According to critics like Finkielkraut, the UN is now committed to the view that norms of multiculturalism "outweigh the rights of man". In fact, the UN's position is just the opposite. For example, UNESCO's 2001 Universal Declaration on Cultural Diversity states that "No one may invoke cultural diversity to infringe upon human rights guaranteed by international law, nor to limit their scope" (Article 4). Similarly, the UN's 1992 Declaration on the Rights of Persons Belonging to National or Ethnic, Religious and Linguistic Minorities states that any rights or duties recognized in the Declaration "shall not prejudice the enjoyment of all persons of universally recognized human rights and fundamental freedoms" (Article 8.2). The International Labour Organization's 1989 Convention on the rights of indigenous peoples says that the right of indigenous people to maintain their cultural practices should be respected "where these are not incompatible with fundamental rights defined by the national legal system and internationally recognized human rights" (Article 8.2). In all of these cases, the UN and its affiliated bodies endorse multiculturalism as a supplement to and expansion of universal human rights, not as an abandonment or abridgement of them.

The same is true of other international organizations. For example, the Council of Europe's 1995 Framework Convention for the Protection of National Minorities says that the Convention must be interpreted in a way that complies with the European Convention on Human Rights (Article 23). In fact, every international declaration and convention on these issues makes the same point – the rights of minorities and indigenous peoples are an inseparable part of a larger human rights framework, and operate within its limits.

At the level of formal international law, therefore, the situation is clear: minority rights are endorsed because and insofar as they extend human rights, and are rejected insofar as they abridge human rights. However, these formal international declarations are unlikely to satisfy the critics of multiculturalism. They will argue that international organizations like the UN are simply hiding the underlying tensions between minority rights and universal human rights, pretending that the two are complementary when in fact they systematically conflict. According to critics, multiculturalism and universal human rights rest on contradictory premises, and so cannot be coherently combined. For example, the former is said to be relativist whereas the latter is universalist; or the former is said to privilege the group whereas the latter privileges the individual. As such, they are inherently at odds, no matter how much the UN pretends otherwise in its official rhetoric.

In order to resolve this debate, therefore, we need to go below the level of rhetorical pronouncements, and look at the way multiculturalism actually works: ie. what sorts of claims are being made by minority groups; how they are framed, defended and debated; how they are legally codified and judicially enforced; how they impact on the rights and resources of different people inside and outside the group; and so on. This is obviously a complicated task, given the immense variety of multiculturalist claims and experiences around the world. In the rest of this chapter, I will offer a preliminary and incomplete attempt to map the many ways in which multiculturalism is tied to broader ideas of human rights. I will discuss these inter-connections along two dimensions. First, I will examine how human rights ideals have served as an inspiration for claims for multiculturalism, through the delegitimation of traditional ethnic and racial hierarchies. Second, I will explore how human rights ideals have constrained claims for multiculturalism, influencing how these claims are framed, channelling and filtering them to accord with the underlying values of international human rights norms. These twin processes of inspiration and constraint are crucial to understanding the sort of multiculturalism that has emerged in the Western democracies, and is now increasingly diffused around the world.

1 The human rights revolution as inspiration

In my view, the trend towards multiculturalism can only be understood as a new stage in the gradual working out of the logic of human rights, and in particular the logic of the idea of the inherent equality of human beings, both as individuals and as peoples.

With the adoption of the Universal Declaration of Human Rights (UDHR) in 1948, the international order decisively repudiated older ideas of a racial or ethnic hierarchy, according to which some peoples were superior to others, and thereby had the right to rule over them. It is important to remember how contested this idea of human equality was. In 1919, when Japan proposed that a clause on racial equality be included in the covenant of the League of Nations, this was soundly rejected by the United States, Canada and other Western powers. Assumptions about a hierarchy of peoples were in fact widely accepted throughout the West up until the Second World War, when Hitler's fanatical and murderous policies discredited them. The whole system of colonialism was premised on the assumption of a hierarchy of peoples, and this assumption was the explicit basis of both domestic policies and international law throughout the nineteenth century and the first half of the twentieth century (including the racially exclusionary immigration laws found in all the New World settler states). In short, prior to the Second World War, "racism around the world was largely socially accepted, politically buttressed, economically supported, intellectually justified, and legally tolerated".[5]

Since 1948, however, we have been living in a world where the idea of human equality is unquestioned, at least officially, and this has generated a series of political movements designed to contest the lingering presence or enduring effects of older ethnic and racial hierarchies. (It has also inspired movements to contest other types of hierarchies, such as gender, disability and sexual orientation.)

In relation to ethnic and racial hierarchies, we can identify a sequence of such movements. The first was decolonization, from roughly 1948 to 1966. Some Western countries that signed the UDHR did not believe that endorsing the principle of the equality of peoples would require them to give up their colonies (e.g. France, Spain, Portugal). But this position was unsustainable, and the link between equality and decolonization was made explicit in the UN's 1960 General Assembly Resolution 1514 on decolonization.

A second stage was racial desegregation, from roughly 1955 to 1965, initiated by the African American civil rights struggles, and partially inspired by decolonization struggles.[6] When the United States signed the UDHR in 1948, it did not believe that this would require abandoning its segregationist laws. But this position too became unsustainable, and the link between equality and racial discrimination was made explicit in the UN's 1965 Convention on the Elimination of All Forms of Racial Discrimination.

The African American civil rights struggle subsequently inspired historically subordinated ethnocultural groups around the world to engage in their own struggles against the lingering presence of ethnic and racial hierarchies. We can see this in the way indigenous peoples adopted the rhetoric of "Red Power", or in the way national minorities (such as the Québécois or Catholics in Northern Ireland) called themselves "white niggers", or in the way Caribbean immigrants to the UK adopted the rhetoric and legal strategies of American blacks. All of these movements were profoundly influenced by American ideas of civil rights liberalism, and its commitment to defend equality for disadvantaged and stigmatized minorities through the enforcement of minority rights.

However, as civil rights liberalism spread, it also had to adapt to the actual challenges facing different types of minorities around the world. For American theorists, ideas such as "civil rights" and "equality" have been interpreted through the lens of anti-discrimination in general, and racial desegregation in particular. For most American theorists, the sorts of rights that civil rights liberalism must defend are therefore rights to undifferentiated citizenship within a "civic nation" that transcend ethnic, racial and religious differences.

In most countries, however, the situation of minorities needing protection differs from that of African Americans, and so too do the sorts of civil and political rights they require. African Americans were involuntarily segregated, solely on the basis of their race, excluded from common institutions and opportunities to which they often wanted access. Many minorities, however, are in the opposite position: they have been involuntarily assimilated, stripped of their own language, culture and self-governing institutions. They too have faced oppression at the hands of their co-citizens, and have had their civil rights denied to them, often with the enthusiastic backing of large majorities, on the grounds of their inferiority or backwardness. They too need counter-majoritarian protections. But the form these protections take is not solely anti-discrimination and undifferentiated citizenship, but rather various group-differentiated minority rights. In the Canadian context, for example, these include bilingualism and provincial autonomy (for the Québécois), land claims and treaty rights (for aboriginal peoples), and various sorts of multicultural accommodations (for immigrant/ethnic groups).

The struggle for these differentiated minority rights must be understood as a local adaptation of civil rights liberalism, and hence as a new stage in the unfolding of the human rights revolution. Just as decolonization inspired the struggle for racial desegregation, so racial desegregation inspired the struggle for minority rights and multiculturalism. This third stage is inspired by the civil rights liberalism of the second stage (as well as the decolonization struggles of the first stage), shares its commitment to contesting ethnic and racial hierarchies, and seeks to apply this commitment more effectively to the actual range of exclusions, stigmatizations and inequalities that exist in Western democracies. Few countries that signed the UDHR expected that endorsing the principle of the equality of peoples would require accepting norms of multiculturalism and minority rights. But that position too has become unsustainable, and the link between equality and multiculturalism has been made explicit in the UN's 1992 Declaration on the Rights of Persons Belonging to National or Ethnic, Religious and Linguistic Minorities.

In all three stages of this struggle against ethnic and racial hierarchy, what matters is not the change in international law per se, which has had little impact on most people's everyday lives. The real change has been in people's consciousness. Members of historically subordinated groups today demand equality, and demand it as a right. They believe they are entitled to equality, and entitled to it now, not in some indefinite or millenarian future.

This sort of rights-consciousness has become such a pervasive feature of modernity that we have trouble imagining that it did not always exist. But if we examine the historical records, we find that minorities in the past typically justified their claims, not by appeal to human rights or equality, but by appealing to the generosity of rulers in according "privileges", often in return for past loyalty and services. Today, by contrast, groups have a powerful sense of entitlement to equality as a basic human right, not as a favour or charity, and are angrily impatient with any lingering manifestations of older hierarchies.[7]

Of course, there is no consensus on what "equality" means (and, conversely, no agreement on what sorts of actions or practices are evidence of "hierarchy"). People who agree on the general principle of the equality of peoples may disagree about whether or when this requires official bilingualism, for example, or consociational power-sharing, or religious accommodations. But there can be no doubt that Western democracies historically privileged a particular national group over other groups who were subject to assimilation or exclusion. This historic hierarchy was reflected in a wide range of policies and institutions, from the schools and state symbols to policies regarding language, immigration, media, citizenship, the division of powers, and electoral systems. So long as leaders of non-dominant groups can identify (or conjure up) manifestations of these historic hierarchies, they will be able to draw upon the powerful rights-consciousness of their members.

2   The human rights revolution as constraint

The human rights revolution is important in another way. It constrains as well as inspires the pursuit of multiculturalism, and this constraining function helps to explain why states and dominant groups have become more willing to accept minority claims.

States are unlikely to accept strong forms of minority rights if they fear it will lead to islands of local tyranny within a broader democratic state. The likelihood that multiculturalist reforms will gain popular support depends heavily, therefore, on confidence that these reforms will not jeopardize human rights and liberal-democratic values. And here, the human rights revolution has served a dual function. If it has helped to inspire minorities to push for multiculturalism, it is equally true that the human rights revolution constrains the way in which minorities articulate and pursue their minority rights. In fact, the human rights revolution is a two-edged sword. It has created political space for ethnocultural groups to contest inherited hierarchies. But it also requires groups to advance their claims in a very specific language – namely, the language of human rights, civil rights liberalism, and democratic constitutionalism, with their guarantees of gender equality, religious freedom, racial non-discrimination, due process, and so on. The leaders of minorities can appeal to the ideals of liberal multiculturalism to challenge their historic exclusion and subordination, but those very ideals also impose the duty on them to be just, tolerant and inclusive.

Of course, the mere fact that minority groups articulate their claims in the language of human rights and liberal constitutionalism is not, by itself, sufficient to generate confidence that these values will be upheld. The use of this language may be merely strategic, adopted purely for public consumption. The traditional leaders of a minority group may wish to contest their subordinate status vis-à-vis the dominant group while still hoping to maintain their own dominance over women, religious minorities, migrants, lower caste groups, and so on.

So the question is whether these values will be respected in practice. And in the established Western democracies, there are often good grounds for confidence on this score. This confidence arises from two sources: the existence of robust legal mechanisms to protect human rights, and the existence of a consensus on liberal-democratic values that cuts across ethnic lines. Put simply, there is no legal space for minorities to set aside human rights norms in the name of multiculturalism, and, in the case of most minorities, there is no wish to do so.

From a legal point of view, policies of multiculturalism operate within the larger framework of liberal-democratic constitutionalism, and as such any powers devolved to autonomous minority institutions are typically subject to the same common standards of respect for human rights and civil liberties as any other public institution. For example, in virtually every case of territorial autonomy for national minorities in the West, such as Quebec or Catalonia, substate governments are subject to the same constitutional constraints as the central government, and so have no legal capacity to restrict individual freedoms in the name of maintaining cultural authenticity, religious orthodoxy or racial purity.[8] In many cases, they are also subject to regional and international human rights monitoring, and more generally are integrated into a dense web of rights-protecting mechanisms (including constitutional courts, human rights commissions, ombudsmen, etc.). People who live in the autonomous entities of Scotland, Catalonia or Quebec have access to some of the most advanced systems of human rights protection in the world.

Not only is it legally impossible for minorities in the West to establish islands of illiberal rule, but in many cases the evidence suggests that they have no wish to do so. In the case of national minorities, for example, all of the evidence suggests that their members are at least as strongly committed to liberal-democratic values as members of dominant groups, if not more so.[9] This removes one of the central fears that dominant groups have about minority self-government. In many parts of the world, there is the fear that once national minorities or indigenous peoples acquire self-governing power, they will use it to persecute, dispossess, expel or kill anyone who does not belong to the minority group. In the established Western democracies, however, this is a non-issue. There is no fear that self-governing groups will use their powers to establish islands of tyranny or theocracy. More specifically, there is no fear that members of the dominant group who happen to live on the territory of the self-governing minority will be subject to persecution or expulsion. The human rights of English residents of

Scotland are firmly protected, not only by Scottish constitutional law, but also by European law, and this would be true even if Scotland seceded from Britain. The human rights of English Canadian residents of Quebec, or of Castilian residents of Catalonia, are fully protected, no matter what political status Quebec or Catalonia ends up having.

Of course, there are illiberal strands within minority nationalist movements – consider the racist and anti-immigrant wings of Basque and Flemish nationalism – as there are within historically dominant groups. And the level of support for liberal-democratic values within some immigrant and indigenous groups is even more contested. There is always the risk that institutions and programmes established in the name of liberal multiculturalism will be captured by such illiberal elements. I will return to this risk below. But the adoption of liberal multiculturalism rests on what Nancy Rosenblum calls the "liberal expectancy"[10] – i.e. the hope and expectation that liberal-democratic values will grow over time and take firm root across ethnic, racial and religious lines, within both majority and minority groups, and that in the meantime there are robust mechanisms in place to ensure that multicultural policies and institutions cannot be captured and misused for illiberal purposes.

This liberal expectancy rests, in part, on the assumption that the public structures and principles of a liberal democracy exert a kind of "gravitational pull" on the beliefs and practices of ethnic and religious groups.[11] As Rosenblum notes, this metaphor of gravitational pull – an all-pervasive but invisible force – obscures rather than reveals the actual mechanisms at work, and indeed many discussions of the liberal expectancy have a somewhat mysterious air to them. However, there is considerable evidence that such a process has indeed operated historically. When Catholics and Jews first started arriving in the United States in the nineteenth century, for example, it was widely believed that their conservative and patriarchal beliefs and authoritarian practices precluded them from truly embracing liberal democracy. And yet most religious groups in America have become liberalized, gradually incorporating norms of individual freedom, tolerance and sexual equality into their own self-understandings. Similarly, there were doubts about whether earlier waves of immigrants to the US and Canada from southern or eastern Europe, where liberal democracy had never taken root, could truly internalize liberal-democratic values. Yet today these groups are often seen as some of the most loyal defenders of constitutional principles. And some substate nationalist groups that had earlier flirted with authoritarian ideologies, such as Quebec between the two world wars, have undergone dramatic liberalization. Recent studies suggest that support for liberal-democratic principles is also increasingly pervasive in self-governing indigenous communities.[12]

These earlier experiences of the liberal expectancy in action have helped generate confidence that multiculturalism can be safely contained within the boundaries of liberal-democratic constitutionalism and human rights norms. In a society permeated by a strong belief in this liberal expectancy, citizens feel confident that however issues of multiculturalism are settled, their own basic civil and political rights will be respected. No matter how the claims of ethnocultural groups are resolved – no matter what language rights, self-government rights, land rights, or multiculturalism policies are adopted – people can rest assured that they will not be stripped of their citizenship, or subject to ethnic cleansing, or jailed without a fair trial, or denied their rights to free speech, association and worship. Put simply, the consensus on liberal-democratic values ensures that debates over accommodating diversity are not a matter of life and death. As a result, dominant groups will not fight to the death to resist minority claims.

3 Multiculturalism and citizenization

This dual role of human rights – both as inspiration and constraint – has been pivotal in enabling the adoption and acceptance of liberal multiculturalism. It legitimizes the claims of historically disadvantaged minorities, yet reassures members of the dominant group that no matter how debates over minority rights are resolved, basic human rights will be protected.

In this way, liberal multiculturalism in the West can be understood as a process of "citizenization", in sociological jargon. Historically, ethnocultural and religious diversity has been characterized by a range of illiberal and undemo-cratic relations – including relations of conqueror and conquered; colonizer and colonized; settler and indigenous; racialized and unmarked; normalized and deviant; orthodox and heretic; civilized and backward; ally and enemy; master and slave. The task for all liberal democracies has been to turn this catalogue of uncivil relations into relationships of liberal-democratic citizenship, both in terms of the vertical relationship between the members of minorities and the state, and the horizontal relationships amongst the members of different groups.

In the past, it used to be assumed that the only or best way to engage in this process of citizenization was to impose a single undifferentiated model of cit-izenship on all individuals. But liberal multiculturalism starts from the assump-tion that this complex history inevitably and appropriately generates group-differentiated ethnopolitical claims. The key to citizenization is not to suppress these differential claims, but rather to filter and frame them through the language of human rights, civil liberties and democratic accountability.[13] And this is precisely what liberal multiculturalism, understood as a third stage in the human rights struggle against ethnic and racial hierarchy, seeks to do.

In my view, the acceptance of liberal multiculturalism in the West, and its attractiveness as a model to be diffused globally, is centrally tied to this process of citizenization. The idea that multiculturalism can serve as an effective vehicle for creating and consolidating relations of liberal-democratic citizenship in multieth-nic states is contested. Indeed, most commentators writing in the 1950s and 1960s would have rejected this idea, fearing that it would simply reproduce relations of enmity or hierarchy. But we now have close to 40 years of experience in the West with various models of liberal multiculturalism, and as I discuss elsewhere, there is growing evidence that these models can indeed serve this function.[14]

Multiculturalism is not the only example of this process of citizenization. On the contrary, the rise and spread of liberal multiculturalism in the West has to be situated within the much broader processes of liberalization and democratization that occurred across virtually the entire range of social policy starting in the 1960s – e.g. liberalizing reproductive rights (abortion laws, contraception), liberalizing divorce laws, abolishing the death penalty, prohibiting gender and religious discrimination, decriminalizing homosexuality, amongst many other such reforms. All of these were intended to replace earlier uncivil relations of dominance and intolerance with newer relations of democratic citizenship. And these legal and policy reforms, in turn, reflected wider processes of liberalization in civil society and public opinion, with the dramatic displacement of conservative, patriarchal, and deferential attitudes with more liberal, egalitarian and autonomous values. The rise of multiculturalism is one dimension of this broad-ranging struggle to liberalize society and to implement the ideals of the human rights revolution and of civil rights liberalism.

4 Multiculturalism and liberalization

The account I have given so far should not be surprising. I have essentially just said that liberal democracies in the West have adopted a liberal-democratic conception of multiculturalism. Surely that is what one would expect, barring clear evidence to the contrary. And yet it is remarkable how few commentators are willing to contemplate the possibility that multiculturalism is a liberal-democratic phenomenon, and how much intellectual energy has been expended in finding or inventing any number of alternative accounts of the intellectual foundations and moral impulses behind it.

As I noted earlier, some commentators have argued that the very idea of multiculturalism is at odds with the logic of liberal democracy, and that the shift towards recognizing group-differentiated rights represents a reaction against human rights. On this view, the first two stages in the post-war struggle against ethnic and racial hierarchy – decolonization and racial desegregation – were inspired by Enlightenment liberalism, but the third stage represents a deviation from, and reaction against, civil rights liberalism.

Commentators disagree about the precise nature of this deviation. Indeed, the academic literature is full of various fanciful theories about where and how multiculturalism departed from the liberal tradition. Some say that multiculturalism is based on a cultural relativist reaction against liberalism, rooted in nineteenth-century German romanticism. According to Finkielkraut, for example, the first two stages were "conceived under the implicit patronage of Diderot, Condorcet or Voltaire", whereas the third stage is driven by the chauvinistic and relativistic thinking of Herder and Spengler.[15] Others argue that multiculturalism is based on a postmodernist and deconstructionist rejection of liberalism, rooted in Nietzschean scepticism. According to Richard Caputo, for example, "proponents of multiculturalism tend to accept and build upon the Nietzschean rejection of rationalism with its notion of universal truth and justice".[16]

While these interpretations are familiar ones in the academic literature, I simply do not believe there is any credible evidence for them, at least within the

Western democracies. I have read literally hundreds of position papers and policy documents produced by the various participants in the policy networks on multiculturalism – governments, professional advocacy groups, philanthropic organizations – as well as the resulting laws and court cases, and I have yet to find a single discussion that expresses any sympathy for either Spengler or Nietzsche, either implicitly or explicitly.

Within the public debate, we can find yet another, more simple, explanation for how multiculturalism has diverged from liberal-democratic values. Multiculturalism, it is said, is about "culture", and culture (at least in the context of ethnic groups) is fundamentally about ancestral "traditions", so that "accommodating cultural diversity" is essentially a matter of preserving "traditional ways of life". This basic idea can be elaborated in various ways. One familiar form argues that while some degree of cultural change is inevitable, there are certain practices that are vital to the "authenticity" or "integrity" of a culture, and which must therefore be protected from change. These "authentic" practices are said to be essential to the identity of the group, and hence to the identity of its individual members. This link between culture and identity is thought to be particularly strong if the cultural practice is "traditional" – that is, deeply rooted in a people's history, and not just the result of recent adaptations or outside influences. On this view, cultural rights and policies of cultural inclusion are presented as primarily or exclusively intended to protect such "authentic" cultural practices from pressures to change.

On this view, multicultural claims are interpreted through a set of ideas relating to cultural authenticity and group identity. "Culture" is typically interpreted in terms of (or reduced to) a set of discrete practices, preferably "traditional" and "authentic" practices. These practices are then said to be essential to the group's identity, and hence to the identity of individual members, and so must be accommodated and protected by multiculturalism policies.

This is a version of what Amartya Sen calls the "communitarian" or "conservative" approach to multiculturalism, or what we might simply call a "traditionalist" approach.[17] It should immediately be clear, I hope, that this account is not only different from, but flatly in contradiction to, the liberal account I have developed. The liberal view of multiculturalism is inevitably, intentionally and unapologetically transformational of people's cultural traditions. It demands both dominant and historically subordinated groups to engage in new practices, to enter new relationships, and to embrace new concepts and discourses, all of which profoundly transform people's identities and practices.

This is perhaps most obvious in the case of the historically dominant majority nation in each country, which is required to renounce fantasies of racial superiority, to relinquish claims to exclusive ownership of the state, and to abandon attempts to fashion public institutions solely in its own national (typically white/ Christian) image. In fact, much of multiculturalism's "long march through the institutions" consists precisely in identifying and attacking those deeply rooted traditions, customs and symbols that have historically excluded or stigmatized minorities. Much has been written about the transformations in majority identities and practices this has required, and the backlash it can create.[18]

But liberal multiculturalism is equally transformative of the identities and practices of minority groups. Many of these groups have their own histories of ethnic and racial prejudice, of anti-Semitism, of caste and gender exclusion, of religious triumphalism, and of political authoritarianism, all of which are delegitimized by the norms of liberal-democratic multiculturalism. Moreover, even where the traditional practices of a minority group are free of these illiberal or undemocratic elements, some of these practices may have emerged as a response to the experience of discrimination, stigmatization or exclusion at the hands of others, and may lose their attractiveness as that motivating experience fades in people's memory. Some minority groups developed distinctive norms of self-help, endogamy, and internal conflict resolution because they were excluded from, or discriminated within, the institutions of the larger society. Those norms may lose their rationale as ethnic and racial hierarchies break down, and as group members feel more comfortable interacting with members of other groups and participating in state institutions. Far from guaranteeing the protection of the traditional ways of life of either the majority or minorities, liberal multiculturalism poses multiple challenges to them.

So the traditionalist conception of multiculturalism stands in sharp contrast to the liberal conception, with different goals and rationales. Indeed, from a liberal perspective, the traditionalist approach to multiculturalism is deeply implausible and unattractive, for several reasons:

- The traditionalist conception assumes that the cultural practices for which state recognition is being sought are "timeless" or "authentic". In reality, however, studies repeatedly show that so-called traditional practices are fairly recent, often themselves the product of earlier cultural interchanges, and sometimes even "invented" by elites to legitimize their position. So ideas of "cultural authenticity" or "cultural purity" are often anthropologically naive. They are also politically dangerous. They imply that there is something abnormal and regrettable about cultural evolution and cross-cultural influence, when in fact such changes and influences are normal, inevitable, and essential to the process of human development. It is cultural hybridity, not cultural purity, which is the normal state of human affairs, and fantasies of cultural purity can only be maintained by artificially cutting off groups from interaction with the larger world, and by instilling xenophobic fear of others.[19]
- The traditionalist conception assumes that there is a neutral or objective way of determining which practices are "authentic" to a group. In reality, this is a matter of political contestation within the group itself. It is often conservative elites within the group who claim the authority to judge what is "authentic" and "traditional", and they do so precisely to suppress demands for change from reformers within the group. Practices that historically may have been variable, evolving, contested and optional are declared by conservative elites to be "sacred", a matter of religious or cultural "obligation", and essential to group membership. To interpret multiculturalism as protecting traditional or authentic practices has the effect of rewarding such conservative elites: it

gives power to those who can claim to be the guardians of ancient traditions, while implying that those people who wish to challenge these traditions are not "true" or "proper" members of the group.[20] In this sense, the conservative interpretation of multiculturalism is more accurately described, not as according people cultural rights, but as imposing cultural duties – i.e. the duty to maintain one's culture, whether one wants to do so or not – and hence as an abridgement not expansion of individual freedom.

- The traditionalist claim that there is a right to preserve one's cultural traditions has been interpreted by some – most famously, by the American Anthropology Association – to preclude the very idea of universal human rights. According to the AAA's statement to the United Nations in 1947, people's identities and personalities are realized through their cultures, and so everyone has the right to live by their own traditions, which means that the very idea of judging local cultures by universal standards of human rights is unsound.[21] More recently, anthropologists have backed away from this extreme relativist view, and have attempted to reconcile support for a right to cultural preservation with support for universal human rights.[22] Anthropologists today are more likely to accept the possibility that some cultural traditions are oppressive, and that universal human rights can help to prevent this oppression. So we now find anthropologists talking about "balancing" human rights and the right to cultural preservation. But this still is a dangerous position if it implies that human rights protection should be sacrificed or compromised (albeit "not too much") in order to accommodate practices that violate those standards.

- The traditionalist claim that respecting a cultural tradition is essential to respecting a person's identity can be invoked as a "trump" to avoid democratic debate. To say that a particular cultural practice is part of my "identity" is sometimes a way of inviting others to consider and debate its value and significance. But in other contexts, this claim is invoked as a way of foreclosing that debate, by implying that any questioning of that practice will be interpreted as a sign of disrespect for me as a person. Where identity claims are presented in this way as non-negotiable "trumps", the result is to erode the potential for democratic dialogue. In multiethnic states where there are diverse and sometimes competing cultural traditions, we need to find a way to talk civilly about our practices, to discuss their benefits and costs, and to think about fair and honourable compromises where these practices conflict.[23]

In short, interpreting multiculturalism as a right to preserve authentic cultural traditions raises several potential dangers: it may inhibit constructive relations between cultures (by privileging cultural purity over cultural hybridity); it may erode the freedom of individuals within groups (by privileging authoritarian or conservative elites over internal reformers); it can be invoked to deny the existence of universal human rights; and it may threaten the space for civil debate and democratic negotiation over cultural conflicts.

Given the profound differences between the liberal and traditionalist interpretations of multiculturalism, it is obviously crucial to determine which of these in fact underpins the recent shifts towards multiculturalism within the West, and within international law. One can find echoes of both views in the public debate, but which of them provides the framework for contemporary multiculturalism policies and international legal norms?

Critics of multiculturalism typically assume that it is the conservative interpretation that underpins the trend towards multiculturalism. I believe, however, that this assumption is implausible, and indeed demonstrably false. For one thing, these critics have not provided any plausible account of how conservative multiculturalism could have become the official public policy of Western democracies, particularly in a 40-year era of wide-ranging liberalization and human rights reforms.[24] How could a "winning coalition" be built in support of conservative multiculturalism in Western democracies? How could it gain the support of the major political parties, or of a majority of members of the national legislature? It is difficult to make political sense of this scenario, and indeed most critics who discuss the adoption of multiculturalism treat it as a mystery, as if gremlins snuck into national parliaments and drafted multicultural policies while no one was watching.[25]

If we look at the actual process by which multiculturalism policies were adopted, a different picture emerges. In reality, virtually everyone involved in adopting multicultural reforms in the West – from the political activists and civil society organizations that initially mobilized for these reforms, to the segment of the public that supported them, to the legislators who adopted them, to the bureaucrats who drafted and implemented them, to the judges who interpreted them – were inspired by the ideals of human rights and civil rights liberalism. These actors viewed multicultural reforms as part of a larger process of social and political liberalization, and embedded these reforms legally and institutionally within a liberal rights framework.

To be sure, the fact that the contemporary wave of multicultural reforms originated in the human rights revolution does not yet tell us anything about its actual effects, including any unintended effects. Once multicultural policy structures are in place, illiberal conservative or authoritarian elites within various communities have often attempted to gain control over them, or at least to influence their implementation and direction. This is a universal phenomenon: once new powers or resources are made available, competition will inevitably arise for control over them. For example, once multiculturalism funds are made available, and multiculturalism advisory councils established, conservative elites within immigrant groups seek access to them. Once institutions of self-government are established for indigenous peoples or substate nationalist groups, conservatives seek to use these new powers to protect their traditional authority. This sort of political contestation is inevitable. Indeed, it would violate every known law of political science if it did not happen. It is even possible that multicultural policies have sometimes, unintentionally, served to strengthen the hand of conservative elites against the forces of liberal reform within various communities.

So one important question we need to ask is to what extent conservative/ authoritarian elites have been successful in capturing these policies, and what safeguards are in place to ensure that the original emancipatory goals and ideals are not subverted. I will return to this question below. But my focus here is on the original goals of multiculturalism policies – the normative principles and political coalitions that underpinned their adoption. And here I would insist that the actors involved in adopting multiculturalism in the Western democracies viewed themselves as expressing and extending the human rights revolution, not reacting against it.

This is obviously a sweeping generalization, and it would ultimately need to be tested on a case-by-case basis for all of the different types of multiculturalism policies adopted for different groups in different countries. But as a first step, let me focus on the Canadian case, where the connection between liberalization and multiculturalism is particularly clear.

Consider the bases of political support for multiculturalism in Canada. If multiculturalism reflected a reaction against liberalization, we would expect to see two competing political camps: a liberal camp in favour of liberalizing reforms on issues of gender equality, abortion, divorce, and gay rights, so as to emancipate individuals; and then a conservative camp in favour of immigrant multiculturalism, aboriginal rights and Quebec autonomy so as to protect these communities from liberalizing reforms. In reality, the situation in Canada is just the opposite.

On the one hand, we have patriarchal cultural conservatives who believe that society is changing too fast, and who believe that more weight should be given to traditional authorities and practices. This is the group Michael Adams has characterized as the "father knows best" crowd, which he estimates at around 35 per cent of the Canadian population.[26] Predictably, they strongly oppose liberalizing reforms about women's equality and gay rights. But they equally oppose immigrant multiculturalism, aboriginal rights and accommodating Quebec. Indeed, the emergence of these diversity policies is precisely one of the changes that they find most distressing. There has not been (and is not now) any significant level of public support for any of these forms of multiculturalism amongst cultural conservatives.

Of course, having lost the battle to block these policies, patriarchal conservatives have not simply disappeared. They are regrouping in order to see how they can now exploit the opportunities created by these policies. For example, conservative Protestants in Canada, who initially fought tooth and nail to block multiculturalism in the public schools since it would strip Christianity of its privileged position, are now regrouping to see whether they can invoke multiculturalism to regain some lost privileges.[27] But this post-facto strategic manipulation of multiculturalism must be distinguished from support for the policy's adoption, which patriarchal conservatives strongly opposed.

On the other hand, we have the liberal wing of the Canadian populace, which has become increasingly egalitarian, anti-authoritarian, and individualistic. Predictably, they strongly support gender equality and gay rights, but they equally endorse multiculturalism policies, and view both sets of reforms as expressions of a single logic of civil rights liberalism.

So both camps have operated on the assumption that multiculturalism is an integral part and parcel of a larger process of liberalization – although of course they differ on how to evaluate this larger process – and changes in support for multiculturalism policies over time track changes in support for liberal egalitarian values more generally.

The link between liberalization and multiculturalism policies can be confirmed by examining the way these policies have been legally drafted and judicially enforced. One of the most striking things about these policies is how tightly and explicitly they are connected to broader norms of human rights and liberal constitutionalism, both conceptually and institutionally.

Consider the preamble to Canada's Multiculturalism Act of 1988. It begins by saying that because the government of Canada is committed to civil liberties, particularly the freedom of individuals "to make the life that the individual is able and wishes to have", and because it is committed to equality, particularly racial equality and gender equality, and because of its international human rights obligations, particularly the international convention against racial discrimination, therefore it is adopting a policy of multiculturalism. It goes on, in the main text, to reiterate human rights norms as part of the substance of the multiculturalism policy.[28] You could hardly ask for a clearer statement that multiculturalism is to be understood as an integral part of the human rights revolution, and an extension of, not brake on, civil rights liberalism. There is not a whiff of cultural conservatism, patriarchalism, or postmodernist deconstructionism in this statement. It is the very milk of Enlightenment liberalism and universal human rights.

In fact, this point had already been made explicit in the original 1971 parliamentary statement on multiculturalism in Canada, which stated that "a policy of multiculturalism within a bilingual framework is basically the conscious support of individual freedom of choice. We are free to be ourselves".[29]

These formulations are obviously intended as an instruction to the relevant political actors, from minority activists to bureaucrats to judges, that multiculturalism must be understood as a policy inspired by liberal-democratic norms. Nor was this left to chance, or to the good will of political actors. The Multiculturalism Act is located squarely within the larger institutional framework of liberal-democratic constitutionalism, and hence is legally subject to the same constitutional constraints as any other federal policy. Any federal action done in the name of multiculturalism must respect the requirements of the Canadian Charter of Rights and Freedoms, as interpreted and enforced by judicial bodies such as the Canadian Human Rights Commission and the Supreme Court.

So the way in which multiculturalism in Canada has been legally defined makes clear that it does not exist outside the framework of liberal-democratic constitutionalism and human rights jurisprudence, or as an exception to it, or deviation from it. Rather, it is firmly embedded within that framework. It is defined as flowing from human rights norms, as embodying those norms, and as enforceable through judicial institutions whose mandate is to uphold those norms.

Of course, this is just one example from one country, and there may be aspects of the Canadian approach that are not found in other Western democracies. Even so, it is an important case to consider, since Canada was the first country to adopt an official "multiculturalism" policy, and as a result has played an important role in shaping international conceptions of what multiculturalism is. As Yasmeen Abu-Laban notes, Canada is widely seen around the world as a country where multiculturalism "exists" – where multiculturalism is a well-established practice, not just a rhetoric – and Canadian formulations are often studied as prototypes.[30] For example, the way multiculturalism is linked to human rights in the preamble to the Canadian Multiculturalism Act is essentially duplicated in the UN's 1992 Declaration on the Rights of Minorities – both insist that the rights of minorities are founded on human rights norms, and so should be interpreted as further extending and implementing these norms.

In any event, Canada is far from unique in the way it ties multiculturalism to liberalism. We see a similar linkage in Australia, for example. According to James Jupp – who played a pivotal role in defining Australia's multiculturalism policy – multiculturalism in Australia: "is essentially a liberal ideology which operates within liberal institutions with the universal approval of liberal attitudes. It accepts that all humans should be treated as equals and that different cultures can co-exist if they accept liberal values".[31]

As in Canada, multiculturalism was introduced in Australia by the same left-liberal or social-democratic political forces that were pushing for liberalization more generally, such as strengthened gender equality, non-discrimination and gay rights.

The same basic pattern can be found in other Western democracies that have moved in the direction of a more multicultural approach. As a general rule, multiculturalism has been adopted by social-democratic or left-liberal parties and coalitions that endorse liberalization more generally, and the resulting policies have been drafted in such a way that makes explicit their foundation in human rights norms. And, as we have seen, it is this same distinctly liberal model of multiculturalism that has been enshrined in international law.

To be sure, public confidence in this "liberal expectancy" varies across time and across societies, and there have been times and places where people have become sceptical that multiculturalism can securely be rooted in liberal-democratic constitutionalism and human rights norms. Indeed, this scepticism helps to explain some of the strong opposition to multiculturalism that has arisen recently, and some of the cases of a "retreat from multiculturalism", particularly in the context of Muslim immigrants to Europe. Many Europeans have come to believe both that Muslims may resist the "gravitational pull" towards liberal-democratic values, and that existing human rights safeguards are insufficient to prevent multiculturalism being abused by Muslim leaders to perpetuate illiberal practices. And indeed there have been several high-profile cases in Europe where the government seemed unable or unwilling to protect girls or women within Muslim immigrant communities from abuse. As a result, support for multiculturalism has dropped in many of the countries of Europe where Muslims are seen

as the main claimants of multiculturalism. Periodic stories about illiberal practices in indigenous communities – including various forms of gender discrimination and religious persecution – have also reduced public support for indigenous
rights to self-government in some countries.

These are important cases, but we should not lose sight of the fact that the
vast bulk of multicultural rights, whether claimed by immigrants, national
minorities or indigenous peoples, operate comfortably within the framework of
liberal-democratic constitutionalism. As I said earlier, we have close to 40 years
of experience with a wide range of minority rights in the Western democracies,
and it seems that the liberal expectancy is holding. Members of minority groups
are internalizing liberal-democratic values, and in those rare cases where minority leaders have attempted to invoke the ideals or institutions of multiculturalism
for illiberal purposes, these attempts have been blocked by the normal safeguards of democratic accountability, the rule of law, and human rights guarantees. To date at least, fears of the illiberal capture of multiculturalism seem
overstated, at least within the consolidated Western democracies.[32]

In any event, these cases confirm the key point: namely, that wherever multiculturalism has been adopted within the West, or endorsed by the international
community, it is a distinctly liberal-democratic model of multiculturalism, supported because and insofar as it is seen as consistent with, and indeed enhancing
of, liberal democratic values and human rights ideals. Where that link is not perceived, either in relation to multiculturalism generally or in relation to the claims
of a particular minority group, public support for multiculturalism drops.

In short, we see varying levels of public belief in liberal multiculturalism
across the West. What we do not see, however, is any other type of non-liberal
multiculturalism, whether rooted in Herderian cultural conservatism or
Nietzschean postmodernism. There are Herderian and Nietzschean multicultural-
ists in academia, but this is not the sort of multiculturalism that has shaped
public policy in the West, or shaped international norms at the UN.

If this analysis is correct, it suggests that multiculturalism should not be seen
as a fad or fashion that will soon disappear. On the contrary, it is rooted in some
of the deepest values and principles of the post-war Western world, and is likely
to endure as long as ideals of human rights and the equality of peoples remain at
the foundation of the international order. In this sense, the suggestion by Finkielkraut and others that we should replace multiculturalism with a renewed
emphasis on universal human rights is deeply misleading. It is precisely the
emergence and diffusion of a human rights culture that has made possible the
rise of multiculturalism, and the more the former takes root, the more it will
inspire and shape the latter.

Notes

1 For an overview of the spread of such policies, domestically and internationally, see
   my *Multicultural Odysseys*, Oxford: Oxford University Press, 2007.
2 Alain Finkielkraut, *The Undoing of Thought*, London: Claridge Press, 1988.

3 Pascal Bruckner, "Enlightenment Fundamentalism or Racism of the Anti-Racists?", January 2007. Available at www.signandsight.com/features/1146.html.

4 Tariq Modood, *Multiculturalism*, Cambridge: Polity Press, 2007, p. 8.

5 Paul Gordon Lauren, *Power and Prejudice: The Politics and Diplomacy of Racial Discrimination* 2/e, Boulder, CO: Westview, 1996, p. 144.

6 On the link between decolonization struggles and the African American civil rights struggles, see Penny Von Eschen, *Race Against Empire: Black Americans and Anti-Colonialism 1937–57*, Stanford, CA: Stanford University Press, 1997.

7 For a discussion of this shift in the Latin American context, see Anke Schwittay, "From Peasant Favors to Indigenous Rights: The Articulation of an Indigenous Identity and Land Struggle in Northwestern Argentina", *Journal of Latin American Anthropology* 8(3) (2003): 127–54. On the "rights revolution" more generally, see Michael Ignatieff, *The Rights Revolution*, Toronto: Anansi Press, 2000.

8 A partial exception concerns Indian tribal governments in the US, which have a limited exemption from some provisions of the US Bill of Rights, and this exemption has allowed some tribes to adopt policies that violate liberal norms. But it is worth emphasizing that, while many tribal governments defend this partial exemption from the US Bill of Rights, they typically do not object to the idea that their self-government decisions should be subject to international human rights norms and international monitoring. See, on this, my *Politics in the Vernacular*, Oxford: Oxford University Press, 2001, chap. 4.

9 For the evidence, see my *Multicultural Odysseys*, chap. 5.

10 Nancy Rosenblum, *Membership and Morals: The Personal Uses of Pluralism in America*, Princeton, NJ: Princeton University Press, 1998, pp. 55–61.

11 William Galston, *Liberal Purposes*, Cambridge: Cambridge University Press, 1991, p.292.

12 Tim Schouls, *Shifting Boundaries: Aboriginal Identity, Pluralist Theory, and the Politics of Self-Government*, Vancouver: UBC Press, 2003.

13 This distinguishes liberal multiculturalism from other forms of "multiculturalism" in history that were not tied to ideas and relationships of democratic citizenship – e.g. the Ottoman millet system, which accorded minorities a number of constitutional guarantees, but defined them in a position of constitutional inequality (e.g. excluded from visible high offices) and unfreedom (eg. not allowed to proselytize).

14 See my *Multicultural Odysseys*, chap. 5.

15 Finkielkraut, *Undoing of Thought*, pp. 54, 64.

16 Richard Caputo, "Multiculturalism and Social Justice in the United States", *Race, Gender and Class* 8(1) (2001): 164.

17 Sen in UNHDR, *Cultural Liberty in Today's Diverse World: Human Development Report 2004*, United Nations Development Programme, New York. The claim that multiculturalism is rooted in cultural conservatism rather than liberalism has a long-standing pedigree. Indeed, many of the earliest academic theorists of multiculturalism in the 1970s and 1980s simply took for granted that multiculturalism arose as a "communitarian" reaction against liberalisation, and as an attempt to contain its corrosive effects on traditional authorities and practices. On this view, multiculturalism was demanded by communitarian or conservative elites who worried that newly emancipated individuals would use their human rights and civil rights to question and reject traditional authority structures and cultural practices. Multiculturalism, in short, was intended to set communitarian brakes on liberalization. I discuss this "first wave" of communitarian theories of multiculturalism, and how it has been contested by more recent liberal theories of multiculturalism, in my *Politics in the Vernacular*, chap. 2.

18 For a discussion of 'white backlash' against multiculturalism, see Roger Hewitt, *White Backlash and the Politics of Multiculturalism*, Cambridge: Cambridge University Press, 2005.

19 See Jeremy Waldron, "Minority Cultures and the Cosmopolitan Alternative", in Will

Kymlicka (ed.) *The Rights of Minority Cultures*, Oxford: Oxford University Press, 1995: pp. 93–119. A related mistake is to view our identities as citizens of larger societies as somehow "inauthentic" and "artificial", as compared to the "true" identity tied up with membership in particular ethnic or religious groups. In reality, wider pan-ethnic civic identities are just as normal and natural – just as common in history – as more particularistic ethnic or religious identities.

20 See Bhikhu Parekh, *Rethinking Multiculturalism: Cultural Diversity and Political Theory*, Cambridge, MA: Harvard University Press, 2000.

21 See American Anthropological Association Executive Board, "Statement on Human Rights Submitted to the Commission on Human Rights, United Nations", *American Anthropologist*, New Series 49 (1947): 539–43.

22 For the evolving and tortured relationship between anthropologists and human rights, see Michael Freeman, "Anthropology and the Democratization of Human Rights", *International Journal of Human Rights* 6(3) (2002): 37–54; R.A. Wilson (ed.) *Human Rights, Culture and Context: Anthropological Perspectives*, London: Pluto Press, 1997.

23 For an eloquent statement of this concern, see Jeremy Waldron, "Cultural Identity and Civic Responsibility", in Will Kymlicka and Wayne Norman (eds) *Citizenship in Diverse Societies*, Oxford: Oxford University Press, 2000: 155–74.

24 For example, critics of Canada's Multiculturalism Act have suggested that its conservative logic of cultural preservation entails that female genital mutilation (FGM) should be permitted within those immigrant groups where it is a "traditional" practice (e.g. Neil Bissoondath, *Selling Illusions: The Cult of Multiculturalism in Canada*, Toronto: Penguin, 1994. But how can we reconcile this with the fact that, at the very same time Canada was adopting its Multiculturalism Act, it also became one of the first countries in the world to accept that a girl should be granted refugee status if she faces a risk of being subject to FGM if returned to her country of origin, even if FGM is "traditional" in that country of origin? It would be self-contradictory for a country like Canada to tolerate FGM within its own borders in the name of cultural preservation, while defining it as persecution overseas. Critics like Bissoondath assume that legislators have in fact embraced this self-contradiction, but they have given no plausible interpretation of how such a self-contradiction could have emerged.

25 For a clear example, see Brian Barry, *Culture and Equality: An Egalitarian Critique of Multiculturalism*, Cambridge: Polity Press, 2001, pp. 292–9.

26 Michael Adams, *Better Happy Than Rich?*, Toronto: Penguin, 2000.

27 Scott Davies, "From Moral Duty to Cultural Rights: A Case Study of Political Framing in Education", *Sociology of Education* 72 (1999): 1–21.

28 The Act is reprinted as an appendix in my *Finding Our Way: Rethinking Ethnocultural Relations in Canada*, Oxford: Oxford University Press, 1998.

29 Pierre Trudeau, "Statement to the House of Commons on Multiculturalism", House of Commons, *Official Report of Debates*, 28th Parliament, 3rd Session, 8 October 1971, pp. 8545–6.

30 Yasmeen Abu-Laban, "Liberalism, Multiculturalism and Essentialism", *Citizenship Studies* 6(4) (2002): 460.

31 James Jupp, "The New Multicultural Agenda", *Crossings* 1(1) (1996): 40.

32 The risk of illiberal capture is obviously much higher in countries that are not yet consolidated democracies. See *Multicultural Odysseys*, chaps 6–7.

6   On postnational identity

Michel Seymour

In this chapter, I would like to respond to some of the criticisms raised against national identity formulated by those who endorse a certain form of postnational identity and who base their critiques either on constitutional patriotism or anti-culturalism. Specifically, I will examine the thesis that we have entered a postnational era. The proponents of postnational identity hold that the contemporary model of political organization no longer requires any kind of national belonging or attachment. Jürgen Habermas and Jean-Marc Ferry, for example, have made such claims in various contexts. First, they assert that the nation-state is no longer, all by itself, adequately equipped to deal with the challenges that come with the globalization of trade.[1] I believe that one must agree with that assessment. They also look favourably on political entities that contain more than one national group. The political community may in the eighteenth and nineteenth centuries have been up to a certain point congruent with the national community, or at least this is how the members of these communities represented themselves, but it is no longer necessarily the case today. I also agree with that idea. However, Habermas and Ferry further argue that, in terms of identity, nationality is no longer an essential ingredient in a political community.[2] Habermas and Ferry recognize that the nation-state is here to stay and that we are not about to see it disappear. However, they argue that it is no longer a leading player on the international scene, and, most importantly, that the endorsement of a constitutional text by the population is what will henceforth increasingly be the cementing factor among citizens in the domestic arena.[3] At least, this is the direction that these authors see now being taken in Europe.[4] Even if European states are still very often understood as nation-states, it is no longer the nation that binds citizens to one another within the state: it is rather the constitution. This, they say, is the reason why the creation of political communities that no longer coincide with national borders can favourably be considered. Instead of acknowledging national identity and nationalism as inescapable political forces, they attempt to get beyond it by postulating identification with more inclusive features of a political community.

There is another argument that also challenges the idea of the nation-state, and more generally of nations as important sources of identity within the political community. It is also a view predicting the decline of national identity as the primary source of citizens' identity, but this time, the authors insist that citizens have fragmented, plural and changing identities. This view can be described as anti-culturalist, since it is simultaneously directed against both national identity and multiculturalism, and it is also a view favourable to narrativism and cosmopolitanism.[5] While the argument based on constitutional patriotism may be understood as a top-down argument, to the extent that it presumes a positive identification with an encompassing political organization that is capable of transcending, broadening and exceeding the national framework, the anti-culturalist argument is a bottom-up argument, that negatively acknowledges the internal crumbling of national identity.

I wish to argue that postnational identity is an illusion, and that we need instead to revisit our concept of the nation and its relationship to the concept of a common public identity. I submit that newly understood national identities could very well be determinant factors for democratic, viable and legitimate types of political organizations, including multination states and supranational organizations. I also want to argue for the existence of various sorts of nations, and this makes it possible to account for the internal national diversity of our societies, as well as identity pluralism and the dynamic nature of national identity, and I wish to do so without having to eliminate the notion of a common public national identity from our account. Nations are omnipresent, both as inclusive entities and as recognized components within these inclusive entities. Rather than seeking to go beyond nationality, we must recognize the diversity of its manifestations. While *the* nation may indeed be "disappearing", it is making way for nation*s*. Nationality is illegitimate only when it denies the various manifestations of nationalism. So it is problematic only when a unique kind of identity is imposed upon everyone without being sensitive to minority nations or other sorts of national minorities. In short, nationality is unacceptable when it denies recognition to minority nationalism. Finally, the legitimacy of common public national identities and minorities who are seeking recognition depends largely on the adoption of a principle of reciprocal recognition. There is no common public national identity without recognition, but there is no recognition without reciprocity.

1 Top-down disintegration of the nation-state?

There are at least three major characteristics associated with constitutional patriotism: (1) rejection of the nationalist principle (i.e. the principle according to which all nations should have their own state), (2) the claim that we can make sense of plurinational political entities, and (3) postnational identity. The essential thesis is the third of the three: postnational identity. The first two claims are not incompatible with recognizing the importance of national identity as a currently acting, ongoing and legitimate political force. Even if we abandon the nationalist principle, nations may be essential, in so far as the exercise of their right to internal self-determination may continue to be a major political issue. And even if we admit the possibility that the borders of the nation and the borders of the state no longer coincide, we may have to recognize the legitimacy of a secessionist movement for a specific people within a state, if the state refuses to recognize the people's right to internal self-determination. Therefore, the first two ideas of constitutional patriotism are compatible with the possibility of putting nationalism at the forefront of normatively important political debates. More is required to justify constitutional patriotism. It must be further argued that we have entered a postnational era.

Because nations very often contain national minorities, it is apparently impossible to preserve the unity of the entire political community by relying on the characteristic attributes of a single nation. That is the first important observation that can be made by the constitutional patriot. When societies deal with immigration, or when they are burdened with frontiers that have been imposed on them as a result of the arbitrary vicissitudes of history, or when we witness movements of entire populations, we simply cannot claim that the borders of a state are at the same time the borders of a single people. Based on these observations, adherents of constitutional patriotism commit an error, perhaps the most fatal one. They believe that we must then minimize the importance of the "national framework". The nation does not disappear, but according to them, citizens henceforth relate to a constitutional text as the source of their allegiance to the political community. I would like to challenge that conclusion. I want to show that the national framework remains an essential frame of reference, including when the state appears to be increasingly diversified. In order to show that the state is able to pass this diversity test, we must introduce the idea of common public identity. To put it succinctly, I believe that the concept of common public identity can be understood as national and be used to avoid two extreme models of political organization: constitutional patriotism, on the one hand, and the "society of identities", on the other.[6]

1.1 Nations as societal cultures

Despite the great diversity among nations, they have common traits. They are all "societal cultures", understood as structures of culture involved in crossroads of influences and offering contexts of choice.[7] The concept that makes it possible to see how a people can pass the diversity test while continuing, in some way, to promote a common public identity is the concept of a structure of culture, because it is the structure of culture that carries with it the common public national identity. In its simplest version, the structure of culture assumes a common public language, common public institutions and a common public history. The common public language is the language mainly spoken in public spaces within a particular territory, by people who have different mother tongues or use different languages at home. The common public institutions within that territory are those in which the common public language is the language primarily spoken. The common public history is the history of the common public institutions, that is, the history that is defined by a certain subject matter, and not a particular history in the sense of a specific narrative. If the common public history had to be a specific narrative, it would presume adherence to a single historical account, and this would amount to admitting a collective narrative identity. There is never, however, a definitive consensus concerning the line taken by history, and it is required that members of the nation be able to criticize the official interpretation without losing their national identity. The concept of a "common public history" must therefore be understood to mean only a commonly shared subject matter, the history of the common public institutions, that can be appropriated in different ways and in different narratives.

Here we have a first case of common public national identity, the one that characterizes the single nation-state, and we have at least four identity traits: a constitution, a common language, a common body of institutions and a common history. The common public identity therefore has sufficient thickness to call it national, at least when the population in question has, in addition, a certain degree of national consciousness, that is, a majority of the population represents itself as a country with a single constitution, a single language, a single body of public institutions and a single public history. National consciousness is as a matter of fact a fifth identity trait. I would eventually also add other important elements, such as the existence of a collective will to live together (Ernest Renan's daily plebiscite), a common crossroads of influences and a common context of choice, but we can already note that common public identity, as I characterize it here, is relatively thick and cannot be reduced to mere adherence to a constitutional text.

It is important to contrast this simple version of a common public identity and a richer version in which people are seen as sharing the same beliefs, values, traditions, customs, goals and ways of life. The difference is congruent with Will Kymlicka's distinction between the structure of culture and the character of culture. In referring to a collective identity, it is not necessary to postulate among the members an agreement or consensus concerning beliefs, values, traditions, customs, goals and ways of life. We may merely be referring to elements belonging to the institutional identity of the group: constitution, language, particular institutions, history of these institutions, national consciousness, collective will, crossroads of influences and context of choice. Sharing a language, institutions and a history of these institutions in a specific crossroads of influences and with a specific context of choice constitutes a fairly thick identity. It involves a certain particularism, even if it is not the rich particularism of a population sharing the same life world. In trying to justify postnationalism, it is fairly easy to criticize a concept of national identity that involves sharing the same character of culture. But it is much harder to do the same when the particularist features are those belonging to the structure of culture, like common public languages, institutions and histories.

Like John Rawls,[8] I endorse a political and not a metaphysical concept of the nation. We need to understand the nation by reference to its institutional identity. This does not mean that we restrict nations only to those groups who already have sovereign political governments. It is rather that we consider nations only as they present themselves in the political arena, without considering their metaphysical nature.[9] To cement the bonds among different individuals within a nation, it is not necessary to postulate that the individual precedes the community or that the community precedes the individual. It is not necessary to choose between the comprehensive definitions that identify the nation either with an association of individuals (ontological atomism), or with a collective organism (ontological holism). Nor do we have to decide between those who feel that persons are prior to their ends, or postulate, on the contrary, a single set of beliefs, values, purposes or projects defining the identity of its members. We do not have to choose between one side or the other in the liberal individualist and communitarian debate. The political definition of a people assumes that what cements the individuals into a single unit is their institutional identity. Just as, from the political standpoint, individuals are understood as citizens, peoples are understood as societal cultures, that is as having a certain institutional identity.

1.2 Seven sorts of nations

It should also be noted immediately that there may be several sorts of common public identities, some of which are more complex than others, even though the simple version that I have just introduced has already made it somewhat clearer. There are in fact various concepts of nation corresponding to various national consciousnesses. Individuals may think of themselves as belonging to ethnic, cultural, civic, sociopolitical, diasporic, multisocietal and multiterritorial nations. We think of ourselves as a member of a single ethnic nation when we represent ourselves as sharing the same ancestral origin (some aboriginal nations). We represent ourselves as a member of a single cultural nation when we think of ourselves as having different ancestral origins but see each other as sharing a single mother tongue, a single body of (non-political) institutions and a single history (the Metis nation in Canada). We represent ourselves as a member of a single civic nation when we share the same country and that country is thought of as a one-nation state (Japan). We represent ourselves as a member of a single sociopolitical nation when we belong to a political community that is not sovereign but that contains within itself the largest sample in the world of a group of people that shares the same language, the same institutions and the same history (Quebec, Catalonia, Scotland). We represent ourselves as members of a single diasporic nation when we belong to a group whose members have the same language, the same culture and the same history, but are spread out over various discontinuous territories and form a minority in each of these territories (the Jewish diasporic nation before the creation of Israel). We represent ourselves as members of a multisocietal nation when the sovereign state appears in the eyes of the majority to be composed of more than one national societal culture (Great Britain, Belgium). And we represent ourselves as part of a multiterritorial nation when the group occupies a continuous territory, but it is one that does not correspond to legally recognized borders. For example, the Kurdish people occupy a non-fragmented territory (Kurdistan) but that territory lies outside the official borders of existing states. Similar remarks apply to the Mohawk nation who happen to live in Quebec, Ontario and New York State in Akwesasne, Kanesa-take and Kahnawake. So there are at least seven distinct sorts of national consciousness that a population may entertain.

These seven sorts of nations form very different kinds of common public identities. For instance, civic and multisocietal nations are different sorts of sovereign countries. Diasporic and multiterritorial nations transcend the actual borders of existing countries. Finally, ethnic, cultural and sociopolitical nations are defined as component entities situated within the confines of sovereign countries. Sociopolitical nations, in particular, are nations that have political self-government but no sovereign state and are defined on the basis of the demarcation lines formally recognized within a sovereign state (cantons, provinces, *länder*, federated states). Of course, not all cantons, provinces, *länder* and federated states are nations, but if a critical mass of the population within a canton, a province, a *land* or a federated state entertains a national consciousness, then the nation is sociopolitical and it may in principle include minorities within its territory.

There is thus a wide variety of common public identities. Some coincide with single nation-states, others with nations without states, and others still with plurinational sovereign states. What, then, can we say about the concept of a common public identity? I wish to defend certain ideas about the different forms of national political organization. Whether it is a civic nation, a sociopolitical nation or a multisocietal nation, the common public identity involved cannot be reduced to the mere endorsement of a constitution. There must also be other important elements that cement the identity of the population, and these must relate to national identity.

1.3 Nations as common public identities

I have described above what is a relatively simple case of common public identity. It is one that we find at the heart of the structure of culture of a relatively simple sort of nation, such as the ethnic nation, the cultural nation, the civic nation (the single nation-state), and the uninational sociopolitical nation, for it presumes the existence of a common public language, a common public set of institutions and a common public history. To consider this question in greater depth, however, we must go farther than that. If we endorse conceptual pluralism with respect to the nation, we must deal with a number of different kinds of common public identities. For example, we have to talk about the common public national identity of the plurinational sociopolitical nation (a politically self-governing nation with no sovereign state containing national minorities), and of the multisocietal nation (a plurinational sovereign state). It will then be important, but also difficult, to identify a common national identity in these societies. When the country is a multination state and has within it several societal cultures, its members have many common public identities, so it is not clear how we could postulate at the same time another encompassing common public identity at the level of the entire state. That is the case in Belgium, Canada, Great

Britain or Spain. In those countries, it is dangerous to equate the nation with one of its component particular societal cultures. If there is a common public identity, it cannot easily be one associated with any particular group. In these societies, it looks as though there is not a common public language, a single body of common public institutions and a single common public history, but as we shall see, we could still conceive these sovereign states as "nations" as long as, among other things, we can describe them as aggregates of national societal cultures.

We have focused on a particular concept of the nation: the civic nation or one-nation state. Now it is fairly easy to describe the common public national identity of a sovereign one-nation state that would be *ethnically* homogeneous. The national identity would be the result of the ongoing presence of an historical community in the country that is reproduced from generation to generation and that is not transformed by contact with any other groups. This is a very easy case, but it is also the rarest case. When we think about what may be a common public identity, do we instead not think of *citizenship*? Now, common citizenship is conferred by a constitutional text or at least a constitutional arrangement, whether written or not. Is this not the real identity, and does it not provide ammunition for those endorsing constitutional patriotism? My own answer is no. As I said, the common public national identity is what provides "homogeneity", and not merely the constitutional text.

But how is it possible to maintain a degree of homogeneity in the contemporary single nation-state while also reflecting the sociological diversity of which it is made up? The common public identity shared by all citizens must on the one hand be a richer identity than the one that would arise out of a constitutional text that guarantees human rights and freedoms, among other things, and on the other hand, must also reflect that sociological diversity. How is this possible? A contemporary one-nation sovereign state is the home of diverse minorities. It often contains contiguous diasporas, that is, extensions of neighbouring nations (or of neighbouring national majorities), and non-contiguous diasporas, that is immigrant communities. It may also contain historical minorities that can no longer be described as immigrant communities but that still identify themselves with a foreign country. Is it possible, within these states, to claim a rich common public identity that would make it possible to preserve an important role for the concept of nation, even when the society appears to be increasingly diversified? As we just saw, the answer is yes. The answer lies precisely in the notion of a common public identity, which implies not only a common constitution, but also common public language, institutions and history.

The expression "common public identity" may seem to be pleonastic, but it really is not at all. It is compatible with minority public languages, institutions and histories that are not shared in common throughout the territory. The perfectly homogeneous one-nation state model is unquestionably a very endangered species. But this does not mean that we have embarked on a postnational era, because the notion of a common public identity in the civic nation still can be thick, and because it is compatible with the recognition of minority public languages, institutions and histories. The civic nation is legitimate provided that it formally recognizes the national minorities that are located within its territory and provided that the institutional implications of this recognition are also accepted by the population as a whole. And my claim is that it can afford to do so as long as it imposes only a common public identity understood as an encompassing societal culture.

What has been said about the one-nation state applies *mutatis mutandis* to "stateless nations" like Quebec, Catalonia and Scotland. These are peoples who provide examples of sociopolitical nations. Here again, we have a common public language, common public institutions and a common public history, in addition to an implicit or explicit internal constitution, that is, laws that are interpretive, as compared to other laws. In these societies, we also find a national consciousness, a collective will to live together, a specific crossroad of influences and a specific context of choice. We can talk about those nations as having a common public identity even though these political communities are not sovereign and even if they are polyethnic, pluricultural, even sometimes plurinational, as in the case of Quebec. The concept of sociopolitical nation is also legitimate provided that the common public identity that it brings into play is accompanied by politics of recognition for the national minorities and/or minority nations that it contains. Those minority public identities must be recognized, but this is not opposed to the idea of a fairly thick common public identity. For instance, the Catalonian people must recognize their Castilian minority and the Quebec people must recognize their Anglophone minority.

Things get more complicated when the sovereign state is a multisocietal nation. In that case, the common public identity cannot be characterized as automatically involving a single common public language, a single body of common public institutions and a single common public history. But these components may still be essential to a multisocietal nation, because this kind of nation may be understood as an "aggregate" of common public identities. In other words, even though we have managed with the multisocietal nations to dissociate the common public identity from a shared common language, institutions and history, it is impossible to represent multisocietal nations without looking at the component common public identities present in their constituent nations.

1.4 Multination states as aggregates of common public identities

With the multisocietal nation, it may seem that we have got to the Habermasian idea of constitutional patriotism, which presumes, precisely, an identity founded exclusively on adherence to a constitutional text. It seems that we must consider this kind of thin identity in order to account for states such as Canada[10] and Spain, or to account for supranational organizations such as the European Union.[11] My first idea, however, is that the common public identity of a multisocietal nation must have a minimum foundation in the existence of peoples who freely choose to associate with one another. This is the first sense in which the multisocietal nation is an aggregate of various national societal cultures. In other words, the common public identities of their constituent societies must be the basic political units out of which a more inclusive public identity has been constructed. This is a democratic procedural requirement. Ethnic, cultural and sociopolitical nations must try to democratically find a common ground, on the basis of which they freely choose to associate with one another by adopting common institutions.[12] Then, and this seems to me to be another condition *sine qua non* for the success of the multisocietal nation undertaking, the populations concerned must also represent themselves in this way. The constituent national blocs underlying the multisocietal nation must be present in the self-representation of the population as a whole. That population, in other words, must see itself as composed of more than one nation. So when I say that the multisocietal nation must be understood as an aggregate of common public identities, I am thinking not only of the democratic procedure that must have been implemented at the origin of the political organization, but also of what goes on in the people's minds. The population must understand the composite nature of the state and represent itself as plurinational. Such a plurinational self-representation determines the viability of the multination state, to the extent that the consciousness of belonging to a plurinational ensemble also makes the political entity in question viable.[13] And finally, the aggregative nature of the multisocietal nation or of the supranational organization must also lead to politics of recognition, that is, politics designed to promote and protect national diversity within society. There must be, among other things, a scheme of collective rights for minority nations within the territory in order to counterbalance the structural inequalities that may arise concerning identity matters, when a majority nation exerts a certain domination over minority nations. The common public identity of the multisocietal nation is not only compatible with the recognition of minority identities, it is also absolutely required. In other words, recognition of their constituent nations makes it possible for multination or supranational political organizations to be legitimate and morally above reproach, and because a lack of recognition of their component nations may be considered to be an injustice that calls for reparation.

In order to properly understand why recognition is essential, let us once again look at the two cases examined earlier: the single-nation state (or civic state) and the uninational sociopolitical nation, which as we said, is a particular sort of stateless nation. The common public identity of the civic nation or of the sociopolitical nation, as we have seen, includes a common language, common institutions and a common public history. Notice however that those various components derive largely from characteristic traits belonging to the majority. They originate from the national majority, even if they can at the same time be shared by all citizens in the public space. They disclose the national majority's collective will to survive as a majority. Since these characteristic traits originate from the majority, recognition of minority languages, institutions and histories becomes an essential moral requirement in order to neutralize the nationalist influence exerted by the national majority. By imposing its own language, its own institutions and its own public history on all citizens, the national majority in the civic nation or in the sociopolitical nation is engaged in a nationalist venture that cannot be legitimate unless it is compensated for by a policy of recognition toward minority groups. It is often said that the ultimate test of nationalism is the treatment of minorities, and it is the politics of recognition that enable it to pass that test.

Does the problem re-emerge in the multisocietal nation? Is the common public identity that it promotes also based on a nationalist act that imposes the rules of a national majority on diverse minorities? We must consider what the common public identity of the multisocietal nation consists of. When the sovereign state is a multination state, we said that the common public identity cannot be characterized as automatically involving a single common public language, a single body of common public institutions and a single common public history – even though that is sometimes the case, as shown by the example of Great Britain. Now since the multination state does not necessarily involve reference to the particularist features of a national majority, it may *prima facie* seem to be a neutral political entity. For that reason, one might be led to believe that the recognition of its constituent nations should not be required. But that would be a mistake. No matter what we come up with in terms of shared identity, the problem is that we are often dealing with national groups that have populations, economic resources and levers of power that are of different strengths. Multination states are only very rarely characterized by a balance among their various national components. They consist of majority societal cultures and minority societal cultures, and the former often exercise a certain domination over the latter. Inevitably, the institutional personality of the multination state will often absorb the directions chosen by the majority. In Canada, for example, the influence of the English Canadian majority is overwhelming. Therefore, recognition is also required even in the case of the multisocietal nation.

Certainly before we can truly talk about a multisocietal *nation* there must be an inclusive public identity at the top of all of the constituent public identities. That amounts to admitting that the nationally diversified character of the political community must be part of its common public identity. The multination state must be understood as an aggregate of nations. The political entity must democratically be grounded on the bedrock of the national constituents, the citizens' self-representation must call on those diverse national components, and politics of recognition must also be in place because of the determining influence of the majority group. In other words, while we have managed with the multisocietal nation to reach a level where we can truly dissociate the common public identity from the idea of a common language, common institutions and a common history, it is, for all intents and purposes, impossible to represent such a nation politically without appealing to its constituent groups and without regard to the balance of power among the diverse national components. To counteract the imbalances that may settle in permanently between the majority and the national minorities, a democratic representation of the component nations and a plurinational consciousness are needed, but also politics of recognition of the national minorities. Otherwise, we are merely surrendering to state nationalism.[14] Because multination states, some nation-states and some stateless nations contain within themselves diverse national components, we have to recognize those diverse national components and accept the institutional consequences that follow from this formal recognition. In this case, we are not merely claiming that national diversity must be part of the citizens' self-representation. We are also saying what the common public identity must be in order to achieve some kind of legitimacy. We are prescribing explicit recognition in a constitution of the diverse national components. Far from achieving postnational identity through a constitution, the constitution must on the contrary reflect national identities.

In order to see how a thick common public identity is legitimate, we also have to call on another principle that is a component of the concept of recognition: the principle of reciprocity. The idea is simply that recognition has to be reciprocal. Once they are recognized in the larger unit, contiguous diasporas within a civic or sociopolitical nation, national minorities within a multisocietal nation, sovereign states within a supranational organization, must in turn recognize the common public identity that transcends them and sign on to the constitutional text in which that recognition is enshrined. There must therefore be a principle of reciprocity applied in tandem with the very policy of recognition. There can be no common public identity without a constitutionally entrenched policy of recognition, but neither can there be a policy of recognition without reciprocity. The principle of reciprocity can be stated another way. If the national minorities and minority nations are not formally recognized by the inclusive states in which they are located, they have no obligation to sign on to the constitutional text of the inclusive state. The corollary is that if the national minorities and minority nations do not want to sign on to a constitutional text in which they would be recognized, the inclusive entities have no obligation to formally recognize their minority national components. Recognition is a tango, and it takes two to tango. Thus there is no common public identity where there is no constitutionally entrenched policy of recognition, but there is no policy of recognition without reciprocity. The identity of the group as a whole is determined by majority adherence of the members within the group, and that comment applies equally to the minority groups. However, the principle of reciprocity makes it possible to assess the legitimacy of that self-representation. A self-representation may be incorrect within a group, even if it is adopted by a majority of its members. If the group as a whole adopts a self-representation that includes the minority, the minority cannot legitimately be included unless the population as a whole formally recognizes the minority and accepts the institutional consequences of that recognition. Conversely, a minority in which a majority rules itself out of the common public identity cannot legitimately do so if its identity has been recognized by the population as a whole.

1.5 How a multination state becomes a multisocietal nation

The cement of identity that is likely to bind citizens belonging to a multisocietal nation to one another of course assumes a constitutional text, but it must be an aggregate in the triple sense just introduced. My idea is thus that a multisocietal public identity cannot escape the presence of its component nations. It is impossible to contemplate, in the medium or long term, common public identities that are completely free from the influence of national majorities (in the case of civic or sociopolitical nations) or of majority societal cultures (in a multisocietal nation). What is very commonly called "majority nationalism" is nothing but state policies that pretend to universality but that inevitably are, at the same time, a vehicle for the interests of a national majority or for a majority nation. For example, the Canadian state must not be understood as a body of neutral common institutions. The Canadian state is inevitably, in large part, a vehicle for the English Canadian national majority, and it is engaged into a nation-building enterprise. Its immigration policy, its multiculturalism policy and the social policies relying on the exercise of the federal spending power can be seen as involving objectives that are partly subordinated to a nationalist agenda. We can therefore see why constitutional patriotism cannot even apply to multisocietal nations. The separation between the political community and specific national identities can only be democratically feasible, politically viable and morally legitimate if national identities occupy centre stage. It is in this sense that multination states are to be seen as aggregates of nations. So this reveals the illusory nature of postnational identity.[15]

As noted above, we can talk of plurinational states as themselves forming nations, by calling them "multisocietal nations". The close connection that holds between the political community and national identity in the case of the multination states is not only that they are aggregates of nations. They also involve other common bonds that go beyond constitutional patriotism. In the case of Canada, for instance, there are of course values that come into play in its constitution: bilingualism, federalism, multiculturalism and to a certain extent (in sections 25 and 35 concerning aboriginal populations) plurinationalism. But in addition to the constitution, there are other features that allow us to describe it as involving a common public national identity. Canada is also a political community, that is, a sovereign country. There is in addition an emerging national consciousness shared among Canadians and there is a common public history shared by these Canadians. If in addition to this, there had been a truly aggregative conception of Canada involving a plurinational democratic representation, a plurinational consciousness and a formal recognition of all its component nations, Canada could have become a democratic, viable and legitimate multisocietal nation. In other words, it would paradoxically achieve a more complete common national public identity by becoming a true aggregate of nations.

1.6 Where constitutional patriotism goes wrong

There are therefore many crucial differences between my approach and Habermas' constitutional patriotism. First, I accept plurinational states, but they must be democratically created by their component national groups, they must involve a shared plurinational consciousness and they must incorporate politics of recognition taking the form of collective rights granted to minority nations and other national minorities. Second, multination states can themselves be described as nations. These two ideas suggest that the multination state has not transcended national identity, and they show that the concept of constitutional patriotism, as defined by Habermas, is entirely inoperative. By definition, that concept meant the possibility of transcending national identity. What we are saying here is that the nation has not been transcended.

In a nutshell then, component nations must be acknowledged democratically, psychologically and legally to secure the creation, viability and legitimacy of multination states. If I am correct on this point, no conclusion can be drawn with respect to the decline of the phenomenon of nationality apart from comments that, quite rightly, recognize the impotence of sovereign states in the fight against the excesses of globalization. Those excesses call for the creation of supranational organizations that are capable of asserting political principles and overseeing development while forcing sovereign states and multinational corporations to comply with labour rights, rights of children, respect for the environment and, more generally, human rights. Obviously, supranational institutions must also be capable of imposing distributive justice measures in North–South relations. This may all be important and true, but it is not possible even for supranational organizations to reach any conclusion that supports postnational identity, and for two main reasons. The first is that supranational organizations themselves owe their existence, their continuation and their legitimacy to nations (civic nations or multisocietal nations). They themselves should be understood as mere aggregates of nations. Contrary to multination states, they perhaps cannot be described as forming nations, for they are not sovereign entities and do not involve a long common history, but they nevertheless cannot be seen as transcending nations. The second reason, which is even more obvious, is that the battle that is going on within the basic global structure against neoliberalism cannot be won unless it is based among other things on a set of principles such as those that affirm the value of cultural diversity, the right of peoples to equal development and the right of peoples to protect the integrity of their national economies. In other words, we must not simply cite human rights; we must also rely on the law of peoples. Supranational organizations must not step in only when there are systematic human rights violations occurring; they must also do so when genocide, racism and minority rights violations are occurring within states. Once again, this brings us back to the nation.

2 The nation: disintegrating from the bottom up?

My rejection of constitutional patriotism is based essentially on the rejection of postnational identity. It amounts to asserting that the nation is somewhat of an "essential" ingredient of liberal democracies, perhaps even, as Liah Greenfeld would have it, a constitutive aspect of modernity.[16] This could remain true even if the nation-state were no longer the only model of political organization. To show this point, I have rebutted arguments that were meant to show that the creation of multination states and supranational organizations could be supported by postnational identity. I have argued that, on the contrary, those entities had to be grounded on the bedrock of national identities and, in the case of multination states, could themselves be seen as nations.

But other objections can also be made that question the force of national identification: in this case, we are no longer arguing, with Habermas and Ferry, that national identification is less relevant from a top-down perspective, but rather from a bottom-up perspective. For instance, Seyla Benhabib argues for a theory of narrative identity and for this reason criticizes any attempt to impose uniform national identities to all the citizens in a given polity, because this implies a problematic collectively shared narrative identity.[17] If collective narrative identities existed, they would be so fragile that they would inevitably be transformed after a short while, and that is why recognition of those identities must remain informal. There are others who think that we are witnessing the presence of the global basic structure within society itself and they believe that the concept of national societal culture with its own context of choice, so vaunted by Kymlicka,[18] no longer has an application.[19] Finally, Anthony Appiah directly attacks the existence of cultures, since according to him they can only be postulated if we subscribe to a problematic essentialist reification and if we endorse preservationist ethics.[20] In other words, these authors suggest that the imposition of a single national identity is incompatible with internal cultural diversity, with the fact of identity pluralism and with the dynamic nature of identity. Those phenomena are increasingly influential in our societies because of the global basic structure. They are essentially eloquent harbingers of the advent of a postnational era.

Anticultural critics give additional credentials to constitutional patriotism. Actually, the two arguments are mutually reinforcing, and not only because both target national identity and argue for postnational identity. Indeed, the more fragmented identities are in a given society, the more it becomes necessary to rely on a tenuous identity in order to include all citizens within a single group. Those individuals will have to refer exclusively to a constitutional text in order to find common ground.

I would like to show that national identity understood as a societal culture and as involving a common public identity is perfectly compatible with diversity in the composition of a people, with identity pluralism (the fact that individuals have multiple identities) and with the dynamic nature of identity.

2.1 Accounting for diversity

On the theme of diversity, it must be emphasized, first, that I have defined a people by making explicit use of structural features such as language, institutions and history of these institutions. I specifically endorsed Kymlicka's distinction between the structure and the character of culture. We are in effect suggesting the adoption at the collective level of what is already accepted at the individual level when we describe persons as citizens. The suggestion is to define peoples in institutional terms as societal cultures. This characterization is compatible with the existence of a wide diversity of conceptions about the common good and about the good life. Subgroups may have different beliefs, values, traditions, customs and ways of life while sharing the same common public language, institutions and history.

Second, I earlier said that we had to recognize at least seven different kinds of nations. If we leave out ethnic nations, all of the other kinds of nations are not ethnically homogeneous. We must therefore necessarily admit the possibility that a people can be polyethnic. For example, cultural, civic, sociopolitical, diasporic, multisocietal and multiterritorial nations can all be polyethnic. But that is not all. If we except ethnic and cultural nations, all of the other kinds of nations can be pluricultural. Also, sociopolitical and multisocietal nations can even be multination societies. Some societies are therefore simultaneously polyethnic, pluricultural and plurinational. Finally, a single nation-state may can contain other types of national minorities, such as historical minorities, contiguous diasporas (extensions of neighbouring nations) and non-contiguous diasporas, that is, immigrant communities. The approach that I take, which admits of at least seven kinds of nations, and acknowledges samples of nations such as contiguous and non-contiguous diasporas, thus provides a fairly good picture of the diversity within existing nations.

I would say that conceptual pluralism is superior, on this point, to most existing approaches that take a doctrinaire stance in favour of a univocal definition of nation, or that fall back on the fine old dichotomy between ethnic and civic nations. Approaches like these do not acknowledge the variety of uses of the word "nation", and they are forced for this reason to prescribe a thorough reform in the use of the national vocabulary. Even worse, they tend, sooner or later, to deny the existence of certain nations, and to oppose to a certain deep diversity, as well as failing to take into account the self-representation entertained by various populations.

On the contrary, the approach I adopt allows for different uses to be recognized and legitimized, and it is able to take deep diversity into account. If nations are partly a function of the self-representations held by its population, we cannot deny the existence of different sorts of nations. So I am, for instance, able to recognize "united nations" – referring to a body of sovereign states, whether they be civic nations or multisocietal nations – as well as aboriginal nations (ethnic or sociopolitical), the Acadian nation (cultural), the Canadian nation (multisocietal) and the Quebec nation (sociopolitical). This approach also recognizes the former Jewish nation (diasporic) and the Kurdish or Mohawk nations (multiterritorial).

A third feature of the present approach is relevant for the question of accommodating diversity. I have described nationality as involving what I have called a common public identity. This account is thus compatible with the recognition of minority public identities. It is not enough to be inclusive of many different minorities within a common institutional identity. There must be a recognition of those minorities within the polity. As a matter of fact, one can safely predict that recognition is a necessary condition for inclusion. Minorities will be more willing to recognize the rules and regulations implemented for the population as a whole if recognition is reciprocal. Conversely, recognition of minorities can be made in exchange for a recognition of the inclusive identity. Inclusion can take place in the context of integration, not assimilation. This can be done as long as the inclusive identity is understood as a common public identity and as long as minorities are recognized.

So there is no reason to conclude that an account that wishes to preserve nationality as an important source of identity is doomed to be exclusivist, ethnocentric or chauvinist. It will not happen if the account of a people is one in which it is understood as a societal culture, if we allow for different sorts of nations and if national identity is understood as a common public identity.

2.2 Accounting for plural identities

I can also demonstrate the advantages of the present approach in dealing with the phenomenon of identity pluralism. Individuals may have different sorts of allegiances: to their sexual affiliations, to their profession, to their city, to their family or to their nationality. This is certainly something that the present account can accept. It could even be claimed that without a societal culture, minority groups and associations could not flourish. Moreover, supposing that individuals have a chart of their different allegiances and that this chart involves a ranking of these allegiances that is dependent on their rational preferences, nations understood as societal cultures providing contexts of choices are necessary conditions guaranteeing the very existence of these charts of group allegiances.

Furthermore, I said that the position taken here recognizes several kinds of nations, and the consequence of this is to authorize "nations within a nation". This has an immediate impact on identity pluralism. I said that we can recognize ethnic nations in a cultural nation; ethnic and cultural nations in a sociopolitical nation; ethnic, cultural and sociopolitical nations in a multisocietal nation. We can also recognize historical minorities, contiguous diasporas and non-contiguous diasporas in most of those nations, including within the civic nation, even though it is by definition a sovereign single-nation state. This means that people who belong to those nations can at the same time be members of other nations. For example, as a member of a contiguous diaspora, a person can be connected with a community of residence, by territory, and with a national majority or a nation located on another, contiguous territory. As well, as a member of an immigrant community, a person can be associated with a new community of residence and an old community of origin. And more generally, a person can be a member of an ethnic, cultural, diasporic, multiterritorial or sociopolitical nation and at the same time be included in a multisocietal nation. Recognition of a variety of nations is what makes it possible to recognize identity pluralism, even concerning national identity. A person can be of one nation within another nation and have more than one national identity. According to certain intellectuals, this seems strange. And yet it is an everyday fact for an immigrant who is attached both to his or her country of origin and to the new community of residence. It is also the case for a person who has several different citizenships because he or she holds many passports. It may therefore also be the case for a person who lives in a multination state.

Now as I said, the approach I favour is one that can involve politics of recognition for component minority nations or other national minorities within the population. It is thus easy to see why it can accommodate plural identities. If all the components of a plural identity are recognized, the plural identity is itself recognized.

2.3 Accounting for the dynamic character of identity

On the question of the dynamic nature of identity, I would simply want to say this. Even if at any point in history, societal cultures have a specific character, this character may change while the structure of culture remains the same. In *Multicultural Citizenship*, Kymlicka acknowledges this fact in terms of the existence of a culture and its character. This has led Appiah to mistakenly attribute to him the view according to which the continued identity of the group is ethnic and based on genetic filiations.[21] But this is a complete misunderstanding that rests on no basis whatsoever. The continued identity of the group through time is institutional not ethnic. The structure of culture roughly remains the same through time. It does not involve any metaphysical essentialism since we are dealing with the institutional personality of groups as they appear in the political realm.[22] We are therefore able to account for the dynamic nature of the character of culture.

Second, at any point in history, there are disputes about how a nation is to define itself. There are diverse self-representations at odds within the society. The official accepted definition is merely the definition that is able to impose itself temporarily, the one having the support of a majority of citizens. This is all possible because of the partially subjective nature of national identity. National consciousness is a subjective factor and it depends on the individual national consciousnesses held by citizens. In Quebec, for example, there were for a long time conflicts among ethnic, cultural and sociopolitical definitions, and there are still debates between some of them. Historically, we have witnessed the slow progression from an ethnic definition of nation – the French Canadian nation – to a cultural definition – the Francophone Quebec nation – and we are now engaged in the slow progression that is taking us toward a sociopolitical definition of nation. Some people claim, however, that Quebec is not yet a nation "properly speaking", and that it will become one only when it is sovereign. Those people then want Quebec to achieve either a civic nation status (a country that includes a single nation) or a multisocietal nation status (a sovereign multination state). To my mind, the civic definition would be illegitimate in Quebec, because there are eleven aboriginal peoples within the territory.

Similarly, the English Canadian nation has gradually given way for a while to the Canadian civic nation, containing a single Canadian nation identified with the country, and also to a certain extent to a multisocietal nation, because of the presence of aboriginal peoples in the constitution of Canada. I would want to argue that the civic definition would not be legitimate and that the kind of multi-societal nation entertained by many is also problematic, because it does not involve the recognition of Quebec and Acadian nations. (The recognition of the Quebec nation by the Harper government is to a large extent merely verbal.) We are therefore witnessing, in Canada, the slow progression from the English Canadian cultural nation to a partly civic and partly multisocietal nation, even though Canada might have transformed itself into a complete multisocietal nation, with the formal recognition of Quebec and Acadian nations. The Acadian people take the form of a cultural nation because, like any nation, it is characterized by a common language, institutions and history, but it does not have its own political institutions, properly speaking. However, it could one day want to do just that, and if it did, it would form a sociopolitical nation. There are also ethnic or cultural aboriginal nations that have become sociopolitical nations (Nunavut), while others are multiterritorial (Mohawks) but are increasingly having to engage in autonomous political organization.

Accordingly, even though the theory I propose puts the nation at the forefront, I can recognize not only the variety of national consciousnesses within the diverse populations that make up Canada, as well as identity pluralism, but I can also acknowledge the dynamic nature of the various identity processes.[23]

3 Conclusion

In this chapter I have criticized the view according to which we are entering a postnational era. My claims are both normative and factual. I am suggesting that we are not entering a postnational era, and I am also suggesting that we should not try to, because the democratic character of multisocietal nations and supranational organizations, their viability and their legitimacy are intimately related to a reckoning of national identity. Even though the nation is under attack from both top and bottom, it is still alive and well and kicking. Societies that fail to acknowledge their minority nations remain unstable. Strategies of assimilation always fail and the minority nationalism that we thought had disappeared sooner or later resurfaces. Despite the numerous attempts to assimilate if not to annihilate Chechnya or Tibet, these nations are still standing. In spite of the genocidal ambitions entertained by the Nazis against the Jews, the state of Israel is now here to stay. Palestinian nationalism is also resilient in spite of all the destruction and deprivation that Palestinians have encumbered. Minority nationalisms in Great Britain, Spain and Canada have not decreased at all. So one can clearly argue that national identity remains a formidable source of group affiliation. It can be a legitimate one even in the contemporary world as long as we introduce the concept of common public identity, see nations as societal cultures, recognize conceptual pluralism and accept the principle of reciprocal recognition. I have also shown that the account could acknowledge the existence of diversity, identity pluralism and the dynamic character of identity.

Common public identity is a kind of "civic" identity, not in the sense of the civic nation, but in the pretheoretical sense of the word. My concept of common public identity is an explanation of the intuitive concept of civic identity. It assumes the rejection of constitutional patriotism, because it comprises a thick identity including one or more common public languages, one or more sets of common public institutions and one or more common public histories (and the same kinds of remarks apply to national consciousness, to the collective will to live together, to crossroads of influences and to contexts of choice). There is a thick identity that proves the vacuity of postnational identity.

Peoples, states and supranational organizations are built on the bedrock of national societal *cultures* understood in the sense of structures of culture. Because nations are kinds of societal *cultures* and because they are not easy to transcend, I have no objection to talking about the concept of a common public *culture*. Common public identity is at the same time a common public culture. The important thing here is not to confuse the structure of the culture and the character of culture, as emphasized by Kymlicka. The structure of culture relates to institutions, while the character is a matter of beliefs, values, traditions, customs and ways of life adopted by a critical mass of the population at a particular time. A structure of culture can last over time, despite changes that may occur in its character. Of course, some institutions may be intimately related to a certain set of beliefs, as for example, with religions institutions, but not all are. It is also true that, in some societies, the majority of institutions are indeed associated with a particular character. If our societies are now on the verge of acknowledging the reasonable and irreversible diversity of characters, other societies may be relatively homogeneous in terms of character, and that may lead to the interweaving of structure and character. However, the distinction between structure and nature is still of analytical relevance, because we can refer to the linguistic, political, educational and cultural institutions of such societies without referring to the dominant nature of a particular character. If we understand culture in this way – as the structure of culture – then we can say that this chapter is not only a critique of constitutional patriotism and postnational identity, but also an argument for the concept of a common public culture.

Notes

1 Habermas (2006, 2000: chap. 3); Ferry (2005a: chaps 1–3, 2005b, 2001).
2 Habermas (1998: chap. 3, 2001: chap. 4); Ferry (2005a: chap. 3, 2005b, 2001).
3 Habermas (1998: chap. 3). For a discussion, see Nootens (1999).
4 Habermas (2006, 1998: chap. 3); Ferry (2000, 2001, 2005a).
5 Appiah (2005, 2006); Seyla Benhabib (2002); Jeremy Waldron (1992, 2000).
6 A "society of identities" is one in which identities are fragmented and where there is no common frame of reference for everyone. For a critical discussion, see Jacques Beauchemin (2004).
7 Kymlicka (1989, 1995).
8 See Rawls (1999).
9 For methodological reasons, Rawls considers only the peoples that are organized into sovereign states, but he acknowledges that a more complex model should consider the issue of self-determination and secession for peoples, and the rules for federations of peoples (Rawls 1999: 38). So it is clear that his political conception of peoples is not meant to be restricted only to those who already have sovereign states.

10 See Leydet (1995).
11 Some have even examined the application of constitutional patriotism to the case of Quebec. See Courtois (2002, 2004).
12 Nations are thus essential players not only in the functioning of nation-states, but also in the functioning of multination states and supranational organizations. Here we might think of the major role played by France and Germany in the European construction. It is these two peoples that have expressed the most enthusiasm for the European construction, but they are also the peoples that, together, enjoy enormous power within the Union. If the powerful nation-states did not find the European Union to their taste, it is a very good bet that their enthusiasm would wane considerably. Even the strongest Europeanists, like Joschka Fisher, who support a pan-European referendum on the reform of European institutions, accept the principle of the double majority under which implementation requires not only an absolute majority of votes cast by European citizens, but also a majority of states in which a majority of citizens are determined to support the reform (quoted in Habermas 2006: 11).
13 On this point, we can again refer to the European Union. There are major differences between representing itself as a Europe composed of 15 countries and a Europe composed of 25 countries. Joschka Fisher's proposal, to which we alluded earlier, assumes that the referendum would be binding only for states in which a majority voted for the reform. That means that Fischer is now prepared to consider a two-tier Europe. While that idea expresses the need to proceed slowly toward expansion, it also shows a significant sensitivity to the self-representation of the populations in question. Ferry (2005b: 28) also appears to be sensitive to criticism of the excessive haste in the expansion process. I see this as an additional indication that the self-representation of the populations plays an important role. To understand the still preponderant role of national consciousness in the European Union, it will be useful to read the empirical study reported in Deflem and Pampel (1996).
14 While the enthusiasm of Ferry and Habermas for the Draft Treaty establishing a Constitution for Europe may be justified in part, it is not accompanied by any criticism mentioning the total absence of any formal commitment by the participating states toward their national minorities. Accordingly, their position is paradoxically de facto in line with the nationalism of the participating states. For an examination of this unsatisfactory aspect of the Draft Treaty, see Seymour (2004).
15 The constitutional patriotism adopted by Ferry (1996) in his reconstructive ethics can be characterized as a sophisticated variant, in that it can go so far as to authorize the introduction of a certain policy of recognition, while for Habermas such a policy appears superfluous (Habermas 2005, 1995, 1994). However, in order for recognition to be compatible with constitutional patriotism, it must not be merely *symbolic* in the sense of Galeotti (2002) and must thus not imply any differential *treatment* in the sense in which it is understood by Arto Laitinen (2002). It must also be resolutely turned toward the past and take the form of an act of contrition (what Yael Tamir (1999) describes as an atonement) or commemoration. This way of understanding recognition is entirely consistent with the postnational identity posited by Habermas, and so it is also perfectly consistent with constitutional patriotism, because it has no impact on the present-day treatment of the national components within a state. But as Pierre Mouterde (2006) wrote in reporting the opinion of Walter Benjamin,

> he [Benjamin] allows us to see, retrospectively, the limits of contemporary political correctness, which, because it is closeted in commemorations divorced from present-day issues and does not combine remembering with doing something about life today, remains a prisoner of the discourse of the victors.

16 See Liah Greenfeld (1992).
17 See Seyla Benhabib (2002).
18 See Kymlicka (1989, 1995).

19 See Waldron (1992, 2000).
20 See Anthony Appiah (2005, 2006).
21 See Appiah (2005: 136).
22 For other arguments against interpreting politics of recognition as involving essentialist claims, see Maclure (2007) and Courtois (2005).
23 I could also spend more time on stateless persons or persons whose identity trajectory is unique and complex. The first can be understood as people who have several national identities, who prefer none of those identities in particular and who consider those identities to be of relatively low importance in their pantheon of allegiances. To understand and define them, we can only look to national identities. We can then acknowledge that there are such people without having to question what has been said here, because such cases are relatively rare. However, the fact is that increasing numbers of immigrants have had a twisting and complex identity trajectory, even though they do not claim an identity self-representation in the nature of statelessness. To incorporate those cases into my model, these individuals need only acknowledge the distinction between immigrant communities and national host communities.

References

Appiah, Kwame Anthony (2005) *The Ethics of Identity*, Princeton, NJ: Princeton University Press.

Appiah, Kwame Anthony (2006) *Cosmopolitanism*, New York: W.W. Norton.

Beauchemin, Jacques (2004) *La Société des Identités*, Outremont: Éditions Athéna.

Benhabib, Seyla (2002) *The Claims of Culture*, Princeton, NJ: Princeton University Press.

Courtois, Stéphane (2002) "Le patriotisme constitutionnel de J. Habermas face au nationalisme québécois: sa portée, ses limites", *Dialogue* 41(4).

Courtois, Stéphane (2004) "Habermas et la question du nationalisme: le cas du Québec", *Philosophiques* 27(2): 377–401.

Courtois, Stéphane (2005) "Are multiculturalist theories victims of the 'Cultural Essentialism' fallacy?", *Human Affairs* 15(2): 149–165.

Deflem, Mathieu and Pampel, Fred C. (1996) "The myth of postnational identity: popular support for European unification", *Social Forces* 75(1): 119–143.

Ferry, Jean-Marc (1996) *L'Éthique Reconstructive*, Paris: Cerf.

Ferry, Jean-Marc (2000) *La Question de l'État Européen*, Paris: Éditions Gallimard, Collection "NRF-essais".

Ferry, Jean-Marc (2001) "Devenons des patriotes européens", *Le Monde des Débats/Le Nouvel Observateur* 23, mars.

Ferry, Jean-Marc (2005a) *Europe la Voie Kantienne. Essai sur l'Identité Postnationale*, Paris: Cerf.

Ferry, Jean-Marc (2005b) "Quelle démocratie postnationale?", *Éthique Publique (International Journal of Societal and Governmental Ethics): Nouvelles Formes de la Démocratie*, Montréal, Québec: éditions Liber, Spring, 7(1): 166–175.

Galeotti, Anna Elisabetta (2002) *Toleration as Recognition*, Cambridge: Cambridge University Press.

Greenfeld, Liah (1992) *Nationalism. Five Roads to Modernity*, Cambridge, MA: Harvard University Press.

Habermas, Jürgen (1994), "Struggles for recognition in the democratic constitutional state", in *Multiculturalism: Examining the Politics of Recognition*, Princeton, NJ: Princeton University Press.

Habermas, Jürgen (1995) "Multiculturalism and the liberal state", *Stanford Law Review*, May, 47: 849.

Habermas, Jürgen (1998) *The Inclusion of the Other*, Cambridge, MA: MIT Press.

Habermas, Jürgen (2000) *Après l'État-nation*, Paris, Fayard.

Habermas, Jürgen (2001) *Postnational Constellation*, Cambridge, MA: MIT Press.

Habermas, Jürgen (2005) "Equal treatment of cultures and the limits of postmodern liberalism", *The Journal of Political Philosophy* 13(1): 1–28.

Habermas, Jürgen (2006) *Sur l'Europe*, Paris: Bayard.

Kymlicka, Will (1989) *Liberalism, Community and Culture*, Oxford: Clarendon Press.

Kymlicka, Will (1995) *Multicultural Citizenship*, Oxford: Oxford University Press.

Laitinen, Arto (2002) "Interpersonal recognition: a response to value or a precondition of personhood", *Inquiry* 45(4): 463–478.

Leydet, Dominique (1995) "Patriotisme constitutionnel et identité nationale", in Michel Seymour (ed.) *Une Nation peut-elle se Donner la Constitution de son Choix?*, Montréal: Bellarmin, pp. 79–93.

Maclure, Jocelyn (2007) "La reconnaissance engage-t-elle à l'essentialisme?", *Philosophiques* 34(1).

Mouterde, Pierre (2006) "Walter Benjamin et la querelle sur l'histoire au secondaire", *Le Devoir*, September, 9.

Nootens, Geneviève (1999) "L'identité postnationale: itinéraire(s) de la citoyenneté", *Politique et Sociétés* 18(3): 101–120.

Rawls, John (1999) *The Law of Peoples*, Cambridge, MA: Harvard.

Seymour, Michel (2004) "Nation-states, national minorities and the draft treaty", in Francesca Astengo and Nanette Neuwhal (eds), *A Constitution for Europe? Governance and Policy-making in the European Union*, Montréal: Chaire Jean-Monnet, Université de Montréal, pp. 280–296.

Tamir, Yael (1999) "L'époque des excuses: l'émergence d'un nouveau paradigme politique", in Michel Seymour (ed.), *Nationalité, Citoyenneté et Solidarité*, Montréal: Liber.

Waldron, Jeremy (1992) "Minority cultures and the cosmopolitan alternative", *University of Michigan Journal of Law Reform* 25: 751.

Waldron, Jeremy (2000) "What is cosmopolitan?" *Journal of Political Philosophy* 8(2): 227–243.

7 Reframing sovereignty?

Sub-state national societies and contemporary challenges to the nation-state

Stephen Tierney

The rise of sub-state nationalism in developed states such as Canada, Spain and the United Kingdom over recent decades has come at a time when the sovereignty of the nation-state is under question as a result both of economic globalisation and of supra-state institutional and legal harmonisation. For many commentators, the re-emergence of sub-state national identities is paradoxical in an age when the state seems to be in decline as a politico-legal force. This chapter contends that in fact the agenda for constitutional reform which is now prevalent within sub-state national societies is in many ways well tuned to a changing world, wherein some features of the state's traditional legal capacity and political competence are in decline, but in the context of which the state continues to retain considerable significance. The chapter also challenges the assumption that the constitutional programmes of sub-state nationalists within these states is predominantly secessionist, and argues that the main challenge to the legal structure of these states comes in calls for the amendment or radical reinterpretation of the state's constitutional arrangements in recognition of its plurinational nature.

1 Introduction

Over the past thirty years, sub-state national societies in a number of developed liberal democracies – particularly Quebec, Catalonia and Scotland within Canada, Spain and the United Kingdom respectively – have both reasserted their national distinctiveness and demanded recognition of it in constitutional terms, a phenomenon that has been termed by some 'neo-nationalism' (Keating 2001a; McRoberts 1997: 55; McCrone 2001: 3–13; Nairn 1977). This re-emergence of sub-state national sentiment within industrially advanced states, and the struggle for constitutional change which has accompanied it, are considered by many observers to be strangely incongruous at a time of economic and cultural 'globalisation' where the power of the nation-state itself seems to be waning.[1] Why do sub-state nations, the common refrain asks, seek statehood when the very concept of state sovereignty is losing its meaning? In this chapter we will argue, however, that the rise of sub-state nationalism even at a time when the resilience of state sovereignty is itself coming into question, is in fact not as paradoxical as it might at first appear, at least insofar as this process is taking place within developed democracies.[2] It will be contended that the elaborate constitutional programmes which are now being advanced by sub-state nationalist movements for the reform of their respective host states are in many respects informed by, and reflective of, wider transformations in the patterns of state sovereignty.

The term 'sovereignty' is of course highly elusive, and in order to capture how it is used by sub-state nationalists in debates concerning the nature of the contemporary state, it is important to note how parties to these debates use sovereignty in a holistic way, embracing both its legal and political dimensions. Here the recent work of Martin Loughlin is illuminating. Loughlin defines sovereignty as possessed of two different dimensions – 'competence' and 'capacity' – which encapsulate, respectively, the concept's legal and political elements. In other words, 'competence' represents 'authority' in a juridical sense, while 'capacity' embodies a more politicised conceptualisation of pragmatic 'power' (Loughlin 2003: 82). This is a helpful model to apply to contemporary nationalism because we can observe in the practice of sub-state nationalists precisely this combination of the legal and the political; each element is combined inextricably in the rhetoric with which these constitutional actors contest traditional narratives of state sovereignty. A second feature of this holistic conception of sovereignty is that by eliding the idea of legal authority and political power it envisages sovereignty as being relational in nature: as Loughlin would have it, sovereignty is 'generated as a product of the political relationship between the people and the state' (Loughlin 2003: 70). Again this relational idea features in the discourse of sub-state nationalists. For them sovereignty has a relational essence, but they demand that when used to describe a plurinational democracy the relationship metaphor be made more complex in order to encapsulate the idea of 'the people' in a pluralistic way; sovereignty within a plurinational state cannot be posited merely as the 'relationship between the people and the state', rather it must be a relationship between the *peoples* who together compose the state, and the state itself. The relational idea of sovereignty therefore must be one which is flexible enough to accommodate a plurality of peoples or *demoi*, each of which might bring with it a differing vision and a variegated set of claims concerning where sovereignty lies within the state.

One common myth which will be challenged in this chapter is the notion that the dominant nationalist voices within territories such as Catalonia, Quebec and Scotland are in fact 'separatist' ones. In fact, sub-state national societies are, with their new visions of what sovereignty can and does mean, presenting very complex claims to greater autonomy and enhanced recognition *within*, or at least *with*, the state, while at the same time attempting to negotiate some measure of discrete personality within the international institutions to which the state belongs; these aspirations therefore represent a deeply ambivalent strategy of operating more effectively inside, and when the opportunity avails itself and is attractive, beyond, the nation-state. As such, these territories demonstrate in many ways that they are fully engaged with the modern challenges which face any polity in an age of 'late sovereignty', where the power of the nation-state is declining through the influence of international normative sites, but where, through playing a full role within these fora, territorial polities can yet retain considerable influence.[3]

Therefore, contemporary sub-state national demands for better constitutional accommodation require to be located within the context of a global political and legal environment which is itself rapidly changing. As Keating suggests: 'We are heading for a new, differentiated, asymmetrical political order in which the old constitutional categories are losing their meaning' (Keating 2001b: 275). As they observe external challenges to the nation-state, sub-state national societies situate their own constitutional aspirations within this environment. It is in this context that their core aims take on an increasingly international flavour. For example: the goal of enhanced constitutional *autonomy* for the society's territorial space now makes reference not only to the state but also to membership of international organisations;[4] the search for improved institutional *representation* for the society now targets not only the central state but also the international community (Heywood 2000: 12; Börzel 2000: 21; Salmon 2001: 63–84; Harel 2003: 4–7); and the desire for general *recognition* of the society's 'national' status similarly looks to both state and international actors for a response (Latouche 1993; Requejo 1999, 2001c: 127).

In Section 2 the chapter will demonstrate how sub-state nationalism within 'plurinational' states relates to wider contemporary challenges to traditionally rendered accounts of the 'Westphalian', statal model of sovereignty itself. It will address the ways in which the new sub-state nationalist agenda constitutes one level of a tri-partite series of issues emerging across supra-state, sectoral and sub-state levels. Any meaningful analysis of the questions posed by sub-state national societies to plurinational states must be contextualised within the framework of broader global challenges to all nation-states. Various matters are at stake here for traditional concepts of statehood, for example: the hierarchy of competing levels of legal authority at supra-state, sub-state and sectoral levels; the normative resilience of state constitutions in the face of these competing authority sites; and the continuing reliability, as explanatory devices, of traditional models of statehood and of their fundamental doctrinal components, such as sovereignty and territorial integrity. It is therefore the central aim of the chapter to situate the contemporary nationalist challenge within this wider condition of global political and constitutional flux and within wider-ranging contemporary debates, particularly in Europe but also in North America, concerning the nature of statehood itself.

Flowing from this analysis, in Section 3 it will be observed how the challenge of sub-state nationalism manifests itself increasingly in demands for improved accommodation *within* the state rather than in the threat of secession. The chapter will conclude by suggesting that although internal accommodation constitutes a seemingly less radical challenge to the state than does 'separatism',[5] in fact the new debates emerging around the nature of the state and its plurinational nature perhaps raise more difficult questions for established conceptions of constitutional sovereignty than does secession.

2 Situating nationalism in an age of 'globalisation'

There are a number of contemporary politico-legal challenges which presently exert themselves upon states, and which together call into question the very via- bility of the nation-state, at least insofar as the state is conceptualised to repre- sent a 'Westphalian' model of absolute sovereignty.[6] These 'challenges' are in fact rival sites of authority which in our time contest constructions of the nation- state as the pre-eminent, or according to certain positivists, the exclusive, site of territorial sovereignty; and which, in doing so, also offer alternative reference points for both the identity and the loyalty of the citizen. These rival sites of authority can be categorised in terms of 'levels', of which, a number of com- mentators agree, there are three. First, and in Europe at least the most topical, is the emergence of supra-state political and legal orders – most prominently the European Union. Although operating at the supra-state level, entities such as the EU remain territorial in their remit. For example, the EU has been described as a 'post-state' polity in that it operates above the state but remains a fully territory- based polity (Walker 2002: 347). Certainly the EU is unique in terms of the sophistication of its institutional infrastructure, and other entities such as the North American Free Trade Agreement could certainly not be described as 'post- state'; however, even in the context of NAFTA, certain comparable issues con- cerning the transference of state sovereignty have arisen (Gagnon 2001: 21).

Second, at a 'sectoral' level (Keating 2001b: 46), there exists a primarily economic challenge to state sovereignty through the extra-territorial dynamic of what is often loosely termed 'globalisation' (Beitz 1994; Waldron 1995: 93–119; Held *et al.* 1999; Moore 2001), but which also embraces a networked and powerful system embracing political and legal dimensions (Habermas and Pensky 2001: 60). This process, although consisting primarily of an economic imperative, can impact on legal authority through regulatory devices (for example, in the practices of the World Trade Organisation) (Weiler 2000; Cass 2001: 42; Habermas 1999: 49), and becomes in many respects politically, if not strictly legally, authoritative. In a sense, therefore, the sectoral challenge is a functional one, affecting more the state's 'capacity' than its 'competence'. As Marks puts it, globalisation 'changes the context in which state functions are exercised' (Marks 2000: 76). This can be distinguished from the supra-state challenge given that the sectoral challenge operates on a largely extra-territorial or deterritorialised basis, creating claims that it constitutes a new form of terri- torially intangible empire which is progressively circumscribing the globe within open and expanding frontiers (Hardt and Negri 2000: xii). The third challenge is that presented by sub-state nationalism. This resembles the supra- state challenge in being territorially based, but is distinctive in so much as it operates primarily *within* the state; although, as will be explored, sub-state soci- eties are also capable of acting beyond the state by building networks and rela- tionships at extra-state level.

A body of literature has built up analysing the implications of these new sites of challenge for the independent operation of municipal constitutional systems.

Questions are now being raised concerning the continuing capacity and competence of the state to manage, or otherwise exercise control over, social and economic relations (McCrone 2001; Held 1988); and this has led in turn both to theoretical deconstructions of established notions of statal authority (in particular, reified visions of the state as *the* receptacle of absolute sovereignty) (Christodoulidis 1998; MacCormick 1999; Weiler 1999; Tierney and Warbrick 2006), and to radical revisions in the study of constitutions and constitutionalism itself (Ladeur 1997; Tully 1995; Curtin 1997; Chalmers 2000; Walker 2006; Choudhry and McGarry 2008). This work has concentrated largely upon either the challenges posed at supra-state level through transnational politico-legal constructs such as the European Union and the North American Free Trade Agreement, or alternatively, upon those challenges presented by economic, political and legal forces operating at the sectoral level and facilitated to some extent by regulatory machinery such as the WTO. This chapter contends, however, that the role played by sub-state nationalism offers an additional radical dynamic which has generally been missed from this debate; in fact, sub-state nationalism poses similar questions about the coherence of the Westphalian model of the nation-state, and as such this phenomenon constitutes a site of authority comparable to these other two sites of challenge.

This task of explaining the role of sub-state nationalism in these great changes begins with a consideration of how this phenomenon, which may seem only to undermine the authority of the specific state within which a particular sub-state national society is located, rather than to raise more fundamental questions about the nature of statehood itself, can be located in juxtaposition to these two other forces. In other words, how sub-state nationalism takes its place as part of a triad of rival sites, linking with the supra-state and sectoral forces in posing broad, structural challenges to the very foundations of the Westphalian statal model. In suggesting this linkage between sub-state nationalism and these other sites it is important to begin by addressing the common preconception that sub-state nationalism does not in fact raise, in any meaningful way, fundamental issues concerning the nature of the nation-state. It is frequently argued first, that as a political strategy sub-state nationalism is in fact driven by, and is dependent upon, the same statal dynamics that motivate existing states; and second, that as a consequence, sub-state nations as territorial sites of constitutional authority are just as likely to be affected in negative ways by new supra-state and sectoral sites of authority as are nation-states themselves. It will be posited that this argument, while correctly identifying ways in which statal and sub-statal polities are each affected by globalising dynamics, goes too far in this process of elision, thereby overlooking or underemphasising important points of demarcation between the effects of globalisation on these differing models of polity.

The starting point in engaging with this argument is to observe the historical relationship between state-nationalism and the construction of the nation-state, whereby nationalism as an instrumental political device of the modern age performed a central task in the state-building project by providing the ideological glue adhering the loyalty of the populace to the physical space of the state

(Gellner 1964: 169; Deutsch 1966; Hobsbawm 1990; Anderson 1991; Weber 1966; Breuilly 1993). In this sense, through the process of state-building (Gellner 1983; Reinhard 1996; Rae 2002), nationalism in the nineteenth and twentieth centuries became the key political device which tied together, in a synergetic relationship, the populace, the territory and the constitutional order of the evolving state. And, for the purposes of this account, it should be recalled also that constitutionalism was central to this process (Holmes 1995: xi; Resina 2002: 381). A comparable process can also be said to have occurred among sub-state nations, with similar dynamics of nation-building at work (McCrone 1998: 11; Smith 1998: 11–16). This is particularly true of those sub-state nations, such as Scotland, which entered the modern era as independent states, but it is also the case in more subtle ways for sub-state nations such as Catalonia and Quebec, which although never independent, did find the constitutional space to build politically and culturally discrete societies, particularly from the nineteenth century onwards.

Therefore, at first glance it appears that the political agenda of sub-state nationalism should not in fact challenge deeper conceptions of statehood; on the contrary, given that the Westphalian state is, according to the constructivist model of Gellner and others, bound symbiotically to the ideology of nationalism, it is widely understood that the principal, if not exclusive, political strategy of sub-state nationalist movements is simply to join the club of nation-states as presently ordered (MacPherson 1998). It follows, therefore, that sub-state nationalism is often considered to be an outmoded political strategy which seeks to secure a seat at the Westphalian table for sub-state national societies at a time when that table is itself being overturned or at least re-ordered. The dismissal of sub-state nationalism (and indeed of state nationalism) as outmoded political strategies is nicely captured in Hobsbawm's famous account: '...the phenomenon [nationalism] is past its peak. The owl of Minerva which brings wisdom, said Hegel, flies out at dusk. It is a good sign that it is now circling round nations and nationalism' (Hobsbawm 1990: 192). According to this account, rather than challenging traditional conceptions of statehood, sub-state nationalism in fact depends upon their survival and is accordingly as much threatened by the supra-state and sectoral rivals to the nation-state model as is the state itself. The death-knell of nationalism, sounded so loudly across the political spectrum in the modern age, and given new force by the political, economic and technological transformations in our time, rings as loudly, by way of these constructions, for the myopia of luddite minority nations, harking sentimentally after a bygone age, as it does for the conceit of the nation-state clinging doggedly to the last vestiges of its own imagined constitutional and political autarchy. And for good measure the dismissal of sub-state nationalism as a practical irrelevance is often accompanied by a normative critique of the phenomenon on the grounds that it is atavistic, reactionary and anti-historical (Ignatieff 1998; MacPherson 1998: 25–26).

It is submitted that this construction of sub-state nationalist movements misses certain important factors which do in fact work to link sub-state nationalism to the other sites of authority that rival the state, and *together* these three forces, albeit in differing ways, constitute a common challenge to the political capacity, and at times also to the legal competence, of the state. Furthermore, this linkage with globalising forces highlights that the reasons behind the re-emergence of sub-state nationalism at a time when the concept of the nation-state is being called into question, are in fact highly complex; and as such, it is simplistic to caricature this phenomenon as a last desperate attempt to leap aboard the sinking ship of statehood, just as this vessel disappears beneath the waves of globalisation. It is possible to turn to three arguments which challenge the stereotypical representation of the constitutional aspirations of sub-state nationalist movements as fatally misguided.

First, it can be argued that the nation-state never was, as statist constructions have assumed, the possessor of untrammelled sovereignty. The narrow positivist construction of sovereignty as the embodiment of absolute legal power seems to miss the relational dimension of sovereignty which has always linked the political and the legal. These aspects have combined in the constitution of sovereignty as (per Loughlin) a thing 'socially constructed' (Loughlin 2003: 73). In terms of this more nuanced politico-legal formulation, we might say that sovereignty has served, and continues to serve, as a *relative* as well as a *relational* concept, its viability dependent upon the strength of the differing factors impacting upon, and limiting the freedom of, the central governmental organs of the state. Therefore, in this sense the classical Westphalian formulation of the state as a legally autonomous unit was always an exercise in hyperbolic self-aggrandisement by states that failed to reflect the reality of international interdependence and the relative strengths and weaknesses of different states at different times (Krasner 1999). Furthermore, the forces which have served to limit the freedom to manoeuvre of particular states, and in doing so to restrict their sovereign sphere of operations in both de facto and at times *de jure* senses, have not been exclusively external. Sub-state forces, including sub-state national societies within plurinational states, have in certain cases been able to negotiate degrees of autonomy within the state. The existence of federal states is an obvious example of this process; but even in unitary states it has been possible for sub-state national societies to secure levels of autonomy, even though in unitary states, such as the UK and Spain, these measures of self-rule may not have been formally entrenched in the state's constitution. For example, Paterson has argued that, even before the devolution settlement embodied in the Scotland Act 1998, Scotland through 'administrative independence' enjoyed a level of autonomy comparable to other small European nations which, despite formal independent statehood, have always had to negotiate their autonomy in relation to big powers (Paterson 1994).[7] Also in Spain, while the Constitution of 1978 does provide for the autonomy of what have come to be known as the autonomous communities, the devolution of powers itself has operated upon an ad hoc basis through the bilateral negotiation of statutes of autonomy with the central state, a process which has been heavily contingent upon the political muscle of the sub-state territory in question (Fossas 1999: 6; Heywood 2000: 6).[8] So successful have Catalonia and other sub-state territories been in establishing strong models of autonomy through this semi-formal and largely unentrenched system that it is now widely argued that Spain, while still in formal terms a unitary state, is now in reality 'quasi-federal' (Moreno 2001a: 31; Heywood 1995: 162; Colomer 1999: 40–52; Börzel 2002).

Another related development has been the way in which sub-state national societies, armed with a sense of their own 'nationhood', have also asserted an international presence through the phenomenon which now enjoys the classification of 'paradiplomacy' (Michelmann and Soldatos 1990; Aldecoa and Keating 1999; Laitin 2001; Mitchell and Cavanagh 2001). In both these ways, sub-state national societies have developed spheres of operation which transcend traditional statal imaginings about political, and perhaps even legal, sovereignty; they have in certain cases been successful in negotiating power both within the supposedly monolithic construction of the sovereign state, and even within the 'billiard ball' world of international law and relations. In fact it is in many respects international law rather than the constitutional order of their own states which has held back radical approaches to shared sovereignty within particular plurinational states. The mythical notion of absolute sovereignty in the municipal sphere is in no small measure a construction of international legal theory which traditionally envisaged personality as a unitary concept and treated the central organs of government within a state as internally sovereign and indivisible. This may have helped bolster monistic conceptualisations of internal sovereignty in a formalistic legal sense even when in de facto terms internal sovereignty had long since been compromised and qualified. For example, a state cannot use federalism or other forms of internally 'divided sovereignty' as an excuse for its failure to comply with international obligations. In the context of the case studies addressed here, this has had serious knock-on effects for sub-state autonomy in those states which are members of strong international legal regimes, in particular the European Union or the Canada–US Free Trade Agreement of 1987 (Leslie 1994: 40).

The efforts made by sub-state nations to develop an international presence may suggest therefore, that as the constitutional authority of states weakens further both in terms of capacity and of formal competence[9] against the backdrop of the contemporary dynamics of the global economic and political environment, sub-state national societies may be well placed to exploit such developments further in order to find governmental space at both the reconstituted state level and at the developing 'extra-state' or 'post-state' levels, provided these opportunities are made available beyond the state. For example, proto-institutions at supra-state level, such as the Committee of the Regions within the EU, are already offering pathways, albeit rather weak ones, for these territories to develop an extra-state presence (Aldecoa and Keating 1999: 7; Azopardi 2009).

Second, although it seems incontestable that contemporary challenges presented at supra-national and sectoral levels do indeed constitute sites of authority which rival that of the nation-state, it is also necessary not to overstate this point, bearing in mind that the state remains in many respects very resilient (Loughlin 2003: 94–95. See also Loughlin 2000: 145; Brubaker 1996; Mann 1993: 118;

Moravcsik 1998). Even in the age of 'late sovereignty', a sense of balance should be maintained, as McCrone reminds us: 'It is too facile to claim that, in a globalised world, the age of the state is dead, although it is also now much harder to sustain the argument that the state is all-powerful' (McCrone 2001: 11). The state continues to perform important economic and political functions: a fact recognised by sub-state nationalist movements anxious to protect and foster their particular societies. Perhaps the main reason for the state's resilience is its control of territory and the continuing normative authority which comes with territorial jurisdiction. There is a strong functional dimension to territorial control. As Gagnon notes, territory, 'remains one of the rare areas within liberal democracies where it is still possible to maintain representation and to demand political accountability from political actors' (Gagnon 2001: 24). In this sense it can be argued that the resilience of the state also has a normative dimension. For example, it may be that a rule-bound international society can itself only be built upon nation-states which themselves respect the rule of law (Hirst and Thompson 1996: 190–194); and that it is only within identifiable territorial units of a manageable size that people can realistically form ties of identity and loyalty through which they can take part meaningfully in the democratic process.

Many sub-state nationalist movements are aware of those aspects of statehood which continue to offer the prospect of institutional defences against globalising tendencies; indeed, it is largely from recognition of the state's enduring potential that nationalism retains its potent political force today. Since the state retains important strengths, either greater autonomy within a strong state or even secession are attractive options for a sub-state national society. The latter option of course promises statehood itself, while the former allows the sub-state national society to govern itself within a host state which is itself a sufficiently robust environment to protect to some extent the autonomy regime from forces external to the state.

The third argument challenging stereotypical presentations of the constitutional aspirations of sub-state nationalist movements is the way in which these movements are both aware of, and prepared to harness for their own purposes, the changing role of the nation-state. In this sense the challenge presented by sub-state national societies to the nation-state does not portend a loss of power *from* the state (as does the challenge at the sectoral level), but rather the redistribution of power *within* it. From this observation it follows that the sub-state challenge is comparable to the supra-state challenge in that both represent the relocation of state power to alternative *territorial* sites; by contrast the sectoral challenge represents the diffusion of power to *deterritorialised* sites. It seems that the new supra-national and sectoral sites of authority which are challenging certain traditional statal roles are not necessarily considered by sub-state nationalists to constitute a threat to their aspirations for constitutional autonomy in the same ways and to the same extent that they are often perceived by state elites to present a danger to state authority. In fact, Keating and others contend that sub-state nationalist movements are developing highly imaginative strategies and progressive political agendas in the face of these globalising forces; and that, given the ways in which these sub-state movements envisage radical reconfigu-rations in the state polity, these strategies and agendas require a rethinking of traditional constitutional doctrine (Keating 2001c: 23; McCrone 1998: 182; Saleé 1996).

Although it is important not to overlook the fact that strains of 'statist' seces-sionism remain strong within nationalist discourse in Catalonia, Quebec and Scotland, in recent constitutional debates it seems that more powerful nationalist forces within these sub-state national societies are increasingly aware of the changing global context within which their political demands require to be artic-ulated, and that this growing realisation is resulting in debates which are far more sophisticated than might have been anticipated by those who consider sub-state nationalist movements to be monolithic in positioning their societies as 'proto-states in waiting'. For example, the European strategy of the independen-tist Scottish National Party is notable in this context, as is the 'Barcelona Decla-ration' of 1998 in which nationalist parties in the Basque Country, Catalonia and Galicia called for a reconfiguration of the Spanish state along plurinational lines and emphasised the increasing orientation of these parties towards the EU. In a related way, during the Quebec referendum campaign in 1995, the Quebec nationalist parties balanced their campaign for sovereignty by emphasising Que-bec's commitment to NAFTA.[10]

A related argument suggests that in some ways sub-state national societies are perhaps better prepared than the state to face these changing realities, because, with a long tradition of advancing strategies for constitutional change, national-ist movements within these territories are already acclimatised to the process of challenging and re-thinking fundamental questions of constitutional authority. It may be, therefore, that these societies are less prone to fetishise existing institu-tions and authority structures than are existing states instilled with a conviction of constitutional absolutism. For example, these territories have been quick to seize upon the opportunities to engage diplomatically beyond the state. These engagements can be formal (one example mentioned above is the Committee of the Regions of the EU), or more informal and bilateral ties as exemplified by the forging of cross-cultural links and economic ties between sub-state nations and regions in Europe; for example, Catalonia has worked through these less formal networks as one of the 'Four Motors of Europe', linking with Baden-Württemberg, Lombardy and Rhône-Alpes to promote itself as an advanced rather than a struggling economy.

At the same time, however, these processes of engaging beyond the state should not be seen as a sign that territorial attachments are no longer important. Instead the sub-state nation continues to provide some stability in an age of transformation. As Keating puts it: 'these identities ... provide a reference point for politics in a confusing world, in which the old concurrent spheres of state, nation and policy making systems no longer coincide' (Keating 2001b: 264). Inherent in this process then is a deep ambivalence which is also present among dominant or statal national societies themselves as they at once seek to take advantage of the opportunities of globalisation, but remain closely attached to their own societies. In this context McCrone suggests that the national unit offers a form of psychological security for the citizen trying to come to terms with an increasingly complex world: 'Nationalist movements can encapsulate cultural defence, the pursuit of political resources, as well as being vehicles for social identity in times of rapid social change...' In short, the sub-state nation, in a way similar to the dominant national society, provides both security and opportunity: 'it provides a sense of historical continuity coupled with strategies for addressing the future' (McCrone 2001: 11).[11]

Furthermore, sub-state nationalist movements are often forced by the logic of their own arguments to recognise that shifting patterns of statal authority also impact upon their own sub-state societies. For example, one nationalist strategy is to argue that external forces such as the EU, in restricting the existing governmental functions exercised by the host state within which the sub-state territory is located, make the state less important in governmental terms to the sub-state nation (hence 'independence in Europe' type arguments). Having recruited the influence of external forces to strengthen its argument that the relevance of the host state is in decline, and in drawing succour from the potential avenues offered to the sub-state national society by alternative normative and strategic sites of authority, it would be disingenuous, and indeed unsustainable, for the nationalist movement not to acknowledge that the pressures which undermine state power will also, albeit in different ways, undermine the scope for action of new, smaller nation-states or increasingly autonomous units within larger states; even if sub-state nationalists will still maintain that such smaller units are better able to cope with, and respond to, these external pressures. Therefore, these groups need to formulate constitutional agendas which, in light of these changes, must be meaningfully contextualised if they are to meet with any possibility of implementation. For example, *realpolitik* applies in any claim to 'sovereignty': 'sovereignty consists of a *plausible claim to ultimate authority* made on behalf of a particular polity' (Walker 2002: 345). This reality serves to condition autonomy claims, rendering terms like 'independence' and 'separation' increasingly redundant, a point that will be developed in Section 3.

Thus far an attempt has been made to introduce the sub-state national challenge to plurinational states in the context of wider forces which today operate to constrict the existing politico-constitutional capacity and competence of the nation-state. It has been argued that in one sense the classical Westphalian formulation of the state as a politically self-contained and legally autonomous unit was always a caricature that failed to reflect international interdependence and the relative strengths and weaknesses of different states at different times (Simpson 2004); and that this characterisation also served to under-estimate the existing role of sub-state territories in limiting central state authority. It has also been suggested however, that this is not the whole story, and that this historical reality requires to be tempered by an appreciation that in many other ways the power of the nation-state endures in important respects. It is therefore within this complex environment of wider global change set against the endurance of state power, that the constitutional agendas of sub-state national societies need to be reformulated. On the one hand, insofar as the state does retain power in the contemporary world, an increasingly autonomous sub-state nation can use this comfort-zone to extend its territorial authority within the state by drawing upon those strategies which it has always used to negotiate governmental space within the state (and indeed beyond it, through paradiplomacy); and on the other hand, sub-state national societies must also attempt to find new opportunities even in the face of those contemporary processes of both deterritorialisation (the sectoral challenge) and reterritorialisation (the supra-state challenge) which do, despite the continuing viability of the nation-state, in many ways both supplant the governmental capacity, and compromise the competence, of the nation-state model in novel and deeply penetrative ways. Thus, sub-state national societies are perhaps in a useful position to produce imaginative governmental strategies, given the predisposition towards constitutional change which has long informed their political practice, and given the practical opportunities which increasingly fluid normative sites now seem to offer to flexible political operators.

Having introduced and attempted to contextualise the sub-state national society challenge to plurinational states in this way, the chapter will now address in more detail the ways in which sub-state national societies themselves represent a rival site of authority which works to bring about a reconception of the plurinational nation-state, in particular by the ways in which they challenge traditional constructions of the state's constitutional self-understanding. In this sense it will be suggested that the constitutional aspirations of sub-state national societies such as Catalonia, Quebec and Scotland are more nuanced than is often thought; and that the models of institutional change now being advocated within these territories focus increasingly upon reconfiguring relations with their respective host states in preference to secession and full statehood.

3 Eschewing secession?: sub-state national societies in a complex world

Insofar as the sub-state national society challenge to the constitutional authority of particular states links with supra-state and sectoral forces in contesting established certainties concerning the nation-state, it does so at the most fundamental level by challenging traditional monistic conceptions of internal constitutional sovereignty with radically reconfigured models of authority.[12] Forces operating at supra-state and sectoral levels clearly challenge the ways in which state sovereignty can manifest itself *externally*. But in penetrating deep into the legislative and executive roles of the domestic branches of government, they also compromise the reality of the state's municipal sovereignty; in other words, they constrict the capacity and at times even the competence of the state constitution to act as the ultimate repository of governmental power which supposedly allocates and co-ordinates in totality the division of public legal functions operating within the state's territory. Elaborating further upon this dynamic, the vision of 'the encompassing constitution' is now called into question both in explanatory terms for its continuing capacity to describe in an authentic way recent and ongoing transformations in the relations of power between the state and external forces; and, in prescriptive terms, for its suitability to meet the changing demands made by citizens which stem from these transforming relations of power. For example, Catalan nationalists argue that the formal description of Catalonia as merely an autonomous community within Spain, fails to take account of its unique 'national' status (a conviction shared by nationalists in the Basque Country and Galicia); similarly Quebec nationalists refute the monistic national assumptions which underpin symmetrical federalism in Canada. Interestingly, by contrast, the highly diverse models of devolution in the United Kingdom are considerably more sensitive to the historical and societal differences which demarcate Scotland, Wales and Northern Ireland both from England and from one another.

It is in the dual context of transforming relations of power and concomitant alterations in the expectations of citizens that the sub-state national society challenge must be cast. It has been noted in passing that the sub-state challenge to the sovereign authority of the state and its constitutional apparatus can manifest itself in two differing aspirations: first, the desire to withdraw from the state, or second the intention to reconstitute intra-state relations through some measure of accommodation short of secession. These aspirations will now be discussed further in order to draw out the implications they might hold for constitutional sovereignty. The former aspiration, secession, is the spectre which sub-state nationalism is so often deemed to represent, and at first sight it seems the more threatening of these two challenges to the state's authority, in particular to its notion of constitutional sovereignty. The second and apparently less radical challenge is posed today by sub-state national society demands for increased autonomy and representation within, and better recognition by, the state. It is becoming ever more the case that both the political strategy of nationalist groups within sub-state national societies and the reality of ongoing processes of institutional accommodation within plurinational states, tend towards the latter process (internal accommodation) through the pursuit of complex and case-specific models for the reconstitution of sub-state – host state relations.

Therefore, while strong separatist movements do exist, nationalist opinion within plurinational states is veering increasingly towards enhanced autonomy and representation within, and better recognition by, the state, in preference to full-blooded secessionism. There seem to be several reasons for this. First, it has been observed that in the modern world, the larger state, insofar as it retains power, might act as a bulwark against external forces which would otherwise undermine sub-state autonomy just as they weaken the state's power. The attractions of such an arrangement have taken hold particularly within Catalan nationalism where the dominant strategy is to develop a stronger role in Europe in conjunction with strong ties to the rest of Spain (McRoberts 2001a: 68).[13] Therefore, even when a sub-state national society advances a strategy which appears to be secessionist, the constitutional outcome it in fact seeks is often a heavily compromised version of statehood which bears little resemblance to the traditional Westphalian model. For example, the three main Quebec nationalist parties in advance of the Quebec referendum on 'sovereignty' in 1995 made a pact whereby, in the event of a victory for the nationalist side, they would seek to negotiate an economic and political partnership with the rest of Canada. As Robert Young observes, this was a notion of sovereignty with a strong insurance policy stemming from continued close association with Canada: 'sovereignty would bring gains on several fronts while the partnership would protect voters from short-term economic losses and eventual isolation from Canada' (Young 1999: 24). With this partnership model Quebec nationalists proposed that Quebec would keep the Canadian currency, maintain free trade between Canada and a 'sovereign' Quebec through joint institutions, and create the option of joint Quebec–Canada citizenship for its residents (Simeon 2001: 51; Seymour 2000: 245–247; Newman 1999: 12).[14] Quebec is but one example; nationalists in Catalonia and Scotland have also developed nuanced approaches to 'independence', in the hope that the sub-state society can negotiate considerable influence within supra-state bodies without seceding from the host state;[15] and in this respect the line between the aspiration for statehood and that for autonomy can itself become blurred.[16]

Another reason why solutions short of full secession are preferred is that there are often strong identity and loyalty ties between the sub-state national society and the host state; sub-state national societies such as Catalonia, Quebec and Scotland see Spain, Canada and the UK respectively, as a product of a union or compact between or among nations (Rokkan and Urwin 1982: 11; O'Neill 2000; Romney 1999; Resina 2002). Certainly resentment may arise from a sense within the sub-state national society that the identity of the state has been appropriated by a dominant society within it. But despite this, the state can remain a constitutional construct which the sub-state national society, as a founding partner, feels a deep bond with and a vested interest in. The lingering attachment which members of sub-state national societies often show to the state can surprise political elites. Indeed, it was evidence of such attachments to the Canadian state, derived from extensive consultation with ordinary Quebecers as to their preferred constitutional options in 1995, which led Quebec nationalists to formulate a pact on economic and political partnership with Canada, and in doing so to water down what had been a much more 'statist' plan for Quebec 'sovereignty'. The results of this consultation process which indicated that attachments to Canada remained strong even among Quebec nationalists, were borne out in opinion polls conducted after the 1995 referendum which have shown that support for 'sovereignty' for Quebec increases when the prospect of partnership with Canada is certain, with one poll suggesting that only 30 per cent would support sovereignty if there was to be no prospect of such a partnership (Young 1999: 41).

Therefore, the complexity in the constitutional models which are now advocated by sub-state nationalists, encompassing as they do radical autonomy combined with continued relations with the state and supra-state bodies, mirrors the deeply complex patterns of identity to be found among members of sub-state national societies in relation to the various 'sites of identity' which attract their loyalty. Recent research highlights identity trends within plurinational states which are to some degree fluid, with complex matrices of shared and multi-layered identities appearing in the data. This level of complexity and fluidity in patterns of identity formation and change provides another link between the sub-state national challenge and the other alternative authority sites which have been mentioned; in particular, it links sub-state nationalism to the supra-state challenge, where observers of, for example, the EU have also identified a relationship between weakening state power and changing identity patterns (Bond and Rosie 2002; McCrone and Paterson 2002). From this it has been argued that national identity is in fact used strategically by citizens for political purposes, and can shift according to the respective political advantages which might be derived from the variegated application of identities in differing political environments. As David McCrone, a sociologist who has carried out extensive empirical research in the area of national identity within plurinational states, argues:

> there is something quite calculative about national identity which shifts according to political circumstances. It is far less a matter of sentiment than it is of political practice ... the issue, in other words, is not which one you are, but which you choose according to circumstance and purpose.
>
> (McCrone 2001: 9)

An example of this is the different voting patterns which occur in Catalonia in general elections as opposed to elections to the *Generalitat*; a phenomenon which suggests that voters use their identities in different, and often opportunistic, ways (De Rafael 1998; Roller 2001: 218.) This has led Moreno to comment:

> I think we ought to reconsider both the premises and implications of all-embracing identities, for they are increasingly untenable. While being corroded by the forces of globalization, these identities are also subject to fragmentation, competition and overlap with numerous other senses of belonging.
>
> (Moreno 2001b: 201)

In this context, the practical difficulties for any territory in becoming a new state – for example, the establishment of a currency, or the problems in joining international organisations[17] – would seem to weigh heavily in any debate over the constitutional future.

A third factor for the increasing preference for accommodation within the state in place of secession is that pre-existing patterns of constitutional accommodation can themselves set new terms for the constitutional debate between sub-state national society and host state. In some sense constitutional reform brings with it what might be called 'institutional capture', whereby future debate on constitutional options is reframed through the prism of already evolving arrangements.[18] For example, the recent implementation of devolution in the UK has established new terms for the nationalist debate on future developments, forcing nationalist groups, not just in Scotland, but also in Wales and Northern

Ireland, to re-articulate their demands for further accommodation in light of the following realities: the perceived success or failure of the new institutional arrangements in meeting sub-state demands; and the extent to which sub-state actors have been successful in managing the new autonomy regimes. For example, by the time of the Scottish parliamentary elections of 2003 it seemed that support for independence in Scotland had waned partly due to a widespread sense of disillusionment with the performance of the devolved Parliament since its inauguration in 1999.[19] In a similar way, the debate surrounding Quebec's aspirations within Canada has been heavily influenced by the constitutional developments of the past twenty years involving the controversial patriation of the constitution from the United Kingdom in 1980, and the failed constitutional initiatives of the draft Meech Lake Accord of 1987 and the draft Charlottetown Accord of 1992, where attempts were made to amend the Canadian constitution in order to meet at least some of Quebec's constitutional aspirations. While these initiatives remained credible, the Quebec nationalist elite approached the issue of constitutional reform in more incremental ways, and although many remained staunchly committed to seeking full statehood for Quebec irrespective of progress made in these constitutional negotiations, moderate nationalists turned to more radical 'sovereignty' options in 1995 largely as a result of the failure of these negotiations. The influence of existing institutions on contemporary constitutional practice is also borne out simply in terms of the level, and sophistication, of constitutional activity in Canada in the 1980s and 1990s. In comparative terms, since the 1970s, the constitutional demands of sub-state national societies in the UK and Spain have tended to be far more restrained than Quebec's and one reason for this is that nationalists in Catalonia and Scotland began their engagement with their respective host state from a position in which they lacked entrenched institutional power, whereas the ambition of Quebec nationalists was in large measure conditioned by the fact that they were seeking to build on an already very decentralised federal model (Meadwell 2001: 56).

Therefore, in light of these three factors, and taking into account what has been said about the context of wider global and regional developments, it is possible to say that the agenda of sub-state nationalism is now being reshaped within the context of two types of highly changeable and widely differentiated process. They are: first, the overarching spectre of external forces at supra-national and sectoral levels which to some extent refine the parameters within which constitutional change is negotiated and implemented; and second, the processes of negotiation and change themselves which, through both the development of a discourse common to all parties, and the evolution of these engagements into substantive outcomes, set both the institutional context, and the patterns of engagement, for their future evolution.[20] It is within these two processes that sub-state nationalists develop ever more nuanced political goals which, in taking account of the complex shifts in institutional and behavioural reality at levels both internal and external to the state, and of the fluidity of identity patterns within the sub-state territory, serve to reconstitute nationalist aspirations. This can lead to the formulation of highly imaginative solutions for the perceived constitutional malaise of the sub-state national society in question, helping to ensure that these prescriptive remedies will be tempered by, and framed against, the *realpolitik* of this broader constitutional and political environment.

In this context it seems that the search for sophisticated models of accommodation within the state may in fact pose a more radical challenge to the state and its constitutional arrangements than does secession. Although sub-state national societies continue to identify with the host state, this should disguise neither the strength of sub-state nationalism nor the increasingly radical demands for a reconfiguration of the state constitution made by sub-state nationalist movements. For many citizens within sub-state national societies, these societies represent alternative *demoi* which should be recognised as constitutional co-equals by the constitution of the state (Requejo 2001a). Such demands, if taken seriously by the state, can call into question many of the constitution's most profound self-understandings including even the conception of unitary citizenship which has been an article of faith for state-building processes (Carens 2000; Tierney 2007).

By contrast, secession need not undermine the state's constitutional self-understanding in a significant way. Here it is helpful to consider the distinction between secession and revolution. On the one hand, secession occurs when a group removes itself and a piece of territory from the jurisdiction of the state. This differs from revolution: 'being aimed only at restricting the scope of the state's power, not dissolving it, [secession] does not, like revolution, require (though in fact it may result in) the overthrow of the government' (Buchanan 1991: 10). Secession, therefore, does not necessarily pose any threat to the state's continuing constitutional authority over the remainder state, and accordingly may not require significant constitutional change beyond recognition, and then only de facto, of the act of secession. It simply involves a reduction in the size of territory over which the state and its constitution have jurisdiction; and in fact, through the withdrawal of a disgruntled minority, the political viability of the existing constitution may be consolidated. There is no doubt that secession can have a profound effect on the collective psychology of the remainder population, but purely in terms of the normative authority of the constitution, the effects need only be minimal. Neither, certainly, is it the case that a radical model of constitutional change designed to accommodate sub-state national societies is equivalent to revolution; once again there is no act of overthrowing the recognised government of the state. However, in their ever more imaginative manifestations, radical demands for constitutional recognition of the plurinational nature of the state do call into question fundamental assumptions about the allocation of normative authority within the constitution, particularly when they involve calls for 'shared sovereignty' by way of, for example, asymmetrical autonomy;[21] sub-state veto rights within the state's constitutional amendment arrangements and/or other decision-making processes;[22] and full and co-equal decision-making powers for sub-state national societies at the centre of the state.[23] Although these demands stop short of calling for a break-up of the state, in seeking a radical reconfiguration of the state's constitution they do call for a conceptual revision of many of the central tenets of the state's dominant constitutional ideology in a way that secessionist demands do not.

4 Conclusion

The contemporary agendas of sub-state nationalist movements within Canada, Spain and the UK are in many ways more complex, and in particular less 'secessionist', than is often assumed. In proposing radical constitutional change within the state, the dynamic of contemporary nationalism also impacts upon the traditional explanatory and prescriptive language through which constitutional arrangements are discussed. It is indeed inevitable that the increasing sophistication of sub-state nationalism which shakes institutional statal certainties such as monistic conceptions of sovereignty, should also challenge existing constitutional theory and discourse. In other words, the challenge to state constitutions is no less a challenge to the way in which these constitutions are articulated and their fundamental principles debated. Therefore, constitutional language as much as political institutions is now also a point of contestation in plurinational states, as a consequence of perceptions within sub-state national societies that the reality of the plurinational state as a union of nations is not adequately represented in established constitutional norms and principles, or at least in the dominant interpretations and narrations of these norms and principles.

These complex constitutional debates *within* the plurinational state also have implications for debates concerning sovereignty *beyond* the state. These implications, made manifest through the ways in which sub-state nationalism links to wider changes at sectoral and supra-state levels, are only beginning to play themselves out. What seems clear is that the full part which sub-state nationalism plays in the debate over globalisation must be recognised if the changing nature of constitutionalism within modern, territorially diverse democracies is to be adequately understood.

Notes

1 For Thomas Franck the phenomenon of neo-nationalism has been termed 'post-modern neo-tribalism' (Franck 1995: 140–141) and for Michael Ignatieff, it is 'the narcissism of minor differences' (Ignatieff 1999: 91–102).
2 This study is restricted to a specific set of liberal democracies and the author makes no claim as to whether or not this analysis might be applied more generally to other cases of sub-state nationalism.
3 The term 'late sovereignty' suggests that the age of state sovereignty, even within the European Union, is far from over (Walker 2003). This term is a more accurate description of our age than the often-used and overstated term: 'post-sovereignty'.
4 This process of 'externalisation' takes place whether the aim is statehood, as in the Scottish National Party's 'independence in Europe' strategy, or increased autonomy within the state which will also involve enhanced powers of 'paradiplomacy', as is to be found in the mainstream Catalan nationalism of the *Convergència i Unió* (Nash 2003).

5 A central contention of the chapter is that sub-state nationalism and separatism are not synonyms.
6 It should be noted from the beginning that any presentation of the Peace of West-phalia of 1648 as the defining moment in the birth of the modern nation-state is of course simplistic and largely inaccurate, but insofar as the term 'Westphalia' has passed into common juridical parlance to encapsulate untrammelled state power it continues to serve as a useful caricature.
7 See also Mitchell (1968: 209), and Walker who notes how historically Scotland has been able to use the unitary state to its advantage (Walker 2001: 112).
8 Note the changes to the Catalan Statute of Autonomy in 2006: Organic Law 6/2006 of 19 July, on the Reform of the Statute of Autonomy of Catalonia, *Parlament de Cat-alunya*. Available at www.parlament-cat.net/porteso/estatut/estatut_angles_100506.pdf.
9 Supra-state organisations such as the EU certainly challenge the constitutional com-petence as well as the capacity of Member States – Case 6/64, *Costa* v. *ENEL* [1964] ECR 1141.
10 See respectively: SNP Election Manifesto, April 2003, and Scottish Executive White Paper (2007), 'Choosing Scotland's Future: A National Conversation', Edinburgh: Scottish Executive, paras 3.21–3.27; *Declaració de Barcelona*, Barcelona: Con-vergència i Unió (1998) at 1; Young (1999: 14).
11 Even current plans for independence refer significantly to an ongoing social union (para. 3.25) and partnership (para. 3.27) with the rest of the UK: Scottish Executive White Paper (2007), 'Choosing Scotland's Future: A National Conversation', Edin-burgh: Scottish Executive. Notably, despite the fact that a SNP government now rules in Scotland support for independence has shown no notable increase and may even be falling away. 'SNP election victory not based on increased support for independence', National Centre for Social Research, paper (2007).
12 The use of the term 'monistic' here denotes a unitary construction of the *internal* sov-ereignty of the state, centred around a singular conception of the *demos*; it is not used in the technical legal sense to describe the domestic legal order's *external* relationship to international law.
13 On the general realignment of sub-state nationalism in the context of Europe see Jeffery (2000).
14 Since then the impetus for another referendum has been weak and the Quebec polit-ical agenda remains predominantly reformist rather than secessionist.
15 The term 'nationalist' is used in a broad sense here to include non-secessionist nation-alist parties such as the Scottish Labour Party, the Scottish Liberal Democrats and the *Convergència i Unió* in Catalonia.
16 Although the success of these ventures by Catalonia, Quebec and Scotland have hith-erto been very mixed. For example, on Catalonia see Balcells (1995: 197).
17 For example, during the 1995 referendum campaign, Canada threatened to veto any attempt by an independent Quebec to join NAFTA. See comments by Minister of Intergovernmental Affairs, Marcel Massé quoted in the *Globe and Mail*, 10 December 1994.
18 This argument draws upon the power of institutions as set out by the 'new institution-alist' school of political science. See, for example, Peters (1999).
19 The SNP did however form the government after 2007 and plans a referendum on independence in 2010. Scottish Executive White Paper (2007), 'Choosing Scotland's Future: A National Conversation', Edinburgh: Scottish Executive. The unionist parties also support further autonomy for Scotland, short of secession. Commission on Scot-tish Devolution, 'Serving Scotland Better: Scotland and the United Kingdom in the 21st Century', Edinburgh: Scottish Parliament (2009).
20 For example, one way in which the legislative power of the devolved Scottish Parlia-ment is limited is that it may not legislate incompatibly with either EC law or 'Con-

vention rights' per the European Convention on Human Rights – (Scotland Act 1998, section 29(2)(d)). Debate on Scotland's future constitutional options will of necessity be framed within these strictures, which also represent the reality for any governmental authority within Europe today (Himsworth 2001; Tierney 2001; Tierney 2009).

21 Catalan arguments for asymmetry within Spain are discussed by: Moreno (2001a); Requejo (2001b); and Villadangos (1999). For similar discussions re Canada, see: Leslie (1994); Resnick (1994); and McRoberts (2001b).

22 Various experiments in this regard were attempted during the final years of the Austro-Hungarian empire, see Plasseraud (2000). Such a right of veto has been a firm demand made by Quebec since patriation of the constitution from the UK through the Constitution Act 1982 (McRoberts 1997: 16–17; Oliver 1999: 534, and 544, fns 106–107).

23 Each of these demands appears in the Barcelona Declaration and in other proposals made by Catalan nationalist parties (*Declaració de Barcelona* op. cit.; Roller op. cit. at 211).

References

Aldecoa, F. and Keating, M. (eds) (1999) *Paradiplomacy in Action: The Foreign Relations of Subnational Governments*, London: Frank Cass.

Aldecoa, F. and Keating, M. (1999) 'Introduction', in F. Aldecoa and M. Keating (eds) *Paradiplomacy in Action: The Foreign Relations of Subnational Governments*, London: Frank Cass, pp. 1–16.

Anderson, B. (1991) *Imagined Communities: Reflections on the Origin and Spread of Nationalism*, London: Verso.

Azopardi, K. (2009) *Sovereignty and the Stateless Nation: Gibraltar in the Modern Legal Context*, Oxford: Hart Publishing.

Balcells, A. (1995) *Catalan Nationalism: Past and Present*, London: MacMillan.

Beitz, C.R. (1994) 'Cosmopolitan Liberalism and the States System', in C. Brown (ed.) *Political Restructuring in Europe. Ethical Perspectives*, London: Routledge.

Bond, R. and Rosie, M. (2002) 'National Identities in Post-Devolution Scotland', Institute of Governance paper, Edinburgh: Institute of Governance, University of Edinburgh.

Börzel, T.A. (2000) 'From Competitive Regionalism to Co-operative Federalism: The Europeanization of the Spanish State of the Autonomies', *Publius* 30: 17–142.

Börzel, T.A. (2002) *States and Regions in the European Union. Institutional Adaptation in Germany and Spain*, Cambridge: Cambridge University Press.

Breuilly, J. (1993) *Nationalism and the State*, 2nd edn, Manchester: Manchester University Press.

Brubaker, R. (1996) *Nationalism Reframed: Nationhood and the National Question in the New Europe*, Cambridge: Cambridge University Press.

Buchanan, A. (1991) *Secession: The Morality of Political Divorce from Fort Sumter to Lithuania and Quebec*, Boulder, CO: Westview Press.

Carens, J.H. (2000) *Culture, Citizenship and Community*, Oxford: Oxford University Press.

Cass, D.Z. (2001) 'The "Constitutionalization" of International Trade Law: Judicial Norm-Generation as the Engine of Constitutional Development in International Trade', *European Journal of International Law* 12: 39–75.

Chalmers, D. (2000) 'Postnationalism and the Quest for Constitutional Substitutes', *Journal of Law and Society* 27: 178–217.

Choudhry, S. and McGarry, J. (eds) (2008) *Constitutional Design for Divided Societies: Integration or Accommodation?*, Oxford: Oxford University Press.

Christodoulidis, E. (1998) *Law and Reflexive Politics*, Dordrecht: Kluwer.

Colomer, J.M. (1999) 'The Spanish "State of the Autonomies": Non-institutional Federalism', in P. Heywood (ed.) *Politics and Policy in Democratic Spain*, London: Frank Cass, pp. 40–52.

Curtin, D.M. (1997) *Postnational Democracy*, Utrecht: Universiteit Utrecht.

De Rafael, G.H. (1998) 'An Empirical Survey of Social Structure and Nationalistic Identification in Spain in the 1990s', *Nations and Nationalism* 4: 35–59.

Deutsch, K. (1966) *Nationalism and Social Communication: An Enquiry into the Foundations of Nationality*, Cambridge, MA: MIT Press.

Fossas, E. (1999) 'Asymmetry and Plurinationality in Spain', Working Paper 167, *Institut de Ciències Politiques i Socials*, Barcelona: Universitat Autònoma de Barcelona.

Franck, T. (1995) *Fairness in International Law and Institutions*, Oxford: Oxford University Press.

Gagnon, A. (2001) 'Quebec: The Emergence of a Region-State?', *Scottish Affairs* 14–27.

Gellner, E. (1964) *Thought and Change*, London: Weidenfeld and Nicholson.

Gellner, E. (1983) *Nations and Nationalism*, Oxford: Blackwell.

Habermas, J. (1999) 'The European Nation-State and the Pressures of Globalization', *New Left Review* 235: 46–59.

Habermas, J. and Pensky, M. (2001) *The Postnational Constellation: Political Essays*, Cambridge: Polity Press.

Hardt, M. and Negri, A. (2000) *Empire*, Cambridge, MA: Harvard University Press.

Harel, L. (2003) 'The International Relations of the National Assembly of Quebec', *Canadian Parliamentary Review* 26: 4–7.

Held, D. (1988) 'Farewell to the Nation-State', *Marxism Today*, December, 12–17.

Held, D., McGrew, A., Goldblatt, D. and Perraton, J. (eds) (1999) *Global Transformations*, Cambridge: Polity Press.

Heywood, P. (1995) *The Government and Politics of Spain*, London: MacMillan.

Heywood, P. (2000) 'Spanish Regionalism, a Case Study', Working Documents in the Study of European Governance, No. 2, Nottingham: CSEG.

Himsworth, C. (2001) 'Rights Versus Devolution', in T. Campbell, K. Ewing and A. Tomkins (eds) *Sceptical Essays on Human Rights*, Oxford: Oxford University Press.

Hirst, P. and Thompson, G. (1996) *Globalization in Question*, Cambridge: Polity Press.

Hobsbawm, E.J. (1990) *Nations and Nationalism since 1780: Programme, Myth, Reality*, Cambridge: Cambridge University Press.

Holmes, S. (1995) *Passions and Constraints: On the Theory of Liberal Democracy*, Chicago: Chicago University Press.

Ignatieff, M. (1998) *The Warrior's Honour: Ethnic War and the Modern Conscience*, New York: Metropolitan Books.

Ignatieff, M. (1999) 'The Narcissism of Minor Differences', in R. Beiner (ed.) *Theorizing Nationalism*, Albany: State University of New York Press.

Jeffery, C. (2000) 'Sub-National Mobilization and European Integration', *Journal of Common Market Studies* 38(1): 1–24.

Keating, M. (2001a) *Plurinational Democracy: Stateless Nations in a Post-sovereignty Era*, Oxford: Oxford University Press.

Keating, M. (2001b) *Nations Against the State – The New Politics of Nationalism in Quebec, Catalonia and Scotland*, 2nd edn, UK: Palgrave.

Keating, M. (2001c) 'Managing the Multinational State: Constitutional Settlement in the United Kingdom', in T.C. Salmon and M. Keating (eds) *The Dynamics of*

Decentralization: Canadian Federalism and British Devolution, Montreal/London: McGill/Queens University Press.

Krasner, S.D. (1999) *Sovereignty: Organized Hypocrisy*, Oxford: Oxford University Press.

Ladeur, K.H. (1997) 'Towards a Legal Theory of Supranationality – The Viability of the Network Concept', *European Law Journal* 3: 33–54.

Laitin, D. (2001) 'National Identities in the Emerging European State', in M. Keating and J. McGarry (eds) *Minority Nationalism and the Changing International Order*, Oxford: Oxford University Press.

Latouche, D. (1993) '"Quebec, See Canada": Quebec Nationalism in the New Global Age', in A.-G. Gagnon (ed.) *Quebec: State and Society*, 2nd edn, Scarborough, Ontario: Nelson Canada.

Leslie, P.M. (1994) 'Asymmetry: Rejected, Conceded, Imposed', in F. Leslie Seidle (ed.) *Seeking a New Canadian Partnership: Asymmetrical and Confederal Options*, Montreal: Institute for Research on Public Policy, pp. 37–69.

Loughlin, M. (2000) *Sword and Scales: An Examination of the Relationship Between Law and Politics*, Oxford: Hart Publishing.

Loughlin, M. (2003) *The Idea of Public Law*, Oxford: Oxford University Press.

MacCormick, N. (1999) *Questioning Sovereignty: Law, State and Nation in the European Commonwealth*, Oxford: Oxford University Press.

MacPherson, J.M. (1998) *Is Blood Thicker Than Water?: Crises of Nationalism in the Modern World*, Toronto: Vintage Books Canada.

McCrone, D. (1998) *The Sociology of Nationalism: Tomorrow's Ancestors*, London: Routledge.

McCrone, D. (2001) 'Neo-Nationalism in Stateless Nations', *Scottish Affairs* 3–13.

McCrone, D. and Paterson, L. (2002) 'The Conundrum of Scottish Independence', *Scottish Affairs* 35–56.

McRoberts, K. (1997) *Misconceiving Canada: The Struggle for National Unity*, Toronto: Oxford University Press.

McRoberts, K. (2001a) *Catalonia: Nation Building without a State*, Toronto: Oxford University Press.

McRoberts, K. (2001b) 'Canada and the Multinational State', *Canadian Journal of Political Science* 34: 683–714.

Mann, M. (1993) 'Nation-states in Europe and Other Continents: Diversifying, Developing, not Dying', *Daedalus* 122: 115–140.

Marks, S. (2000) *The Riddle of all Constitutions: International Law, Democracy, and the Critique of Ideology*, Oxford: Oxford University Press.

Meadwell, H. (2001) 'The Future of Quebec', *Scottish Affairs* 54–64.

Michelmann, H. and Soldatos, P. (eds) (1990) *Federalism and International Relations: The Role of Sub-units*, Oxford: Clarendon Press.

Mitchell, J.D.B. (1968) *Constitutional Law*, 2nd edn, Edinburgh: Green.

Mitchell, J. and Cavanagh, M. (2001) 'Context and Contingency: Constitutional Nationalists and Europe', in M. Keating and J. McGarry (eds) *Minority Nationalism and the Changing International Order*, Oxford: Oxford University Press, pp. 246–263.

Moore, M. (2001) 'Globalization, Cosmopolitanism, and Minority Nationalism', in M. Keating and J. McGarry (eds) *Minority Nationalism and the Changing International Order*, Oxford: Oxford University Press, pp. 44–60.

Moravcsik, A. (1998) *The Choice for Europe: Social Purpose and State Power from Messina to Maastricht*, London: Routledge.

Moreno, L. (2001a) *The Federalization of Spain*, London: Cass.

Moreno, L. (2001b) 'Ethnoterritorial Concurrence in Multinational Societies: The Spanish Comunidades Autónomas', in A. Gagnon, C. Taylor and J. Tully (eds) *Multinational Democracies*, Cambridge: Cambridge University Press, pp. 201–221.

Nairn, T. (1977) *The Break-Up of Britain: Crisis and Neo-Nationalism*, London: New Left Books.

Nash, E. (2003) 'Catalonians Rattle Madrid with Bid for Sovereign Power', *Independent*, 26 March.

Newman, W.J. (1999) *The Quebec Secession Reference: The Rule of Law and the Position of the Attorney General of Canada*, Canada: York University Press.

Oliver, P. (1999) 'Canada, Quebec and Constitutional Amendment', *University of Toronto Law Journal* 49: 519–610.

O'Neill, M. (2000) 'Great Britain', *Parliamentary Affairs* 53: 69–95.

Paterson, L. (1994) *Autonomy of Modern Scotland*, Edinburgh: Edinburgh University Press.

Peters, B.G. (1999) *Institutional Theory in Political Science: The New Institutionalism*, London: Continuum.

Plasseraud, Y. (2000) 'How to Solve Cultural Identity Problems: Choose your Own Nation', *Le Monde Diplomatique*, May.

Rae, H. (2002) *State Identities and the Homogenisation of Peoples*, Cambridge: Cambridge University Press.

Reinhard, W. (ed.) (1996) *Power Elites and State Building*, Oxford: Clarendon Press.

Requejo, F. (1999) 'La Acomodación 'Federal' de la Plurinacionalidad. Democracia Liberal y Federalismo Plural en España', in E. Fossas and F. Requejo (eds) *Asimetría Federal y Estado Plurinacional. El Debate Sobre la Acomodación de la Diversidad en Canadá, Bélgica y España*, Madrid: Trotta, pp. 303–344.

Requejo, F. (2001a) 'Democratic Legitimacy and National Pluralism', in F. Requejo (ed.) *Democracy and National Pluralism*, London: Routledge, pp. 157–177.

Requejo, F. (2001b) 'Federalism and the Quality of Democracy in Plurinational Contexts: Present Shortcomings and Possible Improvements', Workshop Paper, ECPR Joint Sessions of Workshops, Grenoble: ECPR.

Requejo, F. (2001c) 'Political Liberalism in Multinational States: The Legitimacy of Plural and Asymmetrical Federalism', in A. Gagnon, C. Taylor and J. Tully (eds) *Multinational Democracies*, Cambridge: Cambridge University Press, pp. 110–132.

Requejo, F. (2005) *Multinational Federalism and Value Pluralism*, London and New York: Routledge.

Resina, J.R. (2002) 'Post-national Spain? Post-Spanish Spain?', *Nations and Nationalism* 8: 377–396.

Resnick, P. (1994) 'Toward a Multinational Federalism: Asymmetrical and Confederal Alternatives', in F. Leslie Seidle (ed.) *Seeking a New Canadian Partnership: Asymmetrical and Confederal Options*, Montreal: Institute for Research on Public Policy, pp. 71–94.

Rokkan, S. and Urwin, D. (1982) 'Introduction: Centres and Peripheries in Western Europe', in S. Rokkan and D. Urwin (eds) *The Politics of Territorial Identity: Studies in European Regionalism*, London: Sage, pp. 1–17.

Roller, E. (2001) 'The March 2000 General Election in Spain', *Government and Opposition* 36: 209–229.

Romney, P. (1999) *Getting it Wrong: How Canadians Forgot Their Past and Imperiled Confederation*, Toronto: Toronto University Press.

Saleé, D. (1996) 'La Mondialisation et la Construction de l'Identité au Québec', in M.

Elbaz, A. Fortin and G. Laforest (eds) *Les Frontiéres de l'Identité: Modernité et Post-modernisme au Quebéc*, Sainte-Foy: Les Presses de l'Université de Laval.

Salmon, T.C. (2001) 'Oxymorons: The Scottish Parliament, the European Union and International Relations?', in T.C. Salmon and M. Keating (eds) *The Dynamics of Decentralization: Canadian Federalism and British Devolution*, Montreal/London: McGill/Queens University Press, pp. 63–84.

Salmon, T.C. and Keating, M. (eds) (2001) *The Dynamics of Decentralization: Canadian Federalism and British Devolution*, Montreal/London: McGill/Queens University Press, pp. 63–84.

Seymour, M. (2000) 'Quebec and Canada at the Crossroads: A Nation within a Nation', *Nations and Nationalism* 6: 227–256.

Simeon, R. (2001) 'Recent Trends in Federalism and Intergovernmental Relations in Canada: Lessons for the United Kingdom?', in T.C. Salmon and M. Keating (eds) *The Dynamics of Decentralization: Canadian Federalism and British Devolution*, Montreal/London: McGill/Queens University Press.

Simpson, G. (2004) *Great Powers and Outlaw States: Unequal Sovereigns in the International Legal Order*, Cambridge: Cambridge University Press.

Smith, A.D. (1998) *Nationalism and Modernism: A Critical Survey of Recent Theories of Nations and Nationalism*, London/New York: Routledge.

Tierney, S. (2001) 'Constitutionalising the Role of the Judge: Scotland and the New Order', *Edinburgh Law Review* 5: 49–72.

Tierney, S. (2007) 'We the Peoples: Balancing Constituent Power and Constitutionalism in Plurinational States', in M. Loughlin and N. Walker (eds) *The Paradox of Constitutionalism*, Oxford: Oxford University Press, pp. 229–246.

Tierney, S. (2009) 'Federalism in a Unitary State: A Paradox too Far?', *Regional and Federal Studies* 19(2): 237–253.

Tierney, S. and Warbrick, C. (eds) (2006) *Towards an International Legal Community? The Sovereignty of States and the Sovereignty of International Law*, London: British Institute of International and Comparative Law.

Tully, J. (1995) *Strange Multiplicity: Constitutionalism in an Age of Diversity*, Cambridge: Cambridge University Press.

Villadangos, E.S. (1999) 'The Coexistence between one State and Several Nationalities and Regions: The Spanish Case', Workshop Paper, ECPR Workshop, Mannheim: ECPR.

Waldron, J. (1995) 'Minority Cultures and the Cosmopolitan Alternative', in W. Kymlicka (ed.) *The Rights of Minority Cultures*, Oxford: Oxford University Press, pp. 93–119.

Walker, N. (2001) 'Constitutionalism in a New Key', in G. De Burca and J. Scott (eds) *The EU and the WTO: Legal and Constitutional Aspects*, Oxford: Hart Publishing.

Walker, N. (2002) 'The Idea of Constitutional Pluralism', *Modern Law Review* 65: 317–359.

Walker, N. (2003) 'Late Sovereignty in the European Union', in N. Walker (ed.) *Sovereignty in Transition*, Oxford: Hart Publishing, pp. 3–32.

Walker, N. (ed.) (2006) *Relocating Sovereignty*, UK: Ashgate.

Weber, M. (1966) *General Economic History*, New York: Collier Books.

Weiler, J. (1999) *The Constitution of Europe: 'Do the New Clothes Have an Emperor?' and Other Essays on European Integration*, Cambridge: Cambridge University Press.

Weiler, J. (2000) *The EU, the WTO, and the NAFTA: Towards a Common Law of International Trade?*, Florence and Oxford: Academy of European Law, EUI, Florence/Oxford University Press.

Young, R.A. (1999) *The Struggle for Quebec: From Referendum to Referendum?*, Montreal/London: McGill/Queen's University Press.

8 Federalism and the protection of rights and freedoms

Affinities and antagonism

José Woehrling

What are the interrelations between federalism and the protection of human rights? Such a question arises not only in federations in the strict sense, but in all "compound" states that consist of two levels of government, each having substantial powers and enjoying true autonomy in relation to the other (as for example in "regionalized" countries like Spain or Italy). Given such a situation, each level of government can take positive as well as negative measures in respect to human rights: negative, in exercising its powers in ways that restrict the benefit of rights; positive, in so far as each level of government is able to adopt constitutional and legislative instruments aimed at protecting the enjoyment of rights. Thus, we shall examine in turn: (1) The effects that federalism has on the protection of rights and freedoms; we shall see that the division of powers that characterizes federalism has mostly, albeit not only, beneficial consequences for the protection of the rights of individuals and minorities; (2) The effects of protecting rights and freedoms through a national Bill of Rights and judicial review for the balance of powers in a federation. As we shall see, judicial review by federal courts under a national constitutional instrument can lead to more centralization of powers as well as to more legal standardization, both impinging on the values of federalism.

1 The impact of federalism on the protection of rights

Federalism, and more generally the compound nature of governmental power, furthers the protection of rights and freedoms in two different ways. First, from an institutional and political point of view, federalism divides and diffuses – and consequently limits – power, at the same time as it allows people to participate more actively in political affairs within smaller political units. In federations with national, ethnic or linguistic minorities, those groups large enough to form the majority of the population in one or several federated units will be able to attain a position of political majority. Second, from a legal point of view, by superposing two legal systems, federalism also allows for the existence of two layers of constitutional or quasi-constitutional instruments for the protection of human rights that will complement each other and together provide more comprehensive protections. However, in certain aspects the functioning of a federal system can also hamper the protection of rights and freedoms, especially in creating difficulties for the ratification and implementation of international human rights conventions.

1.1 Institutional and political benefits of federalism for the protection of rights

1.1.1 The rights of people in general

In a broad way, the benefits of federalism for the protection of rights and freedoms of people in general can be epitomized by two simple ideas. First, by dividing power, federalism limits and diminishes power and thus helps to prevent its abuse. From this point of view, federalism functions like a second form of separation of powers that complements the separation between the legislative, executive and judicial branches._This concept, which hardly needs further elaboration, has received a classical exposition in a famous text by James Madison, in the *Federalist Papers*:

> In the compound republic of America, the power surrendered by the people is first divided between two distinct governments, and then the portion allotted to each subdivided among distinct and separate departments. Hence a double security arises to the rights of the people. The different governments will control each other, at the same time that each will be controlled by itself.
>
> (Hamilton *et al.* 1987: 321)

Second, by decentralizing power, federalism enhances political and democratic rights inasmuch as citizens can participate more effectively in political life within smaller political units where the *locus* of power is situated nearer to them. Federalism confers more influence to smaller groups by localizing a greater part of political authority at their level. It gives individuals the possibility to exercise more influence and control at the regional or local level than they can conceivably exercise at the national level. As well, by giving people the opportunity to participate in political affairs at more numerous levels of government, federalism helps to educate them in the practice of citizenship. Finally, in a federation, citizens have access to more than one source of governmental services and benefits; if one administration fails to provide a certain benefit, they can turn to another level of government. Thus, federalism forestalls a situation of monopolistic exercise of state power and, instead, creates a competition between different governments to the benefit of the electorate.[1]

However, the localization of a substantial amount of political power at a level that is closer to the local population can also bring negative consequences for the protection of rights and freedoms, by increasing the likelihood of tyranny by sectoral interests. A political majority is easier to gain and to conserve at a local rather than at the national level, thus there are more risks that it is appropriated by a particular faction. Conversely, the localization of political power at the national level is considered to avert the tyranny of local majorities. In a larger context, the influence of the many pressure groups will be better counterbalanced. The national government usually can keep more distance in relation to local quarrels; it is often in a better situation to protect regional or local minorities. At the same time, the centralization of power can also bring a concentration of power that heightens the risks of abuse. A more distant government will also be less responsive to the needs and wishes of the citizens. In consequence, both centralization and decentralization of political power can result in negative as well as positive outcomes for the protection of rights and freedoms. Federalism allows for a combination of centralization and decentralization in proportions that vary with each particular situation.

Finally, in so far as the different governments in a federation act as a check upon one another, there will result a supplementary limitation of political power to the benefit of the citizens. As Alexander Hamilton wrote:

> Power being almost always the rival of power, the general government will at all times stand ready to check the usurpations of the state governments, and these will have the same disposition towards the general government. The people, by throwing themselves into either scale, will infallibly make it preponderate. If their rights are invaded by either, they can make use of the other as instrument of redress.
>
> (Hamilton *et al.* 1987: 206)

Nonetheless, in a well-balanced federation each government must enjoy a sufficient autonomy in relation to the other in the use of its constitutional powers.

1.1.2 The rights of minorities

In a federal state, it is possible to adjust the political divisions of the territory in order to create one or more constituent units in which a group that is a minority nationally will form the majority regionally, and thus be in position to control the political institutions and power at the regional level. Several federal countries, like Canada, Switzerland, Belgium or India, have precisely chosen to become federations because it was considered a solution to the problems arising from the existence of ethnic, religious or linguistic minorities.[2] Of course, this kind of arrangement is only available to national minorities, as distinguished from immigrant groups (which in any case do not claim such territorial autonomy), and is only possible if the national minority is large enough and concentrated on a given territory. Furthermore, when internal federal borders are drawn in order to allow a national minority to become a majority in one or more constituent states, this will often create new minorities within the regional majority.[3]

Another difficulty in using federalism in order to solve problems associated with minorities stems from the fact that the federal principle, as it is normally understood, does not easily admit asymmetric arrangements. In most plurinational federations, only some constituent states, sometimes only one, are controlled by a national minority and thus insist on more local autonomy. The other constituent states, which are inhabited by the national majority, will more easily accept the trend toward a greater centralization of power at the level of the federation. A way of accommodating these different positions could be to accept more asymmetry in the powers allocated to the constituent states inhabited by a national minority, on the one hand, and to the states that serve as territorial subdivisions of the national majority, on the other. However, such an asymmetry is difficult to reconcile with the principle of equality between the constituent states as well as with equality between all citizens of the federation (as long, at least, as equality of treament is understood as identical treatment rather than different treatment according to different situations).

The reluctance to grant territorial autonomy to national minorities is often explained by the fear of the national majority that it will nourish rather than assuage separatist claims or tendencies. Another concern is that an ethnic or religious minority exercising a measure of territorial autonomy may adopt policies or rules toward its own members, or members of the national majority inhabiting the minority territory, that are incompatible with human rights like sexual equality, freedom of religion or freedom of opinion, to the extent that such policies might be considered necessary to uphold traditional institutions and ways of life. Finally, dividing the territory along ethnic lines produces more homogenous majorities and, as James Madison argued, the more homogenous a majority, the greater the risks that it may become tyrannical toward minorities:

> The smaller the society, the fewer probably will be the distinct parties and interests composing it; the fewer the distinct parties and interests, the more frequently will a majority be found of the same party; and the smaller the number of individuals composing a majority, and the smaller the compass within which they are placed, the more easily will they concert and execute their plans of oppression. Extend the sphere, and you take in a greater variety of parties and interests; you make it less probable that a majority of the whole will have a common motive to invade the rights of other citizens; or if such a common motive exists, it will be more difficult for all who feel it to discover their own strength, and to act in unison with each other. Besides other impediments, it may be remarked that, where there is a consciousness of unjust or dishonorable purposes, communication is always checked by distrust in proportion to the number whose concurrence is necessary.
>
> (Hamilton *et al.* 1987: 128)

To protect minorities that cannot benefit from a system of territorial autonomy (or "minorities within the minority" that have appeared as a result of such arrangements), other methods are required. Minorities can be given a guaranteed representation within political bodies like legislatures or executives; veto rights and increased or double majority rules can provide minorities with a protection against injurious majority decisions. Note, however, that such designs are not particular to federal systems. It is also possible to design a system of "personal federalism" (or "personal autonomy") in which a minority group will be given the power to adopt rules whose applicability is determined by membership in the group based on a personal characteristic like religion or language, rather than on residence on a particular territory (Kymlicka 1996: 81). Again, such an arrangement is not limited to federal systems (even though it can be considered inspired by the federal principle) and one of its most interesting contemporary implementations is to be found in Lebanon, which is not a federation. The 18 religious communities existing in Lebanon adopt the rules applying to their members in matters of marriage, divorce, adoption and other questions of personal and familial status. However, implementation of the personal autonomy principle has been quite limited in so far as modern democratic systems function under principles of political representation and criteria for the application of legal rules that are mainly based on considerations of territory.

One way of protecting minorities living within the constituent states of a federation is to give federal authorities the power to prevent, stop or redress the wrongs inflicted on them by the regional government. However, such mechanisms are difficult to reconcile with the autonomy that should be guaranteed in a true federation to each level of government in relation to the other.

Finally, the mobility and establishment rights guaranteed in the federal constitution constitute a last resort protection for minorities against their regional government. Members of a minority that are not satisfied with their position in their state of residence can move to another constituent state where the group they belong to forms the majority or, at least, where they can expect to be treated in a better way. It must be noted that in the United States this "right of exit", which allows a change of legal status through a change of jurisdiction, is often considered to be one of the advantages of federalism for the protection of the rights of people in general, not only of the rights of minorities. Such a view has been put forward by, amongst others, Robert Bork:

> If another state allows the liberty you value, you can move there, and the choice of what freedom you value is yours alone, not dependent on those who made the Constitution. In this sense, federalism is the constitutional guarantee most protective of the individual's freedom to make his own choices.
>
> (Bork 1990: 53)[4]

However, the most effective means for the protection of minorities that cannot benefit from territorial autonomy is the use of a constitutional instrument, applied by the courts, in order to place limits on majority rule. In a federation, this protection of rights and freedoms through judicial review can be enhanced by superposing two levels of constitutional instruments for the protection of rights, be it the rights of people in general or the rights of minorities.

At the same time, there exists a certain tension between the protection of minorities by systems of territorial autonomy, on the one hand, and judicial review, on the other. In so far as judicial review based on rights and freedoms limits majority rule, it will of course limit the powers, and hence the autonomy, of national minorities that form the majority in a constituent state of a federation. Such a "minority–majority" will see its self-rule limited in favour of its own minorities. The most difficult situation appears when the minority living in a unit controlled by a national minority belongs to the national majority (for example, Anglophones in Quebec, Castillanophones in Catalonia or German-speaking Swiss in the French-speaking cantons). Groups that are a majority in a constituent state but a minority nationally will often feel culturally threatened and thus have a tendency to use their majority position to the fullest, in order, for example, to protect their language. Conversely, the majority at the national level, whose members are in the minority in a member state, can use its power position to force on the regional government very stringent obligations toward its minority, which that government will regard as unduly restricting its autonomy.

In sum, national minorities forming the majority on a part of the federal territory will be served best by a system of territorial autonomy that allows them to become a political majority and exercise a partial self-rule. Minorities too small or too scattered over the territory to be able to benefit from such an arrangement must be protected against majority rule by a constitutional instrument combined with judicial review.

1.2 Legal benefits of federalism for the protection of rights: the two layers of constitutional instruments and judicial review

In most federations, there are two layers of constitutional or legislative instruments for the protection of rights and freedoms, one at the national level, the other at the level of the constituent states. To illustrate this situation, we shall use the examples of Canada and the United States. In Canada, all provincial legislatures and the federal Parliament have adopted, in their respective fields of jurisdiction, human rights statutes that are not entrenched through a special amendment procedure, but possess nonetheless a "quasi constitutional" character giving them a limited kind of primacy over ordinary corresponding provincial or federal legislation. In addition, the Canadian Constitution contains, since 1982, a fully entrenched *Canadian Charter of Rights and Freedoms* (Woehrling 2003, 2005). In the United States, the situation is similar; alongside the Bill of Rights entrenched in the American Constitution, one finds a State Bill of Rights in each of the State Constitutions (Collins 1985).

In these two federations, the state or provincial constitutional or "quasi constitutional" instruments often guarantee rights and freedoms that are not guaranteed, or not as effectively, by national instruments.[5] For example, the *Canadian Charter of Rights and Freedoms*, forming part of the Canadian federal Constitution, does not guarantee property rights or, more generally, social, economic and cultural rights, that are contained in some of the provincial Charters or Bills of

Rights, most notably the Quebec *Charter of Human Rights and Freedoms*. In the United States, rights like the right to education are absent from the federal Constitution, but can be found in many of the State Constitutions.

Many other aspects of the complementarity between the federal Constitution and the State Constitutions in their role of protecting rights and freedoms have been documented in the United States (Beasley 1996: 111–118; Howard 1990: 127ff.). In Canada, while the Canadian Charter only applies to public authorities (vertical effect), many of the provincial instruments apply as well to private relations (horizontal effect). In a more general way, Canadian provinces and American States can experiment in the protection of human rights (as in any other area in which they have jurisdiction), with successful experimentation often adopted by other states or provinces and by the federal government. For example, Quebec was the first jurisdiction in Canada to prohibit discrimination based on sexual orientation, resulting in the eventual adoption of this initiative by the federal government and by the other provinces.

The role of provincial and state instruments in complementing national constitutional instruments is enhanced by the fact that the former can generally be modified much more easily than the latter, which makes them more adaptable to changing social problems and needs. In Canada, the provincial quasi-constitutional human rights instruments can be amended like ordinary legislation. In the United States, though the amendment of the State Constitutions requires a special procedure, it is still much easier than the modification of the federal Constitution (May 1987). The introduction of new rights by amendments to the Canadian or American Constitutions that have failed will sometimes succeed at the level of the state and provincial instruments. For example, after the failure of the *Equal Rights Amendment* (ERA) in the United States, which would have added to the Constitution a provision guaranteeing sex equality in a more specific way, a similar provision has been adopted by more than half the American States in their own constitutions.

Furthermore, if for any reason there appears a deficit in the protection of certain rights and freedoms at one level of government, this can be compensated for at the other level. Such a phenomenon (which has been designated the "New Judicial Federalism") occurred in the United States in the 1970s, when the American Supreme Court adopted a less favourable construction of the rights of those accused of criminal offences. State courts later developed a more robust defence of these rights under the State human rights instruments (Tarr 1994; D'Alemberte 1996; Brennan 1977).

It is inevitable that the existence of a double layer of national and State instruments will create some fragmentation in the benefits of rights and freedoms along state lines. Nevertheless, the federal Constitution guarantees a degree of homogeneity, since federal rights apply on the whole territory. Of course, the state or provincial instruments must be compatible with the federal Constitution, which in some cases means that they must provide at least the same protection in their particular field of application. For example, the *Alberta Human Rights Act*, which applies both in private relations and to state action but did not prohibit sexual orientation discrimination, has been declared contrary to the *Canadian Charter* that does prohibit that kind of discrimination but applies only to state action and not in private relations. Instead of striking down the provincial statute, the Supreme Court of Canada decided to "read in" the missing protection, which means that the federal Constitution was used to impose upon the Alberta legislature the obligation to protect homosexuals in private relations, a protection that the federal Constitution itself does not provide (*Vriend* v. *Alberta* 1998).

1.3 The disadvantages of federalism for the protection of rights: the difficulties arising in the ratification and implementation of human rights treaties

Federalism does not only result in positive effects on the protection of rights and freedoms. The existence of a double layer of national and state or provincial human rights instruments provokes legal complexities that burden citizens as well as legal professionals (in particular when it involves an assessment of which of the several instruments is applicable). That same double layer exacerbates the *legalization* of politics that is probably the most regrettable consequence of the generalization of judicial review based on human rights. Social actors have a growing tendency to resort to constitutional provisions in order to formulate their political claims in terms of rights to be respected or won (i.e. they *legalize* the issue by formulating political claims in legal and constitutional terms). Many special interest groups now avoid democratic mechanisms, which they consider too unwieldy or costly, and find it easier to submit their requests to the courts by reformulating them in the language of rights and freedoms (Woehrling 2009).

The most important disadvantage of federalism for the protection of human rights is that it seriously complicates the ratification and implementation, by federal states, of international instruments for the protection of human rights. By its very nature, federalism divides powers between two levels of government. Conversely, international law presupposes the unity of state action in international relations and requires coherent and uniform conduct by the national government. Therefore, the risk is great that if the federation is granted all the needed authority to act effectively in the international area, the exercise of these powers will threaten to disrupt the internal division of responsibilities (by opening a channel for the national government to invade the states' jurisdictions). Most of the matters coming under the jurisdiction of the constituent states, in particular those involving human rights are at the present time subject to international treaties.

These difficulties exist in almost all federations, irrespective of the particular solutions that have been adopted in regards to the relationship between international and domestic law, or to the division of powers between the federation and the constituent states in the matter of ratification and implementation of treaties. Canada, Belgium and the United States are good examples because these three federations cover a good part of all the possible situations. The United States and Belgium have adopted a monist system and recognize direct application of international conventions by domestic courts as well as a certain degree of supremacy of international law over domestic law. Canada, on the contrary, is a dualist country, where a treaty is only applicable by Canadian courts after it has been incorporated in domestic law and can have no higher authority than the incorporating statute. In the United States, the central government possesses all the powers necessary to ratify and to implement treaties, irrespective of their subject matter. In Belgium, the power to ratify, as well as the power to implement treaties is divided between the federation and the constituent states along the internal division of powers. Finally, in Canada there is no such alignment between the power to ratify and the power to implement, as the federal executive holds the power to ratify any treaty, irrespective of the subject matter, while the power to implement, on the contrary, is divided between the federal parliament and the provincial legislatures along the internal division of powers.

In Canada, the absence of any power of the federal government to force provinces to implement a treaty which it has ratified, or to substitute for the provinces to this end, explains the risk that a duly ratified treaty will not be implemented, with such a situation engaging the international responsibility of the Canadian State. In rare cases, the Canadian government has simply abstained from ratifying a human rights treaty to avoid any complications likely to arise from an anticipated negative attitude of the provinces (this has been the case for the UNESCO *Convention Against Discrimination in Education*). But in most instances the federal government will conclude a federal–provincial agreement before the ratification, in which the provinces agree to fulfil their responsibility at the implementation stage. In return, provincial governments are associated in various ways in the negotiations. For example, such a procedure was followed in 1976, for the ratification and implementation of the two United Nations Human Rights Covenants. At that time, a more general federal–provincial agreement was also concluded, under which there is to be ongoing consultation and cooperation between the two levels of government, before as well as after the ratification of human rights conventions. Under this agreement, the provinces are able to prepare their specific part of the Canadian report to the monitoring agencies and are allowed, if they so wish, to have a representative on the Canadian delegation when the report is examined. Moreover, they can also defend their policies when these are attacked before an international body like the United Nations Human Rights Committee. However, some difficulties remain. If a province is found by the Committee to have adopted a policy contrary to the Pact and refuses to amend it, the federal government has no recourse to compel it to act or to substitute its own policy over that of the provincial authorities (Hogg 2003: 285 ff.).

In Belgium, the power to ratify, as well as the power to implement treaties have been divided between the federation and the constituent units along the internal division of powers. In the case of a "mixed" treaty, whose subject matter falls within the jurisdiction of both levels, agreement by both is necessary. Such a requirement will of course cause difficulties when the interests of the federated entities diverge, as is presently the case with the attempted ratification by Belgium of the *Framework Convention on the Protection of National Minorities* prepared by the Council of Europe. At the implementation stage, the Belgian Constitution provides for a power of temporary substitution of the constituent units by the federation when such an action is needed to implement a ratified treaty. However, in order to respect the units' autonomy, rigorous conditions have to be fulfilled before this power can be used. The Belgian situation thus illustrates the fact that the existence of a power of the federation to compel the constituent states to implement a treaty or to substitute for them does not remove all difficulties, nor does it dispense the need for the two levels of government to cooperate (Lejeune 1994).

Finally, in the United States there appear to be no *legal* difficulties in the field of international treaty relations, since the Constitution, as interpreted by the Supreme Court, gives the federal authorities the power to ratify as well as to implement all treaties, irrespective of their subject matter. However, serious problems have appeared on a *political* level (Bradley and Goldsmith 2000; Henkin 1995; Buergenthal 1997). For many complex reasons, including the fear that the treaty power could be used by the federal government to invade the jurisdiction of the States, the Senate, whose approbation is necessary for the ratification of treaties by the President, has blocked or delayed the ratification of many important human rights conventions or has approved such a ratification only after having imposed reservations, understandings and declarations ("RUDs") that diminish considerably the importance of the treaty in its application to the United States. One of the most striking examples of such a situation has been the ratification of the *International Covenant on Civil and Political Rights*, for which the Senate has imposed a set of restrictive clauses, in particular a "federal understanding" under which the Covenant

> [...] shall be implemented by the Federal Government to the extent that it exercises legislative and judicial jurisdiction over the matters covered therein, and otherwise by the state and local governments, to the extent that state and local governments exercise jurisdiction over such matters [...].

Of course, this clause does not diminish the international obligations of the United States under the Covenant, but it conveys the concern that the exercise by the federal government of its treaty powers should not disturb the internal division of powers nor diminish the autonomy of the States in exercising their jurisdictions. It is striking to note that actual practice in Canada and the United States is comparable even if the legal situation is very different, partly because federalism concerns are the same in the two countries.

One can thus conclude that federalism inevitably entails some complications for the ratification and implementation of treaties in general and human rights treaties in particular. However, like other problems deriving from the division of powers in a federation, these difficulties can be overcome by negotiation and cooperation between the federation and the constituent states and, in any case, are not an excuse for not respecting the mutual autonomy of the two levels of government. Respect for human rights should not justify a lack of respect for federalism.

2 The impact of the protection of rights on federalism

Judicial review by federal courts under a national Charter of Rights can lead to more *centralization* of powers as well as to more legal uniformity or *standardization*, with both contradicting some of the objectives pursued through federalism. Centralization consists in a transfer of powers from the federated states towards a federal body; it is antagonistic to the autonomy of the federated states. Standardization involves imposition, by the courts, of uniform values that limit the ability of the federated states to adopt differing policies; it compromises federal diversity.

2.1 Centralizing effect of the protection of rights

The centralizing consequences of the protection of rights take three mainforms.

2.1.1 Transfer of some decisional power from representative bodies of the federated states to federal judicial bodies

Protection of rights by the federal courts implies a transfer of decision-making power over social, economic and political issues from representative provincial bodies to a federal judicial body. This implies a double deficit, first in terms of democracy, second in terms of federalism. As a federal body, the Supreme Court (or the Constitutional Court) is more sensitive to the priorities and concerns of the federal political class and elites than to those of the federated states. Natural and institutional links exist between the members of the Supreme Court and federal political office holders; they share the same political culture. This is even more true in Canada than in the United States and other federations. The Canadian federal executive has complete discretion to appoint members of the Supreme Court without any real input from the provincial governments. In contrast, in the United States as well as in most other federations, the federated states can exercice such influence through the Senate (or Federal Chamber), which participates in the appointment of members of the Supreme or Constitutional Court. Studies show that in federated or regionalized states, Supreme and Constitutional Courts almost always exercise a centralizing influence, and foster a long-term increase in the political legitimacy and powers of the national government (Bzedra 1993; Shapiro 1981: 20).

2.1.2 Consolidation of national identity to the detriment of regional identities

Protection of rights through the federal constitution and the federal courts helps to create and consolidate a shared national identity or, in other words, a feeling of common citizenship. Such nation-building is almost necessarily at the expense of identification with the regional community in the constituent state. Systems for the protection of rights through a national constitution and the federal courts are thus powerful tools for unifying mentalities and loyalties. This then facilitates the centralization of power. It is in this perspective that there is a relatively widely shared opinion that in 1982 one of the primary objectives of the *Canadian Charter* was nation-building: the establishment of an institution that would help to consolidate Canadian identity and the legitimacy of the central government, and thus foster centralization of power (Russell 1983; Cairns 1992).

It is generally agreed that the *Canadian Charter* created new civic awareness among Canadians, based on rights entitlement claims and expression of identity articulated at the national level rather than regionally or provincially (Morton 1995). This role of the federal constitution as an instrument of nation-building has also been noted in the United States, where it can be argued "that, rather than the American nation's creating the Constitution, the Constitution created the nation" (Howard 1996: 23).

2.1.3 Economic and social rights as justification for federal intervention in jurisdictions of the federated states

In many federations, economic and social rights (i.e. primarily health care, social services and education rights) are used to justify federal intervention in areas under the jurisdiction of the federated states. Federal intervention is presented as necessary to redistribute resources among regions with different levels of wealth and to ensure a degree of uniformity in the way states deliver social services. Although economic and social rights are not formally guaranteed in many federal constitutions, like those of Canada and the United States, the need to implement such rights effectively and consistently is an argument used in political discourse to justify the redistributive, harmonizing role of federal authorities. In other words, individual rights discourse has been transposed into the domain of collective social rights and redistribution to provide legitimacy for federal intervention.

The vehicle for federal intervention is the spending power, which refers to the ability of federal authorities to employ financial resources for pupuses under the exclusive jurisdiction of the federated states. The federal government has greater capacity than the states to raise and spend funds. By offering to provide all or part of the funding of programmes under the jurisdiction of the states, and by attaching conditions on the receipt of such money, the federal government is able to intervene in areas under constitutionally exclusive provincial jurisdiction. Federal funding is generally conditional on compliance with certain national standards set by the central government. In many federations, like the United States and Canada, the federal spending power has thus been used to encourage constituent states to create or expand major shared-cost programmes in the fields of education, health care and social assistance. On the positive side, the spending power has allowed the federal government to persuade the states or provinces to provide important services to the population and to secure nation-wide standards of health, education, income-security and other public services. On the negative side, the use of the spending power can be viewed as disturbing the priorities of the states or provinces and undermining their autonomy. An additional criticism of this system is that it creates confusion with respect to accountability for budgetary and political decisions: the real decisions are no longer made by the local political authorities who answer to their constituencies.

To summarize, in this area the problem stems from the opposition between protecting the autonomy of the federated states and the perceived necessity to establish or consolidate national social solidarity and protection programmes.

2.2 Standardizing effect of constitutional scrutiny based on the federal constitution

One of the objectives of federalism is to promote legal, social and cultural diversity. In their areas of jurisdiction, federated states should be allowed to create different solutions to societal problems by taking into account the cultural values specific to each regional political community. Yet protecting rights through national constitutional instruments and the courts has standardizing effects that are obstacles to such diversity.

2.2.1 Why rights protection results in standardization: a transcendental and pre-political conception of rights

The reason rights result in standardization is the way their philosophical nature is perceived: they are considered universal and transcendental (pre-political), particularly in the case of liberal individual rights. The very concept of "fundamental" rights implies that they have to apply to everyone in the same way, with no or very few exceptions. Construed in this way, all variations look like unacceptable forms of relativism.[6] Yet this vision corresponds to only one aspect of the real nature of human rights. In many respects, human rights necessarily result from weighing and balancing interests, which is a process that is largely contingent on context and can legitimately vary over time and from one country or regional context to the next. The logic of a fundamental right is partly dictated by the community's social, cultural and political values.

If we define rights as resulting from balancing interests through a democratic process in a concrete social and political situation, it seems advantageous to be able to adjust the solution to the specific context. Federalism promotes this kind of diversity. On the contrary, if we tend to define rights as intangible universals, they have to be applied in a uniform way by the courts. In this case, federalism is an obstacle because it necessarily results in different legal regimes and some fragmentation of the system of rights.

2.2.2 Legal and political aspects of standardization resulting from rights protection

On the legal level, the standardizing consequences of rights protection take well-known forms. The courts, in particular the Supreme or Constitutional Court, impose uniform norms and standards on the federated states, which limit their choices when exercising their constitutional jurisdictions. Every time a legislation of a federated state is declared unconstitutional, the same automatically applies to the other states. We can thus speak of *negative* standardization. Standardization can also be more invasive. It is well known that Supreme and Constitutional Courts often hand down "constructive" decisions in which they set out in great detail how the legislature should amend legislation to make it consistent with the Constitution. Sometimes courts go so far as to write new legislation themselves by judicially rephrasing the impugned legislative provision (adding to it or deleting part of it). In such cases, the courts impose *positive* uniform standards, sometimes down to minute details, on all the federated states.[7]

The standardizing consequences of rights protection can exist even without any court intervention, state governments adjusting their policies to be compatible with rights and freedoms in an anticipated and preventive way. Observations in Canada show that, at the drafting stage, primary or delegated legislation is often modified or outright abandoned because it is considered as possibly incompatible with the *Canadian Charter of Rights and Freedoms* (Monahan and Finkelstein 1992). The same phenomenon has been observed in the United States (Tushnet 1995). This kind of internal constitutional scrutiny being subject to circulation and imitation among the federated states has also standardizing consequences.

2.2.3 Means of attenuating the standardizing consequences of rights protection

Courts are aware of the potential standardizing effect of human rights protection and in some cases try to reduce those effects in order to protect the diversity goals pursued through federalism. For example, the Supreme Court of Canada has established that the very diversity of *provincial* legal regimes, originating from the fact that provinces exercise their constitutional powers in different ways, cannot be considered to be discrimination based on place of residence, unless the federal system is to be abandoned altogether. The Court also accepts geographical variations in the application of *federal* laws, as long as these can be justified by the interaction between federal and provincial powers and the necessity for the federal Parliament to take into account the diversity of provincial legislation.

There are further ways to attenuate the standardizing consequences of rights and freedom protection. However, in order to use them, one has to be persuaded that a degree of relativism is acceptable in human rights.

First, adopting a less demanding interpretation of a right or freedom leaves greater leeway with respect to how the right is ensured. For example, it might be accepted that the principle of state religious neutrality could be complied with either by total absence of state support for religions or by perfectly equal support for all religions. If this interpretation were accepted, the federated states would have a choice between two policies that would both be equally in compliance with the Constitution; a degree of diversity would remain possible. However, if the neutrality principle were interpreted as requiring total absence of state support in all cases, only one solution would be possible and, consequently, standardization would be imposed on the constituent states. Thus some partisans of maximum protection for rights and freedoms distrust federalism because defence of diversity leads those in favour of federalism to request flexible application of rights and freedoms. The same consideration appears in the case law under the *European Convention on Human Rights*. The European Court recognizes a "margin of appreciation" to the member states so as to allow a diversity of national solutions. Critics of this concept consider that it diminishes the protection of rights (Mahoney 1998: 5–6).

Second, the standardizing effects of rights protection can be attenuated through the criteria applied when limitations to rights are examined for justification purposes. The primary criterion for justification is the concept of proportionality: a limitation is justifiable if it is proportional to important goals of social interest. Yet, the proportionality criterion is normally applied in a "context-dependent" way, in other words, by taking into account the variables of the specific spatial and temporal context. A limitation that would be unreasonable in a normal situation could appear reasonable under exceptional circumstances; a limit could be considered reasonable in circumstances specific to one federated state, but nowhere else in the federation. Thus, for example, the Supreme Court of Canada ruled in a well-known case that the vulnerability of the French language in Québec justified some limitations on freedom of commercial expression (*Ford* v. *Québec* 1998). Without saying so explicitly, it implied that the same measures would not be justified with respect to English in the rest of Canada. This approach thus makes it possible for the scope of rights to vary in accordance with the limitations that can be imposed on them in certain specific contexts. Theoretically, this is a technique that could make it possible to reconcile a degree of universality in rights content with a degree of diversity in concrete application. However, it seems likely that the courts will accept variations in the scope of rights only in exceptional cases. This is because the implementation of criteria for justifying rights infringements inevitably results in a *comparison* between the challenged policy and policies adopted in the same area by other free and democratic societies. When the challenged policy is federal, the criteria for comparison will be sought mainly in comparative law and international human rights instruments, since they are considered a kind of synthesis of national rights protection systems. When the challenged policy is that of a federated state, the comparison will most often be with the law of other states in the federation. The greater the consistency among the various state legislations, the more difficult it will be to justify the challenged measure if it deviates from the common denominator among the states.

In summary, despite the fact that constitutional law contains a number of techniques that make it possible to introduce a degree of relativism into the scope of rights and freedoms, protection of such rights through the constitutional and judicial process will inevitably have standardizing results. The universal, individualistic logic of rights is too powerful for concerns related to federalism and diversity to be able to oppose it effectively.

3 Conclusion

Federalism's greatest merit is that it promotes community values. Yet, just as community values regress before individualism and personal autonomy, federalism loses strength when faced with individual rights. The "rights consumer" takes the place of the deliberating citizen. When rights are seen as resulting from a process in which interests are weighed and opposing claims adjusted in a democratic manner, federalism is an advantage because it promotes participation and thus rights can be expressed, made concrete and adjusted in accordance with the political communities sharing a geographic area. However, when rights are seen as resulting from restriction of the democratic process through anti-majority mechanisms, federalism appears threatening in some respects, for it is at the local level that majorities seem most dangerous. Moreover, if rights are pre-political and transcendental, they will be by definition universal and it will be very difficult for them to vary from one jurisdiction to another.

Notes

1 Conversely in so far as federalism divides powers between two levels of government, its functioning demands a high degree of coordination between the federation and the constituent units. Coordination mechanisms are generally dominated by the executive branch and inadequately controlled by elected assemblies and, thus, subject to a certain democratic deficit. Furthermore, the complexity of intergovernmental coordination mechanisms creates a lack of transparency for citizens, who no longer know which level of government is responsible for certain decisions.
2 However, in other federations like the United States, there has been a conscious effort to avert the possibility of federalism being used in order to allow national minorities to form the majority in one or several constituent units.
3 The political division of the state territory in order to create subdivisions in which a national minority forms the majority of the local population is also possible in "regional" states like Spain or Italy and even in unitary states, where certain regions can be given a special status, like Corsica in France or the Aaland Islands in Finland.
4 On this aspect, see also Stewart (1985: 923–927).
5 In Canada, the federal Supreme Court is the final interpreter of the federal Constitution as well as of provincial human rights quasi-constitutional instruments and the Court shows a tendency to interpret both sets of instruments in a similar way, even in cases where there exist significant differences in their respective wording. Such an attitude has both advantages and disadvantages. The main advantage is that it simplifies the legal situation. The disadvantage is that such an attitude tends in some situations to diminish the complementarity of the two sets of instruments. In the United States, the distinctive character of the State Constitutions is more accented, to the extent that the federal Supreme Court does not, in usual circumstances, interpret and apply these instruments, whose final interpreters are the State Supreme Courts. Nonetheless, the State Courts are of course influenced, when interpreting the State Constitutions, by the case law of the United States Supreme Court.
6 "The idea of justice connotes consistency in the law, the notion that all citizens should envoy the same rights" (Howard 1996: 22). "Proponents of federalism who suppose

that rights should be permitted to vary among the units of a federal system must be prepared to reckon with the power of this concept of justice" (Howard 1996: 23).

> What counts as fundamental rights may differ, and what is deemed the appropriate agent for enforcement of rights may also differ. But to the extent that our rights are portrayed in transcendent, universal terms, they demand a consistency that can only be satisfied by constitutional nationalism.
>
> (Jacobsohn 1996: 36)

7 A well-known illustration is to be found in *Roe* v. *Wade* (1973), where the United States Supreme Court not only invalidated, directly or indirectly, the abortion statutes of a majority of states, but imposed upon all the states a very detailed judge-made regime. In this case, intervention by the Court had the effect of "federalizing" a problem that was traditionaly legislated by the states (criminal law being a state responsibility in the United States). Conversely, in Canada the decision of the Supreme Court in *R*. v. *Morgentaler* (1988), in striking down the abortion section of the federal Criminal Code (criminal law being a federal responsibility in Canada), had the effect of "provincializing" the field, which is now legislated by the provinces as relating to medical care.

References

Beasley, D.T. (1996) "Federalism and the Protection of Individual Rights: The American State Constitutional Perspective", in E. Katz and G.A. Tarr, *Federalism and Rights*, Lanham, MA: Rowman & Littlefield Publishers, p. 101.

Bork, R. (1990) *The Tempting of America. The Political Seduction of the Law*, New York: Simon & Schuster.

Bradley, C.A. and Goldsmith, J.L. (2000) "Treaties, Human Rights and Conditional Consent", *University of Pennsylvania Law Review* 149: 399.

Brennan, W. (1977) "State Constitutions and the Protection of Individual Rights", *Harvard Law Review* 90: 489.

Buergenthal, T. (1997) "Modern Constitutions and Human Rights Treaties", *Columbia Journal of Transnational Law* 36: 211.

Bzedra, A. (1993) "Comparative Analysis of Federal High Courts: A Political Theory of Judicial Review", *Canadian Journal of Political Science* 26: 3.

Cairns, A.C. (1992) *Charter versus Federalism*, Montreal; Kingston: McGill; Queen's University Press.

Collins, R.K.L. (1985) "Bills and Declarations of Rights Digest", *The American Bench*, 3rd edn, Sacramento: Reginald Bishop Forster & Associates, pp. 2483–2523.

D'Alemberte, T. (1996) "Rights and Federalism: An Agenda to Advance the Vision of Justice Brennan", in E. Katz and G.A. Tarr, *Federalism and Rights*, Lanham, MA: Rowman & Littlefield Publishers, p. 123.

Hamilton, A., Madison, J. and Jay, J. (1987) *Federalist Papers*, London: Penguin Books.

Henkin, L. (1995) "U.S. Ratification of Human Rights Conventions: The Ghost of Senator Bricker", *American Journal of International Law* 89: 341.

Hogg, P.W. (2003) *Constitutional Law of Canada*, Scarborough, Ontario: Thomson-Carswell.

Howard, A.E.D. (1990) "Protecting Human Rights in a Federal System", in M. Tushnet (ed.) *Comparative Constitutional Federalism. Europe and America*, New York: Greenwood Press, p. 115.

Howard, A.E.D. (1996) "Does Federalism Secure or Undermine Rights?", in E. Katz and

G.A. Tarr, *Federalism and Rights*, Lanham, MA: Rowman & Littlefield Publishers, p. 11.

Jacobsohn, G.J. (1996) "Contemporary Constitutional Theory, Federalism, and the Protection of Rights", in E. Katz and G.A. Tarr, *Federalism and Rights*, Lanham, MA: Rowman & Littlefield Publishers, p. 29.

Kymlicka, W. (1996) "Two Models of Pluralism and Tolerance", in D. Heyd (ed.) *Toleration. An Elusive Virtue*, Princeton, NJ: Princeton University Press, p. 81.

Lejeune, Y. (1994) "La Conduite des Relations Internationales", in F. Delpérée (ed.) *La Belgique Fédérale*, Bruxelles: Bruylant, p.313.

Mahoney, P. (1998) "Marvellous Richness of Diversity or Invidious Cultural Relativism?", *Human Rights Law Journal* 19: 1.

May, J.C. (1987) "Constitutional Amendment and Revision Revisited", *Publius: The Journal of Federalism* 17: 153.

Monahan, P.J. and Finkelstein, M. (1992) "The Charter of Rights and Public Policy in Canada", *Osgoode Hall Law Journal* 30: 501.

Morton, F.L. (1995) "The Effects of the Charter of Rights on Canadian Federalism", *Publius: The Journal of Federalism* 25: 173.

Russell, P.H. (1983) "The Political Purposes of the Canadian Charter of Rights and Freedoms", *Canadian Bar Review* 61: 30.

Shapiro, M. (1981) *Courts: A Comparative and Political Analysis*, Chicago: University of Chicago Press, p. 20.

Stewart, R.B. (1985) "Federalism and Rights", *Georgia Law Review* 19: 917.

Tarr, G.A. (1994) "The Past and Future of the New Judicial Federalism", *Publius: The Journal of Federalism* 24: 63.

Tushnet, M. (1995) "Policy Distortion and Democratic Debilitation: Comparative Illumination of the Countermajoritarian Difficulty", *Michigan Law Review* 94: 245.

Woehrling, J. (2000) "Convergences et Divergences entre Fédéralisme et Protection des Droits et Libertés: l'Exemple des Etats-Unis et du Canada", *McGill Law Review* 46: 21.

Woehrling, J. (2003) "L'Actualité Constitutionnelle au Canada: la Superposition et la Complémentarité des Instruments Constitutionnels et 'Quasi-constitutionnels' de Protection des Droits et Libertés", *Revue Française de Droit Constitutionnel* 53: 187.

Woehrling, J. (2005) "Superposición y Complementariedad de los Instrumentos Nacionales y Provinciales de Protección de los Derechos del Hombre en Canadá", in M.-A. Aparicio (ed.) *Derechos y Libertades en los Estados Compuestos*, Barcelona: Atelier Libros juridicos, p. 65.

Woehrling, J. (2009) "The *Canadian Charter of Rights and Freedoms* and its Consequences on Political and Democratic Life and the Federal System", in A.-G. Gagnon (ed.) *Contemporary Canadian Federalism: Foundations, Traditions, Institutions*, Toronto: Toronto University Press, p. 224.

Court cases

Ford v. *Québec (A.G.)* [1988] 2 S.C.R. 712
R. v. *Morgentaler* [1988] 1 R.C.S. 30
Roe v. *Wade* [1973] 410 U.S. 113
Vriend v. *Alberta* [1998] 1 S.C.R. 493

9 The myth of *civic patriotism*

Nationalism under the veil of the Republic in France

Ramón Máiz

"I propose to analyse an idea that is to all appearances straightforward, but which can give rise to the most dangerous misunderstandings" (Renan 1947 I: 887). With these words Ernest Renan began his famous lecture at the Sorbonne *What is a Nation?* on 11 March 1882. In this chapter we will examine the idea that in the historical development of the French Republic one finds the archetypal form of *civic patriotism* which, focusing exclusively on the "daily plebiscite" and the juridical–political relationship between the citizenry and the state, dispenses with all substantive ethnic–cultural and nationalist references. We will show that, under the wing of the Republic, the nation and nationalism – "Une Nation une" – through the equation: State = Nation = Citizenship, have always been explicitly or implicitly present, albeit in a variety of forms.

1 The historical nationalisation of the Republic in France

Recent research has highlighted the connection between the "disillusionment of the world" – the move from a society whose structure is based on an external, transcendent principle of order, to another which is structured around an immanent order – and the appearance of the (transcendent–immanent) concept of the nation, as well as the "civil religion" (Rousseau) of love for the homeland and nationalism (Gauchet 1986; Bell 2001).

However, here we are concerned with recalling, as succinctly as possible, that the French nation, the archetype par excellence of the myth of nationalism or civic patriotism and the Enlightenment, was founded during a period of initial religious exclusion. The confrontation between Catholics and Protestants, and even between Gallican and Roman Catholics, was a veritable historical–political driving force for its own particular dual process of nation building and state building and had a greater impact on the future than is commonly supposed. The creation of a shared "French" identity, as Anthony Marx has shown, has a fundamental historical root: the unification at the dawn of the modern era of a *Catholic* nation, symbolised by the myth of Joan of Arc, in opposition to the Huguenot Protestants, within the country, and the English, as external enemies (Marx 2003). This underlying Catholic founding dimension, France as the *La Fille Aînée de L'Église* (Rémond 1992), would give rise, after the Revolution, to a nationally constituent mythical–symbolic coexistence/confrontation between the myth of *La Pucelle d'Orleans* and *Marianne*, between Catholic France and the lay Republic (Winock 1992; Agulhon 1979). This confers a permanent historical divergence and tension on the "French" concept of nationhood between the political–territorial and the mythical–symbolic ends of the continuum of nation-alising factors, which was implicit during most of the period of the Republic (see at the end: Historical map of ideas of nationhood in France). Moreover, the myth of Joan of Arc as a national heroine was introduced by the republicans, as shown by the work of Michelet or the republican statue of the national saint, by Frémiet, which was erected in the Place des Pyramides in Paris in 1874 (Mélonio 2001: 175). This was propagated at the time by moderate republicans (Joseph Fabre's proposal in 1884 for a public holiday in her honour, which was passed by the French parliament in 1894) (Winock 1992: 141) as a way of achieving a consen-sus in a country which at the time was seriously divided both ideologically and socially. Only much later would the myth be reformulated, in a clearly anti-Semitic form, at the time of the Dreyfus Affair and, later still, in anti-Muslim form by the Front National. This reappropriation of the "Bonne Lorraine" would result in a kind of discourse based on the binary logic of oppositions that would structure the mythical–symbolic complex of French reactionary nationalism, par-tially interwoven with a number of republican nationalisms, during most of the twentieth century – "C'est une Celte, Jeanne D'Arc, qui sauva la patrie" (Drumont) – and would be its legacy to contemporary extreme-right national-isms: Joan of Arc/Jews, national/internal enemy, country/town, peasant/nomad, work/speculation, health/morbidity, people/intellectuals, national unity/national disintegration, French/English, Catholicism/atheism, spiritualism/materialism, virginity/prostitution, superior race/inferior race, etc. (Winock 2004).

Even without the anti-Semitic reformulation, that founding religious split which, although distant in time, was no less important in its founding function of the common ascendancy, has survived in stronger or weaker form even the notorious attempts at secularisation of the end of the nineteenth century, exem-plified by the education law of 1882 and the separation of the State and the Church by the law of 1905. In fact, beyond its recovery by nationalist move-ments during and following the Dreyfus Affair – "la nationalité française est liée étroitement au catholicisme" (Barrès 1925: 254) – the religious debt of its origins has inspired a whole series of commitments of the French Republic to the Catho-lic religion which, despite the declaration of the secular State in the 1958 Consti-tution, has remained as an implicit backdrop to this day. Therefore, it is necessary to recall a number of striking practices: although the catechism was not taught in state schools, the national education authorities allowed Wednes-day afternoons to be used for the religious (Catholic) education of pupils. Like-wise, many public holidays are still traditional Catholic festivals: Easter, Ascension Day, Christmas, 15 August. There is, however, a well-known territo-rial exception that is often forgotten, but which is very significant in the "one and indivisible" Republic: since they were returned to France in 1918, Alsace and Lorraine have maintained a special concordat with the Holy See. Moreover, the principle of the "école unique" was finally abandoned, thus permitting not only private Catholic education, but also facilitating public aid for private schools (Barangé law of 1951), introducing a contractual principle of public finance for private education (Debré law of 1959), or even authorising financing, with public funds, for the running of private centres (Guermeur law of 1976). Moreover, and of particular interest here, the Catholic character of 95 per cent of the private centres subsidised with public funds was used by these same centres, during the 1990s, as a reason to be exempted from the application of the Bayrou memorandum on the use of religious symbols (Poulat 1987; Gaspard and Khos-rokhavar 1995; Laborde 2008).

Apart from religion, following the Revolution other ethnic–cultural elements clouded the civic purity of republican ideology which, it should not be forgotten, already bore in its Jacobin version a significant burden of values which referred to an exacerbated idea of the common good (a virtuous citizenry distilled by the Great Terror) and not only a conception of justice, which was equally problem-atic ("La République une et indivisible"). Indeed, tensions stemming from the *nationalist paradox* are clearly perceptible from the very beginning. To be exact, on the one hand, claims are made for the sovereignty and constituent power of a nation that previously existed in history and, on the other, the necessary political production of the French nation through a variety of procedures: national educa-tion by means of the *Projet d'Education Nationale* of Rabaut de Saint-Étienne (1792); the systematic elimination of *patois* and the "creation of republicans, or better still Frenchmen, who will give the nation its own unique physiognomy", demanded by Marie-Joseph Chénier (1792) (Certeau *et al*. 1975); the exclusion of the nobility due to their "faineantisse" and the anti-particularist territorial reorganisation of "L'adunation politique" of Emmanuel Sieyès (1789) etc. The task of forging a collective identity of "Frenchmen" despite religious, class, regional and cultural differences would be regarded by the founders of the Republic as a correlate and pre-requisite for the functioning of democratic insti-tutions and even the healing or tempering of social inequalities.

Even during the most decisionist moments of *La Révolution* – a revolution that was based on both will and reason and, it should be remembered, openly directed against history: "L'histoire c'est pas nôtre code" (Rabaut de Sainte-Étienne) – ethnic and cultural dimensions played a role that was, if not funda-mental, always of some importance. In fact, beneath the revolutionary rupture it is possible to observe a partial continuation of the nation that was the *Ancien Régime*. This can be seen in the syncretism of France's national flag (the colours of Paris and the National Guard, blue and red, in addition to the white of the monarchy). Or the *Marsellaise*, the national anthem, written by the arch-monarchist Rouget de Lisle, who eliminated the initial reference to the demoli-tion of the "thrones of the tyrants" because it was excessively republican and replaced it with another referring to foreign "tyrants", that is, the Prussians, not the French (Verrière 2000: 276). Or, finally, the vicissitudes of the Louvre, which opened on 8 November 1793 as the "palace of the nation", an unmistaka-ble sign of a conception of the republic in which the political legitimacy of the new order included the construction of a French national narrative marked by iconic works of art (Mélonio 2001: 164).

Likewise, despite the fact that Roman roots undeniably predominate as a mythical–discursive reference to Jacobin republicanism, there is another shadowy dimension in which the Celtic chieftain "Vercingetorix" (in 1867 an enormous statue was erected in his honour by Napoleon III in Alise-Sainte-Reine), the "Gallic Cockerel", the Gallic origins of the real France (a creation of the *Academie Celtique* in 1805, destined to "faire la statistique antique des Gaules") (Thiesse 1999: 57) etc., play a by no means insignificant role in the construction of the "Nation Une" (Pomian 1992). In 1802 Girodet-Trioson painted the *Apothéose des Héros Français Morts pour la Patrie pendant la Guerre de la Liberté*, in which Marceau, Kléber and others can be seen being received by *Ossian* (the publication of Macpherson's texts dates back to 1761) in Paradise; the same myth appears in *Le Songe d'Ossian* (1812) by Ingres (Darriulat 2001: 114).

Moreover, the evolution of Jacobin patriotism during the French Revolution covers a whole spectrum which goes from cosmopolitanism to incipient signs of xenophobia, while at the same time displaying an increasing nationalisation of the initial patriotism by means of a variety of different elements:

• The Gallic/Celtic myth of the origins of France.
• An ethical overload of the idea of good community life: virtuous citizenry, religious transfer (worship of the "goddess reason"), the execution of the king as an "acte de providence nationale" (Robespierre) (Nora 1986: 804).
• Reformulation of state education as both a republican and a national institution, exemplified in the significant transition from "Instruction publique" (Condorcet) to "l'éducation nationale" (Rabaut de Saint-Étienne). State education is designed, from the very beginning, to carry out the task of affirming and producing a unitary and homogeneous conception of the national community.
• The construction of the *Republique une et indivisible* in opposition to the cultural and linguistic diversity of France, which was reinterpreted as an obstacle to nation building. Instead of being a *natural* fact, the nation becomes an *artificial* product of political will: cultural homogeneity, unified historical narrative propagated by state schools, centralisation and unitarianism, imposition of the national language, etc. (Bell 2001: 15).
• Close links between citizenship and nationality, to such an extent that civic rights are limited and made dependent on membership of the nation.
• Militarism and universalist expansionism in France's "civilising mission" in the world.
• Production of the figure of the foreigner as "the other", the suspect (*conspiration de l'étranger*): increase in the number of tests of public-spiritedness, prohibition of residence, confiscation of goods, etc. Internal homogenisation that placed the category of citizen of the nation above all particularisms and also involved the reinforcement of the external delimitation of the foreigner (Brubaker 1992: 46).

It is not necessary to refer to the work of Chateaubriand – *Atala*, *Les Natchez*, *Le Genie du Christianisme* or the *Essai Historique* – in order to detect, from the perspective of the counter-revolution, the recovery of national Catholicism and the defence of the "man of nature" in contrast to the disintegrative modernity of one's roots (Thom 1995). It is in the very field of liberal republicanism where, as the century unfolds, we discover the unmistakable signs of a recovery of the organicism of the nation. Without any doubt, the influential work of Madame de Staël provides clear proof of this. In her novel *Corinne ou L'Italie*, but above all in *De L'Allemagne*, the author puts forward a clear conception of nations and national identities based on ethnic–cultural features: "The difference between languages, natural borders, memories of a common history, all contribute to create among men *these great individuals that are called nations* (de Staël 1814: 41). "Ces grands individus qu'on appelle des nations" would receive attention from a variety of intellectual, political, and institutional perspectives in post-revolutionary France.

What can be said, for example, about post-revolutionary historiography? And we are not referring to the work of Taine who, from *L'Histoire de la Literature Anglaise* (1863) to *Les Origines de la France Contemporaine* (1875–1883), develops an idea of the French nation which is openly anti-Jacobin, deterministic and racist. We must confront, once again, the republican legacy, whose early task would be none other than, with the justification of defending the revolution, reinstating the lost affective link of communitarianism to the abstraction of the Republic. Regarding this point, it is necessary to recall that the republican Michelet – who, incidentally, wrote that "Le Dieu des nations a parlé par la France" – explicitly dedicated his work to reconcile "dogmas and principles" with "legend" (from Joan of Arc to the Revolution). It is from this perspective of *republican nationalism*, for which the nation constitutes the supreme truth built on the myth of the origins, that a text like *Le Peuple* (1846) should be read as well as two of its themes that would subsequently be more influential: (1) France as a *universal nation*: "asile du monde", "bien plus qu'une nation: la fraternité vivante", etc. (Michelet 1846, 1: 229); and (2) France as a *One and Indivisible Nation*, built by the suppression of "nationalités intérieures": "it is when France eliminates from its midst all the divergent Frances that it attains its highest and most original revelation" (Michelet 1846: 216). Initially conceived as an intermediate stage between tribe and Universal Republic, the *nation* was gradually filled with solid (linguistic, historical, affective, etc.) content as the century progressed. In fact, from Michelet onwards it can be said that a movement in search of organicism begins for the French nation which, recognisable earlier in Ferry, is more clearly visible in the work of Renan and Thierry.

It would, however, be with the Empire and the Restoration, especially in the romantic historiography of Thierry, when, in opposition to the civic nationalism of Michelet – *nationalism* in its strict sense, not mere "republican patriotism", because it reinforces the idea of the nation granting it a highly affective content, transforming national history into a national (and, at the same time, universal) *Destiny*, introducing the myth of the "chosen people" etc. – the theme of the "struggle of races" is recovered as the driving force of French history, and the reason for loyalty to the "primitive race". In the same way, the reformulation of the founding Celtic myth returns the French nation to the common Aryan trunk and thus to an equal footing with Germany. The mythical conflict between Franks and Gauls, between nobles and serfs ("la race conquise") (Poliakov 1971) reverberates even in such influential historical accounts as Guizot's. But, moreover, the relative influence of the Celtic myth of the origins, in the version of Reynaud and Martin, regarding French republicanism, as the century unfolds, illustrates the in no way marginal ethical background of the most "civic" of nationalisms. The obvious, and in principle unthinkable, presence of a form of "Celtic republican patriotism" exemplifies the inseparability between the historical–cultural and mythical dimension and the civic dimension of the nation. In fact, from 1830 onwards, it is possible to observe how a defence of "instinct" and "love for the homeland" overwhelm, in the republican youth, the purely rational dimension of citizenship and the state (Darriulat 2001: 115).

The vicissitudes of *jus solis* bear witness, likewise, beyond the stereotypical, to the narrow limits of French civic patriotism. In effect, the pre-revolutionary tradition of *jus solis* was rejected by jurists, against Napoleon's wishes, and replaced by the *jus sanguinis* in the Code of 1803. In fact, *jus solis* would not be recovered until the 1889 law, but complicated, moreover, by the additional requirement of socialisation in French customs and culture. Finally, in 1927, as an instrument of a demographic policy for dealing with depopulation, a third stage to facilitate access to nationality was opened (through naturalisation or marriage). To all this must be added, from the end of the 1920s, a racist perspective that would triumph in Vichy after 1940, a form of racism that would not disappear with the Liberation, but would re-emerge occasionally in the policy of quotas imposed by Georges Mauco, in the forced repatriation of North Africans carried out by d'Estaing between 1978 and 1980, in the attempts to suppress the *jus solis*, etc. (Weil 2002). In fact, as Brubaker has shown, even the recovery of *jus solis* formed part of a wider national–republic consciousness-raising ("moral and civil indoctrination") (Brubaker 1992: 45), by means of a national education system that imposes at one fell swoop a single language (the dialectal variety of L'Île de France), an account of history and a number of common national myths and symbols for all French people.

Meanwhile, the slow nationalisation of France in opposition to the traditional territories and internal regions, merged together, as we well know from Eugen Weber among others, civic patriotism with (1) organisation through radial road networks to unify the territory, with (2) an education system to generalise the language, history and symbols of the nation, and (3) the army, *La Grande Armée* elevated to become a key instrument for the nationalising socialisation of the *Grande Nation* (Weber 1976: 493).

A fundamental part of this process was the construction of the "national heritage" which stemmed from Guizot's encouragement in 1830 of the conservation and cataloguing of the historical monuments of France. In 1838, Hugo, Montalambert and Merimée were appointed members of the historical committee of the monuments and artistic treasures of France. One of the most important events in this regard was, thanks to Villet Le Duc, the "invention of cathedrals" as national monuments; that is, as symbols of national unity in a secularised and divided society, by means of a discourse based on the own/Gothic – alien/neo-classical dichotomy, which established itself after 1848 (Mélonio 2001: 156).

It is not, therefore, necessary to wait, as is usually the case, for the nationali-sation of France during the Third Republic, for the trauma of the 1871 defeat, for the appearance of the "nationalist" party towards the end of the century (Birn-baum 1993: 88), for Maurice Barrés' famous article in *Le Figaro* in 1892, which introduced the term "nationalist" (Girardet 1966: 221), in order to detect, from the beginning of the Revolution, a process of the progressive incorporation into the republican programme of a strictly nationalist content (values, narratives, myths and symbols of a common ancestry, mission and destiny). On the con-trary, one can discern how, from an early stage, a peculiar attempt to equate the universal with the particular gradually establishes itself: the history of France with universal history, human rights with the "rights of man" and the citizen. Put another way, a growing synthesis of the abstract universal with the specific uni-versal. If, on the one hand, the Revolution was against tradition, with the need to complete the abstract skeleton of principles with flesh and blood, following the mobilisation there was a growing recovery of history, the myth of the Golden Age, of a common ancestry, of the glorious tradition of a language and culture with universal value (Nora 1986).

This is the ideological national–republican formula that, in essence, existed at the time of the July Monarchy and the Restoration, Armand Carrel and the "the nationals". It is possible to read in the pages of *Le National* this singular synthe-sis of the republic and the French nation, citizenship of rights, on the one hand, and *chauvinisme cocardier* and militaristic humanitarian messianism, on the other. These themes were later reformulated, although they already appear in Quinet (Herder's translator, incidentally), after the 1848 Revolution: France's destiny illuminates, at that time, a new providential universal "Mission", which would no longer be the *Code Civil* and the Enlightenment, but the liberation of oppressed nationalities.

But at the same time the ethnification of the republican concept is reinforced: the right to self-determination slowly ceases to be the property of the "peoples" understood as the citizenry, in order to become the right of oppressed nations, which possessed a particular culture, language, history, etc. which forged their collective identity. In relation to this, a highly significant event is the progressive semantic replacement of the term "nation" by that of "nationalité" in the 1840s, because it confirms the weakening of the universalist and cosmopolitan concept of the homeland at the end of a long road. In synthesis: the long journey from: (1) *national sovereignty*, where the nation is an abstract entity of reason, for the sole purpose of imputation of sovereignty and the foundation of censual suffrage (1791); to (2) *popular sovereignty*, or the nation understood as a specific popula-tion of citizens, although semiotically representing itself, in peculiar synecdoche, by the Jacobin vanguard, by the virtuous minority (1793) (Máiz 2007); (3) to the *sovereignty of the nation*, but now as a unanimous and homogeneous community of destiny, endowed with a universal civilising and colonial mission; (4) to the ethnic–cultural *French nation*, with its specific language, history, traditions, myths and symbols, at the heart of a conflicting friend and enemy logic, now external (England, Germany), now internal (Jews).

It was from 1870 onwards, however, during the war with Germany and the subsequent loss of Alsace Lorraine, that the ethnification and nationalisation of French political thought became properly established. This would ultimately have a significant effect on republican ideology itself: such as the drift from *opportuniste* republicanism, to Littré's *Republique conservatrice*, including Gambetta's *République transactionnelle* (Nicolet 1982).

All this took place during the "German crisis of French thought" which makes cultural nationalism of a German nature compatible with political, intellectual (Momssen, Strauss) and military confrontation with Germany (Digeon 1959), blurring once again the myth of the ethnic–civic dichotomy. For this reason it is necessary to look behind the supposed transparency of the civic narrative, the ambiguities and the internal tension that exist following the statements which, at first sight, seem to have an unequivocally strong political accent of a territorial and liberal nature: "What distinguishes nations is not race or language … but a community of ideas, interests, affections, and hopes. … Race and language are history and the past … what is current and alive are will, ideas, interests, affections" (Fustel de Coulanges 1870, in Girardet 1966: 213).

Above all we must pay attention to the traditional "voluntarist" reading of Renan. In effect, with the famous phrase from his lecture in the Sorbonne in 1882: "The existence of a nation is (if you forgive the metaphor) a continual plebiscite" (Renan 1947 I: 904), one can deduce a whole supposedly "voluntarist" and "civic" conception of the nation. Thus, the confirming element par excellence of the nation would be the freely expressed consent of the citizens. However, if one looks a little more closely, his position is far from being as unequivocal and political as many have tried to make it (Finkielkraut 1987).

Above all, his idea of the nation should be contextualised at the heart of a body of work that, from *L'Avenir de la Science*, including *Philosophie de l'Histoire Contemporaine*, to *La Réforme Intellectuelle et Morale de la France*, its explicit objective, despite its deceptive anti-clericalism, is a critique of the entire legacy of the Enlightenment and the Revolution. Thus, in *La Réforme…*, the critique of materialism and "French democracy" is extended to a demand for the late-feudal principle of "hierarchy" (Renan (1859) 1947 I: 29–68) and a historical determinism with Herderian roots. Despite the undeniable subsequent evolution of his thought as a result of the Franco-German conflict, Renan never accepted the legacy of the Enlightenment and the Revolution (Sternhell 1983: XXVII).

This provides a number of keys to why, first of all, there are many instances in his work of uses of the concept of nation which are a long way from the democratic and plebiscitary voluntarism that is attributed to him. Thus, for example, in a text of 1871, *La Réforme Intellectuelle et Morale de la France*, one can read "A nation is not the mere addition of the individuals that it comprises; it is a soul, a consciousness, a person, a living result" (Renan 1947 I: 361). This "soul of the nation", however, cannot survive on its own, but requires the help of a "college" that is officially responsible for ensuring this. Without this institutional support, our author continues, cemented by a single will, "like the dream of our democrats", that is, as the mere "national reason of the people" it will become, in a highly graphic description, a perishable house of sand (*une maison de sable*). In order to maintain the time-line that links the living with the dead the nation must be institutionalised, not forgetting that, unlike what is usually attributed to him "the current will of the nation, the plebiscite, even when it is seriously implemented, is not sufficient". The alternative leaves little room for doubt with regard to the author's conservative liberalism. As is demonstrated by his rejection of the "majorité numerique" and universal suffrage, any trace of the Republic and the nation that rose up against the King has disappeared: "A dynasty is the best institution to achieve this" (Renan 1947 I: 375). The relationship between the traditional dynastic institutions and the nation becomes so fundamental for the existence of the nation because the dynasty, in some way, precedes and is superior to the nation. In fact, it was the dynasty that produced the nation: "*le roi a fait la nation*" (Renan 1947 I: 380).

Second, even in *Qu'est-ce qu'une Nation?* the political–voluntarist conception is the result, above all, of the historical circumstances of Germany's annexation of Alsace Lorraine and the "objective" (linguistic, ethnic) arguments used to justify it by German intellectuals. Moreover, this is heavily nuanced by the surprising presence of elements coming from the very same ethnic, Germanic tradition, which had, in principle, been rejected by the voluntarist, civic concept. The idea is put forward here, for example, that "A nation is a soul, a spiritual principle" (Renan 1947 I: 903). In fact, for Renan, there are not one but two elements that confer nationalising charisma: (1) the past, history "the common possession of a rich legacy of memories (*d'un riche legs de souvenirs*); that is, "a heroic past, great men, glory … here lies the social capital on which the national idea is based" (Renan 1947 I: 904); and (2) consent, the explicit desire of co-nationals to live together.

Politics is clearly insufficient for Renan; common interests are not enough: "a *Zollverein* is not a homeland" (Renan 1947 I: 902); unexpectedly, the "complications of history" are also required. History as a narrative; that is, the "history" of past glories created explicitly as a national mythical story as opposed to history as a science, which often dilutes and clouds the singularity of the homeland: "Oblivion, even historical error, are an essential factor in the creation of a nation. That is why the progress of historical studies is often a danger for nationality" (Renan 1947 I: 891). Moreover, one should not disregard the culturalising essentialism that lies behind the argument of 1882. How, if he is unable to fully realise the omnipresence in his reasoning of history, tradition, the common ancestry; in short, the undivided legacy on which the nation is built: (*l'heritage qu'on a reçu indivis*) (Renan 1947 I: 904)?

The critique, in this particular text, of race as a nationalising factor, and its terrible result, the "zoological wars" (Renan 1947: 456), should not lead to the oblivion of its substantive racism: "the absence of healthy ideas about the inequality of races may lead to total decadence," he states in *Dialogues Philosophiques* (Renan 1947 I: 591). Also his militant anti-Semitism – "la race sémitique représente une combination inférieure de la nature humane" (Renan 1947 VIII: 144), which is evident in works like *Histoire Générale et Système Comparé des Langues Sémitiques*. Both elements would have an enormous influence on anti-Semitism (Jules Soury, Édouard Drumont) and on subsequent French nationalism (Barrès).

Let us concentrate now on the supporters of the Republic. The figure of Leon Gambetta is perhaps the one which best illustrates the nationalisation process of republicanism. This is because, in the 1870s, the leader of the Republican party not only reasserts the French nation, but also reformulates nationalism to suit the realities of the present, by contrasting the stereotypical "France Glorieuse" with the victim mentality of "la France vaincue et humiliée".

In short, what needs to be highlighted in the nationalisation process of French republicanism after 1870 – throughout the Third Republic – is the fact that, without initially renouncing revolutionary patriotism and the republican heritage of the Revolution, or at least not completely, the concept of the French nation undergoes a definitive shift towards the mythical–symbolic sphere, at the same time as the initial liberal–voluntarist articulation is diluted, through the following movements:

- Growing accidentalism of the forms of government: progressive diluting of the founding antagonism between monarchy and republic.
- Reinforcement of French particularism (*reserrement*) and ethnification of the concept of nation – the idea of "race" in Thierry and Taine, "history" in Renan (*souvenirs*), influence of Darwinism and positivism – at the same time as the appearance of a nationalism of the European retreat in the face of the universalism and civilising expansion of the Revolution and the Empire. It could be exemplified as the shift from the "révolutionner l'Europe" (Sieyès) to "mon patriotisme est en France" (Clemenceau).
- State education will be clearly conceived as the fundamental nationalising institution. Thus, a nationalist pedagogy goes beyond mere civic education (history, geography, imposition of the French national language over the *patois*, cultivation of national values, etc.). The Ferry law of 1882 synthesises all this with its explicit statement of "the wish to found a national education system" (Ferry 1996: 109).
- Dissemination of a new synthesis between the idea of *Justice* or liberal-democratic ideal (a unitary and indivisible republic) and an idea of *Common Good* based on the new hegemonic social classes (the traditional bourgeois moral values: discipline, work, saving, *chauvinisme*, etc. raised to "national values").
- Reinforcement of militarism, not only by means of the key role of the army at the heart of the state, but also with the partial militarisation of the national education system (the "school battalions" of 1882). It should not be forgotten,

in this regard, that in 1882 Jules Ferry ordered the distribution of 20,000 copies of the *Soldiers' Songs* to schools. The books of Paul Déroulède, an admirer and vulgariser of Renan, founder of the Ligues des Patriotes – *De l'Éducation Militaire* (1882) or the *La Défense Nationale* (1883) – demonstrate the extreme dilution of republican patriotism in the search for a "strong regime", but without renouncing universal suffrage yet (Winock 1982: 293). What appears here, beyond the militarisation of the education system, is a whole idea of the nation; a new, united France founded on military virtues, the values of sacrifice and discipline, worship of the leader, support for coups d'état. The slogan "Pour la patrie, par le livre et par l'epée" of the education *Leagues* perfectly synthesises the new form of nationalism that was developing.

• Colonialism: hand in hand with the European retreat before Germany (which would firmly establish the nationalism of "la revanche") came a new impetus for colonialism in Africa and Asia: France receives a new "Mission", the "civilisation of inferior races" in Ferry's words when extending the French education law to include Algeria.

• Definitive prominence of "la Nation" in contrast to "the Republic". As the early republicanism and secularism had previously cleared the way, and as neither God nor the monarch are able to obstruct the new direction, the nation emerges as the destination community, as a collective being generated by "solidarité nationale". From this stems the new synthesis of the *Republican Nation* as "cultural, spiritual and moral Unity", as stated in J. Barni's *Manuel Republicain* (1992). Or, put another way, the French Republic now reformulated, in a very significant way, as a "moral person", as "la plus haute expression de l'esprit humain", in the words of Gambetta during his famous speech at Annecy (1872).

Finally, towards the end of the century, starting with *Boulangisme*, "protestation nationale" (1888) and the "parti national" (1888–1889), including what occurred before and after the Dreyfus Affaire, until the *Action Française*, the Nationalism of the "nationalists" would take a step towards the predominance of mythical–symbolic factors and a clearly organicist bias of the idea of the nation, even in some cases anti-Semitic and authoritarian, which would end up eroding republicanism once and for all (Tombs 1991). It should be stressed, however, that only Maurras, with the formulation of "nationalisme intégrale", would make a definitive break with the republican regime, declaring democracy itself "anti-national": neither Barrès nor Péguy would nominally renounce the Republic.

It is worth highlighting the following elements of the new national–republican synthesis:

• Absolutisation of French cultural uniformism (communitarian essentialism): "une chaire et un cimetière" (Barrès) as fundamental factors of the nation.

• Culturalist and biological racism, depending on the case, based on Drumont's anti-Semitism, *La France Juive* (1886), and the historical anti-

Semitism (in its anti-capitalist version) of the republican and socialist left, which would make even Jaurés hesitate (Birnbaum 1993).

• Catholic reaction, recovery of religion as a national trait (Péguy) and diffusion of the Jeanne d'Arc myth (La France Catholique) vs. Marianne (the Republic) and from that, once more, regarding Jews as internal enemies (the Other) of France.

• Reinforcement of militarism (Barrès' "La République armée") and revenge nationalism against Germany as the historical enemy (Maurras' "La révanche reine de France").

• Change from *jus sanguinis* to *jus solis*, although corrected by a key factor: the necessary socialisation required by the 1989 law, concession of nationality to second-generation immigrants to prevent foreigners who had been resident for a long time from being excluded from military service. In the words of the Conseil Constitutionnel in 1993, the *jus solis* "is not a fundamental principle of the Republic", and would be introduced quite late (1889) and "pour répondre notamment aux exigentes de la conscription". And, moreover, it was a form of *jus solis* conceived as a unifying instrument and to block the creation of ethnic–cultural minorities at the heart of France (Brubaker 1992: 105), an ethnic–cultural complement of the centralism of the "République une et indivisible" and, as a result, with clearly racist features: the law would only apply in Algeria, despite the fact that it was a wholly French territory, to Europeans of the *Hexagone* and not the indigenous Algerians (Weil 2002: 61).

• Predominance of openly ethnic nationalism: the past, myths of a common ancestry, the narrative of palingenesis, discourse of decadence and resurrection (Barrès' "la terre et les morts").

• Juridical–political construction of the figure of the "foreigner" (Noiriel 1988): colonialism and assimilationism as two aspects of the same process of the fusion of citizenship/nationality.

• It should be stressed, however, that there were important differences between Barrès' and Maurras' ideas of the nation and previous French nationalism, both in its republican and counter-revolutionary versions. Barrès, in fact, retains an large component of traditionalism which, along the road that takes him from Renan to Taine, leads him not only to deplore modernity, democracy, and parliamentarianism, but to yearn for the old France, its traditions – "je me baigne dans la tradition française", he wrote in his *Cahiers* (IV: 67) – and its values (order, hierarchy, honour). In the exceptional trilogy of the *Roman de l'Energie Nationale* (1897–1902) we find a superb synthesis of the past components of his nationalism: (1) the decontextualisation of French tradition and history as the principal evil that modernity causes in its rootless young protagonists ("étrangeres à nos habitudes traditionelles"). The loss of roots of these "déracinés" young people, of the umbilical link with regional and national reality, is presented as a genuine loss of the meaning of life, of personal alienation ("un jeune isolé de sa nation ne vaut guère plus qu'un mot detaché d'un texte" (Barrès 1994

I: 1109); (2) The cause of all this is a French political and education system imbued with rationalist abstraction, derived from the triumph of disastrous enlightened philosophy, exemplified in *Les Déracinés* in the character of Boutiller, a reflection of the Kantian professor of philosophy Burdeau. With this education system, the bourgeois state produces a denationalised France, "dissociée et descerebrée" (Barrès 1994 I: 616); (3) This universalism of reason leads to the illusion of cosmopolitanism, to "se passer de la patrie", to the falsity of the "citoyens de l'humanité", of the "affranchis"; (4) The loss of the nation is articulated by the open rejection of the liberal state, of individual rights, of constitutional guarantees and, above all, by an omnipresent anti-parliamentarianism ("le parlamentarisme n'est qu'un systéme de chantage") (Barrès 1994 I: 1075).

But, on the other hand, Barrès' radical nationalism indicates a way to "refaire la substance nationale entamée" (620), which markedly breaks away from French counter-revolutionary traditionalism: (1) above all because its anti-Cartesianism and comprehensive critique of the Enlightenment extends into open irrationalism, anti-intellectualism, and support for the unconscious and instinct; (2) which, in turn, leads to partisan thought, to the rejection of objective and universal values, to particularism, to the chauvinist bias of moral and political judgement; (3) the nation becomes nature which imposes itself on the individual, in the irresistible determinism of "une nation de chaire et d'os", in anti-voluntarism based on the mythical–historical legacy of "la terre et les morts"; (4) having rejected the class struggle, the question of the nationalist discourse turns determinedly towards populism; (5) the repertoire of action leads to the spontaneity of the masses, which expresses "national energy", revolt, street-fighting against the established order: ("le plaisir instinctif d'être dans un troupeau", he wrote in *Mes Cahiers* (I 1929: 39)); (6) the theme of the removal of heterogeneity from the heart of the people and xenophobia emerge ("reagir contre les étrangers qui nous envahissent"), which overflows into open racism and anti-Semitism; (7) radical anti-Protestantism and agnostic and instrumental Catholicism towards nationalism, conceived strategically as "l'expression de notre sang".

Maurras' "integral nationalism" shares a number of the postulates mentioned above. Among other features common to anti-Protestantism, we might mention anti-individualism, anti-Semitism, xenophobia, and anti-parliamentarianism. But there are also marked differences between the two. Of course, Barrès' refusal to condemn the Republic and the Revolution as an indivisible and unavoidable heritage of the history of France is a long way from the recovery of the monarchy and the explicit condemnation of the French Revolution espoused by Maurras and the ideology of *Action Française*. But we must look more deeply into the roots of this disagreement, as they are highly revealing of the ideas of nationhood and nationalism that are at stake.

Of special interest is the scope of the equivocal Maurrasian postulate: "Politique d'abord". On the one hand, Maurras breaks with the counter-revolutionary postulates of De Maistre and Bonald, not with regard to the political supremacy of religion but, and above all, because it overcomes the substantial alien nature of the very idea of nation typical of counter-revolutionary thinking, for which the very concept of nation synthesised the entire legacy of the Revolution. But this break does not mean that Maurras opts for an authoritarian form of political voluntarism in his concept of the nation, neither can he be considered a precursor of fascism. Above all, his integral nationalism is aimed against the key synthesis of the French Revolution: reason and will. But he does this using rationalist philosophy, which is diametrically opposed to that of Barrès, as a starting point in order to rob the revolution of the monopoly of reason and thus justify the idea of the nation with a certain kind of modernity that is not unrelated to the world of science. But, on the other hand, it is decidedly anti-voluntarist. In fact, "Politique d'abord" has nothing to do with the ontological primacy of politics, that is, of decision, of the artificial versus the natural, but quite the contrary: "politique la première, la première dans l'ordre du temps, nullement dans l'ordre de la dignité" (Maurras 1972: 172). That is, against revolutionary ideology, the immutable being, the nature of things should prevail over the duty of being and the nation as the unanimous organic totality should prevail over the individual and his will. The Maurrasian nation differs from the republican nation in that the latter was based on "l'impieté vers ce qui est".

For this reason, despite the fact that in the *Enquête sur la Monarquie* Maurras introduces the concept of "revolution conservatrice", does not hesitate to advocate coups d'état, postulates the determined and energetic action of a vanguard that imposes monarchy on the masses, etc., he fails to take the final step towards total rupture with conservatism's and counter-revolutionary traditionalism's idea of the nation, nor does he accept a reading of the national dimension based on artificialist voluntarism. Maurras' integral nationalism is heading down this road but does not go very far. Thus, for example, in the novel *Dilemme de Marc Sangnier* he defends "l'absou l'inmouable" of "l'être français", shades of Maistre or Le Play, by returning to the same ontology that advocates an immutable order of the French nation around the hereditary, traditional, anti-parliamentarian and decentralised monarchy. All this is expressed through a form of discourse that weaves a semantic web of oppositions that reflect the servitude of tradition in integral nationalism, at the same time as its great originality: nature/artifice, nation/state, monarchy/republic, Catholicism/Protestantism, Provence/Paris, Mediterranean/Atlantic, centralisation/local liberties, vanguard/masses, coup d'état/democratic elections, etc.

The real break in French nationalism, which is hardly hinted at in the work of Barrès and Maurras, would occur with fascist nationalism, the anti-nationalist radical nationalism of the revolutionary right: Georges Valois, Thierry Maulnier, Pierre Drieu La Rochelle, Robert Brasillach, etc. Only with these authors will the "besoin d'action" and a *decisionist* conception of the nation evolve towards an extreme antidemocratic and violent "voluntarism". Thus, paradoxically, at the end of a long road which started with the revolutionary concept of the nation in Sieyès – a road that saw the gradual ethnification of the republican concept of nation until the final expulsion of all forms of republicanism – the only French voluntarist and political concept of the nation would be that of a decisionist, anti-republican, authoritarian and fascist form of nationalism (see below, Historical map of ideas of nationhood in France). Leaving the very interesting controversy regarding the existence and features of French fascism (Lévy 1981; Milza 1987; Winock 2004; Dobry 2003), let us now turn to the highly illustrative cases of Maulnier and Drieu La Rochelle in relation to the issues that interest us here.

Thierry Maulnier, despite being highly influenced at first by Barrès, formulates a different version of "néo-nationalisme français" in which the traditionalist articulation of the nation gives way to a revolutionary, voluntarist, agonistic, authoritarian and violent vision; a kind of neo-nationalism that, representing a clear break with previous French nationalisms, regards itself as "anti-nationalist" as is revealed by the title of his most important work *Au Delà du Nationalisme*.

Above all, Maulnier's nationalism completely abandons all links with the past or Arcadian dreams of returning to the traditional France: "the nation no longer lies in the current state of things but in the will to change them" (Maulnier 1938: 230). For him, nationalism consists, above all, in an "action politique créatrice" which, faced with tradition and restoration, proposes the creation of a new order through which the community of the nation recovers the possibility of deciding its own destiny and triumphing in a "new synthesis of the antagonisms that tear it apart. The nation can only be rebuilt through a liberating metamorphosis" (Maulnier 1938: 227). It is important to highlight this synthesis of the palingenetic myth of decadence and resurrection, and the radical novelty of the new world of the nation which springs from revolutionary action. In this way, nationalist *will* and revolutionary *will* come together in the act of historical creation of the nation: "la seule voie politique du nationalisme est la voie révolutionnaire", "une revolution ne peut être que nationale", etc. (Maulnier 1938: 226). Hence the strategic political objective of neo-nationalism:

> to interest the nation in the revolution in an organic way, as it is the only one that can carry it out; and to interest the nation in the revolution, as it is the only thing that can save it.
>
> (Maulnier 1938: 249)

Only in this decisionist context of national political mobilisation is it possible to comprehend his undisguised admiration for some aspects of Marxism: "théorie grosière de l'histoire et la societé, mais théorie géniale de l'action revolutionnaire" (Maulnier 1938: 232). However, this does not prevent the prediction that the era of class struggle must end in order to foreground the new nationalist driving force of history, which is: "l'infrastructure organique ou biologique des communautés humaines" (Maulnier 1938: 198). However, the "revolution nationale" which is advocated does not harbour any dream of France as a reconciled community, but is based on an agonistic idea of the nation as an "equilibre féconde d'antagonismes": "Revolutionary and totalitarian action, as the embodiment of supreme efficacy, only attains (aboutit) a valuable political creation insofar as it constructs a national structure based on natural antagonisms" (Maulnier 1938: 239).

But it is in the prolific literary and political work of Pierre Drieu La Rochelle that *anti-nationalist neo-nationlism* reaches its highest levels of authoritarian modernism, voluntarism, anti-traditionalism, revolution, and purifying and nihilistic violence. A form of radical nationalism which is, in all other respects, explicitly directed against those who, like Maurras, have not learnt the terrible lesson of the century: "un monarchiste n'est jamais un moderne: il n'a point la brutalité, le simplisme barbare d'un moderne" (Sterhnell 1978: 285).

Both in his essays *Socialisme Fasciste* (1934), *Chronique Politique* (1943) etc. and in his novels, above all the extraordinary *Gilles* (1939), we find the most extreme expression of this kind of revolutionary and anti-nationalist French nationalism: "le nationalisme est perimée" (Drieu 1939: 56). In Drieu's work the absolute imperative of French national unity, a lyrical vision of the regenerated and purified nation as opposed to the decadence and rottenness of liberal modernity – "une conception spirituelle, esthétique de la nation" (Drieu 1934: 221) – links up with the principal themes of contemporary fascism: "Ce parti ne peut être que national et socialiste" (1934: 96). Thus, among others, we could mention: the cult of youth and the new; justification of violence, cult of the body and physical strength – the contrast of "la fiertè du corps", of "le bon athlete" with the bourgeois "intellectuel ventripotent" (Drieu 1943: 45); the foregrounding of revolutionary spontaneity ("les forces spontanées de la vie, de la santé, du sang" (Drieu 1943: 50); contempt of material well-being and rejection of the mediocrity of bourgeois values of the *Revêuse Bourgeoisie* (Drieu 1937: 89): profit, obsession with money, usefulness, tedium ... which are contrasted with the heroic values of action against the established order, and "une disposition au sacrifice, une volonté de combat" (Drieu 1934: 202); support for war ("La Guerre c'est ma patrie") (Drieu 1939: 75), and as a consequence, for the archetype of the "guerrier" in contrast to the "clerc"; antagonistic proximity to Marxism (je n'en veux pas moins comme les marxistes détruire la société actuelle, constituir une force de combat..." (Drieu 1939: 521), and admiration of Lenin and his "politique au lieu de commandement"; an obvious irrationalism and taste for instinct and the aesthetic of the myth, directly straight against "une conception intellectualiste et rationaliste de la vie qui est tout à fait perimée" (Drieu 1934: 53), bearing in mind that "La rationalisme c'est l'agonie de la raison" (Drieu 1939: 560); overcoming class struggle through nationalist populism: "renverser la dictature francmaçonne par une coalition de jeunes bourgeois et jeunes ouvriers" (Drieu 1939: 421); not forgetting, finally, anti-Semitism and racism, based not on theories of race, but on the enemy within, the complete opposite of the nation: "je ne peux pas supporter les juifs parce qu'ils sont par excellence le monde moderne" (Drieu 1939: 112).

As a result of this long evolution, throughout the nineteenth century and the first half of the twentieth, and despite important differences that cannot be overlooked, France accumulated a penetrating sediment of organicism in the concept of the nation that would cement a hidden consensus which, from the beginning of the 1914–1918 war onwards, would partially affect both the right and the left and would project its implicit interpretative norms of the nation and the republic over contemporary France. Even among the most ardent defenders of republicanism and peace between nations such as Jaurés, Allemane, Hervé, Vaillant, etc. one can discern the footprint not only of civic patriotism, but also of this nationalist ethnification of republicanism. The words of Jean Jaurés in *L'Armée Nouvelle* of 1911 show how far this process had gone:

> The homeland is not exclusively founded on economic categories … it possesses much greater organic depth and much greater idealistic height. Its roots go deep into human life itself and, in a manner of speaking, into the physiology of man.
>
> (Jaurés 2001: 326)

We find a indissoluble ethnic–civic discourse that articulates cultural and linguistic absolutism, anti-particularist centralism and unitarianism, historical narrative of military and civilising *Grandeur* and, finally, designation of the "other", the immigrant, as culturally alien and inferior, although there are two alternatives: republican and assimilationist, on the one hand, and "nationalist" and exclusive, on the other.

It is quite significant that the work of Mauco, *Les Étrangers en France*, the first study of immigration in France, by an author with decisive influence in the public policies of immigration during the Vichy period and the early years following the Liberation (Weil 2002), does not establish a *biological* criterion for exclusion, one of racial purity, but of *cultural* superiority, when diagnosing the dangers that immigration represents, as the carrier of "the contrary of reason and sense of finesse characteristic of the French people" (Mauco 1932: 557). Hence the, sometimes deceptive, cultural, not biological, factor, of this – in a strict sense – *raceless racism* and its criteria for exclusion: "the others" do not share, nor will ever be able to share completely, the same past, the same memories, the same culture. For this reason it is by no means accurate to talk about *jus solis* in the French republican tradition, but of *jus solis* plus assimilation (second generation immigrants). That is, the acquisition of nationality requires socialisation in French culture. In short, we are seeing the roots of a new equation: assimilation = naturalisation (Silverman 1992: 32).

"Français de papier" was the expression of Action Française, "Être français: ça se mérite" is the slogan of Lepenism. That is, immigrants may be juridically naturalised, but would nevertheless remain alien to the French nation, that is, to its memories, narratives and symbols. But the republican criteria, adopted during the Third French Republic, is that residence and work are not sufficient criteria for naturalisation, but that cultural assimilation is necessary through the two fundamental devices of nationalisation: state education and the army. Both of these state apparatuses have nationalising missions as transmitters of the history, myths, values and symbols of the nation, and although the latter loses importance after the 1914–1918 war, the education system would continue until the present as the *lieu sacré* of the République. The idea that being educated in the society creates a national bond is the corollary of the republican conception that nationality is founded on socialisation: not on ethnic data, and not on a voluntary or contractual act either (Weil 1999: 61).

Assimilationism and *jus solis* for the second generation of immigrants would remain as a republican constant – apart from during Vichy – from the 1889 law onwards, surviving the successive reforms to broaden the citizenship law in 1927, 1945 and 1973, and the more restrictive 1993 law (Hargreaves 1995: 161).

2 Republicanism, nationalism and immigration in contemporary France

From the 1980s onwards, several political conflicts related with immigration had an impact on this historical legacy of the ethnic–cultural concept of nation hidden behind the seamless veil of the republic, which indissolubly links nationality and citizenship, and would reveal all the contradictions of the "civic" French model. It is worth remembering that in the 1980s there were a number of protests by young Algerian immigrants regarding the automatic concession of French citizenship, which some considered to be a violation of their Algerian identity. *Civic* inclusion thus became the ethno-cultural exclusive imposition of French nationality (Mangin 1981). But, moreover, it would soon be clear that, beneath the shiny surface of republican universalism of rights, in the shadows there lurked a nationalist particularism of cultural assimilationism.

Three successive debates took place with regard to this issue:

1   the debate regarding immigrants' right to *vote* (since 1981 and still unresolved);
2   the debate regarding *nationality* (from 1985 until the 1998 reform, which has established the principles of (a) equality of access to nationality for resident foreigners and (b) autonomy of explicitly stated will of belonging);
3   the debate regarding *secularism* (from the first *affaire du foulard* in 1989).

Here we will focus on the last of these, with occasional reference to the second when necessary, due to the links between the two. First of all, we should synthesise the fundamental factors of change, with regard to the immigration problem, which appeared in France during the 1980s (Brubaker 1992; Silverman 1992; Hargreaves 1995; Geddes 2003):

•   A previous element dates from earlier decades: immigration comes to be regarded as a structural rather than a temporal phenomenon. As a result, it is no longer tackled according to the current needs of the labour market, but is seen as a social and political problem, involving the issues of coexistence, public order and education (Noiriel 1988).
•   The existence of a large population of North African immigrants (850,000 Algerians, 27,000 Moroccans, 150,000 Tunisians), many of them second-generation.

- The realisation that Islam had become France's second religion, made official in the President of the Republic's speech of 17 December 2003 during the reception given for the report of the Stasi commission.
- The growth of the National Front with its xenophobic and exclusionist programme, which was aimed directly at the eradication of *jus solis* and the expulsion of immigrants.
- Rise of the left's discourse regarding multiculturalism and the right to be different, and tolerance of socialist policies with regard to immigration (specifically, those of Lionel Jospin, which were continued by Jack Lang).
- Increase in social and political conflicts: terrible living conditions in the ghettoes, lack of safety in neighbourhoods inhabited by North Africans, as well as growing mobilisation and political protests by these sectors.

The debates would initially involve the nationality code, based on the *assimilationist jus solis* mentioned earlier, above all regarding articles 23 (which awarded French nationality at birth to third-generation immigrants) and 44 (which gave French nationality to second-generation immigrants born in France and resident in the country during the previous five years) (Geddes 2003: 63; Weil 2002).

The debate arose both in the ranks of the republican right and those of the socialist republicans and not only affected the automatic nature of acquiring citizenship (which was finally eliminated in the 1998 reform) and the competition that immigrants represented for a labour market in crisis, but also the accusation that the republican political system as a whole, with regard to immigrants, was *insufficiently assimilationist*. In other words, an old *both ethnic and cultural nationalist* concern re-emerged: that immigrants only became "Français de papier", without becoming, if not "Français de souche", at least "Français de coeur". Thus, following the attack on the French formulation of *jus solis* (residence + socialisation), another hidden dimension needed to be addressed: the questioning on the grounds of the assimilationist shortcomings of the current legislation and the policies of the socialist governments that tolerated the instrumental acquisition of French citizenship by immigrants who were not socialised in the national culture.

One of the arguments was shared by a wide range of sectors, albeit with different nuances and articulations, in the 1980s. This was: (1) on the one hand, the assimilation institutions, mainly the education system, had ceased to fulfil, thanks to an angelical "prejudge post-colonialiste" (Kintzler 1996: 106), its nationalising responsibilities and it was necessary to recover these functions, by means of re-secularisation, in opposition to the multiculturalist discourse (Laborde 2008); (2) on the other hand, the fundamentalist homogenisation of Islam had begun and it was conceived as a whole, explicitly and implicitly, to be alien to French culture and national values (Tribalat 2002) and, in consequence, as difficult to assimilate, which meant that it was necessary to be on the defensive with regard to the formation of Islamist community ghettoes.

The left's difficulties in all this debate sprang from the fact that, despite maintaining a clearly differentiated political position on other issues, the majority of its leaders share with those of the right the unquestioned core idea of a national-ist/assimilationist articulation of the republic, the "French model", which leads inexorably to the common ground of cultural monolithism and assimilation as pillars of citizenship (Tournon 2005). In other words, it is not only, nor even fundamentally, reasons of a liberal or republican nature that underlie the critique of difference and particularism by French republicanism. Rather it is reasons based on culturalist nationalism – "Le monde de gauche, secrètement national..." wrote Drieu La Rochelle with exceptional acuity in the 1930s (Drieu 1934: 86) – that had gradually installed itself at the heart of republicanism, para-sitising "civic patriotism". The debate regarding the *affaire du foulard* would thus prove to be not only extraordinarily divisive within the republican left, but revealing of the untenability of its conception of "civic–nationalist" *soi-disant* nation.

In fact, despite the undeniable differences, it is of prime importance to recog-nise the common *nationalist assumptions* shared by most republicans, socialists or liberals, many of whom became, at the time, a kind of *enragés de la Répub-lique* (Mounier 1999). Everyone from the "Socialism and Republic" group led by Jean Pierre Chevènement, intellectuals such as Regis Debray, Finkielkraut, Elisabeth Badinter, Alain Renaut, Catherine Kintzler and others, to highly authoritative figures with great political–institutional weight such as Dominique Schnapper. For all of them, the *superimposition of nationality and citizenship* led over and over again to a dual conflict of republic/particularism and secular-ism/difference.

It is significant, in this respect, both because of the personality of the authors and the media impact it had, to point out that in relation to the *affaires du foulard* five influential philosophers, including Finkielkraut, Debray, Kintzler and Bad-inter, published a manifesto in *Le Nouvel Observateur* on 2 November 1989 (Kintzler 1996: 78). The article denounced, above all, the unacceptable conces-sions in the education system that had been made by republican France in the interests of cultural diversity:

> the Republic is not a mosaic of ghettoes ... trusting exclusively in the natural light of human beings. The education system is at the root of the Republic, and for that reason the destruction of the education system means the beginning of the end of the Republic.

As a result, secularism was pushed to centre stage in the French contemporary debate. In fact, even according to the highly nuanced document produced by the Stasi commission, "laïcité" possesses "the rank of founding value" around which the French Republic has been constructed and represents "a conception of the common good" which rests on three inseparable values: freedom of conscience, equality of rights of all spiritual options and the neutrality of the state.

However, secularism as a representation of "a conception of common good" is historically articulated in France, at the heart of a wider ethic–political con-ception: unitarian nationalist, culturally absolutist, enemy of all forms of particu-

larism or difference ... which results in the empirical–transcendental nationalist
pair of *assimilationism/centralism*. It is true that in the past there was a difference between the militant anticlerical secularism of Emile Combes or Gambetta
himself ("Le cléricalisme voilá l'énemi") and the more neutralist version of
Aristide Briand, Jules Ferry or Jean Jaurés. But it should not be forgotten that
the two are reconciled at the last moment on an underlying premise, which is: a
homogenising cultural–nationalist vision of French society, which produces
assimilationism and acculturation as the only form of *nationalist integration* of
citizenship for immigrants.

Apart from the gender criticism ("le foulard symbole de la soumision
féminine"), the manifesto not only regarded education as the *sacré republicain*
par excellence with the burden that that represents, but also accepts the main
characteristics of the nationalist version of republicanism of the Third Republic
which we have synthesised earlier: cultural absolutism, centralism, an essentialist and trans-historical notion of the French nation, citizenship equivalent to
nationality and consequent exclusion of cultural differences, substantivity of
shared national values, threat of the Other (Islam understood homogeneously as
Islamic fundamentalism), etc. In short, it left no room for dialogue and connection with the debates on secularism in the Muslim world (Bencheikh 1998).

However, one of the missions of secularism is precisely the creation of a
public arena that is common to and shared by all cultural and religious differences (Laborde 2008). However, when articulated within French nationalist discourse of the "défense de l'unité du corps social" – which is riddled with
ethnic–cultural mythical elements and organicist postulates – it becomes a sec-
tarian principle directed in a militant fashion against the public presence of cultural and religious pluralism, which is the result of the complexity of
contemporary French society.

Other infringements of the principle of republican secularism had occurred
beforehand, but had not caused any alarm: the existence of subsidised private
Catholic schools, the use in state schools of symbols and emblems of other
(Christian and Jewish) religions, or even the use of the veil by the mothers and
grandmothers of North African adolescents, which had failed to arouse any conflict whatsoever. If, on the other hand, the *affaire du foulard* has provoked conflict this is because it is attacking, in our opinion, the roots of the nationalist
discourse underlying French republicanism. The veil threatened, in the privileged public arena of the republic, to cause a crisis in the education system,
which is the model of French national citizenship. In other words, the possibility
of integration without assimilation or, put another way, integration as citizens
without national–cultural assimilation. It is not so much an alarmist form of
secular fundamentalism that underlies the republican denouncements of the
foulard, but that behind the universalist republicanism invoked there is the fear
that anti-particularist republican nationalism is being called into question. Following the republic, it is the French nation that feels threatened, not the universal
republic, but the "cultural identity of France" (Táguieff 1996). The Islamic veil
of the "les filles voilées de Creil" shows up the *persona ficta*, the homogeneous,

unitarian and centralist collective identity of the French nation. Paradoxically, the veil is criticised as a symbol of the (particularist) communitarianism of Islam in the name of an implicit and unquestioned (national/universal) French communitarian nationalism. In the end, the ethnicism of minorities is denounced in the name of the *majority ethnicity*, to use the term introduced by Smith and refined by Kaufmann, of the "dominant ethnic group" (Smith 2004; Kaufmann 2004).

But, moreover, the supreme levelling of differences, the construction of a culturally homogeneous, French national republic, by definition alien to ethnic or territorial particularism, is reinforced through the creation of an "Other", Islam, equally homogeneous, with a very similar format, although not in its content, to the way "the Jew" was constructed during the Dreyfus Affair.

Sociological and political studies, however, reveal a very different picture. Above all, they underline the diversity of the collective identities of the North African immigrants with regard to the French nation: from assimilation into the majority culture to Islamic communitarianism, including diverse kinds of accommodation and compatibility between both identities (Venel 2004). This calls into question, incidentally, the close link between the nationalist interpretation of the co-implication of nationality and citizenship. Moreover, the veil, far from exclusively representing an "act of political militancy" (Kintzler 1996: 106), is worn for a variety of very diverse reasons: (1) those of a traditional nature, from the immigrant mothers and grandmothers who have always worn it; (2) those of a family nature, of acceptance of loyalty to the family, but as a way to integrate and embrace the French world; (3) those involving individual assertiveness, as an anti-anomic and dual sign (conciliation of the veil and situated modernity); (4) those of a fundamentalist nature (Gaspard and Khosrokhavar 1995; Cesari 1998). However, all these nuances are overshadowed by the reduction to fundamentalist communitarianism, renunciation of republican ideology and ingenuousness in the face of the dangers of radical Islam, etc. and only two alternatives: "republican assimilation or community chaos" (Cesari 1998: 192). Here the adolescents are homogenised and essentialised, as a danger to the republic, and are subsequently collectively stigmatised in a chain of equivalences that go beyond the borders of France: from Creuil and Aubervilliers to Kabul and Teheran.

It is striking that even in the responses to the text of Finkielkraut *et al.* by "multicultural intellectuals" such as Táguieff, Touraine or Henri Lévy, there is a predominance of considerations of opportunity and strategy: reinforcement of fundamentalism, yielding to the Nationalism of Le Pen, etc., but neither the assimilationist model – the myth of the secular republic – nor the nationalised republicanism in which the postulate of French-style secularism attains its full political significance, are questioned in any depth. And, nevertheless, only this nationalism can fully explain the significant disregard (stated, in fact, by the Conseil d'État) of the fact that secularism is an obligation of the education system and teachers and of the State; not of the students, nor of the society. Moreover, texts denouncing the ethnification of the *affaire du foulard*, such as the recent one by Bouamama, inexplicably reject the relevance of the debate "in essentialist terms" (referring to the nation, identity and community), and express in terms of "social criticism" (class, injustice, domination, etc.), when it is precisely this essentialism which needs dismantling (Bouamama 2004).

All this is not so surprising, however, if we investigate the self-clarification process of prominent republican intellectuals who, in relation to the debate regarding the veil, have shifted, with exceptions such as that of Catherine Kintzler, from a universalist liberal–republican position to the implicit assumption, to a greater or lesser extent, of a French culturalist communitarianism or nationalism. This is true of, say, R. Debray, A. Finkielkraut or D. Schnapper, for whom the classical liberal arguments: separation of the public sphere (justice), as a neutral space of the state, from the private sphere (ideas of good), as a social space of pluralism; autonomy, as a capacity for revising ends and ideas of good, in contrast with authenticity, that is, loyalty to tradition, etc. increasingly give way to an uncritical rediscovery of ethnicity as a founding principle of the French nation. As Debray (Debray 2006) always displayed a greater weakness for the "group instinct", as Finkielkraut denounced, let us briefly focus, for illustrative reasons, on the two other thinkers.

Finkielkraut became famous due to *La Défaite de la Pensée*, an influential neo-enlightened attack, based on the "immutable values" of republicanism, against the romantic spirit of *Volksgeist* that resides in contemporary policies of identity. All this was based on a hyper-voluntarist, and according to what we have seen earlier, a partial and, in the final analysis, incorrect reading of Renan (Finkelkraut 1987: 31). The rehabilitation of Dreyfus was made to equate to that of universal values with regard to chauvinism, the triumph of the contractual definition of the nation as opposed to the collective soul and tradition, while multiculturalism testifies to the disappearance of the Drefusards and the end of French loyalty to the universal (Finkielkraut 1987: 106). However, that which he detested in 1987, "the reduction of France to its Frenchness", years later turns into an unequivocal culturalist defensive turn, in defence of this "little nation" (sic) faced with universalist cosmopolitanism and the loss of roots: "variations of the same discourse: everything is the same because all men are the same. Faced with this triumphant nihilism, only small nations and weak inheritances remain. We are all Quebecois". In *L'Ingratitude*, the scene we find is characterised by an undisguised French cultural nationalist discourse denouncing the "cosmopolitan ecstasy" and "French francophobia", which contrasts belonging to autonomy, communitarian allegiance to indifference to all temporal or geographical attachment, the USA as a "country of communities" in contrast to France, a paradise, it would appear, of "the passion of equality against cultural preference" (Finkielkraut 1999: 153). All this taken to the extreme of inverting, without quoting him, the words – a synthesis of the nascent republican ideology which has already been mentioned – of Rabaud Saint-Étienne: "Whether we like it or not, our history is our code" (Finkielkraut 1999: 97). In short, all the themes of culturalist ethnic nationalism are successively recovered here: history, language, tradition, cultural conservationism, true "conservatism" ... at the service of a French culture not only pre-designed but, to use Renan's words, as an "undivided heritage", a homogeneous and seamless whole, which only permits the passive socialisation in school of the new generations which are obliged to "feel completely at home in the French language". This French national preoccupation, also in the words of Renan, can be seen in the interviews of the programme "Répliques" which Finkielkraut directed in France Culture and were published with the title *Qu'est-ce que la France?* (Finkielkraut 2007).

For her part, Dominique Schnapper, a prominent exponent of the so-called civic–republican nationalism, undergoes a somewhat similar evolution. Thus, in works like *La France de l'Integration* (1991) and especially *La Communauté des Citoyens* (1994) she theorises about a civic concept of the nation as the "fruit of political will" linking "nationality and citizenship" as the "foundations of political legitimacy" (Schnapper 1991: 63, 143), so that "particularisms are relegated to the private sphere" (Schnapper 1991: 101). In *La Communauté des Citoyens*, based on an individual and universalist concept of citizenship alien to any cultural feature whatsoever, and a notion of the public sphere as a space that "transcends all particularisms through citizenship", she proposed a concept of the nation "defined by a form of sovereignty that integrates peoples in a community of citizens, whose existence legitimises the internal and external action of the State" (Schnapper 1994: 48). Here the author postulates a national model that "transcends nationalities", conceived as a "public project", a "universal national project". A form of nationality that is the horizon of the defence of liberty, equality and human rights. This "republican model" of the nation is linked, finally, to "strong state institutions that justify themselves through a system of values" (Schnapper 1994: 96).

A few years later, however, in *La Relation à l'Autre*, Schnapper accentuates the cultural dimension of the republican concept of the nation. It is true that in her earlier books she mentions the necessary "acculturation" of immigrants, the replacement of the "right to difference" by the "right to indifference" (Schnapper 1991: 95), the impossibility of maintaining "particular political identities" in order to prevent the "Lebanonization" of France, the "reduction of cultural differences as the most economical and probably the most effective way of overcoming ethnic identities" etc. But in 1999 the weight of cultural and communitarian nationalist factors is accentuated definitively in contrast with the universal dimension of public order:

> the society of citizens has always been a national society, a particular political organisation, born at a given moment and in a particular region, none being identical to any other and the national dimension constitutes a dimension (sic) of the identity of all individuals.
>
> (Schnapper 1998: 446)

Thus, now she postulates that "all democratic societies indissolubly involve ethnic elements. Political organisation cannot neglect what Elias calls the affective desire of human society" (Schnapper 1998: 455). Finally, she lucidly recognises a tension and the fact that "individuals belong to particular groups".

3 Conclusion

It is clear that recognition of the ethnic–cultural dimension of the nation poses a serious problem for French republicanism: it questions the notion of the one and indivisible republic, its endemic unitarianism, as there is no intrinsic reason whatsoever for believing that sub-national cultures possess less or no political importance with regard to the national culture (Laborde 2008). But this also raises a related question which is of key significance for the issue of immigration which interests us here: faced with the *nationalist* concept of cultural homogeneity, why not recognise diversity as an intrinsic dimension of the French nation?

In conclusion, the *affaire du foulard* has highlighted, first, the historical *nationalisation* of French republicanism in its different political versions and its contemporary reinforcement by a ethno-cultural and assimilationist concept of the nation, in defiance of the proclamations of universalism and the "civic" conception of patriotism. Second, the explicit or implicit postulation of a series of cultural and national concepts that rest on normatively nationalist pre-political assumptions (of a barely pluralist and deliberative nature): (1) the belief that cultures (both French and North African) and the nation are organic, integrated and homogeneous wholes, ignoring or marginalising internal diversity, the plurality of interpretations and concurrent national and interpretive projects, as well as the conflict between them; (2) the belief that cultures and nations are clearly individualised and distinguishable entities, underlining the difference which separates "us" from "them", "what is ours" from "what is theirs", and homogenising both extremes of the duality; (3) the view that nations and cultures are entities crystallised by history, as pre-packaged objective wholes that are essentially alien to any possible process of evolution, change or reformulation; (4) the conviction that belonging to a culture or a nation is related to the passive socialisation in tradition, immersion and uncritical acceptance of the guidelines and formulations

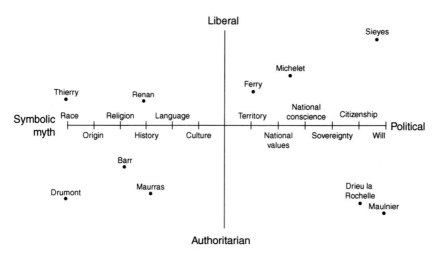

Figure 9.1 Historical map of ideas of nationhood in France.

provided by historical legacies, ignoring any free, adaptive and creative participation of its members in its construction; (5) an isolationist and conservationist perspective of culture and nations, as if debate, change, or non-assimilationist mixing of races or incorporation would put them at risk of degeneration and that they should be protected in their supposed pristine purity ("cultural exception"); (6) a conservative communitarian culturalism that leaves little room for relating demands for recognition with basic and closely linked dimensions of republican democratic politics: equality, participation and political deliberation in all the spheres of social and cultural life, including the pluralist, even plurinational definition of "us".

Bibliography

Agulhon, M. (1979) *Marianne au Combat. L'Imagerie et la Symbolique Républicaines de 1789 a 1880*, Paris: Flammarion.

Balibar, E. (1990) *Race, Nation, Classe*, Paris: La Découverte.

Balibar, E. (1992) *Les Frontières de la Démocratie*, Paris: La Découverte.

Balvet, M. (1984) *Itinéraire d'un Intellectuel vers le Fascisme: Drieu La Rochelle*, Paris: PUF.

Barni, J. (1992) (1872) *La Morale dans le Démocratie, suivi du Manuel Républicain*, Paris: Kimé.

Barrès, M. (1925) *Scènes et Doctrines du Nationalisme* Paris: Plon, dos vols.

Barrès, M. (1994) (1897–1902) *Le Roman de l'Énergie Nationale* in *Romances et Voyages* II, Paris: Lafont, pp.493ss.

Beaune, C. (1985) *Naissance de la Nation France*, Paris: Gallimard.

Bell, D. (2001) *The Cult of the Nation in France*, Cambridge, MA: Harvard University Press.

Bencheikh, S. (1998) *Marianne et le Prophète. L'Islam dans la France Laïque*, Paris: Grasset.

Birnbaum, P. (1993) *La France aux Français*, Paris: Seuil.

Bouamama, S. (2004) *L'Affaire du Voile, ou la Production d'un Racisme Respectable*, Paris: Edi. Du Geais Bleu.

Bouamama, S., Cordeiro, A. and Roux, M. (1992) *La Citoyenneté dans tous ses États: de l'Immigration à la Nouvelle Citoyenneté*, Paris: L'Harmattan.

Brubaker, R. (1992) *Citizenship and Nationhood in France and Germany*, Cambridge, MA: Harvard University Press.

Certeau, M., Julia, D. and Revel, J. (1975) *Une Politique de la Langue*, Paris: Gallimard.

Cesari, J. (1998) *Musulmans et Républicains. Les Jeunes, l'Islam et la France*, Paris: Complexe.

Darriulat, Ph. (2001) *Les Patriotes. La Gauche Républicaine et la Nation 1830–1870*, Paris: Seuil.

Debray, R. (2006) *Ce qui nous Voile le Voile*, Paris: Gallimard.

Digeon, C. (1959) *La Crise Allemande de la Pensée Française*, Paris: PUF.

Dobry, M. (comp.) (2003) *Le Mythe de l'Allergie Française au Fascisme*, Paris: Albin Michel.

Drieu la Rochelle, P. (1934) *Socialisme Fasciste*, Paris: Gallimard.

Drieu la Rochelle, P. (1937) *Rêveuse Bourgeoisie*, Paris: Gallimard.

Drieu la Rochelle, P. (1939) *Gilles*, Paris: Gallimard.

Drieu la Rochelle, P. (1943) *Chronique Politique*, Paris: Gallimard.

Ferry, J. (1996) *La République des Citoyens*, Paris: Imprimerie Nationale.

Finkielkraut, A. (1987) *La Défaite de la Pensée*, Paris: Gallimard.

Finkielkraut, A. (1999) *L'Ingratitude*, Paris: Gallimard.

Finkielkraut, A. (2007) *Qu'est-ce que la France?*, Paris: Stock.

Gallo, M. (2007) *L'Âme de France. Une Histoire de la Nation des Origins à nous Jours*, Paris: Fayard.

Gaspard, F. and Khosrokhavar, F. (1995) *Le Foulard de la République*, Paris: La Découverte.

Gauchet, M. (1986) *Le Disenchantement du Monde*, Paris: Gallimard.

Geddes, A. (2003) *The Politics of Migration and Immigration in Europe*, London: Sage.

Girardet, R. (1966) *Le Nâtionalisme Français*, Paris: A. Colin.

Hargreaves, A. (1995) *Immigration, "Race" and Ethnicity in Contemporary France*, London: Routledge.

Hargreaves, A. and Leaman, J. (1995) *Racism, Ethnicity and Politics in Contemporary Europe*, London: E. Elgar.

Huguenin, F. (1998) *Á l'École de l'Action Française*, Paris: Lattès.

Jaurès, J. (2001) *Oeuvres*, Tome IX, Paris: Fayard.

Kaufmann, E. (ed.) (2004) *Rethinking Ethnicity*, London: Routledge.

Kintzler, K. (1996) *La République en Questions*, Paris: Minerve.

Laborde, C. (2008) *Critical Republicanism. The Hijab Controversy and Political Philosophy*, Oxford: Oxford University Press.

Lamchichi, A. (1999) *Islam et Musulmans de France*, Paris: L'Harmattan.

Lévy, B.H. (1981) *L'Idéologie Française*, Paris: Grasset.

Máiz, R. (2003) "Politics and the Nation. Nationalist mobilization of ethnic differences", *Nations and Nationalism* 9(2): 115–214.

Máiz, R. (2007) *Nación y Revolución: la Teoría Política de Emmanuel Sieyès*, Madrid: Tecnos.

Máiz, R. (2008) *La Frontera Interior*, Murcia: Tres Fronteras.

Mangin, S. (1981) "Le statut des jeunes Algériens nés en France depuis l'independence", *Hommes et Migrations* 10: 21–25.

Marx, A. (2003) *Faith in Nation. Exclusionary Origins of Nationalism*, New York: Oxford University Press.

Mauco, G. (1932) *Les Étrangers en France*, Paris: A. Colin.

Maulnier, Th. (1938) *Au-delà du Nationalisme*, Paris: Gallimard.

Maurras, Ch. (1923) *Mes Idées Politiques*, Paris: Fayard.

Maurras (1972) *De la Politique Naturelle au Nationalisme Intégral*, Paris: Vrin.

Mélonio, F. (2001) *Naissance et Affirmation d'une Culture Nationale. La France de 1815 à 1880*, Paris: Seuil.

Michelet, J. (1974)(1846) *Le Peuple*, Paris: Flammarion.

Milza, P. (1987) *Fascisme Français*, Paris: Flammarion.

Mounier, P. (1999) *Les Enragés de la République*, Paris: La Découverte.

Nicolet, C. (1982) *L'Idée Républicaine en France*, Paris: Gallimard.

Nicolet, C. (2003) *La Fabrique d'une Nation*, Paris: Paerrin.

Noiriel, G. (1988) *Le Creuset Français*, Paris: Seuil.

Nora, P. (1986) *La Nation*, Paris: Gallimard.

Poliakov, L. (1971) *Le Mythe Aryen*, Paris: Calmann-Lévy.

Pomian, K. (1992) "Francs et Gaulois", in P. Nora, *Les Lieux de Mémoire. Les France* III.1, Paris: Gallimard.

Poulat, E. (1987) *Liberté et Laïcité. La Guerre des deux France et le Principe de la Modernité*, Paris: Cerf.

Rémond, R. (1992) "La fille aînée de l'église", in P. Nora, *Les Lieux de Mémoire. Les France* III.3, Paris: Gallimard.

Renan, E. (1947) (1859, 1871, 1882) *Œuvres Complétes*, Tome I, Paris: Calmann Lévy.

Said, E. (1997) *Orientalism*, New York: Vintage.

Sarkozy, N. (2004) *La République, les Religions, l'Espérance*, Paris: Cerf.

Schnapper, D. (1991) *La France de l'Intégration*, Paris: Gallimard.

Schnapper, D. (1994) *La Communauté des Citoyens*, Paris: Gallimard.

Schnapper, D. (1998) *La Relation à l'Autre*, Paris: Gallimard.

Sieyes, E.J. (1991) (1789) *El Tercer Estado y Otros Escritos de 1789*, R. Máiz (comp.), Madrid: Espasa.

Silverman, M. (1992) *Deconstructing the Nation. Inmigration, Racism and Citizenship in Modern France*, London: Routledge.

Smith, A.D. (2004) *The Antiquity of Nations*, London: Polity.

Stäel, Madame de (1807) (1985) *Corinne ou l'Italie*, Paris: Gallimard.

Stäel, Madame de (1814) (1968) *De L'Allemagne*, Paris: Flammarion.

Sternhell, Z. (1972) *Maurice Barrés et le Nationalisme Français*, Paris: A. Colin.

Sternhell, Z. (1978) *La Droite Révolutionnaire. Les Origines Françaises du Fascisme*, Paris: Seuil.

Sternhell, Z. (1983) *Ni Droite ni Gauche. L'Idéologie Fasciste en France*, Paris: Seuil.

Sue, E. (2003) *Les Mystères du Peuple ou l'Historire d'une Famille de Prolétaires à Travers les Âges*, Paris: Laffont.

Sutton, M. (1994) *Charles Maurras et les Catholiques Français. Nationalism et Positivisme*, Paris: Beauchesne.

Táguieff, J.P. (1996) *La République Menacée*, Paris: Textuel.

Thiesse, A.M. (1999) *La Création des Identités Nationales*, Paris: Seuil.

Thom, M. (1995) *Republics, Nations, and Tribes*, London: Verso.

Tombs, R. (ed.) (1991) *Nationhood and Nationalism in France. From Boulangism to the Great War*, London: Routledege.

Tournon, J. (2004) "Ethnicisme et nationalisme dans les professions de foi des candidats á l'élection présidentielle française en 2002", in R. Máiz and J. Tournon (eds) *Ethnicité et Politique*, Paris: L'Harmattan.

Tribalat, M. (2002) *La République et l'Islam. Entre Crainte et Aveuglement*, Paris: Gallimard.

Venel, N. (2004) *Musulmans et Citoyens*, Paris: PUF.

Verrière, J. (2000) *Genèse de la Nation Française*, Paris: Flamarion.

Weber, E. (1976) *Peasants into Frenchmen*, Stanford: Stanford University Press.

Weber, E. (1986) *L'Action Française*, Paris: Fayard.

Weil, P. (2002) *Qu'est-ce qu'un Français? Histoire de la Nationalité Française depuis la Révolution*, Paris: Grasset.

Weil, P. and Hansan, R. (1999) *Nationalité et Citoyenneté en Europe*, Paris: La Découverte.

Weyembergh, M. (1992) *Charles Maurras et la Révolution Française*, Paris: Vrin.

Wieviorka, M. (1992) *La France Raciste*, Paris: Seuil.

Wieviorka, M. (1993) *La Démocratie à l'Épreuve. Nationalisme, Populisme, Ethnicité*, Paris: La Découverte.

Winock, M. (1982) *Nationalisme, Antsémitisme en France*, Paris: Seuil.

Winock, M. (1992) "Jeanne D'Arc" in P. Nora, *Les Lieux de Mémoire* III.3, pp. 675–732.

Winock, M. (2004) *Nationalisme, Antisémitisme et Fascisme en France*, Paris: Seuil.

10 From quid pro quo to modus vivendi

Can legalizing secession strengthen the plurinational federation?

Wayne Norman

1 Political and academic contexts for theories of secession

The twentieth century produced waves of 'secessions'. Most of these – especially in the aftermath of the First and Second World Wars, and again in the late 1950s and early 1960s – involved the creation of new states from crumbling empires. Many of these new states had never existed as independent states before, and most were not carved out to create homelands for any particular ethnocultural group. The wave of secessions in the 1990s, however, had a distinctly ethno-nationalist flavour, with numerous formerly independent states, kingdoms, or federal units fleeing the Soviet Union, Yugoslavia, and Czechoslovakia to form homelands for self-declared 'nations' or 'peoples', where these titular nationalities typically did not include all of the inhabitants of the new states. Coincidentally, we saw a dramatic rise in the popularity of secessionist or 'autonomist' movements within long-standing Western democracies, including the Basque Country and Catalonia in Spain, Corsica in France, Scotland in the UK, Quebec in Canada, Flanders in Belgium, and the Faeroe Islands and Greenland in (or perhaps vis-à-vis) Denmark, among other places. During each of these waves it has no doubt seemed to many observers as if the world order was unravelling and that the burning desire to carve new states out of old ones might spread like wildfire across the globe. With at least 5,000 ethnocultural groups in the world, including perhaps 500 with some kind of national identity, and with 90 per cent of states including more than one nationality, the prospects of a global pandemic of secession can be very frightening indeed. But within a few years each secessionist wave subsides and a decade or two or three follow in which the historic distaste for secession in international law once again becomes the powerful norm.

One decade into the twenty-first century, it now seems as if that secessionist wave of the 1990s has also largely subsided. With a few exceptions here and there, the new states born (or in some cases 'reborn') in the last decade of the twentieth century seem to have consolidated their frontiers and held off further cascading secessionist or irredentist movements. The autonomist movements within Western democracies also, by and large, seem less threatening to their central governments than they did five or ten years earlier. One legacy of this last wave has been the emergence and growth of an impressive body of normative legal and political theory about secession. There are also signs of a burgeoning interest among political philosophers for normative theories about some of the chief alternatives to secession, especially federalism.[1] As I have argued in numerous places over the past two decades, our theoretical reflections on secession and federalism in plurinational states should be closely linked.[2] Contemplating the conditions (if any) under which secession should be permitted is one way to think deeply about the nature of the plurinational state and of the bonds between its constituent parts. This is analogous to the way in which the rules and conventions about divorce in a given jurisdiction reveal a lot about the institution of marriage there: knowing how something comes apart, or is allowed to come apart, tells us much about how or why it is put together.

In a number of long-standing democratic plurinational states today – including the United Kingdom, Canada, Belgium, Spain, and India[3] – secessionist movements have enduring 'hard-core' levels of support in the 20–40 per cent range within at least one of the territories controlled by national minorities; and where opinion polls sometimes register levels of support above 50 per cent. This kind of support for secession should not be seen as surprising or ephemeral. It poses a challenge for federal architects or reformers; a challenge that will take up the rest of this chapter. My primary aim is to show that by bringing the topic of secession 'out of the closet' and dealing with it explicitly in the process of constitutional reform, a plurinational federation can become both more robust and more just.

The treatment of secession in international law is a background condition for any treatment of the topic in constitutional law, because any successful secessionist movement must eventually make its case on an international stage. I shall not, however, deal at any length with the status of secession in international law here (see Buchanan 2004 for the definitive account, and Norman 2006: 170–173 for a summary of some of my own thoughts). It is just a plain matter of fact that international law is not sympathetic to the demands of secessionists in reasonably just, democratic states. As James Crawford, the Whewell Professor of International Law at Cambridge University put it (in effect, drawing out the implications of the *UN Declaration on Friendly Relations* from 1966):

> In international practice there is no recognition of a unilateral right to secede based on a majority vote of the population of a sub-division or territory, whether or not that population constitutes one or more 'peoples' in the ordinary sense of the word. In international law, self-determination for peoples or groups within an independent state is achieved by participation in the political system of the state, on the basis of respect for its territorial integrity.
>
> (Crawford 1997: Summary)

In short, barring extreme brutality, secession is permitted only by mutual agreement between a central government and a regional minority. If the majority of citizens in a federal province[4] of a plurinational democracy voted for independence tomorrow, they could not realistically expect to be recognized by a significant number of states (if any) until they had negotiated the terms of secession with their own central government and that government formally recognized the new state. According to Crawford,

> Outside the colonial context, the United Nations is extremely reluctant to admit a seceding entity to membership against the wishes of the government of the state from which it has purported to secede. There is no case since 1945 where it has done so.[5]

If the central government simply refused to negotiate secession, and did not respond with a brutal or prolonged military repression, then secession would not happen. This is, if you will, the predictable scenario that both secessionists and the central government could anticipate.

It does not follow, however, that central governments in democratic states hold all the cards, or that they can simply ignore secessionist demands. In purely practical terms, a clear majority within a province demanding independence – especially if their preference is revealed in a truly democratic referendum – will give rise to an uncomfortably high level of uncertainty. Economic consequences will be felt in both minority and majority territories, and the possibility of political violence cannot be ruled out in even the most peaceful of political cultures. This kind of status quo is simply unsustainable. The terms of federation (or union) will lose democratic legitimacy – which is why Prime Ministers in both the UK and Canada have publicly declared in recent years that they would allow their minority nations (Scotland or Northern Ireland, and Quebec, respectively) to secede if this was their clear desire.[6] Stonewalling the secessionists can be expected to strengthen, not weaken, the movement's support. The fact that international law would allow this situation to fester is almost beside the point. After all, international law does not demand that states grant national minorities *any* forms of autonomy or recognition; but that is no argument for why these groups should not have access to these things under constitutional law. A just plurinational federation should be designed and run in a way that both: (1) discourages such secessionist resentment in the first place, and, when this is not successful; (2) allows for the possibility of secession in accordance with norms of democracy, justice and the rule of law.

My aim in this chapter is to sketch an argument for why a well-designed secession clause in a federal constitution could potentially contribute to both (2) and (1), in that order. Put very simply, it could facilitate secession, and in so doing discourage it. That said, it is far from clear how the 'norms of democracy, justice and the rule of law' apply to attempts to secede from a reasonably just plurinational federation. It is often noted, for example, that there is a real problem trying to understand how democratic intuitions can be used to justify procedures for changing borders. Democratic procedures presume we know who the 'people' are who must decide; but when it comes to contemplating changing borders the precise set of people who should be self-governing is contested, so it is not clear who should vote on such an issue (see Barry 1991: 162; Moore 2001: 152; Norman 2006: 103). Examples of fair and functional secession procedures in the real world are also problematic. Although there has been a wave of secessions recently – from the Soviet Union, Yugoslavia, Czechoslovakia, Ethiopia and Indonesia – these are hardly examples of states with long-standing histories of democratic federation (and many of these secessions were, in fact, bloodstained). There are also relatively few examples of democratic constitutions with detailed provisions for managing secessionist politics within the rule of law.[7] Most constitutions are silent on the issue, and there are numerous examples of constitutions that seem expressly to forbid secession by declaring the state to be 'indivisible'.

2 What would a constitutional secession clause look like?

Before proceeding with enquiries about whether a constitutional secession clause might be inconsistent with norms of constitutionalism, or otherwise inappropriate or ill advised, it is worth pausing to consider what such a clause might look like. From the small number of states that have 'legalized' secession we can discern three typical approaches: (1) entrenching a concise principle of the right of secession; (2) entrenching a detailed procedure for secession; or (3) interpreting a constitution in a way that 'reads into it' a right of, or procedure for, secession.

1   The most famous and notorious example of an entrenched principle of secession was in the constitution of the Soviet Union. Article 17 of Stalin's 1936 constitution, and article 72 of the constitution that replaced that one in 1977; both proclaim that 'Each Union Republic shall retain the right freely to secede from the USSR'. Of course, as with many of the high-minded principles in the Soviet constitutions, it is presumed that Kremlin leaders did not seriously entertain the possibility of this right actually being exercised. The provision in Article 1 of the Anglo-Irish Agreement of 1985, which grants Northern Ireland the right to secede from the UK in order to join the Republic of Ireland, serves a similar function (Moore 2001: 212). One of the drawbacks with legalizing secession with a concise principle, even if this is done non-cynically, is that it leaves a tremendous number of questions unanswered.

2   Hence, a second approach to constitutionalizing a right to secede spells out in much more detail the *process* that would have to be followed for a secession to take place. As far as I am aware, the two best examples of this approach are to be found in the eight clauses and three sub-clauses in section 113 of the 1983 constitution of Saint Christopher and Nevis (or St Kitts and Nevis; both names are official), and in the five sections and five subsections of Article 39 of the 1994 constitution of Ethiopia. In both cases, these provisions were demanded at a time of founding these federations by the nervous

minorities themselves as a condition of their participating in the new federations.[8]

3   A third approach is more likely in countries with lively secessionist movements but without explicit mention of secession in their constitutions. It is possible that judges in the constitutional court can use other constitutional principles and conventions to *read* a secession clause *into* the constitution. French judges have done this in a way that gives 'Overseas Departments' the right to independence from France.[9] And as we will discuss below, in 1998, in response to a reference from the federal minister of justice, the Canadian Supreme Court gave an *Opinion* running over 25,000 words on what steps would be required for Quebec legally to secede. Even if a country had some kind of secession clause in its constitution it is entirely possible that the constitutional court would have to rule on specific disputes (say, on how to divide assets or debts) that arise over matters that can never be fully spelled out in text of the constitutional.

There is no consensus among constitutional scholars whether it is appropriate or advisable for constitutions to deal explicitly with secession, and there has been virtually no scholarly discussion about what a good secession clause might look like. Assuming for a moment that it is *not in*appropriate for a federal constitution to contain a secession clause (and I will be arguing for this assumption over the course of this chapter), it is reasonable to suppose that the details of the clause could vary as much from state to state as do the details of other aspects of 'federal plumbing', like the division of powers, design of central institutions, the amending formula, etc.[10] For the purposes of the discussion to follow, I shall assume that federal architects, negotiators or reformers contemplating the inclusion of a secession clause would have to come up with provisions that answer one or more of the following questions (so clauses would differ depending on which questions they chose to address explicitly and which answers they provided to these questions):

- Is the right to self-determination or to secede for groups or territories trumpeted as a *fundamental feature* of the federation (e.g. in the preamble or the opening articles, as it is in Ethiopia), or is it treated merely as a *remedial provision* in the bowels of the constitution, so to speak (as it is in St Kitts and Nevis)?
- What specific groups or kinds or groups or territories have access to the right? Does it name one entity in particular (like Nevis or Northern Ireland), or is the right granted symmetrically to all units of a particular kind (Overseas Departments, federal provinces), or to all groups of a particular kind (such as national minorities)?[11]
- What roles are given to provincial or federal assemblies in demanding or approving the initiation of secession proceedings? What special voting rules, if any, are required in these assemblies?[12]
- What roles are given to the people in either the potentially seceding region or in the country as a whole, for example, in a referendum or referenda?[13]

- If there is to be a referendum in the potentially seceding region, how is the precise question to be determined? For example: (a) is it fixed in the constitution, (b) determined by the government or parliament in the secessionist region, or (c) determined by the federal government or parliament?
- What level of support within the secessionist region is deemed sufficient to trigger either negotiations leading to secession or secession itself?[14]
- Who sets the rules for the referendum campaign (e.g. the provincial government or the federal government?), and who organizes, counts, or supervises the actual vote (e.g. either the provincial or federal governments, or both, or even international observers)?
- Is there one referendum only, or more than one with a mandatory waiting period between them? If there is a series of referenda, do they re-pose the same question, or is an initial one merely for a mandate to negotiate secession and the last one an approval of the terms negotiated?[15]
- Is there a provision for sub-regions within the seceding region to opt to stay with the rump state, or for sub-regions in the future rump state to join the seceding region?[16]
- How are federal debts, assets and properties to be divided? Is there a specific formula, or a process for negotiations? If the latter, how is 'good faith' enforced? Is there a provision for binding impartial arbitration?
- Who has the authority to negotiate on behalf of the (potential) rump state? It may not be the federal government or parliament if too many of its members represent the seceding region. Are there provisions for the election of a special negotiating body from the rump?
- How would any final deal providing for secession be approved by the rump state? Would it require a constitutional amendment using the normal amending formula? Or would this be circumvented in the case of secession?
- Is there a 'waiting period' (say, ten years) from the time of ratifying the initial constitutional clause before secession may be attempted? Is there a waiting period after an unsuccessful secession attempt before the same unit may attempt secession again?
- What rights would the new state have to the use of the existing state's currency? What role (if any) would it have in the management of the currency?
- What rights would citizens of the new state have to retain citizenship in the rump state?
- Could the rump state carry on with the same constitution, or would the extraction of the seceding region necessitate immediate adjustments (e.g. to the amending formula or the composition of the constitutional court) that should be either spelled out in advance or dealt with by a constitutional convention at the time of the secession?

Now, obviously, we would not expect *all* of these questions to be answered explicitly in a secession clause in any given constitution. At this stage I would like to highlight two reasons why it might be important to have explicit answers to at least some of the key questions agreed in the constitution. First, in one way or another, most of these questions would in fact have to be answered during the process of an attempted secession from a well-established federal state. If the answers are not clear and specific, many of the questions will be 'answered' (or ignored) by whichever side of the dispute has the power to impose its will. Second, by entrenching very explicit answers to some of these questions into the constitution, federal architects have the opportunity to do more than prepare the way for orderly secessionist politics, should a popular enough secessionist movement arise. They can also establish a pre-emptive impact on the very nature of nationalist–secessionist movements that might arise.

Consider two such impacts. First, as I will explain below, the wording of a secession clause can be part of the special recognition that a constitution bestows on specific minority nationalities, and in so doing it may appease minority nationalism rather than fuel it. Second, some specific answers to these questions may have the effect of making secession possible but rather difficult: for example, by requiring enhanced-majority support in a referendum, or a series of referenda that would make it harder for minority nationalists to capitalize on fleeting passions, or by alerting secessionists that they would be sitting across from quite-possibly-hostile negotiators elected specially to represent the interests of the rump state. We will call this a '*rigorous* secession clause', which could be defined as one designed to make secession less likely or more costly for the secessionists than would the procedures that secessionists themselves might 'propose' in the absence of explicit rules to the game. And in this way, it might discourage minority-nationalist leaders and movements from 'playing the secessionist card' to begin with.[17] These two features of a secession clause – its ability to serve as a powerful symbol of recognition and its ability to discourage the formation of secessionist politics – will figure prominently in my case in favour of a secession clause for plurinational federations.

3 Designing and justifying a secession clause

The full case for constitutionalizing secession requires a complex blend of normative arguments about justice, democracy, recognition and the right to self-determination, along with conjectures about the political sociology of multiethnic societies and the dynamics of nationalist politics, as well as views about constitutionalism and statecraft in federal democracies. It is an understatement that this case has yet to be made in a systematic fashion in the existing literature. So far we have little more than bullet-point-like considerations intended to show that one is not necessarily *crazy* to think that constitutionalizing secession will have numerous benefits, including the possible benefit of making secession less likely in the democratic plurinational state.[18] The reason for the ragged state of this case is (I believe) relatively easy to identify, but difficult to rectify. So far we have tended to treat the issue of whether (and if so, how) to constitutionalize secession as *an application of a moral theory of secession*. In other words, we develop a theory to identify under what conditions territorially concentrated groups have a *moral right* to secede, and then we ask whether this right should be entrenched in constitutions for plurinational states.[19] Instead, I will argue that we have to treat this issue as part of a much broader discussion (or theory) of plurinational federalism and constitutionalism: what forms of recognition and political autonomy are appropriate for territorially concentrated minority groups, and how do we balance these forms of minority self-determination and nation-building with the need for stability and some kind of common identity and equal citizenship across the larger federal state?[20]

In other words, I will argue that we should treat the issue of constitutionalizing secession as one part of a possible answer to this complex question, rather than as a kind of institutional application of a special normative theory of secession per se. To return to that sometimes misleading metaphor, it has more to do with how we think about the terms of *marriage* in the plurinational state than *divorce* from it.[21]

So what is the appropriate normative theoretical underpinning for a constitutional arrangement in a diverse democratic federal state? Surprisingly, there has probably been even less scholarly work on this question in recent years than there has been on the more specific question of secession – at least by political theorists and political philosophers. (See Karmis and Norman 2005 for an annotated intellectual history of normative theories of federalism from the Renaissance to the present.) Let us begin with the model of democratic constitutionalism developed by Cass Sunstein. We start here in part because he is a leading normative theorist of constitutionalism, and in part, as we shall see, because he has also applied his theoretical reflections directly to the question of whether to constitutionalize secession. Sunstein argues that 'the central goal of a constitution is to create the preconditions for a well-functioning democratic order, one in which citizens are genuinely able to govern themselves' (Sunstein 2001a: 6). Now while this may be the – or at least *a* – central goal of constitutions, there are a number of other purposes for constitutions that are either derived from this goal, or sit alongside it. Sunstein himself emphasizes that 'a constitution should promote deliberative democracy, an idea that is meant to combine political accountability with a high degree of reflectiveness and a general commitment to reason-giving' (2001a: 6–7). And that it should create 'structures that will promote freedom in the formation of preferences and not simply implement whatever preferences people have' (2001a: 8).

More specifically, Sunstein urges that constitutional clauses should aim for:

- the protection of rights central to self-government;
- the creation of fixed and stable arrangements by which people order their affairs;
- the removal of especially charged or intractable questions from the public agenda;
- the creation of incentives for compromise, deliberation, and agreement; and
- the solution of problems posed by collective problems, myopia and impulsiveness.

Let us call Sunstein's view 'deliberative constitutionalism'. It does not deal directly with any of the symbolic and recognition goals of a plurinational constitution, but it is a clear articulation of the all-important democratic features. As it turns out, Sunstein believes that these goals collectively suggest 'that a right to secede does not belong in a founding document' (2001a: 114).

I would like to criticize this argument of Sunstein's in two rather different ways. First, in effect, by accepting his premises but denying that they lead to his conclusions. That is, we can accept his goal of deliberative constitutionalism but deny that a properly designed secession clause would undermine it. And second, we will consider the inadequacy of deliberative constitutionalism, on its own, for thinking through the constitutional challenges of the plurinational state.

The basic argument against Sunstein's case is this: he is absolutely right about the pernicious effects of on-going secessionist *politics* on democratic deliberation and political stability – indeed, he may even underestimate the variety and potency of these effects – but he is too quick to assume that secessionist politics is necessarily encouraged by a secession clause and discouraged by its absence.[22] Secessionist *politics* can do all of the things Sunstein fears from an entrenched right to secede; namely:

> increase the risks of ethnic and factional struggle; reduce the prospects for compromise and deliberation in government; raise dramatically the stakes of day-to-day political decisions; introduce irrelevant and illegitimate considerations into those decisions; create dangers of blackmail, strategic behaviour, and exploitation; and, most generally, endanger the prospects for long-term self-governance.
>
> (Sunstein 2001a: 96)

If anything, Sunstein and others *underplay* the corrosive effects of secessionist politics on deliberative democracy. One cannot fully understand the psychological and sociological dimensions of secessionist politics merely by imagining rational bargaining situations where one party threatens exit (cf. Sunstein 2001a: 102). This is because of the ethno-nationalist context of virtually every modern secessionist movement. In order for even cynical threats to secede (i.e. threats by those who do not really want to secede but who want to increase their bargaining power for other demands) to be credible, secessionist leaders must first mobilize 'their people' on inherently divisive nationalist lines. This kind of mobilization can take years, and involves continuous agitation by secessionist entrepreneurs and other minority nationalists. They have an incentive to portray almost any decision or action by the central government as an example of insult, ignorance, humiliation, aggression, exploitation or oppression. But unlike some other forms of 'posturing' to back up threats in political bargaining, this kind of nationalist sentiment is not easily turned off; it can become a background feature of the political culture that ensures that the pernicious effects described in the quote from Sunstein, above, become more or less permanent features of the political landscape. Even non-secessionists in the political culture will find themselves appealing to these sentiments in the course of political argument.

So what can be done through the constitutional engineering of a plurinational state to take away the incentives for minority leaders to engage in secessionist politics? *One* part of the answer to this question – perhaps only a small part – is the question of whether a legitimate secession clause would increase or decrease incentives for secessionist politics. This last question is, of course, largely an empirical matter, and the results would vary with the nature of the secession clause, and the historical setting for which it is proposed. Much of Sunstein's argument is directed against entrenching what might be called a 'simple right to secession'; one that presumably could be exercised with something like bare majority support in the seceding province (the Ethiopian clause seems to be like this). But none of the federalist supporters of constitutionalizing a secession clause are arguing for a simple right to secede. As I noted at the beginning of this chapter, the principal advocates for a secession clause have been political theorists who are philosophically opposed to secession in reasonably just democratic states. They propose what Sunstein calls a 'qualified right to secede', or what I am calling a 'rigorous secession clause', one that would be constructed from answers to many of the questions posed in section 2, above, requiring, perhaps, a substantial majority (two-thirds or three-quarters support) in the seceding region to be exercised, among other hurdles and qualifications. The hope would be that the qualifications on secession would be such that minority-nationalist leaders could not expect to mobilize enough support to make secessionist threats credible in the absence of genuine oppression by the central government. And with the prospects of a credible secessionist threat not in the cards, there would be less incentive to engage in the kind of nationalist mobilization that drives secessionist politics. (At the same time, removing this strategic option would have few implications for the otherwise legitimate nation-building projects within the scope of provincial government powers.)

Sunstein does consider the usefulness of a qualified right to secede that required a supermajority or an extended deliberation period. He dismisses both qualifications with a sentence or two. He notes that:

> [a] requirement of a supermajority would certainly limit the occasions for, and seriousness of, secession threats. But in cases in which the subunit can be energized – for reasons of economic self-interest or ethnic or territorial self-identification – the protection would be inadequate.
>
> (Sunstein 2001a: 112)

But this is too breezy a reply. Surely we cannot dismiss a piece of constitutional engineering simply by imagining low-probability situations in which it might be used to overturn something we like about the status quo. We do not dismiss the legitimacy of a rigorous amending formula (such as that in the US Constitution) simply by imagining that it could potentially be used to repeal some fundamental right or to amend the constitution in some reactionary way.

There are empirical conjectures relevant here. It is significant that there has never been a substantial majority within a subunit voting to secede from a federal state with a long history of liberal democracy.[23] And again, none of the most popular Western secessionist movements today – among the Québécois, Flemish, Scots, Catalans, Spanish Basques, and so on – has ever shown sustained levels of support for secession above 50 per cent. It is also significant that there are virtually no serious examples of secessionist movements within flourishing constitutional democracies that are based purely on economic self-interest – the other motivation cited by Sunstein, and also by economists who assume that this would be the natural and compelling reason for a territorial group to want to secede.[24] All of this suggests that a secession clause that demanded a supermajority significantly higher than 50 per cent might be just the sort of mechanism that could help to do something that Sunstein elsewhere cites as a legitimate aim of constitutional engineering: it would amount to 'a decision to take certain issues [in this case secession] off the ordinary political agenda'.[25] In Sunstein's own words, taking issues off the agenda in this way 'protects' and 'facilitates' democracy. But the issue of secession cannot be removed from the agenda merely by having the constitution turn a blind eye to it. If we learn nothing else from the history of politics in Quebec and the Basque Country, it is that. The fact that many of the new multiethnic democracies in Eastern Europe (which were the explicit targets of Sunstein's advice in the original 1991 version of his arguments) have avoided public secessionist debates is surely explained less by their constitutional prohibitions of secession than by the often heavy-handed intimidation of minorities by majoritarian nationalists.

In short, there is good reason to think – at least in the sorts of countries I am addressing here, in the first instance – that a 'qualified right to secede' can serve as part of a constitutional pre-commitment strategy of the sort that Sunstein himself generally recommends. A crucial question, then, is *who* should be doing this pre-committing? In particular, an important consideration is whether the potentially secessionist minority itself would ever voluntarily pre-commit to an arrangement that made exit significantly more difficult. This question leads to a range of issues that are largely absent from most discussions of constitutionalism in the American tradition, where plurinational constitutional accommodation has never really been on the table.

4 Beyond (or beside) deliberative constitutionalism

All democratic states have an interest in constitutional structures encompassing pre-commitment strategies to facilitate stable, deliberative democracy. In multilingual, plurinational federations, there is a range of constitutional issues that cannot be fully articulated in the language of deliberative democracy – even if addressing these issues successfully will also help facilitate stability and deliberation. Elsewhere I have articulated and defended at length a number of ideals or principles of 'recognition', of both minority and majority identities and communities in a plurinational state (Norman 2006: 156–169). Rather than describe each of these ideals and principles here in abstract, let me simply explain how I believe they would help us understand the positive role that a well-designed secession clause could play in the constitutional order of a plurinational state.

4.1 Removing secession as a realistic objective of ordinary politics

Thus far, I have repeatedly drawn attention to one striking way that a rigorous secession clause might reduce the incentives for secessionist politics – namely, by making the conditions for secession significantly more difficult than those that would be insisted upon by secessionist entrepreneurs in the absence of explicit rules. We have already discussed this argument in some detail. It is time to explore some less obvious ways a secession clause could facilitate a just federal union.

4.2 A symbol of voluntary assent

Even in the democratic world, almost none of the existing national minorities ever gave their initial, democratic assent to their membership in the larger state; and few have had a formal opportunity to assent since. In the less-than-fully democratic world, of course, the situation for minorities is much worse. Most plurinational states are the result of conquests, royal marriages, arbitrary colonial boundaries, and the like, from the distant past. When such conquests are of relatively recent vintage, as they were in the Baltics, minority nations will usually take their first democratic opportunity to exit – and rightfully so. In general, though, when peoples have been sharing the state for many generations, especially under conditions of equal citizenship and democratic elections, exit is not the preferred option. The larger state provides more opportunities, and the intertwining of political and economic systems, not to mention populations and families, make dismemberment messy and risky. There are too many 'both–and' options for most members of well-treated national minorities for them to want to have to face an 'either–or' choice. But this acquiescence does not necessarily imply voluntary or enthusiastic assent on the part of minorities. When states are undergoing fundamental constitutional reforms, occasions for genuine assent present themselves. And an agreement between national minorities and the central government on a qualified right to secede is a powerful symbol of assent. Why is this? For one thing, it approximates a condition that would now be insisted upon by a sovereign state agreeing to enter a federation. Some kind of qualified escape clause would almost certainly be necessary today to get any independent state to agree to surrender a significant degree of its sovereignty to join a new state or superstate organization, even a free-trade agreement. Second, an unused escape clause can become a symbol of continuous voluntary cooperation – roughly in the way that an amendable constitution is usually seen as tacitly accepted over generations even if it is only rarely amended. Placing the possibility of a secession clause on the table during major constitutional reforms can provide a powerful means for making progress on other constitutional issues; as I shall describe below.

4.3 Partnership and recognition

In addition to federations being voluntary arrangements, it is symbolically important for many minority groups to be recognized as full and equal *partners* in the federation. There are, of course, many symbolic and concrete ways that a constitution can enshrine ideals of partnership and recognition – including declarations in the preamble that the country is a partnership, a 'community of communities', a federation of peoples, or what have you; or with specific roles for groups or subunits in, for example, constitutional amendment. Declaring that certain federal partners – whether by name, or by subunit status – have a qualified right to secede is another meaningful way of recognizing such territorial groups as full and willing partners in the state. This is especially true in so-called asymmetrical federations (those in which one or more federal subunits are recognized as homelands for particular national minorities and receive powers not shared by subunits occupied by members of the state's majority group). If only the national minorities' subunits are granted rights to secede, this will help satisfy their desire to be recognized as 'not just another province' – but as, at least symbolically, a nation-to-nation partner.

4.4 Trust-building, anti-assimilationism, loyalty and stability

At the point when states are refounded – especially when this is an opportunity for the democratization of a previously undemocratic state – national minorities are often looking to emerge from a long history of oppression by the majority. In Communist Eastern and Central Europe (ECE), as well as in Franco's Spain, for example, national minorities were subjected to extremely coercive assimilationist projects, typically including the denial of the right to use their minority language in schools and in public life (and much of this has continued in the post-Communist era in ECE). For true, voluntary, democratic cooperation to work after such a history, an extended period of good will and trust-building is needed (Weinstock 1999). The minority is rightly suspicious of the majority; but the majority also has a long-standing suspicion of the 'loyalty' of the minority. In such a situation, an appropriately tailored secession clause could build trust in both directions. For example, in addition to a supermajority requirement, such a clause might also preclude any secession process for the first ten or 20 years of a newly founded or refounded federal arrangement. This might assure the minority that the majority would change its assimilationist habits, and it could assure the majority that the minority would not use any breathing space it got to plot its immediate escape. 'Stability' is hardly a principle of recognition, but in volatile plurinational states it is likely to assume the status of a basic principle by members of majority and minority communities alike. The kind of secession clause just mentioned could help secure a good measure of it.

4.5 Facilitating *fair terms of partnership*

A secession clause need not be thought of as merely a constitutional *artefact*: it can serve a critical role in a negotiating *process* leading to constitutional reform. For example, some kind of escape clause would almost certainly be demanded by independent states agreeing to join a new partnership, as there is implicitly in the European Union.[26] But for the foreseeable future, federations are more likely to arise (or be reformed) by decentralization than by the voluntary union of previously independent states or colonies. And putting a secession clause on the table in such processes of reform creates some intriguing and largely unexplored possibilities. In effect, as the title of this chapter implies, a minority could agree to accept a rigorous secession clause as a kind of *quid pro quo* in exchange for greater autonomy and recognition. Or to look at it from the other side, majorities are often reluctant to offer minorities a significant degree of autonomy or recognition (e.g. constitutional recognition of the minority as a 'people' or a 'nation'), because they fear that this autonomy and status will be used by minority-nationalists in nation-building projects leading to secession. Of course, individual minority leaders demanding autonomy and recognition will often verbally renounce secessionist ambitions, but by agreeing to accept a secession clause that would make secession an unrealistic goal in the absence of central government oppression, minority groups would be making a concrete, long-term commitment to the larger state; and in so doing they would be acknowledging the fairness of *a particular level* of autonomy and recognition. Roughly speaking, the greater the realm of recognition and autonomy (and the nation-building powers that come with it) that the minority demands, the higher the threshold of 'obstacles' (e.g. the higher the level of a qualified majority vote) the majority could demand in the correlative secession clause. A constitutional accord understood in part as a result of this kind of good faith bargain would legitimize many of the ideals of mutual recognition:

- It would show the 'normalness', for both the minority and majority, of minority nationhood and autonomy within a larger federal state. By accepting a difficult secession procedure in return (in part) for national recognition, the minority itself would have committed itself to the rejection of the belief that the only 'normal' condition for a nation is to control a state of its own. Similarly, the majority could grant this kind of recognition (which they may acknowledge de facto in any case) because they no longer have to fear that it will necessarily lead to demands that, as a nation, the minority has an automatic right to its own state.
- Similarly, it could help uncouple, in the eyes of both majorities and minorities, minority nation-building from secessionist politics. And this in turn could help to establish the legitimacy of both orders of government using their sovereign powers in projects with foreseeable and reasonable identity-shaping effects.[27] In other words, it could facilitate an understanding of an equal right of nation-building; nation-building that aimed for neither the assimilation of, nor the escape by, the national minority.

• Both of these potential benefits of a constitutional accord balancing autonomy and recognition, on the one hand, with a pre-commitment to a rigorous
secession clause, on the other, should also facilitate the more healthy acceptance and development of overlapping national identities among members of
the national minority: they can be committed to their larger state in part
because they appreciate the respect and autonomy it accords to their
(primary) national affiliation.

In short, *thinking about the terms of secession may be a very helpful way to think
about the terms of federation.* It is a common refrain in the literature on secession that one of the reasons secession is not usually justified is that it is possible
for national minorities to enjoy a sufficient degree of self-determination and self-
government within some kind of federal system. Some theorists go even further
by suggesting that a national minority is done an *injustice* if it is not granted a
sufficient degree of autonomy and recognition within the larger state (see
Bauböck 2000; Weinstock 2001a: 189; Costa 2003: 69–71; Moore 2001: 15).
But thus far political philosophers have given very little indication of how to
evaluate whether *the degree* of autonomy and recognition, and *the terms* of federation more generally, are just or appropriate. When is enough, enough? Rawl-
sian 'veil of ignorance'-style contractual reasoning might give us some very
general guidelines, but there will always be too much particular socio-historical
information, and too much room for empirical speculation, for us ever to hope to
determine precisely from behind a veil of ignorance the best terms of federation
for any particular plurinational state (e.g. its division of powers, constitutional
amending formula, provincial representation in the second chamber of parliament, etc.).[28] But in the rough-and-tumble world of actual constitutional negotiations between national minorities, federal provinces, and central governments,
the creative use of a secession clause can help nudge a federation in the direction
of arrangements that enhance both the autonomy of minorities and the stability
of the state.

Now it could be objected that if a central government is looking for some
kind of guarantee that a minority would not use its newly granted autonomy and
recognition in a nation-building project leading to secession, then it would be
better to have the minority agree not to a rigorous secession clause, but rather to
a clause that explicitly rules out secession altogether.

The first response to this objection is simply to accept that in certain situations there might be nothing wrong, from the perspective of plurinational federalism, for a group to renounce all rights to secede in exchange for other forms of
autonomy, status or recognition. I am not arguing that a just plurinational federal
constitution *must* contain a secession clause, but only that such a clause is potentially beneficial in a number of ways that matter in plurinational democracies.
That said, many minority groups can foresee no likely circumstances in which
they will favour seceding from their larger state (perhaps this is the way most
Welsh, French Bretons, the Dutch Friesians, and Spanish Galicians or Majorcans
feel), so in their constitutional negotiations they may very well be happy to

renounce permanently a right to secede in order to receive other things they do desire. Other national minorities (and the politicians negotiating on their behalf), however, will find it much more difficult to renounce permanently the independence option, even if they are willing to agree to a clause that would make secession next-to-impossible.[29] So a second response to the objection is that it may be easier for a central government to secure a minority's agreement to a package of reforms if it demands that the minority accept a rigorous secession clause rather than renounce secession entirely. In circumstances where both sides are looking for an agreement – to end years or decades of constitutional disputes, from the point of the federal government, and to secure a more favourable status, from the point of view of the minority – the *quid pro quo* with a rigorous secession clause should look mutually advantageous.

It may also be a better hedge against secessionist politics in the (distant) future. In stable democracies, constitutional procedures have a way of gaining significant legitimacy over time, no matter how arcane. A secession clause that required, say, a three-quarters majority in the seceding province, might sit almost unnoticed for generations. But should a secessionist movement ever arise, it is very likely, in a society that respects the rule of law, that most citizens would see the secessionists as bound to meet those conditions in order to trigger secessionist negotiations. (Consider how nobody seriously suggests ignoring the Electoral College rules in US Presidential elections, even when these rules dictate a result that goes against the more intuitively legitimate popular vote. People may advocate reforming the rules for future elections, but not ignoring them while they are in place.) On the other hand, it is not inconceivable that a secessionist movement could arise long after the inclusion of a constitutional ban on secession, claiming the usual extra-constitutional legitimacy. Simply put: we know that long-standing constitutional procedures – even arcane and inconvenient ones – are almost always adhered to in constitutional democracies, but also that explicit bans on secession in otherwise open societies do not prevent the emergence of secessionist movements willing to move beyond the rule of law.

Perhaps the principal advantage to using a rigorous secession clause, rather than an outright ban, as a *quid pro quo* exchange for more autonomy or recognition for national minorities, is that this allows for some of the other important symbolic benefits just described (voluntary assent, loyalty, recognition, and so on). Entrenching even a heavily qualified right to secede in the constitution – especially if such a right is only granted to particular, named groups or subunits – can serve as a powerful and permanent symbol of that group's national status *and* willing partnership in the state. For a group to accept such a clause is also a significant gesture of commitment to the state and to a political culture that precludes secessionist threats in negotiations between the provinces and the federal government.

5 Conclusion

In this chapter I have argued for two points: first, that it would often make sense to include a secession clause in the constitution of a plurinational federal state;

and second, that the reasons for this are best understood not so much by thinking about the morality of secession, but by thinking through the moral logic of plurinational constitutionalism. If the case for the second point is plausible, then the case for the first point will necessarily be rather sketchy at this stage – because we are still a long way from having a very sophisticated theory of plurinational constitutionalism. Indeed, when it comes to issues about 'entrenching institutional arrangements and substantive rights ... constitutional theory remains in a surprisingly primitive state' (Sunstein 2001a: 97), even in the 'cleaner' case of constitutional theorizing for the 'uninational' state. I have argued that an appropriately qualified right to secession would often make sense within the framework of the deliberative constitutionalism that Sunstein advocates: it could provide a better disincentive for secessionist politics than would constitutional silence on the issue. It makes even more sense once we consider the additional roles a constitution plays in states containing more than one significant national homeland. In these plurinational states, we should think through the issue of whether or not to entrench a secession clause in much the same way we think through issues such as whether to have a centralized state or a federation, how to divide the powers between federal and subunit governments, how to represent subunits in federal institutions, what role to grant subunits in the process of constitutional amendment, whether to give special powers or forms of recognition to particular groups or subunits, and so on. In a plurinational state where these issues are open to free and fair negotiation, the demands of minority national communities will reflect their identities as peoples with their own needs for self-government and recognition; needs that must be balanced against their interest in participating within a stable, self-governing sovereign state with which most of their members also have some level of overlapping national identification. My argument does not conclude that plurinational states *must* include a secession clause, nor does it have anything to say about whether 'uninational' states would benefit from such a clause (presumably most would not).

The argument for constitutionalizing secession is still quite incomplete. But we do have a sense of what a much more definitive case for or against such a clause, or for or against certain design options for such a clause, would look like. This case may be a mixture of considerations of justice and minority rights, democracy, recognition, stability, pragmatism and group-interest; but the precise normative cocktail need not look arbitrary, and in particular, there are grounds for believing that, at least under favourable conditions, representatives of national minorities and majorities could agree on both a clause and its moral and political rationale.

Notes

1 Despite a long 'parallel history' of political thought that took 'unions of states' and federations seriously (see Karmis and Norman 2005), contemporary political philosophers largely ignored this subject matter until recently. A very incomplete list of recent normative theories of federalism includes Bauböck (2000); Burgess (2000); Elazar (1987); Filippov *et al.* (2004); Follesdal (2003a and 2003b); Forsyth (1981);

Kymlicka (2002); LaSelva (1996); Levy (2007); Norman (2006); Requejo (2005); Smith (2000); Tully (1995); Weinstock (2001b).

2 In general, this chapter draws on, revises, and updates arguments that were laid out rather more expansively in Norman (2006). I will indicate here and there where particular themes could be pursued further within that book.

3 It goes without saying that this list could be expanded with perhaps many dozens of others in Eastern Europe, Asia, and Africa with less well-established democratic traditions. My theoretical reflections throughout this chapter will be most directly applicable in the long-standing constitutional democracies of the sort mentioned in the text, although they should at least point in the direction of future reforms in other states as they join this 'club'.

4 For the sake of brevity, I will refer to federal subunits generically as 'provinces', although, of course, in particular federations they may be called 'states', 'cantons', 'autonomous regions', 'republics', etc.

5 Crawford (1997: summary). The widespread recognition of Kosovo after its UDI in 2008 may be the first such case in recent history.

6 See Moore (2001: 212); and 'Notes for a Statement by Prime Minister Jean Chrétien in Response to the Supreme Court Ruling in the Reference on a Unilateral Secession' from 21 August 1998 (www.pco-bcp.gc.ca).

7 For good international surveys of this aspect of constitutional law, see Suksi (1993) and Monahan and Bryant (1996).

8 See Griffiths (2002a) and Pätz (2002). In 1998, 61.7 per cent of voters on the island of Nevis voted to secede (only 58 per cent of registered voters actually voted), but this fell short of the two-thirds majority required by section 113(2)(b) of the constitution. Note that Eritrea declared independence from Ethiopia in April 1993, a year before the official ratification of the current constitution, after a UN-supervised vote with 99.81 per cent of Eritrean voters opting for secession. Nevertheless, it was through the process of Article 39(4) 'that Eritrea gained *de jure* independence in May 1993. No other member state [of Ethiopia] has ever attempted to secede' (Pätz 2002: 193).

9 See Moyrand and Angelo (1999) for an excellent description of the details and logic of this 'reinterpretation' of the 1958 constitution of the Fifth Republic.

10 I have discussed the options and justifications for such 'federal plumbing' in Norman (2006: chapter 4 and 5).

11 The Ethiopian constitution grants the right to secede to 'Every Nation, Nationality and People in Ethiopia' [Article 39(1)] where these are defined very sociologically as

> a group of people who have or share a large measure of a common culture or similar customs, mutual intelligibility of language, belief in a common or related identities, a common psychological make-up, and how inhabit an identifiable, predominantly contiguous territory.
>
> [39(5)]

12 E.g. the Nevis Island Legislature must pass a bill demanding secession from St Kitts and Nevis, the final reading of this bill must be supported by two-thirds of all the elected members of the Assembly, and there must be at least 90 days between the first and second reading of the bill. Then, after a successful referendum, the bill is submitted to the Governor General. There appears to be no role in this process for the federal legislature of St Kitts and Nevis.

13 The United States seceded from Great Britain, and Slovakia seceded from Czechoslovakia, without referenda, to mention but two examples.

14 The Ethiopian constitution demands simply majority support. In Nevis, as noted, two-thirds of the voters must be in favour. The Canadian Supreme Court says repeatedly that the secession of Quebec would require a 'clear majority', and it gives reason to think that this means more than 50 per cent + 1. Another possible threshold in a secessionist referendum might be 50 per cent of eligible voters rather than of votes cast.

15 Both of the quasi-secessionist referenda in Quebec, in 1980 and 1995, have asked merely for a mandate to negotiate a new confederal arrangement with the Government of Canada.

16 I discussed this issue briefly in Norman (2006: 101–106), in the context of the question of how to determine borders for federal provinces.

17 Constitutionalism has always been partly about trying to push certain kinds of issues off the table, to remove them from 'normal politics'. Consider the way a rigorous amending formula can discourage political actors from 'playing the constitutional-amendment card'. For example, both liberals and conservatives in the USA would love to have, respectively, a woman's right to an abortion or a foetus's right to life, entrenched in the constitution. But they also know that it would be impossible to get three-quarters of the state legislatures and two-thirds of both houses of Congress to pass either such amendment. So consequently there is no significant movement to amend the constitution in either of these ways. Pro- and anti-abortion activists devote their energies and resources to other battles. (Alas, one such battle is the attempt to alter the 'living constitution' by appointing Supreme Court judges who will 'read into the constitution' their preferred interpretation.)

18 There was truth-in-advertising in the original working title of Daniel Weinstock's important article 'Constitutionalizing the Right to Secede' (2001a). In draft form it was called 'On some advantages of constitutionalizing the right to secede'.

19 It is definitely not my contention that moral theories of secession of this sort are otiose. I have tried to contribute to them myself (e.g. Norman 1998). See also Buchanan (1991, 1998); Gauthier (1994); Philpott (1995); Moore (2001); as well as Horowitz's dismissal of much of this literature (Horowitz 1998).

20 I lay out the shape and justification of such a theory in chapters 4 and 5 of Norman 2006. A rationale for building a theory of secession out of a theory of federation that differs significantly from mine can be found in Baubӧck (2000: 366–371).

21 For cautionary advice about how not to be misled by this metaphor, see Aronovitch (2000).

22 I have explored this argument in greater detail in Norman (2001).

23 The attempted secession of the southern US states is a problematic example, of course, but also one that is not particularly relevant to the understanding of rival nationalism in plurinational states today. At any rate, no country that permits slavery can possibly be described as a liberal democracy.

24 The example of the Northern League secessionist movement in Italy in the 1990s is a fascinating example. It is generally presumed that northern and southern Italians share the same ethnicity, though some secessionist entrepreneurs behind this movement have at times played with the idea that there is in fact an ethnic distinction between the two groups (e.g. that northern Italians are descended from Celts). It has also seemed clear that a critical mass of supporters of the movement had no real interest in seceding from Italy, but rather wanted to reform the system (perhaps by federalizing it) in order to reduce their 'subsidizing' of the south. So it may not be a *genuine* secessionist movement. But even if it is an example of a genuine secessionist movement that is *not* derived from a minority national identity, it is clearly an exception that proves the rule. Another exception is the southern secession in the US. Of course, at least part of the explanation for the attempted secession of the southern states during the US Civil War is economic. This is one of many ways the case of the US Civil War is virtually *sui generis* in the history of secessionist movements.

25 In a reply to Weinstock, Sunstein concedes that he 'cannot prove the (thoroughly empirical) conjecture that' a secession clause would be more likely to fuel than dampen secessionist politics. And indeed he cites no empirical evidence. He concludes his reply to Weinstock's case for constitutionalizing secession by merely reasserting that 'the more sensible prediction is that [a constitutional right to secede] would undermine, rather than promote, the enterprise of democratic rule' (Sunstein 2001b: 355).

26 'For the European Community, for example, a right to secede may therefore be more sensible, and indeed it will provide a greater incentive to join in the first instance' (Sunstein 2001a: 105).
27 For more detailed discussion of the dynamics of nation-building and identity-shaping, see Norman (2006: chapter 2).
28 I discuss this pattern of reasoning, derived from Rawls (1971), in Norman (2006: 152–156).
29 See Weinstock (2001a: 201) for an explanation of the moral psychology involved in this position.

References

Aronovitch, H. (2000) 'Why Secession is Unlike Divorce', *Public Affairs Quarterly* 14(1): 27–37.
Barry, B. (1991) 'Self-Government Revisited', *Democracy and Power*, Oxford: Oxford University Press, pp. 156–186.
Bauböck, R. (2000) 'Why Stay Together? A Pluralist Approach to Secession and Federation', in W. Kymlicka and W. Norman (2000) pp. 366–394.
Buchanan, A. (1991) *Secession: The Morality of Political Divorce from Fort Sumter to Lithuania and Quebec*, Boulder, CO: Westview Press.
Buchanan, A. (1997) 'Theories of Secession', *Philosophy & Public Affairs* 26(1): 30–61.
Buchanan, A. (1998) 'Democracy and Secession', in Moore (1998) pp. 14–33.
Buchanan, A. (2004) *Justice, Legitimacy, and Self-Determination*, Oxford: Oxford University Press.
Burgess, M. (2000) *Federalism and the European Union: the Building of Europe, 1950–2000*, London: Routledge.
Costa, J. (2003) 'On Theories of Secession: Minorities, Majorities, and the Multinational State', *CRISPP* 6(2): 63–90.
Crawford, J. (1997) *State Practice and International Law in Relation to Secession*, Report to Government of Canada concerning unilateral secession by Quebec, 19 February 1997. (Reprinted in Crawford, J. (2002) *International Law as an Open System. Selected Essays*, London: Cameron & May, pp. 199–242.)
Elazar, D. (1987) *Exploring Federalism*, Tuscaloosa: University of Alabama Press.
Filippov, M., Ordeshook, P. and Schvetsova, O. (2004) *Designing Federalism: A Theory of Self-Sustainable Federal Institutions*, Cambridge: Cambridge University Press.
Føllesdal, A. (2003a) 'Subsidiarity', *Journal of Political Philosophy* 6(2): 190–218.
Føllesdal, A. (2003b) 'Federalism', *The Stanford Encyclopaedia of Philosophy* (winter 2003 edn). Available at http://plato.stanford.edu/archives/win2003/entries/federalism/.
Forsyth, M. (1981) *Union of States: The Theory and Practice of Confederation*, London: Leicester University Press.
Gauthier, D. (1994) 'Breaking Up: An Essay on Secession', *Canadian Journal of Philosophy* 24: 357–372.
Griffiths, A. (ed.) (2002a) *Handbook of Federal Countries, 2002*, Montreal and Kingston: Forum on Federations and McGill-Queen's University Press.
Griffiths, A. (2002b) 'St. Kitts and Nevis', in Griffiths (2002a) pp. 269–281.
Horowitz, D. (1998) 'Self-Determination: Politics, Philosophy, and Law', in Moore (1998) pp. 181–214.
Karmis, D. and Norman, W. (eds) (2005a) *Theories of Federalism*, New York: Palgrave.
Kymlicka, W. (2002) 'Western Political Theory and Ethnic Relations in Eastern Europe',

in W. Kymlicka and M. Opalski (eds) *Can Liberal Pluralism be Exported? Western Political Theory and Ethnic Relations in Eastern Europe*, Oxford: Oxford University Press, pp. 13–105.

Kymlicka, W. and Norman, W. (eds) (2000) *Citizenship iin Diverse Societies*, Oxford: Oxford University Press.

LaSelva, S. (1996) *The Moral Foundations of Canadian Federalism: Paradoxes, Achievements and Tragedies of Nationhood*, Montreal and Kingston: McGill-Queen's University Press.

Levy, J. (2007) 'Federalism, Liberalism, and the Separation of Loyalties', *American Political Science Review* 101(3): 459–477.

Monahan, P. and Bryant, M. (1996) *Coming to Terms with Plan B: Ten Principles Governing Secession*, Toronto: C.D. Howe Institute.

Moore, M. (ed.) (1998) *National Self-Determination and Secession*, Oxford: Oxford University Press.

Moore, M. (2001) *The Ethics of Nationalism*, Oxford: Oxford University Press.

Moyrand, A. and Angelo, A. (1999) 'International Law Perspectives on the Evolution in Status of the French Overseas Territories', *Revue Juridique Polynésienne* 5. Available at www.upf.pf/recherche/IRIDIP/RJP/RJP5.htm.

Norman, W. (1998) 'The Ethics of Secession as the Regulation of Secessionist Politics', in Moore (1998) pp. 34–61.

Norman, W. (2001) 'Secession and (Constitutional) Democracy', in F. Requejo (ed.) *Democracy and National Pluralism*, London: Routledge, pp. 84–102.

Norman, W. (2006) *Negotiating Nationalism: Nation-building, Federalism, and Secession in the Multinational State*, Oxford: Oxford University Press.

Pätz, T. (2002) 'Ethiopia (Federal Democratic Republic of Ethiopia)', in Griffiths (2002a) pp.132–146.

Philpott, D. (1995) 'In Defence of Self-Determination', *Ethics* 105: 352–385.

Rawls, J. (1971) *A Theory of Justice*, Cambridge, MA: Harvard University Press.

Requejo, F. (2005) *Democracy and National Pluralism*, London: Routledge.

Smith, G. (2000) 'Sustainable Federalism, Democratization, and Distributive Justice', in Kymlicka and Norman (2000) pp. 345–365.

Suksi, M. (1993) *Bringing in the People: A Comparison of Constitutional Forms and Practices of the Referendum*, London: Martinus Nijhoff.

Sunstein, C. (2001a) *Designing Democracy: What Constitutions Do*, New York: Oxford University Press.

Sunstein, C. (2001b) 'Should Constitutions Protect the Right to Secede?', *The Journal of Political Philosophy* 9(3): 350–355.

Supreme Court of Canada (1998) *Reference re Secession of Quebec*, SCC no. 25506 (20 August).

Tully, J. (1995) *Strange Multiplicity: Constitutionalism in the Age of Diversity*, Cambridge: Cambridge University Press.

Weinstock, D. (1999) 'Building Trust in Divided Societies', *Journal of Political Philosophy* 7(3): 287–307.

Weinstock, D. (2001a) 'Constitutionalizing the Right to Secede', *Journal of Political Philosophy* 9(2): 182–203.

Weinstock, D. (2001b) 'Towards a Normative Theory of Federalism', *International Social Science Journal* 53(167): 75–83.

11 Nationalism and cosmopolitanism in the global age

Montserrat Guibernau

Nationalism and cosmopolitanism are often portrayed as radically opposed to each other and scholars defining themselves as 'cosmopolitans' tend to display a very critical attitude towards anything that includes the word 'nationalism' and/ or 'national'. Following current debates on these issues, this chapter aims to shed some light into the main differences between national and cosmopolitan identity, and to establish under which circumstances, if any, nationalism and cosmopolitanism may become compatible.

The chapter is divided into two parts. First, it examines the relevance of the psychological, cultural, historical, territorial and political dimensions I attribute to national identity (Guibernau 2004: 135) when applied to cosmopolitan identity. Second, it offers a careful analysis of the specific conditions in which nationalism and cosmopolitanism might become compatible.

1 National identity versus cosmopolitan identity

Various forms of cosmopolitan identity, restricted to a selected elite, have existed since ancient times. In its modern form, cosmopolitan identity is intrinsically bound up with the intensification and expansion of globalization processes allowing us, for the first time in history, to have a reasonably accurate idea of the composition, numbers and features of humanity. Previous images of the world were incomplete to the point of neglecting millions of peoples. Limited awareness of other cultures and civilizations resulted in partial accounts of human diversity entirely mediated by the particular experiences and circumscribed knowledge of various peoples who sought to describe the world from their own perspective and according to their own cultural parameters.

By definition, a cosmopolitan identity is fluid, dynamic, open and a prerogative of a selected elite. Today's cosmopolitans belong to the middle and upper classes, tend to speak English (Norris 2003: 294) as a mother tongue or as a *lingua franca*, enjoy sufficient resources to take advantage of the goods and life-styles associated with post-industrial societies, and feel comfortable using the continuously emerging new ranges of sophisticated information technology and communications goods bombarding the market. Cosmopolitans represent a new class free from national attachments and eager to transcend the limits of their national and local communities. They enjoy travelling a world that, for them, has truly become a single place.

In my view, it is necessary to move beyond a type of cosmopolitan identity blind to the ethical principles of philosophical cosmopolitanism. Praising and savouring cultural diversity for their own sake regardless of the social inequalities and injustices which might, in some cases, be associated with it, should be replaced by a greater concern for global social justice. Further to adopting a critical and constructive attitude toward existing national cultures – one's own as well as those of others – a truly cosmopolitan identity should engage in an active struggle against those ideologies, value systems and social practices impeding the fulfilment of human freedom and equality. The desire to transcend ethnocentrism, while achieving a radical transformation of the social can never be achieved if cosmopolitan identity is made to fit the outlook of a single culture.

Steps towards the construction of an incipient cosmopolitan identity should involve dialogue, exchange, understanding and the reciprocal respect for each other's cultural practices while taking into account the specific temporal and geographical social *milieu* within which they have been constructed. At present, I consider cosmopolitan identity the privilege of an elite and I do not envisage its expansion among the masses in the foreseeable future.

1.1 Psychological dimension

National identity is extremely valuable to individuals because it provides them with a sense of dignity regardless of their class, gender, achievements, status and age. By belonging to the nation individuals identify with and, up to a point, regard as their own the accomplishments of their fellow nationals. It is by identifying with the nation that individuals' finite lives are transcended and that the nation comes to be revered as a higher entity. One of the most outstanding features of national identity is its ability to cut across class divisions while strengthening a sentiment of belonging to an artificial type of extended family, the nation.

As Margalit and Raz (1990: 447ff.) argue, a 'people's self-respect is bound up with the esteem in which their national group is held. If a culture is not generally respected, then the dignity and self-respect of its members will also be threatened'. It is my concern that when this occurs, in some cases, the national elite constructs a victimizing discourse founded on the promotion of a *siège* mentality based on the real or potential threat posed by those who do not 'comprehend and value' the nation's qualities. This involves closing down the community to external influences – in as much as this remains a feasible alternative, portraying certain nations or particular groups as enemies, and promoting a sense of hostility and lack of trust towards foreigners as bearers of a real or potential threat to the besieged nation. The power and resources enjoyed by the nation, as well as its predominant political ideology, strongly contribute to determine the extent of the closure and the mechanisms applied to set it up and maintain it.

In other cases, nationals lose their self-esteem; they adopt a passive attitude and become either isolated or engaged in a rampage of socio-political and cultural decay while often enduring external domination. Sometimes external power acts as a *stimulus* and contributes to awake a resistance movement.

National identity fosters closeness, empathy and solidarity among fellow nationals. By emphasizing what is unique about a specific nation, it singles it out from the rest and generates a sentimental attachment to it. But, does awareness of being 'citizen of the world' foster sentiments of solidarity and closeness among human beings? I do not think so, at least not in the first instance, although up to a point, usually a theoretical point and among certain sectors of the population, it might. In practice, it is incredibly hard to sustain an emotional attachment to such a vast number of unknown people. Indeed, we could consider whether humanity forms a community and feels as a community or, quite the opposite, it stands as a large aggregate of individuals forming myriad of distinct and separate peoples. If the latter is true, then what are the mechanisms, which could promote the rise of some incipient solidarity and a shared sense of identity among peoples who throughout history have spent most of their time fighting each other?

To identify with somebody we need to speak his/her language, understand his/her culture and, above all, we need the sensitivity to know how it would feel like to be in his/her place. We also need the capacity to suffer and rejoice with the other. In my view, most people do not tend to identify with those deemed too different, remote or alien. Nonetheless, an entirely different matter concerns whether people should, in spite of all differences, be able to share an attitude in favour of the recognition and promotion of respect, dignity, equality and freedom for all.

Relations among people, in particular among strangers, do not tend to be based on cosmopolitan principles; the contrary seems to be the norm. To illustrate this, let us just consider the incredible amount of violence present in human relations – personal and collective: a degree of violence that if we were to truly identify with the other would not exist.

A raw test assessing the degree of mutual identification among people could consist of analysing whether individuals are able to inflict pain and use violence against those they identify with. It is my view that only by emphasizing the otherness of victims, individuals are capable of inflicting pain and suffering upon them.

There are numerous examples – war, conflict, crime, repression, rape and torture – in which individuals – pursuing their own private interest or just for the sake of it – strip fellow human beings of their human condition. In order to justify their violence, they degrade their victims by turning them into strangers, enemies, animals or even monsters.

Individuals have a limited capacity to feel for others, or at least to feel with intensity. This is not to deny that people can empathize and, in a superficial manner, identify with strangers whenever their humanity – limited to those traits they can relate to – is brought to the fore. For example we can, up to a point, feel for – that is identify in some unspecified manner – the hunger, suffering, illnesses and deprivation endured by others when they are made visible to us. But the enormous amount of avoidable suffering which continues to exist, not only miles away from us but also within our own societies, shows that identification with strangers is light and often remains associated with the belief that people should take responsibility for their own lives and that we cannot aspire to resolve social problems simply because these are huge and there are far too many.

Acquiring a cosmopolitan identity is a matter of personal choice; in this respect it differs from national identity, which most Westerners have experienced since the moment when they were born and socialized within specific cultures endowed with their own languages.

The eventual materialization of a genuine cosmopolitan identity, in my view, would involve a militant attitude in favour of human freedom and equality. I am aware of the controversial character of these assertions because first of all cosmopolitan principles ought to be defined cross-culturally and they cannot be implemented until a global shared meaning is agreed. I envisage a process similar to that resulting in the Declaration of Human Rights to be applied to the search for genuinely cosmopolitan principles.

But, does cosmopolitan identity require the weakening and even the renunciation of national identity? In my view, cosmopolitan identity urges a critical attitude towards non-cosmopolitan principles present within national cultures as well as the commitment to change them. This does not imply the renunciation of national identity, nor does it denote the outright condemnation of a particular culture, but preparedness to change it from within. I do not regard cosmopolitanism as a synonym of disengagement with the national; on the contrary, I regard it as founded upon a set of ethical principles able to inform political action with the aim of permeating national and other forms of culture with a cosmopolitan outlook.

For example, let us imagine a citizen of a country where after a *coup d'état* a dictatorship has taken over. Would this justify some citizens in being disloyal to the dictator's rule? From a cosmopolitan perspective, we obtain a positive response since disloyalty to a specific political regime on the grounds of its anti-democratic non-cosmopolitan credentials should not be confused with disloyalty to the nation.

A response from a nationalist perspective has to be nuanced. Yet, whenever a nation is defined as an open, democratic society, all attempts to reverse this are to be condemned. It is from this perspective that disloyalty to a non-democratic regime might become an ethical imperative.

1.2 Cultural dimension

The quest for a cosmopolitan identity should be best described as the endeavour towards the addition of a moral layer, defined by respect for cosmopolitan principles, to national, ethnic and other cultures.

While key components of national identity such as culture, language, national symbols, heroes, rituals, sacred places, memories, traditions and ways of life are internalized by individuals and emotionally charged, so far, a comparable process concerning cosmopolitan identity has yet to take place.

An eventual cosmopolitan identity could only come to light within societies endowed with sophisticated telecommunications and information technology networks enabling simultaneous interaction between the peoples of the world. In a similar manner, the construction of national cultures and identities has evolved within industrial societies competent to effect the cultural and linguistic homogenization of their citizens.

A sense of common nationhood acts in tension with deep societal cleavages preventing fellow citizens from identifying each other as members of the same nation. National cohesion can only be attained if differences among citizens are upheld within certain limits and, it seems to me that a similar point including the whole of humanity should be made regarding the eventual rise of a cosmopolitan culture and identity.

The worldwide expansion of cosmopolitan principles, including access to sufficient resources for all to live with dignity, is indispensable for the eventual raise of an incipient cosmopolitan identity. The unlikely fulfilment of this condition stands as a serious obstacle to the advent of cosmopolitanism in the near future. In so far as humanity remains fractured by deep social, political and economic cleavages, such as those currently in place, it will be impossible to envisage the coming into light of a cosmopolitan identity beyond the remit of a privileged elite. Let us bear in mind that throughout history, the progress and advantage acquired by some nations as well as by some social classes has almost invariably been built on the disadvantage and the exploitation endured by others, and this continues to be the case.

1.3 Historical dimension

Antiquity acts as a source of legitimacy for the nation and the national identity associated with it. Elites are eager to remind their fellow nationals that the nation pre-dated their very existence and will transcend their own life span. Instead of looking at the past, a cosmopolitan identity will focus on the future since turning back in time would reveal a fragmented picture dominated by memories of war, conflict, alliances and rivalries among various peoples.

The history of humanity is based upon the immemorial division of its peoples. To the present, conquest, war and conflict have contributed to the emergence of distinct national and ethnic identities. Opposition to the other has proven key to fostering particular identities – individual as well as collective.

Identifying with our ancestors by celebrating their successes and remembering their tragedies is central to the construction of national identity; however, from the perspective of a cosmopolitan identity, such activities can only contribute to further consolidate and deepen existing divisions among various peoples.

If cosmopolitan principles were to be taken seriously, then, how could Spaniards celebrate the conquest of the Americas after the devastation it caused to the indigenous populations of the New World? To what extent could the British Empire be celebrated after the suffering it inflicted on millions of people in India alone? How could slavery be integrated into a colonial history to be proud of? Or indeed, how could the British, French, Dutch and other European peoples engaged in the colonization of North America ignore that the actions and policies of their ancestors brought indigenous peoples – First Nations – to their near extinction? Similar remarks could be made about the Maori and the Aboriginal peoples in New Zealand and Australia, as well as regarding the effects of European colonization upon the peoples of Africa and the Middle East. The list of events reinforcing a view of the world based on the primacy of some peoples over others is long and tainted with blood.

The collective memory shared by the national community emphasizes continuity over time and differentiation from others while strengthening its unity. The selective use of the past – including some joyous as well as some painful events – makes up the backdrop against which intellectuals engage in the construction of a shared national history, one usually based on a myth of common origin connected with a sentiment of forming an extended family. Besides, the experience of sharing the present and a sense of mission, including a common project for the future, crucially reinforces the sentimental bond uniting fellow nationals. Of course, the intensity and specific content of this sentiment varies among individuals, but in spite of this, a sufficiently strong sense of communality tends to remain in place.

The consciousness of forming a nation, once acquired, remains alive for generations, although in some instances, it may remain hidden for a long period of time and then, suddenly, re-emerges as a response to particular events or to the call of some national mobilizers.

1.4 Territorial dimension

Within a cosmopolitan identity, the sentimental attachment to the nation's territory should be replaced by an attachment to the whole planet. Probably the cosmopolitan principle, which has gained greatest prominence worldwide in the last few years, is the principle of sustainability. The reasons for its current relevance derive from serious concerns about global warming and other irreversible alterations of the ecological equilibrium prompted by human action. For most peoples and their governments, the preservation of the environment becomes a priority only and in so far as its continuous degradation poses a direct threat to themselves and to their successors.

The relationship with territory established by a cosmopolitan identity would be founded on the 'lifting out' of cultural experiences from their traditional anchoring (Tomlinson 2003: 273). It is envisaged that a cosmopolitan identity will entail disembedding cultural practices from the territories – spaces – within which they have emerged, and portray them as shared by all without privileging specific groups and peoples.

1.5 Political dimension

The nation is a political community willing to decide upon its future, be it as an independent nation-state, an autonomous entity, a member of a federation, a province or a region. The terminology is subject to various nuances according to each particular case. Those sharing a distinct national identity regard themselves as forming a *demos* with the capacity to reach and express a common will and act upon it. As previously indicated, nations may or may not have a state of their own.

In contrast, the human community has never regarded itself as a single *demos* or acted as one. The eventual rise of a cosmopolitan identity would change this. By emphasizing the significance of sharing the human condition and the dignity, respect, freedom and equality attributed to it, humanity as a whole would be able to express itself as a single *demos*. But, hitherto, the mechanisms for cosmopolitan political representation as well as the institutions and political culture associated with them remain largely undefined. I expect that the emergence of an incipient cosmopolitan identity would, in time, foster the constitution of cosmopolitan institutions with legislative, executive and judicial powers; a move burdened with issues concerning how to make compatible and adapt the value systems of particular national cultures to the requirements of cosmopolitan principles.

Currently, not only national and local interests but also international and transnational ones take precedence over the common interests of humanity as a whole and, only rarely, shared global interest such as the need to preserve the environment has been identified. A cosmopolitan identity would call for a shared language to further communication and understanding among world citizens. Even if English is spoken by large sections of the world's population, it is still far from being a *lingua franca* at global level. In my view, it is impossible to generate a shared sense of identity among people who do not understand each other.

Sharing a vernacular language is paramount to national identity. Conversely, whenever a nation enjoys a distinct language this becomes a strong, if not the strongest, marker of the community, one that allows individuals to recognize each other as fellow nationals.

The minorization of vernacular languages spoken only by a small percentage of the population could be a product of different reasons, among them: the current or past proscription of the language leading to a reduction in the number of its speakers, the influx of a large number of immigrants unwilling or unable to learn the vernacular language of the host society and the influence of a non-vernacular which progressively takes over as the primary language. The replacement of a vernacular by another language almost invariably weakens the sense of distinctiveness attributed to the nation in the eyes of its own members and others.

Wherever a vernacular language has ceased to exist or has been brought to practical extinction while being replaced by another nation's language – usually a nation occupying a position of power over it – the specific accent adopted by individuals speaking the 'foreign' language turns into an identity marker for insiders and outsiders. For instance, usually English speakers from Scotland can easily be identified by their distinctive accent. Even more crucially, the use of a common language among those sharing a national identity confirms that 'the political community really does belong to the people and not to the elite' (Kymlicka 2001: 218).

Sharing a national identity facilitates a mutual understanding between fellow nationals and contributes to the unfolding and consolidation of democratic citizenship. It is difficult to envisage how such a function might be performed at a cosmopolitan level. As argued by Kymlicka (2001: 239), 'democracy requires the adjudication of conflicting interests, and so works best when there is some sort of common identity that transcends these conflicting interests'.

2 Nationalism: an uncomfortable theory

Nationalism has traditionally been an uncomfortable topic for social scientists. In the nineteenth and early twentieth centuries, we encounter numerous examples of major scholars who paid scant attention to what clearly was one of the major political forces of their time. As I have shown elsewhere, Max Weber, a German nationalist himself never provided a systematic theory of nationalism (Guibernau 1996: 40). Weber revealed his German nationalism through his opposition to Polish immigration in eastern Germany, his support of German nationalists during the First World War, and his reaction against the Treaty of Versailles. He encouraged and correctly foresaw a movement of German irredentism after the First World War.

Émile Durkheim and Karl Marx predicted that nationalism would soon disappear and they understood it as an ideology which needed to be transcended. Durkheim's and Marx's approaches are slightly different. Durkheim's position could be described as 'pan-nationalist'. By this I mean that his stance puts 'human' aims above 'national' ones. According to Durkheim, the 'patrie' has a key role in the process of moralization since it is the 'highest organized society that exists' (Giddens 1987: 202).

In contrast, Marx's attitude can be described as 'internationalist'. His main objective was 'universal emancipation' and he envisaged some kind of world solidarity. But he recognized that this could only be possible if nations were free from their conquerors, because only then could the workers think in international terms about a working-class solidarity (Guibernau 1996: 41).

History has proved Marx and Durkheim to be wrong. Instead, nationalism has played a key role in the modern age and it currently manifests itself as a potent force. Nationalism, however, has often been portrayed in intellectual circles as a sign of backwardness and as a doctrine opposed to the cosmopolitan ideal once formulated by Kant (1996 [1795]: 311–352). Such uneasiness towards nationalism stems from its potent emotional dimension, which clearly differs from the ideal of rationality defended by the *philosophes*, which has up to now remain unchallenged. On these grounds, the indiscriminate rejection of all forms of nationalism, including the democratic nationalism of some nations without states, should be carefully assessed, since it often hides a simplistic approach to one of the most influential ideologies of our time.

The study of nationalism requires a thorough analysis of the specific situations in which it arises. The political ideologies to which nationalism is attached are crucial to understand the significance and character of nationalism in each particular case. Above all, we should realize that the complexity, flexibility and great appeal of nationalism are connected to its multifaceted character. Therefore, nationalism is sometimes associated with those who advocate xenophobia and ethnic cleansing, while in other cases, it is applied to describe those who defend their right to exist and peacefully cultivate a particular culture which makes them 'different' from other groups.

The eighteenth century concept of popular sovereignty was designed for the 'whole people'. When the revolutionaries stated that the principle of sovereignty resides essentially in the nation, they may be taken to have asserted that the nation was more than the king and the aristocracy. National self-determination turned out to be one of the most frequent interpretations of popular sovereignty.

The spread of the new ideas of the *philosophes* emphasizing the cult of liberty, equality and in particular the idea of state power rooted in popular consent, were initially applied to the construction and consolidation of the nation-state.

At present, democratic nationalist movements in nations without states invoke the principle of consent and the idea of popular sovereignty to legitimate their claims for self-determination, a concept embracing a wide range of options encompassing political decentralization, devolution, federation and independence. The recognition of the right to self-determination has the capacity to challenge the nation-state as a political institution, which, in most cases, has been created upon the attempt to seek the cultural and political homogenization of its citizens, paying scant attention to its own internal national diversity.

3   Democratic nationalism and cosmopolitanism

A type of nationalism based on the believe in the superiority of a particular ethnic group – ethnocentrism – aiming to dominate and exploit other peoples economically, culturally, military or politically, is not compatible with cosmopolitanism. This type of nationalism which I refer to as 'non-democratic nationalism' wants to expand its nation's borders and is primarily concerned with acquiring sufficient power to achieve its aims. Non-democratic nationalism tends to embrace political ideologies infused with authoritarian, dictatorial or fascist ideas. It fosters unequal relations and tends to promote illiberal and undemocratic forms of government. But not all nationalisms define their objectives and the means to achieve them by subscribing to the use of force and the disregard for the well-being of strangers.

When studying the possible compatibility between nationalism and cosmopolitanism, the sometimes almost visceral rejection of anything related with nationalism on behalf of some defenders of cosmopolitanism for whom nationalism is merely associated with backwardness, ethnocentrism, emotions and violence has to be acknowledged. Instead of engaging in a serious analysis of the

meanings of nationalism, they tend to stick to inaccurate and simplified definitions of it and ignore that cosmopolitanism and democratic nationalism share
some powerful common enemies; these are xenophobia, intolerance and
injustice.

Being a cosmopolitan involves a commitment to global equality, but is it possible to sustain such a commitment and defend a preferential treatment for fellow
nationals? This is the crux of the matter when analysing whether cosmopolitanism and nationalism can be compatible. The response is a nuanced one. Basically we need a definition of global equality and also an account of the meaning
and limitations of the so-called 'priority thesis' for fellow nationals.

To define global equality is a difficult task because the meaning of words
such as 'sufficient' and 'basic needs' is subject to variations according to different cultures and locations; still, this should not prevent us from offering a more
general definition. I understand that the basic tenets of global equality are the
avoidance of death by poverty and the fulfilment of human rights as defined by
the UN.

A clash between cosmopolitanism and nationalism comes to light whenever
the nation, through its policies, contributes to global poverty and the transgres-
sion of human rights. Pogge (2003: 550) writes: 'Our failure to make a serious
effort toward poverty reduction may constitute not merely a lack of beneficence,
but our active impoverishing, starving, and killing millions of innocent people
by economic means.' In my view, whether nationalism is compatible with cosmopolitanism or not depends on the political ideology nationalism is associated
with. This is a democratic form of nationalism – associated with social democracy, socialism or liberalism, to mention but a few political ideologies that
usually inform nationalist political action – subscribing to the principles of social
justice, deliberative democracy and individual freedom plainly shares its values
with cosmopolitanism. In contrast, non-democratic forms of nationalism associated with fascist and authoritarian ideologies stand in opposition to cosmopolitanism and democratic nationalism alike.

Among the arguments commonly neglected by cosmopolitans when assessing
the moral value of nationalism and its nuanced compatibility with cosmopolitanism are:

- The idea that many nationalists perceive national membership as a good in
  itself and not as a mere instrument.
- The assumption that the solidarity bonds shared by members of the nation
  make national belonging valuable and meaningful to individuals.
- The conviction that the attachment to a national culture provides individuals
  with a 'context of choice' (Tan 2004: 91) and a basis for self-identity.
- The belief that sentiments of national belonging generate a 'community of
  obligation in the sense that their members recognize duties to meet the basic
  needs and protect the basic interests of other members' (Miller 1995: 83),
  thus providing a foundation for the development of social justice.
- The idea that national attachments have moral value since, by instilling

social justice, trust and respect among fellow citizens, they are setting up the foundations for a democratic society.

Yet, the compatibility between nationalism and cosmopolitanism still hinges on whether the cosmopolitan commitment to global equality can be reconciled with the nationalist principle of granting priority to fellow nationals. At this point, we could push this a bit further and ask whether the commitment to global equality is compatible with giving priority to family members and friends. Cosmopolitans adopt two broad positions concerning this issue: basically they all accept the principle of egalitarian individualism, and nevertheless, they attribute different weight to the various modes of interpretation of other principles.

David Miller establishes a distinction between 'strong' and 'weak' versions of cosmopolitanism (Held 2005: 17). According to the former,

> all moral principles must be justified by showing that they give equal weight to the claims of everyone, which means that they must either be directly universal in their scope, or if they apply only to a select group of people they must be secondary principles whose ultimate foundation is universal.
>
> (Miller 1998: 166–167)

In contrast, 'weak' cosmopolitanism 'holds only that morality is cosmopolitan in part; there are some valid principles with a more restricted scope', so that

> we may owe certain kinds of treatment to all other human beings regardless of any relationship in which we stand to them, while there are other kinds of treatment that we owe only to those to whom we are related in certain ways, with neither sort of obligation being derivative of the other.
>
> (Miller 1998: 166)

Among the main advocates of 'strong' cosmopolitanism are Martha C. Nussbaum and Bryan Barry; defenders of 'weak' cosmopolitanism include Michael Walzer and Kor Cho Tan.

I agree with Tan (2005: 164) in that a theory of global justice should accommodate and properly account for the special ties and obligations established among fellow nationals and I would also add among members of the same family and people sharing friendship bonds.

In this respect, some liberal nationalists argue that the subordination of national commitments to cosmopolitan justice fails to properly accommodate people's national allegiances and undervalues the moral significance of national identity. Moreover,

> nationalists who reject the subordination of nationality to cosmopolitan justice do not necessarily reject the idea of global justice per se. What they reject is the cosmopolitan egalitarian ideal that the terms of distributive justice ought to be defined independently of people's national commitments

... National allegiances must be allowed to shape the terms of global justice, and not the other way round as cosmopolitans hold.

(Tan 2005: 167)

By being able to develop a sense of national solidarity and duty towards their fellow nationals, individuals move beyond the immediate family circle of solidarity and trust. In a similar manner, a nationalism embracing cosmopolitan values will efficiently contribute to the generation of attachments stretching from the national to the global level. Attachment to fellow nationals does not imply denigration and disrespect for others. On the contrary, the main argument for defending the so-called 'compatriot priority claim' assumes that we have a duty towards compatriots because they are members in a democratic political body that we, as active citizens, have a duty to sustain and improve (Kleingeld 2000: 327).

In my view, the 'priority thesis' is founded on the specific type of relationship established among individuals forming a community, in this case, the nation. It is my concern that the sentiments of solidarity that individuals tend to develop towards members of their own community have the capacity to generate a sense of special duty and care towards them. Being prepared to support your fellow nationals as well as the expectation that one would be assisted by them when in need constitutes a major tenet of social cohesion; this is, a situation in which a minimum set of values and principles able to maintain a sense of unity and common purpose are shared among the members of a particular society who are also prepared to make sacrifices for the well-being of the community.

But, why is national solidarity so important? Basically, because we do not live in a cosmopolitan world within which individuals feel free, equal, secure and are treated with dignity wherever they go regardless or their origin, gender, age, class and culture. Nations are engaged in constant competition with each other, their relations being determined by their own power and status within the international community. Most of the time, nations feel threatened in political, economic or cultural terms and their members rely on, identify with and contribute to their own nations as the communities within which they matter and enjoy certain rights.

4 The nation versus global society

Tönnies' distinction between *Gesellschaft* and *Gemeinschaft* becomes relevant when trying to account for the relationship between the nation and the global society. The former is a community – with a shared history, culture, territory and the wish to decide upon its political destiny – capable of creating a bond of sentiment and a sense of belonging among its members.

The term 'Global society' refers to humanity as a whole. It embraces the wide range of cultures and peoples sharing the planet which, so far, have proven unable to both imagining themselves as forming a single community and acting as a single *demos*.

Tönnies' distinction between community (*Gemeinschaft*) and society (*Gesellschaft*) is based on the different degree of coherence and solidarity, which regulates life in both situations. He writes:

> The theory of the *Gesellschaft* deals with the artificial construction of an aggregate of human beings, which superficially resembles the *Gemeinschaft* in so far as the individuals peacefully live, and dwell together. However, in the *Gemeinschaft* they remain essentially united in spite of all separating factors, whereas in the *Gesellschaft*, they are essentially separated in spite of all uniting factors.
>
> (Tönnies 1955: 74)

In *Gesellschaft*, individuals are isolated and 'there exists a condition of tension against all others'. People only have and enjoy what belongs to them to the exclusion of all others, 'something that has a common value does not exist' (Tönnies 1955: 74–75). A contractual relation lies at the basis of *Gesellschaft*.

In my view, some useful parallels could be drawn between the attributes of *Gesellschaft* and those defining the global society. For instance, although some basic human rights are theoretically granted to all – as established by the UN and sanctioned by most nation-states – within the global society, no contractual relation exists among the peoples of the world, and there are no global legislative and judicial institutions recognized and respected worldwide.

The global society is formed by an aggregate of human beings whose interaction is often mediated by the nation-state and, increasingly, by other international and supranational organizations and institutions. Social coherence is inexistent and some type of 'global' solidarity only tends to materialize in extremely specific circumstances.

Gesellschaft describes a society in which individuals compete most of the time, except when they form a coalition to confront a common enemy. All relations are permeated by material interests and 'based upon comparison of possible and offered services' (Tönnies 1955: 90). Tönnies would go even further and argue that 'before and outside convention and also before and outside of each special contract, the relation of all to all may therefore be conceived as potential hostility or latent war' (1955: 88).

Finding a common enemy to the global society, one capable of triggering a global response is not easy. For instance, global warming and environmental degradation could be regarded as potential common enemies; even so, not all nation-states are prepared to endorse global measures to fight them, primarily because the commitment to such measures would almost invariably come at an economic cost to the nation and its citizens. Moreover, the 'potential hostility' that Tönnies attributes to *Gesellschaft*, with few exceptions, accurately describes global relations.

Let us now turn to Tönnies' conception of *Gemeinshaft* and explore its relevance when seeking to understand the nation. 'Blood, place (land), and mind, or kinship, neighbourhood, and friendship' are, according to Tönnies, the three pillars of *Gemeinschaft*, which are encompassed in the family. He stresses the primordial role of the land, as the place where the community's life evolves. The land is the area occupied by the community throughout different generations, and links individuals to their ancestors prompting the sacralization of certain shrines. What Tönnies writes about the land when applied to *Gemeinschaft* can perfectly be applied to the territory of the nation as portrayed in nationalist discourses.

Habits, mores and folkways are also attributed particular significance in a *Gemeinschaft*. Similarly, customs and beliefs are an important component of the nation. The image of the family, employed by Tönnies to exemplify *Gemeinschaft*, has often been used to portray the nation. But, this does not preclude that nations are ideal communities free from internal conflict and diversity, rather their members may hold conflicting images of the nation and envisage dissimilar national projects.

Democratic nationalist movements accept and encourage dialogue between people who may differ in their conception of the nation but who share a sense of belonging. They conceive national membership as open, and are prepared to engage in a dialogic process leading towards national development. Though, it would be naive to ignore that non-democratic forms of nationalism do not subscribe to these principles and that some nations seek to enhance their unity and identity by implementing undemocratic homogenizing policies.

5 On liberal nationalism and cosmopolitanism

It is the concern of some liberals that a particular type of nationalism, this is, liberal nationalism, is compatible with cosmopolitanism since 'it is within the context of a national culture that the core liberal values of individual autonomy and self-identity, social justice and democracy are best realized' (Kymlicka 2001; Gutman 1996; Tamir 1992; Miller 1995; Nielsen 1999).

Liberal nationalism focuses on the connection between liberal democracy and the nation. Three basic principles define liberal democracy – social justice, deliberative democracy and individual freedom – and it is the liberal nationalists' view that they are all better achieved within the nation. These principles are:

5.1 Social justice

It is the concern of many liberals that moral cosmopolitanism – that is the commitment to global social justice – is better accomplished by fostering it within the nation-state rather than by the creation of some kind of – still so far inexistent – global state. The construction of a welfare state can be regarded as a step toward social justice within a particular society and, as its name indicates, the state is its creator and designer. A 'nebulous cosmopolitan order does not provide welfare state programs, public education, religious liberty, tolerance or the prohibition of racial and sexual discrimination' (Himmelfarb 1996: 77).

Furthermore, a theory of social justice ignoring the particular ties and obligations shared by fellow nationals cannot be considered suitable for humanity since it blatantly ignores the role of the nation as the political space within which social justice emerges as a consequence of the bonds of solidarity uniting nationals (Tan 2005: 164).

Liberal nationalism depends on the sovereign state to implement its principles and relies on national identity as the glue holding together an otherwise diverse population. It is through the commitment to liberal democratic values that the state becomes an organ of global social justice. But it is also through the commitment to liberal democratic values that the state creates the conditions of possibility for its citizens to become sensitive to the spread of democratic values beyond their national borders and prepares them to embrace cosmopolitanism as an attitude in favour of freedom and equality for all.

Although some relevant attempts have been made recently aiming at the adoption of principles destined to promote global social justice, the scope of their impact is minimal when compared with those principles according supremacy to the nation-state. Currently sovereign states have the greatest power to grant and sustain rights, and it is hard to see how this could be fundamentally changed in the foreseeable future. In addition, it would be naïve to ignore that all nation-states' actions are not necessarily conducive to social justice. For instance, it is true that, in some cases, nation-states seeking their own benefit or trying to protect themselves have sabotaged global initiatives destined to tackle specific transnational issues related to social justice such as global warming, genocide, the status and treatment of immigrants and refugees as well as national minorities, to mention but a few.

5.2 Deliberative democracy

It entails 'a system of collective deliberation and legitimation that allows all citizens to use their reason in political deliberation' (Kymlicka 2001: 226). It requires a high level of trust and a mutual understanding among citizens, which, so far, only the nation has been able to generate. In a corresponding manner, global democracy 'is best achieved through the promotion of democratic citizenship at national level. If anything, the goals of moral cosmopolitanism are furthered rather than thwarted by liberal nationalism' (Tan 2004: 96).

Democracy, tolerance and respect within a given society can never be fully attained through the strict compliance with the law – although the law and in particular the threat of punishment tend to persuade those inclined to act otherwise to comply with it. These are attitudes and values that need to be learned, internalized and regarded as so precious that individuals should be prepared to make sacrifices to preserve them.

In my view, a democratic political culture is difficult to achieve; it cannot be improvised and relies heavily on democratic values being introduced through education, political practice and public debate. A commitment to democracy presupposes readiness to engage in a dynamic process which recognizes dialogue as a means to reach solutions and overcome differences. Democracy, if only applied to the political arena, does not guarantee the construction of a democratic society. I regard democracy as a vital attitude defining private and public relations and occurring in the political, social and economic milieu.

5.3 Individual freedom

The relationship between individual autonomy and national culture is a complex one. Liberals argue that national identity 'makes individual freedom meaningful' (Kymlicka 2001: 227). By offering individuals a specific value system, a way of life and traditions, national culture bestows meaning upon specific social practices and situates the individual on a vantage point from which to relate, understand and value those of others. This is why national culture makes individual freedom meaningful.

National identity offers a moral anchor to individuals by means of the specific corpus of knowledge and values it embodies. This represents the context within which individuals make choices and foster solidarity bonds with fellow nationals. Trust and mutual respect are likely to emerge among people socialized within a shared culture including a value system. In this regard, learning to be an active member of a national community ruled by liberal principles prepares the individual for active membership of the world community by 'providing the requisite grounding and motivation for social justice commitments among citizens' (Tan 2004: 91).

In Nielsen's view (1999: 448–450), 'a truly liberal nationalist should also be a cosmopolitan nationalist and cohere with the quintessential cosmopolitan principle of normative individualism and ethical universalism'. Thus the cosmopolitan commitment to global egalitarianism can be reconciled with the national principle in so far as this is informed by liberal nationalism, as an ideology prepared to protect the integrity of the nation while adopting an internationalist and egalitarian outlook.

In my view, one of the major weaknesses of liberal nationalism is its emphasis on individual rights and its disregard for collective rights, a concept of uppermost significance for democratic nationalists. I consider that individual rights cannot be fully enjoyed if they are not conceived in a context of respect for collective rights. Thus, for an individual to be able to develop all its potentialities, he or she cannot be considered in isolation but as a member of one or more groups. Two sets of different rights which complement each other need to be taken into account: those concerning the individual as a free agent, and those related to the social dimension of individuals who live within specific communities. In late modernity, these communities tend to be nations.

After years of developing and promoting individual rights, we are now confronted with the socio-political need to counteract an exceedingly individualistic society threatened by a fragmentation resulting from a growing lack of civic coherence.

6 Conclusion

We live in a world of nations within which national identity compels individuals to social and political action and where national loyalty takes precedence over cosmopolitan allegiances. We do not live within a cosmopolitan order and I do not envisage it emerging in the foreseeable future.

At present, the cosmopolitan ideal remains a utopia far removed from the constant competition, conflict and war defining international relations. It is within this context that individuals turn towards their own nations as a source of identity but also as an environment within which they enjoy some rights.

Democratic nationalism and cosmopolitanism agree in their commitment to human rights, tolerance, cultural interchange and international peace and cooperation and I believe that they both share sufficient aims to coexist. Cosmopolitanism, that is, world citizenship free from national prejudices, could only emerge under the following conditions:

- The establishment of democratic constitutions in all nation-states as a guarantee of respect for freedom, equality before the law, and national, ethnic, cultural and gender diversity.
- The predominance of democracy as the principle governing international relations, which should involve a relationship of equality between nations.
- The enactment of a 'cosmopolitan law', which would provide for what Immanuel Kant called 'universal hospitality', that is the right of any foreigner – not a citizen of the specific state – to be treated without hostility in the country of arrival, supposing that he or she behaves peacefully (Kant 1996: 329).

A cosmopolitan order could only come into light if the above conditions were to be fulfilled. In such an ideal situation the discrimination, repression and attempted annihilation endured by some nations and ethnic groups will cease to exist. It is not morally sound to demand from a nation engaged in a struggle for its own cultural and political survival to declare itself 'cosmopolitan' (*kosmos polites*), simply because to be able to do so this nation should be free, and freedom is not an option for a nation faced by constant threats to its own social, cultural, economic, political or territorial existence while being denied the right to form a part of this 'cosmos'.

This is a point totally ignored by Martha C. Nussbaum who offers a largely US centred analysis. She considers patriotic pride as 'both morally dangerous and, ultimately, subversive of some of the worthy goals [it] sets out to serve' (Nussbaum 1996: 4), insists on the need to encourage a sense of world citizenship among US students – a laudable thing to do – but never talks about how students from 'other' countries – developed or not – may feel about her insistence on world citizenship. She ignores what Tagore clearly spelled out at a time fraught with internationalist discourses:

> Races, communities, nations were constantly urged to abolish their frontiers, destroy their distinctive attributes, cease from mutual strife, and combine

into one great universal society. This was well enough as an ultimate ideal: it would fit a world where peoples were of approximately equal strength and status; but so long as vast inequalities existed, these sermons addressed to the weak – who are still seeking recognition, or even elementary justice, or the means of survival – had they been listened to, would merely ... have achieved for them the unity which the kid achieved with the tiger when it was swallowed by it.... Those who are scattered, weak, humiliated, oppressed must first be collected, strengthened, liberated, given opportunity to grow and develop at least to some degree by their own natural resources, on their own soil, in their own languages, with unborrowed memories, and not wholly in perpetual debt, cultural or economic, to some outside benefactor.

(Berlin 1996: 264)

Democratic nationalism is legitimate. It defends the right of nations to exist and develop while recognizing and respecting internal diversity. It rejects the territorial expansion of nations and shows a commitment to increasing the morality of the nations' citizens by promoting democracy, social justice, freedom, equality, and mutual respect concerning cultural and other differences. Only by being committed to these principles can democratic nationalism become cosmopolitan.

In my view, all nations – with and without states – should be encouraged to set up the conditions favouring the emergence of cosmopolitanism as an attitude compelling individuals to add a further dimension to their care and concern for fellow nationals by raising awareness about the respect, dignity, freedom and equality that should be granted to all human beings.

I am convinced that the political agenda for the future of nations should include the commitment to cosmopolitan ideals and values capable of informing political action and adding a new moral dimension to national identity. The advent of cosmopolitanism requires the pledge to eradicate social, political and economic ideologies based upon the exploitation of individuals and nations. In so far as this remains out of reach, cosmopolitanism will remain a utopian ideology. Its strength as a political and moral ideology will depend on its own ability to act as a transformative force leading a multidimensional process destined to change the relations of power in society. I envisage it to encounter fierce opposition.

Bibliography

Appiah, K.A. (2006) *Cosmopolitanism: Ethics in a World of Strangers*, London and New York: Allen Lane-Penguin Books.

Barry, B. (1979) 'Statism and Nationalism: a Cosmopolitan Critique', in I. Shapiro and C. Beitz, *Political Theory and International Relations*, Princeton, NJ: Princeton University Press.

Beitz, C. (1998) 'Philosophy of International Relations', *Routledge Encyclopedia of Philosophy*, London: Routledge.

Berlin, I. (1996) *The Sense of Reality: Studies in Ideas and their History*, H. Hardy (ed.) London: Pimlico.

Brilmayer, L. (eds) (1999) *Global Justice*, New York: New York University Press.

Brock, G. and Brighouse, H. (2005) *The Political Philosophy of Cosmopolitanism*, Cambridge: Cambridge University Press.

Delanty, G. (2005) 'The Idea of a Cosmopolitan Europe: On the Cultural Significance of Europeanization', *International Review of Sociology* 15(3): 405–421.

Giddens, A. (1987 [1972]) *Durkheim on Politics and the State*, London: Fontana Paperbacks.

Grande, E. (2006) 'Cosmopolitan Political Science', *The British Journal of Sociology* 57(1): 87–111.

Guibernau, M. (1996) *Nationalisms*, Cambridge: Cambridge Polity Press.

Guibernau, M. (2004) 'Anthony D. Smith on Nations and National Identity: A Critical Assessment', *Nations and Nationalism* 10(1/2): 125–141.

Guibernau, M. (2007) *The Identity of Nations*, Cambridge: Polity Press.

Gutman, A. (1994) *Multiculturalism*, Princeton, NJ: Princeton University Press.

Habermas, J. (2001) *The Postnational Constellation: Political Essays*, Cambridge: Polity Press.

Held, D. (2002) 'Cosmopolitanism: Ideas, Realities and Deficits', in D. Held and A. McGrew (eds) *Governing Globalization: Power, Authority and Global Governance*, Cambridge: Polity Press, pp. 305–324.

Held, D. (2005) 'Principles of Cosmopolitan Order', in G. Brock and H. Brighouse, *The Political Philosophy of Cosmopolitanism*, Cambridge: Cambridge University Press, pp. 10–27.

Himmelfarb, G. (1996) 'The Illusions of Cosmopolitanism', in J. Cohen (ed.) *For Love of Country: Debating the Limits of Patriotism/Martha C. Nussbaum with Respondents*, Boston, MA: Beacon Press, pp. 72–77.

Kant, I. (1996 [1795])'Toward Perpetual Peace', *Practical Philosophy*, Cambridge: Cambridge University Press, pp. 311–352.

Kleingeld, P. (2000) 'Kantian Patriotism', *Philosophy and Public Affairs* 29(4): 313–341.

Kymlicka, W. (2001) *Politics in the Vernacular: Nationalism, Multiculturalism and Citizenship*, Oxford: Oxford University Press.

Margalit, A. and Raz, J. (1990) 'National Self-Determination', *Journal of Philosophy* 87(9): 439–461.

Miller, D. (1995) *On Nationality*, Oxford: Oxford University Press.

Miller, D. (1998) 'The Limits of Cosmopolitan Justice', in D. Mapel and T. Nardin (eds) *International Society: Diverse Ethical Perspectives*, Princeton, NJ: Princeton University Press, pp. 166–167.

Nielsen, K. (1999) 'Cosmopolitan Nationalism', *Monist* 82(1): 446–490.

Norris, P. (2003 [2000]) 'Global Governance and Cosmopolitan Citizens', in D. Held and A. McGrew, *The Global Transformations Reader* (2nd edition), Cambridge: Poilty Press, pp. 287–297.

Nussbaum, M.C. (1996) 'Patriotism and Cosmopolitanism', in Joshua Cohen (ed.) *For Love of Country: Debating the Limits of Patriotism/Martha C. Nussbaum with Respondents*, Boston, MA: Beacon Press, pp. 2–20.

O'Neill, O. (1990) 'Enlightenment as Autonomy: Kant's Vindication of Reason', in L. Jordanova and P. Hulme (eds) *The Enlightenment and its Shadows*, London: Routledge.

Pogge, T. (1994a) 'Cosmopolitanism and Sovereignty', in C. Brown (ed.) *Political Restructuring in Europe: Ethical Perspectives*, London: Routledge, pp. 89–102.

Pogge, T. (1994b) 'An Egalitarian Law of Peoples', *Philosophy and Public Affairs* 23: 195–224.

Pogge, T.W. (2003 [2000]) 'Priorities of Global Justice', in D. Held and A. McGrew, *The Global Transformations Reader* (2nd edition), Cambridge: Polity Press, pp. 548–558.

Roy, O. (2004) *Globalized Islam: The Search for a New Ummah*, New York: Columbia University Press.

Schmidt, J. (1998) 'Civility, Enlightenment and Society: Conceptual Confusions and Kantian Remedies', *American Political Science Review* 92: 419–427.

Smith, A.D. (2003 [2000]) 'Towards a Global Culture?', in D. Held and A. McGrew, *The Global Transformations Reader* (2nd edition), Cambridge: Polity Press, pp. 278–296.

Sypnowich, C. (2005) 'Cosmopolitans, Cosmopolitanism, and Human Flourishing', in 'Principles of Cosmopolitan Order', in G. Brock and H. Brighouse, *The Political Philosophy of Cosmopolitanism*, Cambridge: Cambridge University Press, pp. 55–74.

Tamir, Y. (1995) *Liberal Nationalism*, Princeton, NJ: Princeton University Press.

Tan, K.C. (2004) *Justice without Borders: Cosmopolitanism, Nationalism and Patriotism*, Cambridge: Cambridge University.

Tan, K.C. (2005) The Demands of Justice and National Allegiances', in G. Brock and H. Brighouse, *The Political Philosophy of Cosmopolitanism*, Cambridge: Cambridge University Press, pp. 164–179.

Tomlinson, J. (2003 [2000]) 'Global and Cultural Identity', in D. Held and A. McGrew, *The Global Transformations Reader* (2nd edition), Cambridge: Polity Press, pp. 260–277.

Tönnies, F. (1955) *Community and Association (Gemeinschaft und Gesellschaft)*, London: Routledge and Kegan Paul.

12 Democracy, federalism and plurinational states

Miquel Caminal

In liberal democracies *unitary federalism* has made it possible to achieve compatibility between national union and territorial division of state power. *Pluralist federalism* may be the new way to permit the plurinational transformation of nation-states as it promotes compatibility between the plurinational *demos* and the *demoi* of which it is composed. Federal unions have either been constructed and consolidated on the foundations of the permanence of pre-existing state entities or are the result of a territorial transformation of the unitary state, which recomposes itself federally in a process of recognition and guarantee of self-government of the autonomous or federal entities that comprise it. In both cases it is necessary to extend the debate about how to go beyond the concept of the *sovereign state* and the *state means nation* equivalence. Its effect is the federalist institutional transformation of the nation-state by means of two principles: (1) national pluralism; (2) federal division of powers. Together these two principles lead to the replacement of the concept of the sovereign state, which has characterised the formation and development of the modern state, by that of the federal union of states and nations based on divisible and shared sovereignty.

Thus, federalism has two options when it is faced with nationalist hegemony. It can opt to continue to be a juridical–political technique for the territorial organisation of the nation-state which does not get involved in political matters or in their nationalist justification. This is the case of a supposedly neutral form of federalism which does not participate in questions of an ideological nature, but which in reality accepts nationally dominant ideas and projects. On the other hand, it is possible to opt for a plurinational form of federalism which aims to change the foundations of the nation-state and fix an expiry date for dominant nationalism. This is a kind of federalism that accepts the challenge of transforming the nation-state in the context of democratic, multicultural and plurinational societies. The first kind of federalism is national federalism, which has proven its validity in the past, continues to be useful as a demonstration of the compatibility between national unity and the federal division of powers, but is insufficient and inadequate when faced with the new problems and demands of contemporary society. On the other hand, plurinational federalism aims to seek out these problems and at the same time find ways and means to address them through pluralist democracy.

1 The three fallacies of the nation-state

Nation-states still live inside the cage constructed by Bodin in *Les Six Livres de la République* (1576) as they understand sovereignty to be absolute, indivisible and perpetual power when economic, social and political reality has long ago freed itself of the idea of sovereignty that he postulated. Francisco Tomás y Valiente was right when he wrote:

> Regarding sovereignty, it is necessary to distinguish between the concept itself and its holder; what sovereignty is and who the holder of sovereignty is are questions that one should not confuse. Since the end of the 16th century until now there have been many and much more profound changes regarding the holder of sovereignty than regarding the content of the concept of sovereignty itself within the state sphere.[1]

Indeed, during the modern era we have moved from the absolute power of the monarch to sovereignty of the people. In other words, the holder of sovereignty has changed. But the concept of sovereignty remains essentially unaltered in public law. It is time to forget Bodin and, perhaps, recover more of Althusius, who refuted the Bodinian concept of the state and sovereign power in his work *Politica*. In many ways there are no frontiers to the state and yet, in contrast, we continue to refer to state independences that no longer exist and national sovereignties that have diminished. This should not worry us and we must avoid reverting to neo-conservative and exclusive nationalisms, but be able to understand and defend these changes, which lead us towards interdependent societies and shared forms of sovereignty. Three fallacies that have formed the foundations and legitimacy of the nation-state can be overcome: (1) indivisible sovereignty, (2) the equivalence between state and nation, and (3) national uniformity.[2]

1.1 Absolute and indivisible sovereignty

Indivisible sovereignty is a concept inherited from absolute monarchy which has lasted until liberal-democratic constitutionalism. The holder of sovereignty has changed (king, parliament, king–parliament, nation, people), but most people, even in federalist circles, still believe that sovereignty is not divisible, despite Tocqueville's comparison between the *divided sovereignty* of the United States of America (USA) and the *compact sovereignty* of France: "La souveraineté, aux Etats-Unis, est divisée entre l'Union et les États, tandis que, parmi nous, elle est une et compacte."[3] He had previously approached the problem in the following way:

> Une première difficulté dut se présenter à l'esprit des Americains. Il s'agissait de partager la souveraineté de telle sorte que les differents États qui formaient l'Union continuassent à se governer eux mêmes dans tout ce

qui ne regardait que leur prosperité intérieure, sans que la nation entière, représentée par l'Union cessât de faire un corps et de pourvoir à tous ses besoins généraux. Question complexe et difficile à resoudre.[4]

Indeed, the American founding fathers' starting point was the absolute and indivisible conception of sovereignty that dominated European thought which held that there was no middle ground between the confederal position of sovereign states that joined together federally without ceding sovereignty and unitary national sovereignty represented by the unitary state. But the federative process of the constitution of the United States of America itself culminated in a federal system that was halfway between the options mentioned above and at the same time overcame the indivisible conception of sovereignty.

Montesquieu had already made some progress in this direction and was a key point of reference for Madison and Hamilton having defined the federative Republic in 1748 as:

Cette forme de gouvernement est une convention par laquelle plusieurs Corps politiques consentent à devenir citoyens d'un État plus grand qu'ils veulent former. C'est une société de sociétés, qui en font une nouvelle, qui peut s'agrandir par de nouveaux associés qui se sont unis.[5]

According to Montesquieu, this republican design displayed all the internal advantages of republican government and the external power of monarchic government. Internally speaking, power was divisible and distributable; externally speaking, it was unitary and compact. In this way, different policies of government were possible between the states of the federative republic and a single foreign policy.[6] Montesquieu did not say much more about this type of state, but his definition has more things to say that it would seem, and these reappear four decades later in the theses of *The Federalist*.[7] It is worth highlighting the following: (1) the republican model of government; (1) the state conceived as an association of states; (3) the federative republic understood as constituting a society of citizens; and (4) the open possibility of an enlargement of the federative republic through the incorporation of new associates. Montesquieu did not develop a theory regarding the distribution and territorial balance of powers[8] to the same extent as his famous division of legislative, executive and judicial powers, but before this division he did establish a very important maxim for understanding the opportunity and possibility of the divisibility of sovereignty, a general law to guarantee the liberty of citizens, which is the aim of a legitimate state: "Pour qu'on ne puisse abuser du poivoir, il faut que, par la disposition de les choses, le poivoir arrête le poivoir."[9] If this is a basic principle of the unitary state, there is even more reason for it to be the same for the federative republic.

In this respect, the federal Constitution of the USA has already shown the possibility of dividing sovereignty, understood as the exercise of power in representation of the people and by means of the direct election of the powers of the two territorial institutions of government: the Federation and the States. At the same time, Tocqueville related sovereignty and suffrage in his work, by considering the process towards universal suffrage irreversible, as the legitimising foundation of the government of citizens and the distribution of state political power. Sovereignty should not be held by a single power (king or legislative assembly in Hobbes' *Leviathan*) and, in any case, the depositary of this sovereignty is always the people as they are the constituent power. The American federalists used this principle in order to break and overcome the parliamentary sovereignty of Locke and Blackstone. It is the people that yield and distribute the exercise of sovereignty to their representatives through elections. As Chevrier points out:

> Thanks to the transfer of sovereignty of parliament to the American people, the federalists were also able to conceive of a political order without any true sovereign in the classic sense. In other words, without a third party to resolve conflicts in the last resort. From then on it was conceivable that the legislative power, which was indivisible according to the English theory, could be divided between two different orders of government, each one of which possessed the definitive authority to legislate with regard to specific matters. And it is for this reason that they are regarded as "sovereign" in their respective spheres of responsibility, in the second sense of the term, since in the first sovereignty is held by the people.[10]

There is, therefore, not one sphere of government, but two or more that are interdependent and interact together and are able to intersect in the execution of their functions.

The essential qualitative leap towards federation, which so concerned Hamilton, and which Stuart Mill and Tocqueville believed to be the necessary element for the shift from confederation to federation, was the direct legitimisation of federal powers by means of elections, without the mediation of the states. It was at this precise moment that the true divisibility of sovereignty manifested itself, compatible with the unity of the constitutional code. The people elected and simultaneously and dually legitimised the authorities of the Federation and its member states. In the Swiss constitutional reform of 1999 the sense and the rule of constitutional unity compatible with the divisibility of sovereignty was maintained. Thus, article 3 of the federal Constitution states: "The cantons are sovereign in the sense that their sovereignty is not limited by the federal Constitution and they exercise all the rights that are not delegated to the Confederation." Moreover, article 1 of the Constitution of the Republic and Canton of Geneva states:

> 1. The Republic of Geneva is one of the sovereign cantons of the Swiss Confederation. 2. Sovereignty lies with the people; all the political powers and all public duties are no more than the delegation of the supreme authority. 3. The people comprise the totality of the citizens. 4. The form of government is representative democracy.

The unity of the Swiss Confederation is not at risk as a result of this limited and divisible conception of sovereignty.

Federal unions, which are the result of the decentralising transformation of the unitary state; that is, following the reverse process of confederation to federation, equally demand a process of divisibility of sovereignty if we wish to speak of composite states or federations. Belgium, Spain, the United Kingdom and Italy have chosen this way to transform and territorially reform the state. It is not possible to talk about federal union in these cases either if there is no direct and dual legitimisation of the authorities and, at the same time, a dual distribution of powers. Both processes, that which has its origins in the confederation (with several original sovereignties) and that which comes from the unitary state (with sole and compact sovereignty) must lead to the federal principle based on self-government and shared government. This dualism, which is related to the divisibility of sovereignty, has been present in Spanish federalism since its origins. This is how Valentí Almirall expressed it in the *Rules for the Federal Constitution of the Spanish Nation and for the State of Catalonia* (1868), when he states in article 1 that: "They are sovereign States insofar as their sovereignty is not limited by this Constitution..."[11]

The problem that may emerge in this second process or form of federal construction is two-fold: (1) reluctance to divide and limit the original sovereignty of the nation-state; (2) a centrifugal force towards confederation, including the possibility of secession.

Reluctance to yield power and the centralist inertia of the nation-state are serious obstacles to real territorial redistribution of the state's power. At this point it is advisable to distinguish between administrative decentralisation and redistribution of political power; that is, the possibility of taking one's own political decisions by law within a horizontal conception of the territorial organisation of the state, the federal distribution of powers and fiscal federalism. Administrative decentralisation maintains a hierarchical and vertical conception of the territorial model and, therefore, decentralised territorial public powers are dependent on the decisions of the central power. Therefore, the federal transformation of Spain, Italy or the United Kingdom must still overcome considerable obstacles in order to progress towards a real and functional federal union. This is not true in the case of Belgium, where the bipolar federative process has resulted in an asymmetric type of federation with binational foundations.

It is also true that the federal transformation of a unitary state runs the risk of being overtaken by centrifugal processes activated by opposition nationalist movements. This risk is very real in Belgium. It is present in Spain, particularly in Basque nationalism and sectors of Catalan nationalism. In the United Kingdom Scottish nationalism is also growing in strength and there is a complex political negotiation in progress in Northern Ireland. To a lesser degree this also occurs in Italy, which does not have a history of national conflicts as precedents for territorial conflicts. These have arisen and are related to the general crisis in the political system and with the political transition process in the 1990s. Opposition nationalism leans towards a pro-sovereignty position, with the aim of establishing a confederal type relationship, or even of approaching secession through a referendum for national self-determination. This trend clearly goes beyond federation and aspires to the creation of an independent sovereign state.

Both centripetal pressure, fuelled by state nationalism, and centrifugal pressure, fostered by opposition nationalisms, stifle any possibility of constructing a plurinational federation, which demands polycentrism and asymmetry as essential conditions for it to work.

Federations are constructed on the foundations of different centres of political decision, articulated in such a way as to form a constitutional union. Autonomy is inherent in a centre of political decision, which is able to implement its own political policies which are not necessary for, or simply not adopted by, other centres of political decision. Thus, polycentrism, as a federal institutional structure, and asymmetry, resulting from the exercise of self-government, go hand in hand in pluralist federalism.

Polycentrism not only implies asymmetry in the exercise of government, but also the asymmetric distribution of powers among the different territorial spheres of government. Each territorial sphere, whether it be municipal, regional, state or supra-state involves a specific series of powers of government. This affects neither the equally democratic legitimisation of all public powers, from the local to the continental spheres, nor their capacity for autonomy. Symmetry and asymmetry should not be confused, as is often the case, with equality and inequality. They are so different from each other that symmetry can produce inequality, and asymmetry equality. These are independent concepts which may be complementary or contrasting, depending on the case or the problem that is being addressed.

But if we are dealing with the institutional organisation and distribution of powers of a federation, the symmetry–asymmetry relationship must be based on the equality of the citizenry of all the territory which comprise the *demos*, without any form of discrimination. There can be no inequalities in the recognition and exercise of rights based on the fact that citizens belong to different *demoi*. However, this is not at variance with the fact that there may be an asymmetric institutional organisation and, moreover, an asymmetrical distribution of powers within the federation. In order to ensure the stable functioning of the federal system, it is not necessary for there to be a symmetrical concept of the institutional structure and the distribution of powers. It is normal for there to be differences as a reflection of the plural reality of the *demos*, and because "constitutional asymmetry is less related with the citizens gaining *more* power than with *where* that power is exercised".[12] The institutional locality from which specific powers of government are exercised affects the organisation and functioning of the federal system as a whole, but not the rights and freedoms of the citizens or federal equity.

Notwithstanding, the coherence of pluralist federalism itself establishes the institutional structure and the distribution of powers in a balanced way by combining asymmetry with symmetry in the institutional structure and the distribution of powers. Too much asymmetry would prove right those who believe that the federal system could become destabilised and centrifugal, but a certain degree of asymmetry is even highly positive for the federal union, because by recognising differences the will to coexist federally is strengthened. At the same time, asymmetry slows centralising processes, as has been shown by the "Quebec factor" in the way Canadian federalism functions in comparison with that of the United States. It is possible to say exactly the same with regard to the "Catalonia factor" in the way the State of Autonomies functions in Spain. Asymmetric pressure, exercised through the recognition of differences, acts as an anti-centralising factor to the benefit of the territorial democracy.

It is a different matter if asymmetry and asymmetric federalism are used to resolve nationalist conflicts. They are of no use for this. When asymmetry and nationalism are linked, two reactions immediately occur: (1) the other parts of the federation oppose or demand the same treatment; (2) the state nationalism–opposition nationalism dialectic is not exhausted, but revitalised. This is the Achilles heel of asymmetric federalism. Nationalisms can only be deactivated by adopting a new approach to the very foundations of the nation-state as a sovereign state and, as a result, rendering meaningless unilateral demands for the national self-determination of the opposition nationalisms.

Co-sovereignty and co-determination form part of the federalist and pluralist territorial conception of the political organisation of society, which needs to overcome sovereign nationalism as a starting point for federal agreement. Pluralist federalism may be an alternative to sovereign and federative nationalism by deconstructing or making the nation-state plurinational, by moving from a form of sovereignty that is singular and indivisible to one that is shared and divisible. The immediate consequence is the territorial division of powers and the organisation of the federation based on principles of power, coordination and solidarity between the federated units. This territorial division of powers implies the freedom for governments to exercise their powers within the constitutional framework. This is a kind of freedom that includes the capacity to take the initiative; that is, to adopt an enterprising style in order to effectively and efficiently develop one's own powers of government in competition with others. Regarding this matter, it is useful to refer to the contributions of *Public Choice*, applied to the federal process and governance by the public powers of the federation. For many people, the concept of *competition* has a bad reputation, says Albert Breton in *Competitive Governments* (1996). But competition is part of the society of free individuals and of all governmental organisations that are based on the plurality of the public authorities. Without competition there would be a monopoly in the economic and political spheres. Moreover, the free action of individuals and institutions in an inter-institutional society is the first premise for the construction of a society characterised by equality and solidarity between its citizens. Hierarchical submission is contrary to polycentric federalism. Nevertheless, competition precedes but includes inter-governmental coordination and collaboration between the public authorities.

However, polycentrism not only affects the division of powers between the federation and the federated territories, but also, on the one hand, the municipal powers and, on the other, the supra-state powers, as equally fundamental parts of the federal structure. The enlargement of the federal space, by giving greater political projection to the municipal and supra-state spheres, has the democratic virtue of deepening the territorial division of powers. That in itself is positive. But there is another equally important aspect, above all in relation to the main thesis defended in this chapter: it defuses and weakens the nationalist dialectic. Dual federalism has a centre–periphery dynamic, which complements the nationalist pole very well. Conversely, a conception of federal polycentrism that is not exclusively asymmetric but also multilateral works against state centralism and, at the same time, against all forms of national and regional centralism. In short, it is an antidote against all forms of nationalism. Moreover, non-concurrent elections, the possibility of there being different political majorities among the distinct territorial spheres of government, the possibility of the existence of regional, national and state-level political parties and diverse party systems[13] or, in sum, each territory's own inter-institutional network, shows the multilaterality and asymmetry of pluralist federalism.

All this requires intergovernmental coordination and political cooperation between the various authorities of the federation. Polycentrism, asymmetry, bilaterality and multilaterality constitute the plural structure of federations that permit initiative, competition and innovation in government. They are as essential for pluralistic federalism as liberty is for democracy. Liberty and competition within the federal culture have a fundamental starting point: there can be no federation without a free and voluntary accord in favour of the union. The feeling of belonging to a common political community is essential for the unity and stability of federations. Unity cannot be imposed and, at the same time, no part of a democratic federation should confuse free competition with the appearance of relationships of dominance within the federal process. In this pluralist framework, the federal union is not simply the result of the conciliation of interests, or of the convenience and usefulness of being part of the same political organisation, but of the will to form a political community, the *demos*, that unites everyone and with which the citizens identify as members of a community with a plurality of identities.

1.2 The equivalence between state and nation

There is a misunderstanding in the debate regarding the definition of nationhood: this is due to the fact that wherever there is a sovereign state there is also a nation, whereas when a nation is not a state it must assert its right to be recognised as such. As long as the nationalist conception that there must be a correspondence and equivalence between state and nation or between nation and state continues to exist, we will live in a vicious circle of nationalisms in potentially permanent confrontation, with no possible ultimate solution. Lord Acton was right when he remarked:

> The greatest adversary of the rights of nationality is the modern theory of nationality. By making the State and the nation commensurate with each

other in theory, it reduces practically to a subject condition all other nationalities that may be within the boundary. It cannot admit them to an equality with the ruling nation which constitutes the State, because the State would then cease to be national, which would be a contradiction of the principle of its existence. According, therefore, to the degree of humanity and civilization in that dominant body which claims all the rights of the community, the inferior races are exterminated, or reduced to servitude, or outlawed, or put in a condition of dependence.[14]

The insoluble contradiction among nations or, to be precise, between the nation-state and the other stateless nations within the state's territory, is clearly shown by the fact that only the former involves the subjection to authority of the government by law, with the possibility of imposing obligations and of establishing a binding ethical and political relationship; that is, a patriotic relationship, between the nation-society and the nation-state: "The nationality formed by the State, then, is the only one to which we owe political duties, and it is, therefore, the only one which has political rights."[15] As soon as a nation becomes the state all the others are cancelled or rejected, or reduced to being a cultural entity to the extent that the official nation recognises them as such. Thus states are juridically uninational despite the fact that they are sociologically plurinational. This is the error, the great discriminating error of the modern state in its capacity as a national state.

The vast majority of states are really plurinational, as is the case of the Spanish state. This makes it imperative, in a democratic and pluralist sense, for there to be plurinational representation based on equality of rights among its citizens. Diversity can be represented despite the fact that modernity has dictated the imposition of national uniformity as the basis for political representation. How can we progress towards the recognition of the multinationality of the state? The ideal solution would involve the separation of state and nation, in the same way that state and official religion have been separated through the evolution of liberal-democratic constitutionalism. First of all, this separation would inescapably involve the recognition of national diversity when this is the social reality of the state; second, the full equality of rights among the citizens, without any discrimination on national grounds; third, the existence and development of a common public culture with rights and duties as the foundations of a shared citizenship; fourth, the federal organisation of the authorities, without it having to adapt necessarily and exclusively to the territorial principle of recognition of the nationalities. As Otto Bauer believed, the future solution to national conflicts makes it imperative to promote the community principle, before the territorial one, as a way to recognise national diversity.

Citizenship involves self-government because a people are not free if they do not govern themselves. It is the citizens on whom sovereignty is bestowed, not on the nation as an abstract entity, or as a juridical subject outside the real nation; that is, that which is expressed by each and every one of the citizens. The citizens of a democracy do not grant power exclusively to an all-powerful centre, which legitimises itself as the sole and absolute representative of the nation-state. Rather it distributes decision-making power by representative mandate territorially to its (direct and indirect) representatives in the different territorial spheres or *demoi* which make up the *demos* as a whole. In the same way that the liberal state, which signified the end of a sole, absolute and sovereign centre which held all the power, distributed this power among the different public powers that coordinated and balanced each other in the exercise of their functions, so the democratic state must take the following step: the citizens do not transfer their original power to an imagined sovereign nation, but decide for themselves or through representatives whose mandates are limited in time and in the extent of their powers. The constitutional code ensures and guarantees the citizens' liberty, at the same time as it establishes the rules by which they govern themselves or regularly and periodically delegate government to representatives elected through democratic suffrage.

When republicanism renews the democratic debate regarding the concept of liberty and also its relationship with republican government, it should not overlook the foundations on which the *demos* is based. Wherever a group or community of independent and free men and women decide that they constitute a political community, no one can democratically prevent this, provided that this decision does not involve dominating others or the wish to do so. A people's liberty springs from its very right to form and remain as a people, provided that the exercise of this right does not involve the oppression or negation of others. Furthermore, peoples subjected to domination and oppression have even more right to independence and self-government. The political community is democratic to the extent that its citizens, or the vast majority of them, express the wish that this be the case. When one group wishes to detach itself in order to form another independent political community nothing can oppose them if this group of citizens fails to identify with or feel represented by the *demos* to which it belongs. Until now, this issue has been absent from the modern debate regarding the constitution and extension of the model of the nation-state. The origins of the state have not been based on democratic decisions, but on historical circumstances or on force. There is little point now in attempting to delegitimise this fact or, conversely, to ignore it. It is enough to use the current position as a starting point in order to progress towards greater degrees of representativeness and legitimation based on the will of the citizens or, on the other hand, to explore the possibility of democratically exercised self-determination if political union is not desired.

According to a republican conception of citizenship, the equivalence between state and nation is nonsense. The nationalist principle according to which the political nation is equivalent to the cultural nation is incompatible with republicanism. From the republican perspective it is citizenship that constitutes the *demos* on which the state is based, not the cultural nation. Citizenship implies self-government because there is no liberty if the citizens do not constitute the *demoi* in the different territorial spheres of government, from which the public authorities are derived and to whom they are responsible. At the same time, there is no liberty without self-determination, in the sense that each and every one of the citizens has a right to his or her identity, and for this to be recognised as a nationality. As Yael Tamir has pointed out, people are related with self-government, nation with self-determination.[16] Citizenship and self-government imply *territoriality* and, therefore, the precise definition of the different levels and territorial spheres of government. Self-determination and nationality are inherent conditions of the citizens as individuals with rights, whatever their place of residence in the *demos* may be, and in relation to whom the authorities cannot intervene except to recognise, protect and support the free development of diversity.

National self-determination that joins and fuses citizenship and dominant nationality is incompatible with the conception of pluralist and republican federalism that is defended here. Regarding this key point, it is worth repeating that the canvas of pluralist and plurinational federalism is Kokoschkian not Modiglianian, in line with Gellner's description of the multicultural and plurinational society. Nationalities come in extremely diverse territorial sizes and forms and always exceed territorial borders that are supposed to be pure in cultural and linguistic terms. It is not possible to compact them into *demoi*. It is not even possible to do so in the *demos*. And it will be increasingly unthinkable to do so, as the world has become communicatively smaller and more interactive among different national cultures. In the same way that sovereign national states, in response, generated (stateless) nations with their right to self-determination, overcoming the first concept (sovereign nation-state) makes the demand for and the proclamation of the second meaningless. But it is not essential to recognise national self-determination as territorial self-determination, but to permit nationalities to express themselves freely as free communities that can be present in different *demoi*; that is, under different self-governments. With regard to our society, why should it not be possible to achieve compatibility between the Catalan–Valencia–Balearic nation in terms of three peoples each of whom governs itself? Would it not be more in tune with social and political reality to distinguish between the Catalan, Valencian and Balearic peoples instead of arguing about the national nature that unites them? As different peoples they are distinguished territorially, while the national characteristics they share identify them communally.

If we confuse citizenship and nationality, self-government and self-determination within a nationally demarcated territory, majority and minority cultures, strong nations and weak nations, the central nation and the other satellite nations automatically appear, and the latter persist in their desire to become separate nations. And all this leads to nationalist conflict. If each nationality has a territory and, at the same time, nationalism desires compatibility between political nation and cultural nation, together in the national state, the vicious circle of nationalisms and national conflicts continues indefinitely. At this point it is worth quoting the words of Jacob T. Levi:

> Nationalism cannot be universalized. One can be nationalist of one's own nation and friendly to the nationalisms of some or many other particular

nations. But even if every nation and every nationalism is liberal and humane, a nationalism of all nations is not possible.[17]

To clarify this even further: Levy cannot see how it is possible to make nations' right to self-determination universally applicable. There will always be "Bosnias", and not as exceptions. It is necessary to change the paradigm, to go beyond the equivalence between state and nation, to replace the uninational state with the plurinational state. Federalism can transcend and take over the role historically played by nationalism. But to do so it must free itself of its dependence, its submission to state nationalism.

The aim of the *demos* of pluralist federalism is not to "manufacture" its "national" man and woman, nor should this be the aim of one or more *demoi*. Nationality understood as identity affects the liberty of each person and cannot be imposed from outside, nor deduced territorially. The institutionalisation of nationality and the recognition of the rights of its members must be based on the communal principle of personality, not the principle of territoriality. A plurinational state would logically take into account the territorial distribution of the national communities in its federal organisation, but not in order to achieve the nationally uniform symbiosis between each *demoi* and each nationality. One thing is self-government of a given territory and the equality of rights and duties among the citizens in addition to their identity or national sympathies; and quite another is the recognition, within the *demos*, of equality among all the nations which comprise it. Pluralist federalism is the symbiosis in the *demos* of the recognised and consotionally institutionalised nationalities, together with the recognition of the territorial self-government of the members of the federation, who represent the citizenry without there being any discrimination on grounds of nationality or cultural identity.

Nevertheless, this horizon does not exclude existing states and nations, which have been created and have confronted nationalism. While one is forced to live under the hegemony of nationalism it is necessary to find ways to separate the state and the official nation as well as citizenship and nationality. One possible way is by means of the federal nation or the *nation of nations*. This is a name that is prone to confusion and a variety of different interpretations, but may be useful given the current predominance of the *state equals nation* equivalence in an exclusive sense. The mere possibility of ending this exclusivity with regard to the nation, which corresponds to the sovereign and independent state, is a giant leap in itself. The nation of nations supposes that it is possible to use the same word to refer to the equality and reciprocity of different nations, in the same way as the federative republic first appeared as the *states of states*. The nations that make up the plurinational state unite federally by forming the federal nation or the nation of nations as they all display the three characteristics of a juridical, cultural and political nation in the same way as the federal nation, which corresponds to the plurinational state.

In this sense, the contrast between the *political nation-state* and other nations, as *cultural nations* and members of the political nation, is incorrect, discriminatory and exclusive. It is incorrect because at the very moment that self-government is recognised, even if this is at a low political level, the juridical and political condition of the nation is affirmed; discriminatory because it reduces the nations that constitute the political nation or state to the condition of cultural national communities with no chance of also being political nations and, consequently, of being able to decide freely with regard to their own affairs; and exclusive because by limiting national recognition to cultural features, the other cultures that are present in the territory of each nation are excluded. For example, the distinction between political nations to refer to Spain and cultural nations to refer to the nationalities or nations that make up the Spanish nation is incorrect and fails to describe what is indicated by social and political reality: first, because Spain, like all political nations which are also states, has attempted and continues to attempt to be a cultural nation if we analyse retrospectively what has occurred in modern and contemporary Spanish history; and second, because it is false that the nations that make up political nations are only cultural nations. This is a confusion or, to be more accurate, a fallacy, because it is surprising that Spanish liberal nationalism, which does not wish to share the concept of political nation, pays for this exclusivity with the acceptance of a dangerously uniform alternative, by referring to Catalonia and the Basque Country as cultural nations. This is clearly false because Catalonia and the Basque Country are not homogeneous, monolingual cultural nations.

If the will exists to confront the *nation equals state* prejudice in order to make multinationality just, there will be no excuse to refuse to recognise the fact that the self-government of national groups, or the shared government of the federal nation, are equally political and, at the same time, juridically linked. All nations are political if nationhood includes the right to decide about one's own issues. In this sense, Spain, Catalonia and the Basque Country are all equally political and juridical nations, because they are three national communities in which the citizens decide directly and through their representatives regarding issues that affect them, and because the law regulates the system of government and awards and distributes their corresponding powers. All federations and, by extension, all composite states, including the Spanish autonomous state, are made up of parts that govern themselves and, therefore, decide regarding the limits of the Constitution. It is therefore logical to refer to the Catalan people or the Basque people, as political and lawful subjects, with regard to all that which the 1978 Spanish Constitution and the respective Statutes of Autonomy recognise as their rights, and allow them to decide on by means of the system of government, which was freely and democratically created. Where there is a territorial distribution of the state's power, where different public authorities are legitimised through elections, the citizens do not comprise a single national body, there may be more than one. Thus the citizens of Catalonia make up the Catalan nation in a political and juridical sense and, in political and juridical terms, they are also part of the Spanish nation. During the autonomous elections they express the political will of the Catalan people; during the legislative elections they participate in the political will of the Spanish people.

The distinction between juridical nation and political nation is necessary, despite the fact that many authors have confused the two, or have situated the former within the latter.[18] And it is not the same to be forcibly linked to a nation-state as to be linked voluntarily. In the first case, there is no consultation but the registration of the national condition of the citizens and of their compulsory loyalty to the nation-state; in the second, it is the citizens who feel or do not feel linked to the political and national principles that identify the nation-state. The juridical nation does not ask the citizen, it counts him and binds him to its laws. The political nation does ask, because it springs from the will that is freely expressed by the citizenry. It is possible to be part of a nation-state without feeling a member of it; that is, it is possible to be part of the juridical nation without feeling part of the political nation. When the latter occurs in a significant way in parts of the state's territory, there is very likely to be a national problem there: there is a certain number of citizens, they may be many or relatively few, who do not feel identified with the official nation and, on the other hand, feel that they belong to another nation. This nation is *their* political nation, regardless of whether or not it is recognised juridically, because it is national conscience that makes the political nation. Notwithstanding, all national states that are recognised by the international community of states are obviously juridical nations, and all their citizens are linked to them through the juridical code, whatever they may think or feel. But this juridical nation is not, at the same time, a political nation without the free expression of the will of the citizens, which is the source of the legitimisation of the state.

The cultural nation is another thing which invariably goes beyond the territorial borders of the state, above all when one wishes to include it with the other two (juridical and political) senses of the nation. The territorial borders of the cultural nation are normally exceeded because not all the individuals who are resident within the territory demarcated by the cultural nation are members of it and, at the same time, there are bound to be individuals linked to the cultural nation who live outside its territory. Territories marked or identified as nations are normally multicultural and, in exceptional cases, monocultural. This does not detract from the fact that the cultural nation is present in all political nations. The restricted division between political nation and cultural nation is incorrect. The French nation, like the German nation, the Spanish nation, the Scottish nation or the Catalan nation (regardless of whether they are states or not) include, at the same time, both the cultural and the political elements, but there is no political nation that is, to a greater or lesser extent, a cultural community. The three senses of nation (juridical, political and cultural) search for one another and, if they meet and fit together well, make a complete and stable nation.

However, the fact that the cultural nation, or the cultural characteristics of the majority of the population, are present in the identification of the political nation, whether we are referring to the *demoi* or the *demos*, should not lead to the neglect of the cultural minorities within the "national territory". Moreover, culture and language should not be used as instruments by the authorities to assert the political nation. Citizenship comes before nationality, and it is (culturally plural) citizenship which forms the base of the authorities and elects its legitimate representatives. This is why all cultures and languages must ensure complete equality based on the fact that citizenship makes everyone equal in terms of our rights and duties, whatever our national identity or cultural condition may be. In order for this to be possible, three interdependent and complementary steps are necessary:

1   The equal recognition of the cultures and languages of the *demos*, expressed and regulated in the federal constitution. All the languages of a plurinational state must enjoy the same rights, and there can be no discrimination regarding duties nor in the recognition of their official nature.
2   Languages and cultures are the expression of cultural communities that have collective rights which must be recognised and protected by the authorities. Cultural communities can opt for their consociative institutionalisation and participation in self-government with regard to language, communication, culture and education, and it is the duty of the authorities to ensure this, in accordance with the federal constitutional code.
3   The authorities of the *demoi* must take into account the socio-cultural and socio-linguistic specificity of their people in order to ensure that there is no discrimination on cultural or linguistic grounds. Moreover, the particular or majority language of each *demoi* will be the official, common and preferred language for public use and in education.

These three conditions must ensure the survival of the cultures and languages of the *demos* and guarantee that no one will be discriminated against on these grounds. Multicultural richness is not an obstacle for democracy, but a positive fact which, by means of federal agreement, displays the compatibility between cultural diversity and political union and between plurinational and citizenship.

1.3 The cultural uniformity of the modern state

An open society is a society based on diversity and on the recognition and representation of difference. However, the history of the modern state has been characterised by the construction of a uniformity, of a monocultural *us*, in which diversity has been rejected and persecuted through the repression, expulsion or assimilation of those who are different. Cultural homogeneity is constructed among equals, among those who are recognised by the principle through which they are born free and equal. The struggle for equality and for shared liberty by a greater number of people has been a long and controversial process, one that T.H. Marshall expounded in his famous lecture on citizenship and social class at the University of Cambridge in 1949.[19] The civil, political and social dimensions that Marshall pointed out corresponded to three main phases or stages in the recognition of human rights. The eighteenth century was the century of the recognition of civil rights; the nineteenth century saw progress towards the general right of citizens to political participation and the recognition of public liberties; the twentieth century was the century of the welfare state and the development of economic and social rights. These three stages or phases in the development of rights have resulted in more democratic societies and improved quality of life for a significant proportion of the population, although a more rigorous and in-depth study of what has taken place reveals a number of shortcomings in this process, above all the displacement of exploitative and dominant relations to the so-called Third World and the unequal distribution of the enlargement of rights in the First World.

Marshall's genius consisted in discovering a trend, not in photographing social and political reality. The law continues to protect inequality and the lack of liberty for many people (in reality, for the majority). Despite this, there is no doubt that in wealthier and more advanced societies there has been a trend, punctuated by steps forward and backwards, towards a greater degree of liberty for an increasing number of people. It could be said that democracy has been extended to include the civil, political and social dimensions, but it is also true that it has lost intensity. The free men who experienced censitary suffrage were more complete citizens than the free men and women of democratic suffrage. Quantity and quality have not gone in the same direction.

Democracy and federalism are not static systems. They are living processes that mutate and reflect societies' pulse. Within this dynamic conception there should be a *fourth phase* or stage in the development of rights: the recognition of difference. The fourth phase of rights asks directly about the *others*, that is, about those who manifest their right to be different and to be recognised as such in their identity. As long as we are able to include or integrate this difference into the *us*, there is no problem. But what if we cannot? The history of the liberal state provides us with a number of responses, but not enough. The integration and extension of civil and political rights to women, to other races or cultures, has been understood as the incorporation of the national *us*. There has not therefore been any significant progress regarding the recognition of difference, but a process of integration–assimilation.

Two great liberal-democratic republicans, Jefferson and Stuart Mill, were ahead of their time in the analysis of the complex relationship between equality and difference. The passage in Jefferson's *Autobiography* on the American nation, slavery and the negro race is well known:

> Nothing is more certainly written in the book of fate, than that these people are to be free; nor is it less certain that the two races, equally free, cannot live in the same government. Nature, habit, opinion have drawn indelible lines of distinction between them. It is still in our power to direct the process of emancipation and deportation, peaceably, and their place be, *pari passu* (on an equal basis), filled up by free white laborers. If, on the contrary, it is left to force itself on, human nature must shudder at the prospect held up. We should in vain look for an example in the Spanish deportation or deletion of the Moors. This precedent would fall short of our case.[20]

So, the founding fathers of the American Constitution could not imagine, under any circumstances, that there could in the future be a plurinational and multicultural federation. There is no need here to go into the elimination and confinement of the American Indian peoples, but it is worth stressing that it never crossed the minds of those liberal patriots to construct a society of free and equal men and women based on multiculturality.

Precisely when slavery began to be abolished in the liberal societies of the New World, John Stuart Mill was writing his work *The Subjection of Women* (1869).[21] Such was the author's scepticism regarding the intellectual venture of convincing his fellow citizens that there was no reason for discrimination and inequality on grounds of sex that he conceded defeat on the first page of the first chapter of the book:

> ...the principle which regulates the existing social relations between the two sexes — the legal subordination of one sex to the other — is wrong itself, and now one of the chief hindrances to human improvement; and that it ought to be replaced by a principle of perfect equality, admitting no power or privilege on the one side, nor disability on the other. The very words necessary to express the task I have undertaken, show how arduous it is. But it would be a mistake to suppose that the difficulty of the case must lie in the insufficiency or obscurity of the grounds of reason on which my convictions rest. The difficulty is that which exists in all cases in which there is a mass of feeling to be contended against. So long as opinion is strongly rooted in the feelings, it gains rather than loses instability by having a preponderating weight of argument against it. For if it were accepted as a result of argument, the refutation of the argument might shake the solidity of the conviction; but when it rests solely on feeling, worse it fares in argumentative contest, the more persuaded adherents are that their feeling must have some deeper ground, which the arguments do not reach; and while the feeling remains, it is always throwing up fresh entrenchments of argument to repair any breach made in the old. And there are so many causes tending to make the feelings connected with this subject the most intense and most deeply-rooted of those which gather round and protect old institutions and custom, that we need not wonder to find them as yet less undermined and loosened than any of the rest by the progress the great modern spiritual and social transition; nor suppose that the barbarisms to which men cling longest must be less barbarisms than those which they earlier shake off.[22]

This opinion of John Stuart Mill, which was shared by his wife Harriet Taylor,[23] clearly illustrates the difficulty of introducing something as reasonable as gender equality into the civil, cultural and political life of one of the most advanced societies of its time. Prejudices were too profound; so profound that he had no hope that good judgement would prevail. The homogeneously masculine and masculinised society could not accept the evident diversity of real society, made up of men and women with the fundamental right to live in liberty and equality.

The dominant culture of the early liberal societies was classist, racist, male chauvinist and nationalist. The first three adjectives implied political exclusion and economic, social and cultural domination, while the fourth ensured an *us* that formally included the whole nation despite the fact that it was represented and controlled by only a few. The formal nation was a fiction that made everyone equal, when the real nation was characterised by multiple divisions. These divisions were directly related to social inequality and economic dependence. What was woman's place in the liberal societies of the nineteenth century? What was the social place of the cultural communities that did not correspond to the dominant national culture? Political exclusion and cultural submission. Thus, the uniformity of the modern era has been constructed on the foundations of unequal and exclusive societies.

The democratisation of the liberal state has been carried out in successive inclusive phases which have made it possible to partly overcome what worried Jefferson and Stuart Mill. Within the framework of the welfare state in the second half of the twentieth century not only has a social agreement been reached between capital and labour, middle-class women have been progressively incorporated into the labour market,[24] and the recognition of civil and political rights without discrimination on grounds of gender or ethnic group have been prior and necessary conditions for the debate on the recognition of diversity. Without making progress in the equality of rights it is impossible also to advance in the recognition and representation of diversity.

Therefore, the debate regarding diversity has begun in those liberal societies where a number of the conditions for material well-being have been met for a large majority of the population, despite the fact that this is not necessarily a sufficient indicator of cohesion and social inclusion, or of a closing of income gaps, as the distance between the rich and the poor and social marginalisation has increased. The distance between the poorest and the wealthiest has widened even more, but between these two extremes there is a very large social group that sustains the economic and social system. It is this centre that has uncovered all its internal diversity and has promoted the debate on the recognition or not (and to what extent) of diversity. The works of Taylor, Kymlicka, Walzer, Parekh, Wieviorka, Miller, Young and Nussbaum are examples of the numerous contributions that have been made on the issue of pluralism, politics of difference and recognition of diversity in the 1990s and the early years of the twenty-first century. Here I wish to address only two questions: (1) who are we referring to when we talk about diversity?; (2) what relationship is established between individual rights and collective or group rights?

Among the different classifications which have been proposed in the field of cultural pluralism movements, Parekh's[25] is, in my opinion, the most accurate, given the great multicultural complexity of advanced modern societies, when he describes cultural diversity on the basis of the object rather than the subject. He thus distinguishes between three types of cultural diversity or cultural pluralism movements: (1) The phenomenon of *subcultural diversity*, which refers to those movements which demand pluralism within the hegemonic or national culture;

that is, recognition of relatively different styles of life. They do not represent an alternative culture, but propose the pluralisation of the existing one, so that different lifestyles and forms of coexistence, of an individual and group nature (sexual minorities, or other minority cultural groups that demand recognition and protection for their identity and style of life), may be possible and compatible. (2) The phenomenon of *diversity of perspective*, which characterises those movements which are especially critical of the dominant values of society, and which put forward an alternative cultural discourse, a desire for radical change in the dominant or hegemonic culture (ecologist movements, or feminist movements, for example). (3) The phenomenon of community diversity, which refers to cultural communities that share territory with the dominant culture, and which display their own characteristics that define a separate culture which has a right to recognition, representation and, in some cases, self-government. In this third kind of cultural diversity, the aim is essentially to question the monocultural society, which is subordinate to the dominant national culture, so that all cultures are recognised as possessing equal rights, as an expression of the multiculturality that really exists (indigenous communities in territories subjected to colonisation; cultural communities which have their origins in forced or voluntary immigration; cultural communities reborn in modern times as national communities that wish to govern themselves).

This classification is debatable, as are all the others, and each of its sections could be the subject of a long debate. Here I will focus exclusively on the third type of cultural diversity for the logical reason that it is related to the main issue addressed in this chapter. Clearly, we are not talking about the same thing when we refer to indigenous communities, national communities and cultural communities. They are three types of community diversity that are sufficiently different that they should not be confused. In any case, at the outset it is necessary to exclude the label or stigma of the word *immigrant* when we refer to cultural communities which have been resident for a long time and wish to remain in the society they have joined. This is a discrimination that is revealed by contrasting these "immigrant communities" with the descendants of the first white, Christian, European settlers who spoke European languages and who proclaimed independence, from Paine to Simón Bolívar, as *Americans*, despite the fact of their very obvious ancestry and origins. Why are some "immigrants" and others "Americans"? Are their origins not equally foreign? Is it not their original slavery or forced immigration which continues to distinguish one group from the other? Is it the fate of non-Wasp cultural communities to be integrated into and assimilated by the dominant culture? From the perspective of pluralist democracy, the starting point can be none other than the fact that all citizens are equal regardless of their cultural identity. Therefore, in a democratic and multicultural society no culture, language or religion can impose itself on others. Multiculturality must, on the one hand, be guaranteed constitutionally, so that all cultures enjoy the same degree of protection. On the other hand, it is necessary for there to be a series of shared values and institutions in order to ensure that multiculturality does not result in disintegrative multiculturalism, but in a form of interculturality that provides the base for and promotes the existence of a common public culture which is compatible with the preservation of the cultural identities of each and every person or community.

A multicultural and intercultural democratic society may make national–territorial identities based on the cultural community unnecessary over time. Is it possible to imagine a stable and just multiculturally composed and federally organised political community? To a certain extent, they already exist. Canada is an example. A democratic, republican and federal future implies an intercultural mix, in such a way as to overcome the correspondence between cultural community and territory. This means that the territory ceases to be the "property" of any particular culture, and obliges the dominant cultures to dissociate themselves and stop putting their own stamp on a state or a given territory. At best this is a horizon, not a current reality or an aim that can be realised in the short term. But it is essential in the normative debate to know where one wants to go. In fact, the very logic of advanced capitalist society and post-industrialism is multiplying migrations in such a way that the classical version of the monocultural nation-state no longer corresponds to today's multicultural societies.[26] The same changes in the multicultural composition of Catalan society (and in other parts of Spain) which have occurred as a result of immigration in the last fifteen years are a example of this, even though Spain still has difficulty recognising its own cultural diversity. The de-territorialisation of cultural and national communities is an unavoidable step if we wish to overcome the nationalist paradigm.

The right and the aim of all cultural communities is their recognition and equality in an intercultural world. Nevertheless, until that is achieved and we continue to live under the hegemony of nationalism, the cultural community may be (and usually is) the instrument and the argument for stating the right to self-determination over a given territory. This is the same whether we are referring to indigenous communities or national communities. In both cases we are dealing with a cultural community that is linked to its own history and territory which, through the national consciousness of its own existence, states and demands an inalienable right to self-government. The differences between the two communities are based on the type of constitutional recognition they receive. While indigenous communities approach their recognition from the perspective of historical communities that wish to remain and prevail with their own customs, values and norms, national communities are modern recreations of the cultural nation which wish to achieve self-determination and the right to constitute their own state, based on the values and principles of liberal-democratic constitutionalism. Indigenous communities protect themselves from the state; national communities want to have a state.

The complexity of cultural communities of immigrant origin which are subordinated by a dominant culture is greater. This is because we are dealing with people and communities that are outside their historical territory of origin, and who have been forcibly transferred or have voluntarily moved to another land where they have settled and, normally, remained for many generations. Clearly, the immigrants are only the first group and at the beginning. After that the land has no colour or tongue, however difficult this may be for society to accept, or whether some create obstacles to safeguard their privileges. The history of colonisation separated free Americans and enslaved Americans from the beginning. That is why Jefferson feared the day after the slaves were freed. Nowadays, the United States is a multicultural society, but social differences and racial and cultural discrimination still exist. As a result of the existing inequality, it may be logical for cultural communities to wish to integrate, in the sense that the constitutional code ensures the end of all discrimination, and equality of rights for all the citizens, whatever their particular cultural condition may be. Until this objective, which is inseparably linked with eradication of social inequality and cultural discrimination, is reached there is every justification for the recognition and guarantee of community or cultural group rights for those cultural communities that suffer discrimination, marginalisation or inequality in relation to the dominant culture. The scope of these collective rights is the community, not the territory, but one should not exclude a territorial option (such as indigenous communities or national communities) if a cultural group considers that this is the only or the best way to preserve its identity or continued existence as a group. As long as a dominant state nationalism which is confused with a culture that identifies and occupies all the state's territory persists, one cannot exclude the demands of other cultures, not only to defend their common identity, but also to include territorial and governmental claims. However, as discriminatory barriers are overcome, claims for both self-government over a territory and for collective or non-territorial group rights may over time cease to be necessary.

If we imagine an intercultural society, in which the political community represents diversity and a form of homogeneity based on a dominant culture is not imposed, it is perfectly reasonable for everyone's original cultural community to give way to citizenship, which makes all members of the political community equal in terms of their rights and duties. A society of free men and women predominates over one's cultural identity. All multicultural societies demand and need a common culture of shared values and principles of justice. In this sense individual rights and collective or group rights are compatible, provided that one's individual liberty as a citizen predominates. This is a form of liberty conceived in the republican sense, and should not be confused with Berlin's negative liberty.

From Hobbes to Hayek conservative liberalism has understood liberty to be the absence of external opposition or impediment to thought and individual action. This idea of liberty has also been embraced by the liberal-democratic tradition from Constant to Berlin when it distinguishes between the liberty of modern man and that of the ancients and makes negative liberty predominate over positive liberty. Liberal thought in its internal plurality continues to conceive society as the joining or aggregation of free individuals, a form of individualism that promotes security, liberty and property as the paramount values of the political community. As Andrés de Francisco has pointed out, for Berlin there is no necessary relationship between liberty and democratic self-government.[27] As long as the private sphere is respected and individual rights guaranteed; that is, as long as the government passes laws that respect and protect the individual values mentioned earlier, or does not interfere in the private domain, it is less important who governs and how they have acceded to and maintain themselves in government.

For republicanism there is no division or predominance between individual liberty and self-government, but interdependence.[28] The law as an expression of the interests of all the citizenry makes us free. But this law can only come from the will of all, either through the direct participation of the citizens, or through their representatives. Therefore, there can be no separation between negative liberty and positive liberty; the liberty of each and every one is part of the general law of liberty. At the same time, in a multicultural society it is not possible to coexist and share a common public culture if this is not the product of the recognition and representation of multiculturality. Republicanism or republican patriotism may be the way to make the recognition of cultural diversity compatible with the construction of a federal union based on shared cultural values and a republican ethic.

2 Epilogue: pluralist democracy and plurinational federalism as approaches for overcoming the three fallacies of the national state

In the sections above, an alternative model for the political organisation of plurinational and multicultural societies has been described. The sovereign and monocultural national state is a thing of the past. The future is federal and plurinational, within the framework of the development of pluralist and republican democracy, and is given practical expression through the possibility and feasibility of plurinational states organised according to the principles of federalism. It is true that while we live under the hegemony of nationalism the traditional solution will continue to be put forward: the right to constitute one's own national state. The numerous national movements that exist around the world defend objectives that are in line with pro-sovereignty nationalism, and only accept federalism in instrumental terms. The right to self-determination does not, in normative theory, allow for areas where it can be applied and areas where it cannot be applied. Another thing is political practice and empirical theory, as a analysis of why and in what circumstances national self-determination has been possible in some cases and not in others.

Having said that, is this the most suitable way within the framework and development of pluralist democracy? Perhaps it is not a good idea to create more nation-states, but to transform existing states into plurinational ones. The historical dilemma facing us nowadays, while processes of supra-state political union are taking place, when interdependence between states is increasing, when it is indispensable to progress towards an international order based on international law and on a United Nations with enough authority to ensure it is respected,[29] is that it is the transformation of the states themselves that is necessary. In fact, this is already happening in the worlds of communication, economy and finance, and culture. States have inevitably become porous to external changes and have had to adapt to new historical circumstances. We are living in a period of profound changes in the material and intellectual conditions of life, in which it is no longer possible to live monoculturally or in isolation, in which flexibility and the capacity to adapt to changes has become a necessary condition for the very existence of peoples and societies. Periods of transition and change generate opposition, fears about uncertain futures which are resolved by applying old recipes, and even accentuating them.

Therefore, we should not be surprised by this new outbreak of neo-nationalism, racist reactions against immigration and multiculturality, pressure for a reinforcement of national states. It is clear that this is not the path towards a more secure international society. At some moment it will be necessary to rectify and deal with the security of states and nations through the development of global democracy. Nationalism has been the *international* ideology of a global order based on relative (national) force between states, with the possibility of the outbreak of nationalist wars, the maximum expression of which were the First and Second World Wars in the twentieth century. The establishment of a democratic and plural international order will demand a change of territorial paradigm as regards the organisation of states, based on federalism as the alternative and successor to the nationalist era. Pluralist federalism is the means by which it is possible to transform national states into plurinational ones; that is, the replacing of the uninational state through national pluralism. There are two main adversaries to this: state nationalism and opposition nationalism(s). Pro-sovereignty nationalism must step aside before a federal pact is possible. This means that state nationalism must disappear in order for opposition nationalisms to become meaningless. The first step cannot be taken before the first.

A political community of free and equal men and women in the twenty-first century should move towards national secularisation and the divisibility of the *demos*; towards national secularisation in the sense of putting an end to the equivalence between official state and official nation, or between official state and culture; towards the divisibility of the *demos* in the sense of basing territorial political organisation on polycentrism, taking into account that in advanced societies division of labour, economic organisation and social structure have become so globally complex that they demand greater interdependence in the different territorial spheres of government. This global framework affects existing national states, in such a way that sooner or later they will have to adapt to the changes taking place in the societies that they organise and govern. In a democratic and pluralist sense this adaptation can be none other than the national secularism of the authorities, and their territorial organisation into spheres of interdependent government based on federalist principles.

Notes

1 Tomás y Valiente (2000: 70).
2 In the second part of Caminal (2002) I develop three alternative proposals: (i) national secularisation and the divisibility of the *demos*; (ii) the separation between citizenship and nationality and between self-government and self-determination; (iii) the organisation of the federal union based on polycentrism, symmetry and asymmetry.
3 Tocqueville (1842: 198).
4 Ibid. (183).
5 Montesquieu (1964: 577).
6 "Dans la république de Hollande, une province ne peut faire une alliance sans le consentement des autres. Cette loi est très bonne, et même necessaire dans la république fédérative" (Ibid.: 578).
7 Hamilton devotes the whole of chapter 9 of the *The Federalist* to Montesquieu's definition. He criticises those who misinterpret Montesquieu when they state that the republican model is only possible in small states, and, mentioning Montesquieu, he replies that federal union by means of a written constitution can enable the establishment of large federally united republics.
8 Montesquieu's points of reference as federative republics were Switzerland, Holland and Germany: "La république fédérative d'Allemagne est composée de villes libres et des petits États soumis à des princes. L'experience fait voir qu'elle est plus imparfaite que celles de Hollande et de Suisse" (Ibid.: 577).
9 Ibid. (586).
10 Gagnon (2007: 46).
11 González Casanova (1974: 420).
12 Webber (1999: 99).
13 Caminal (1998a).
14 Lord Acton (1908).
15 Ibid.
16 Tamir (1993).
17 Levy (2000: 69).
18 To see the distinction between the three senses of the concept of the nation (juridical nation, political nation and cultural nation), see Caminal (1998b). It is also worth mentioning Levy's critique of civic nationalism for confusing two different meanings: one thing is national loyalty linked to specific values and political principles, and another is the necessary link that law establishes between the state and the nation, in such a way that loyalty to the nation is automatically loyalty to the state, and the reverse (Levy 2000).
19 Marshall (1965: chap. 4).
20 Jefferson (1944: 51).
21 Mill (1869).
22 Ibid.
23 See Hayek (1969).
24 This statement does not ignore the over-exploitation of the working woman in the origins of industrial capitalism. For example, Ildefons Cerdà gives the following figures regarding the working population in the city of Barcelona in 1856: 32,228 men and 22,040 women. For the same job the men earned ten times more than the women. (Cerdà 1972: 252).
25 Parekh (2000).
26 See Rogers Brubaker and his vision of Gellner's contrast between the Kokoshka-type cultural model and the Modigliani-type model in "Myths and misconceptions in the study of nationalism" (Hall 2000: 272–306).
27 de Francisco (2007: 182).
28 Miller (1995); Viroli (2007).
29 Held (1995).

Bibliography

Acton, Lord (1908) *Historical Essays and Studies*, London: Macmillan.

Almirall, V. (1886) *La Confederación Suiza y la Unión Americana: Estudio Político Comparativo*, Barcelona: Librería de López Bernagossi.

Almirall, V. (1978) *Lo Catalanisme*, Barcelona: Altafulla.

Anderson, B. (1991) *Imagines Communities. Reflections on the Origin and Spread of Nationalism*, London; New York: Verso.

Arendt, H. (1978) *The Jew as Pariah*, New York: Grove-Press.

Breton, A. (1996) *Competitive Governments*, Cambridge: Cambridge University Press.

Brubaker, R. (2000) "Myths and misconceptions in the study of nationalism", in J.A. Hall, *The State of the Nation*, Cambridge: Cambridge University Press.

Burgess, M. (2006) *Comparative Federalism. Theory and Practice*, London: Routledge.

Caminal, M. (1998a) *Nacionalisme i Partits Nacionals a Catalunya*, Barcelona: Editorial Empúries.

Caminal, M. (1998b) "Nacionalismo y federalismo", in Joan Anton, *Ideologías y Movimientos Políticos Contemporáneos*, Madrid: Editorial Tecnos.

Caminal, M. (2002) *El Federalismo Pluralista. Del Federalismo Nacional al Federalismo Plurinacional*, Barcelona: Paidós.

Caminal, M. (2007) "Una lectura republicana i federal de l'autodeterminació", *Revista d'Estudis Autonòmics i Federals*, no. 5, Barcelona: Institut d'Estudis Autonòmics, Generalitat de Catalunya.

Cerdà, I. (1972) "Monografía estadística de la clase obrera de Barcelona en 1856" (Statistical monograph of the working class of Barcelona in 1856), *Teoría General de la Urbanización y su Aplicación al Proyecto de Ensanche de Barcelona (General Theory of Town Planning and its Application to the Urban Expansion Project of Barcelona)*, Madrid: Institute of Fiscal Studies, Vol. 2, p. 252.

Francisco, A. de (2007) *Ciudadanía y Democracia. Un Enfoque Republicano (Citizenship and Democracy. A Republican Approach)*, Madrid: Catarata.

Gagnon, A. (dir.) (2007) *El Federalisme Canadenc Contemporani. Fonaments, Tradicions i Institucions (Contemporary Canadian Federalism. Foundations, Traditions, Institutions)*, Generalitat de Catalunya: Institut d'Estudis Autonòmics.

González Casanova, J.A. (1974) *Federalisme i Autonomia a Catalunya (1868–1938) (Federalism and Autonomy in Catalonia 1868–1938)*, Barcelona: Curial.

Hall, J.A. (2000) *The State of the Nation. Ernst Gellner and the Theory of Nationalism*, Cambridge University Press.

Hamilton, A., Madison, J. and Jay, J. (2009) *The Federalist*, Cambridge: Belknap Press of Harvard University Press.

Hannun, H. and Babbitt, E. (2006) *Negotiating Self-Determination*, EUA: Lexington Books.

Hayek, F.A. (1969) *John Stuart Mill and Harriet Taylor*, London: Kelley.

Held, D. (1995) *Democracy and the Global Order. From the Modern State to Cosmopolitan Governance*, Cambridge: Polity Press.

Jefferson, Th. (1944) *The Life and Selected Writings of Jefferson*, New York: The Modern Library.

Levy, J.T. (2000) *The Multiculturalism of Fear*, Oxford: Oxford University Press.

Máiz, R. (2006) "Federalismo plurinacional: una teoría política normative", *Revista d'Estudis Autonòmics i Federals*, no. 3, Barcelona.

Máiz, R. (2000) "El lugar de la nación en la teoría de la democracia y el nacionalismo liberal", *Revista Española de Ciencia Política*, no. 3, Madrid: AECPA-Marcial Pons.

Marshall, T.H. (1965) "Citizenship and social class", *Class, Citizenship, and Social Development*, New York: Anchor.

Mill, J.S. (1970[1869]) *The Subjection of Women*, London; Cambridge, MA: MIT Press.

Miller, D. (1995) *On Nationality*, Oxford: Oxford University Press.

Montesquieu (1964) *Oeuvres Complétes*, Paris: Editions du Senil.

Norman, W. (2006) *Negotiating Nationalism*, Oxford: Oxford University Press.

Parekh, B. (2000) *Rethinking Multiculturalism: Cultural Diversity and Political Theory*, Cambridge, MA: Harvard University Press.

Pi i Margall, F. (1986) *Las Nacionalidades*, Madrid: Centro de Estudios Constitucionales.

Pi i Margall, F. (1982) *La Reacción y la Revolución*, Barcelona: Anthropos.

Requejo, F. (2005) *Multinational Federalism and Value Pluralism*, London; New York: Routledge.

Tamir, Y. (1993) *Liberal Nationalism*, Princeton, NJ: Princeton University Press.

Tocqueville, Alexis de (1842) *De la Démocratie en Amerique*, Paris: Librairie de Charles Gosselin.

Tomás y Valiente, F. (2000) "Sobirania i autonomia en la Segona República i en la Constitució del 1978" (Sovereignty and autonomy in the Second Republic and in the Constitution of 1978) in Enric Fossas (dir.) *Les Transformacions de la Sobirania i el Futur Polític de Catalunya* (*Transformations of Sovereignty and the Political Future of Catalonia)*, Barcelona: Temes Contemporanis-Proa.

Viroli, M. (2007) *Republicanisme*, Barcelona: Centre d'Estudis de Temes Contemporanis-Editorial Angle.

Webber, J. (1999) "Una Constitución asimétrica" (An asymmetric Constitution), in Fossas/Requejo, *Asimetría Federal y Estado Plurinacional (Federal Asymmetry and the Plurinational State)*, Madrid: Editorial Trotta.

Index